Paradigm Debates
in Curriculum
and Supervision

PARADIGM DEBATES IN CURRICULUM AND SUPERVISION

Modern and Postmodern Perspectives

Edited by
Jeffrey Glanz
Linda S. Behar-Horenstein

Foreword by Robert J. Starratt

BERGIN & GARVEY
Westport, Connecticut · London

Library of Congress Cataloging-in-Publication Data

Paradigm debates in curriculum and supervision : modern and postmodern
    perspectives / edited by Jeffrey Glanz, Linda S. Behar-Horenstein ;
    foreword by Robert J. Starratt.
        p.   cm.
    Includes bibliographical references and index.
    ISBN 0–89789–624–6 (alk. paper)
    1. School supervision—Social aspects.   2. Curriculum planning—
Social aspects.   3. Postmodernism and education.   4. Multicultural
education.   I. Glanz, Jeffrey.   II. Behar-Horenstein, Linda S.
LB2806.4.P37   2000
371.2′03—dc21   99–33207

British Library Cataloguing in Publication Data is available.

Library of Congress Catalog Card Number: 99–33207
ISBN: 0–89789–624–6

First published in 2000

Bergin & Garvey, 88 Post Road West, Westport, CT 06881
An imprint of Greenwood Publishing Group, Inc.
www.greenwood.com

Printed in the United States of America

The paper used in this book complies with the
Permanent Paper Standard issued by the National
Information Standards Organization (Z39.48–1984).

10 9 8 7 6 5 4 3 2

Every reasonable effort has been made to trace the owners of copyright materials in this book, but
in some instances this has proven impossible. The author and publisher will be glad to receive information leading to more complete acknowledgments in subsequent printings of the book and in
the meantime extend their apologies for any omissions.

Contents

Foreword *by Robert J. Starratt*   ix

Preface   xv

Part I
Modern Conceptions of Curriculum and Supervision

Introduction   3

1   Can the Modern View of Curriculum Be Refined by
        Postmodern Criticism?   6
    Linda S. Behar-Horenstein
    Case Study 1: Teacher Challenged by Student Diversity Issues

2   Shifting Paradigms: Implications for Curriculum Research
        and Practice   34
    Edmund C. Short
    Case Study 2: The Role of Knowledge in Curriculum Decision-
    Making

3   The Common Unity and the Progressive Restoration of the
        Curriculum Field   54
    Peter S. Hlebowitsh
    Case Study 3: High School Curriculum Promotes Gender Bias

4   Supervision: Don't Discount the Value of the Modern   70
    Jeffrey Glanz
    Case Study 4: Assessing Gender Influences in the Classroom

5   Supervisory Practices: Building a Constructivist Learning
         Community for Adults   93
     Sally J. Zepeda
     Case Study 5: Ethical and Political Challenges of Supervision

6   Collaborative Supervision: Implications for Supervision
         Research and Inquiry   108
     Martha N. Ovando
     Case Study 6: Supervisor Challenged by an Experienced Teacher

Part II
Postmodern Conceptions of Curriculum and Supervision

Introduction   129

7   Postmodernism as a Challenge to Dominant
         Representations of Curriculum   132
     Patrick Slattery
     Case Study 7: Resisting Traditional Approaches to Curriculum
     Implementation

8   Informing Curriculum and Teaching Transformation
         through Postmodern Studies   152
     James G. Henderson
     Case Study 8: Assuming the Transformative Curriculum Leadership
     Challenge

9   Postmodern Visions in Multicultural Education
         Preparation and Practice   169
     Geneva Gay and Pamula Hart
     Case Study 9: Curriculum Activity Inspires Students to Display
     Multiple Perspectives

10   Complicity in Supervision: Another Postmodern Moment   190
     Duncan Waite and Margarida Ramires Fernandes
     Case Study 10: A Dialogic Approach to Supervision

11   Possibilities of Postmodern Supervision   212
     Patricia E. Holland and Maryalice Obermiller
     Case Study 11: Collaborative Visions and Challenges for the Future
     of Technology in Post Middle School

12   Communicative Action: A Postmodern Bridge for
         Supervision in School Organizations   229
     Edward Pajak and Karen K. Evans
     Case Study 12: *Teacher Think Tank*: Postmodern Supervision
     in Action

Part III
Practitioner Responses

Introduction 247

13 Modern and Postmodern Perspectives on Curriculum and
   Supervision: *A View from the Top* 249
   Osborne F. Abbey, Jr.

14 Paradigms of Curriculum and Supervision: A Practitioner's
   Viewpoint 257
   Frances M. Vandiver

15 Student Empowerment through the Professional
   Development of Teachers 265
   Eric Nadelstern, Janet R. Price, and Aaron Listhaus

Afterword: Closing Reflections 277

Index 281

About the Contributors 291

Foreword

Robert J. Starratt

For the past two decades the attention of educators, policy makers, political interest groups, legislators, school boards, and parents has been concentrated on school renewal. This concentration has not been guided by any overarching philosophy. Rather, the national effort has been made up of a cacophony of voices: the business community calling for greater concentration on school-to-work skills; parent groups calling for greater school discipline, security, and concentration on the basics; various interest groups demanding an end to bilingual education or, on the contrary, for greater resources for bilingual programs to accommodate more diverse groups of immigrants; states' initiation of high-stakes testing, with the attendant concentration on curriculum guidelines and protocols necessary to prepare youngsters for those tests; legal wrangling in state legislatures with court-ordered equalization of financing for all children; groups calling for more charter schools and for greater flexibility for home schooling or for Christian academies; local school councils concentrating on specific local issues. Practitioners are overwhelmed by the intensification of the environment and the fragmented agenda of schooling. There is no time to sort out or fashion a guiding philosophy for the school reform agenda.

In the meantime, well beyond the attention of practitioners, policy makers, political interest groups, and the average teacher or parent, there has been a growing conversation/debate among scholars about a philosophical interpretation of the contemporary human and social condition. Many would contend that the philosophical worldview that has dominated the West since the European Age of Enlightenment, a worldview loosely defined as *modernism,* is no longer able to provide either a legitimating rationale for maintaining the human and social status quo or an effective rationality leading toward necessary improvements in the human and social condition. As academics in the field of education have become aware of these philosophical arguments, they have recreated the debate insofar as the interpretations of modernity imply a view of how schooling should be conducted. More specifically, these educational scholars have developed an awareness of how the rationality of the modern world, a rationality grounded in a view of science and the individual and progress in social life, has shaped the beliefs and assumptions of schooling in modern societies. For some, this awareness has led to a critique of those beliefs and assumptions and to the practices they engender. For others, it has led to an awareness of how these beliefs and assumptions need to be made more explicit, to perhaps be modified or developed, and be more consistently applied in the curriculum and pedagogy of the schools.

This book helps to bring that debate closer to the realities of practice, closer to the reform agenda so that the stakeholders may be led to consider these larger questions. The reform or improvement of schooling practices needs to be fashioned against a large social purpose that is itself informed by a realistic assessment of the conditions of society. Are we dealing with conditions of advanced or high modernity (as opposed to early or naive modernity), or are we dealing with conditions of postmodernity, conditions that can no longer be interpreted, legitimated, or solved by categories or epistemologies of modernity? If schools are functioning according to and, in fact, teaching a rationality grounded in the assumptions and beliefs of modernity when society is already facing the conditions of postmodernity, then schools may indeed be dysfunctional—may be, to use a phrase intended for an entirely different criticism, placing the nation at risk. If, on the other hand, conditions in American and Western society are exhibiting strains and struggles that can be understood and addressed by simply (though it is not at all simple) applying the rationality (now understood as more tentative and conditional) and advanced (not, indeed, the previously naive, perhaps arrogant) scientific and technological resources of modernity, then the schools need to work more diligently at preparing youngsters for ever-evolving careers in the knowledge industries and a modulated participation in the construction of themselves in a culture of identity diffusion as they accommodate to the managed political evolution of economic globalization. If that sounds like a mouthful, then it may prepare the reader for the abstract analyses of scholars on both sides of the debate represented in this book. There is a lot at stake in this debate, not simply the judgment over who wins in the rarefied stratosphere of academia—amid the leisure of the theory class, as Bruce Cooper likes to label it—but the debate as it works itself out in the winning and losing within political and economic and cultural arenas of society. Fundamentally, the debate is about the setting of the direction of the country for the next several generations.

One of the compromises of the debate format is that the debaters see their job as having to defeat their opponents. Debaters usually spend at least half their time trying to discredit their opposition. By stretching the position of their opponents to its extremes, they are able to construct a stereotype, a caricature, which is easily rejected as silly, dangerous, pathological, reckless, unpredictable, or, perhaps most reprehensible, "radical." These distortions creep in, I believe, from time to time in this book, without being particularly helpful. More helpful would have been a more generous referencing of whose position was being defended or attacked. For example, I would place the philosopher Charles Taylor within the modernist camp, as I would Anthony Giddens and Jurgen Habermas. I am not sure whether their extensive analyses of modern conditions enter into the arguments of the defenders of modernism. Neither do I find the postmodernists, with few exceptions, engaging the arguments of those authors.

On the other hand, the debate format forces the differences between the positions to become clarified, if only by presenting themselves in an exaggerated, idealized intelligibility. This work of clarification is indeed helpful, and it leads some authors to develop very insightful interpretations of educational practice. As some authors admit, however, elements of modernism and postmodernism overlap, intermingle, and dance together in novel combinations within social reality. Real history is intellectually messy; academic history divides into more artificially orderly periods of identifiable worldviews. Several authors seek to incorporate insights of their opponents in the debate into their own proposals for redesigning curriculum, supervision, and assessment protocols, thus moving beyond the need to win the debate towards some common ground dedicated to improving learning in the schools.

Let me close with two observations. The first concerns what Anthony Giddens calls "ontological security" (Giddens, 1984, 1991). Giddens postulates that humans have a very basic need to feel secure in their social relationships. They need to feel that social life is reasonably ordered and predictable. If their social context appears arbitrary, with no rules, no clues for what is expected, then they won't know what to do, they won't know how to behave or present themselves. Such indeterminacy threatens their sense of identity. If, from hour to hour in the day they do not know how to behave or what to do, then other people will know that they "don't know what they are doing." They will be thought fools, misfits, perhaps crazy. They will lose all confidence in themselves as competent social actors. They will flee that situation and return to more familiar terrain, where they know the routines, the shared definition of things, where they can read the cues and signals from the environment so that they will know what is called for. Because of the universal need for ontological security, humans tend to reproduce the conditions and structures of their social context. Thus, innovations, either in thought or in practice, will be spontaneously resisted if they take them too far beyond the familiar and routine.

Insofar as postmodern rhetoric suggests a sharp break with the accepted ways of modernity as they are embedded in the practice of schooling, that rhetoric will threaten people's ontological security. This suggests that conversations about "the postmodern condition" with parents and teachers and public officials need to begin with the familiar vocabulary of modernism. The whole point is to have people become aware of the dysfunctions and contradictions within ordinary practices of schooling. It is important to affirm the stake that everyone has in the effort to make schooling better serve the needs of the whole community by encouraging everyone to name their reality in their own terminology. The specialized vocabulary of the academy allows professors to short-circuit entire paragraphs or chapters of explanatory text when pursuing a train of thought with another professor; one facility in weaving new arguments with even more abstruse abstractions may even impress one's academic colleagues. Academics, however, need to rehearse a more common vocabulary and a less judgmental attitude when conversing with the so-called ordinary people about what's wrong and what's right for the schools.

In this regard, I find the description of the partnerships and dialogue described in the final chapter of this book refreshing. It reveals a community of diverse people experiencing a particular set of postmodern conditions who come together and pragmatically discuss what they think the situation calls for. There is no inflammatory rhetoric about oppressive regimes of language, hegemonic interests, emancipatory rituals. These are people who cannot afford the luxury of ideological debates. They simply put their heads together and decided what needs to be done. By avoiding the inflammatory rhetoric that might challenge the ontological security of the authorities, they engaged in truly emancipatory activity without needlessly calling attention to the revolution they were enacting by taking charge of their own lives.

The second observation has to do with the intellectual horizons of this book. The book is framed as a debate about the usefulness and legitimacy of working within one perspective or another, within either the frameworks of modernity or the frameworks of postmodernity. That debate, while important and useful, does not exhaust the options for defining the intellectual landscape. An underlying philosophy for schools in the twenty-first century is not necessarily or exclusively to be found in either modernism or postmodernism or a healthy synthesis of the two.

At least two other frameworks deserve attention. One may be called the *new pragmatism*, championed by Richard Rorty (1982, 1991) (even though Slattery in Chapter 7 refers to Rorty as a moderate postmodernist), and in which I would include the new sociology of knowledge (McCarthy, 1996). The second may be called the *new science*. That perspective would include, for example, those philosophical positions based on quantum physics and on ecological frameworks derived from microbiology and paleontological biology (Bateson, 1991; Lovelock, 1979; Prigogine & Stengers, 1984; Turner, 1991; Whitehead, 1925; Zohar & Marshall, 1994). On the other hand, one can ask only so much of a book. This book indeed serves the field well by raising for readers unfamiliar with the philosophical developments of the recent past many of their implications in the field of curriculum and supervision. Although the curriculum field has been challenged for the past twenty years by contact with some of these philosophical currents, the supervision field has remained relatively isolated from them (with the notable exception, perhaps, of the work of John Smyth). This book brings many of the prominent scholars in the curriculum and supervision field, especially, into dialogue with philosophical perspectives that may help to guide the school renewal effort into the next century.

Boston, Massachusetts
February 1999

REFERENCES

Bateson, G. (1991). *A sacred unity: Further steps to an ecology of mind* (edited by R. E. Donaldson). New York: HarperCollins.

Giddens, A. (1984). *The constitution of society.* Cambridge, MA: Polity Press.

Giddens, A. (1991). *Modernity and self-identity: Self and society in the late modern age.* Stanford, CA: Stanford University Press.

Lovelock, J. (1979). *Gaia: A new look at life on Earth.* Oxford: Oxford University Press.

McCarthy, E. D. (1996). *Knowledge as culture: The new sociology of knowledge.* London: Routledge.

Prigogine, I., & Stengers, I. (1984). *Order out of chaos: Man's new dialogue with nature.* New York: Bantam.

Rorty, R. (1982). *Consequences of pragmatism.* Minneapolis: University of Minnesota Press.

Rorty, R. (1991). *Objectivity, relativism, and truth.* Cambridge: Cambridge University Press.

Turner, F. (1991). *Rebirth of value: Meditations on beauty, ecology, religion and education.* Albany: State University of New York Press.

Whitehead, A. N. (1925). *Science and the modern world.* New York: Macmillan.

Zohar, D., and Marshall I. (1994). *The quantum society.* London: HarperCollins.

Preface

Paradigm debates in the educational research community are a frequent if not common occurrence. How do paradigm debates in educational fields such as curriculum and supervision shape educators' understanding and practice? In this volume, it is suggested that educators' adherence to particular views of curriculum and supervision is influential in guiding their beliefs and subsequent actions. For example, a widely accepted belief is that if an individual adopts a mechanistic view of the curriculum, then s/he is likely to deliver a curriculum grounded in preestablished objectives and to evaluate student achievement in relationship to formulated objectives. Many postmodernists contend that such educators are bound by rigid bifurcation and a constrictive linear logic. In supervision, educational leaders who favor leadership styles comprised by autocratic behaviors tend to create school climates that favor a top-down approach to human relationships. Autocratic leaders rely on hierarchical organizational structures and styles that seek to instill compliance and subordinance. Yet prospective administrators who want concrete proposals put into practice find modern perspectives of supervision helpful. In contrast, postmodern supervisors allege that such leaders disallow the emergence of relevant and authentic relationships that might occur when conventional hierarchical structures are diminished and open lines of communication between teachers, students, and administrators become normative.

The contributors in this book present an in-depth analysis of how an individual's predisposition towards modern and postmodern views of curriculum and supervision are likely to influence (1) curriculum development, (2) teaching styles, (3) leadership styles, (4) teacher and student evaluation, and (5) the missions intrinsic to the creation of professional preparation programs that serve to promulgate existing practice or create a new order of teachers and administrators. Hence, paradigm debates between modern and postmodern conceptions of curriculum and supervision and the impact on school practice are the primary contributions of this volume.

The book is divided into three parts. Each part is preceded by an introduction that provides a brief overview of the chapters and focuses the reader's attention to significant issues to be discussed. Each chapter in the first two parts begins with a set of guiding questions and ends with a case study and follow-up questions. Each contributor presents a definite point of view, an explanation of how the paradigm affects practice, and a case study embedded in a realistic context that demonstrates the paradigm in action. Part III presents three practitioner responses to the issues highlighted in this volume regarding modern and postmodern views of curriculum and/or supervision. The book closes with an afterword that summarizes the views expressed by contributors and offers a perspective on modern and postmodern paradigm debates in curriculum and supervision.

The book is written for colleagues in the field and graduate students at the doctoral and master's levels enrolled in programs of curriculum, educational leadership, administration, supervision, and organization development. A secondary audience consists of students enrolled in foundational courses in school curriculum, school and organizational theory, school supervision, problems in educational administration, supervision and curriculum, educational leadership, and the administration of school systems.

We acknowledge the professors and practitioners who so willingly contributed to this volume by expressing their views forthrightly and intelligently. We hope that the issues raised in this collaborative project will lead to continued improvements of curriculum and supervision practice.

Jeffrey Glanz dedicates this, his fifth book, to his wife, who has established a conducive environment for him to continue his scholarly interests, and to his children, Daniel, Joshua, Noah, and Rena, who he wishes will one day read at least one of his books. Linda Behar-Horenstein dedicates this book to her husband for lovingly helping her balance the challenges associated with their dual academic careers and parenting and for supporting and encouraging her scholarly endeavors and to her children, Rachel and Max, whose curiosity and exuberance have deepened her perspectives of what curriculum is, should be, and can be.

PART I

MODERN CONCEPTIONS OF CURRICULUM AND SUPERVISION

Introduction

In Part I, scholars in curriculum and supervision promulgate the benefits of the modernist view for school practice. They describe how practical guidance and strategies culled from modernism has aided teachers and students. Several authors decry some postmodernists for their penchant to ignore the contributions of modernist thought and caution that much can be lost through implementation of the idiosyncratic and elusive practices that the latter advocate. Some authors advance the perspective that a synthesis of principles within modern and postmodern paradigms would be in the best interest of students. While unification may be repugnant to many postmodernists, these modernists advocate for processes characterized by dialogue, deliberation, and reflection to promote equal educational opportunities for all students. The authors call for the identification of common purposes and goals while maintaining a commitment to fostering the growth of all members who work together in learning communities.

In the first chapter, Linda Behar-Horenstein analyzes the suitability of the modern and postmodern paradigms for enhancing school-based curriculum practices. She asserts that the time to move discussions beyond debate passed a long time ago. She advocates for the development of an intentional curriculum grounded in the principles forwarded by modernism that incorporates the flexibility, dynamics, and responsiveness called for by postmodernists. Following the identification of challenges associated with this type of synthesis, Behar-Horenstein offers the readers a set of questions designed to augment an authentic critical analysis of contemporary school-based practices and to hasten the development of curriculum that emanates from a broadly conceived, problem-centered perspective.

In the next chapter, Edmund Short asserts that curriculum research and inquiry should focus on contextually based activities that are important to curriculum practitioners. He asks readers to consider the following question: How do curriculum research and practice inform each other? He highlights flaws in the research paradigms that have guided inquiry and claims that the dominant knowledge production and utilization model is moribund. Short suggests that a new paradigm of curriculum research and inquiry is evolving. He recommends that a deliberative approach, one that is grounded in the careful consideration of understanding how knowledge is comprehended, defined, used, and analyzed, become the focus of inquiry.

In Chapter 3, Peter Hlebowitsh contends that the variance in paradigmatic conceptions of curriculum prompted by postmodernist rejection of the field is likely to bring about adverse outcomes in efforts directed at the improvement of public school education. While pointing out that their movement is built upon unsustainable premises, ideological criticism, and atheoretical notions, he criticizes postmodernism for failing to articulate ideas that are of practical use or to offer an agenda that addresses mutual concerns. Hlebowitsh argues that modernist principles central to curriculum design and development have advanced curriculum scholarship. He argues for the conception of deliberate and conscious design and development, decisions that are responsive to the mission of public school education in a democracy. He urges curriculum scholars to recognize the centrality of curriculum design and development and to refocus their energies on securing a commitment to its historical mandate.

Next, Jeffrey Glanz argues that a common postmodern inclination to criticize the modernist view of supervision can be shortsighted, misguided, and even dangerous. He claims that postmodern advocacy of collegiality in the absence of systematic efforts aimed at improving teaching, instruction, learning, evaluation, and leadership is unresponsive to the reality of teachers' lived experiences in contemporary classrooms. He also contends that this approach abrogates a commitment to ensuring that students have meaningful learning experiences. Glanz asserts that teachers want and need practical guidance and strategies that are grounded in the technical-rational view of supervision. While recommending an approach to instructional supervision that is contextually appropriate and diverse, yet responsive, he offers readers a unified view of supervision that is broad, inclusive, and liberal.

In Chapter 5, Sally Zepeda suggests that effective supervisory practices should encourage teachers to direct their energies towards professional growth, promote the discovery of meaningfulness in their work, and resonate with the principles of adult learning theory—interpersonal sensitivity, collaboration, self-analysis, and autonomy. She maintains that effective supervision is an amalgam of modernist practices, tenets of constructivist learning theory, the practice of collaboration evidenced in job-embedded supervision, and a commitment to enhancing the growth of all members of the learning community. Zepeda calls for a movement away from the hierarchies that divide teachers and principals and foster animosity. She argues for supervisory practice that is reflective, authentic, humane, collegial, and supportive of teacher-initiated innovation.

In the final chapter of Part I, Martha Ovando demonstrates the necessity for collaborative forms of supervisory leadership. Arguing that effective collaboration exceeds the aims of cooperative and collegial relationships, she asserts that collaboration is essential to interorganizational relationships and the legitimization of teachers' practical understanding. Specific attitudes and behaviors characteristic of a collaborative supervisory approach can lead to the development of an educational alliance. She describes the multiplicity of observational techniques available, but cautions teachers and supervisors to select the format that is appropriate to the purpose of formative evaluation. Ovando recommends that further research is needed to illuminate how collaborative supervisory practices enhance equal and equitable learning experiences for all students.

Can the Modern View of Curriculum Be Refined by Postmodern Criticism?

Linda S. Behar-Horenstein

GUIDING QUESTIONS

1. *Why is it important to identify your paradigmatic conception of curriculum?*
2. *What is a modern view of curriculum?*
3. *In what ways does the modern view of curriculum benefit teachers?*
4. *What is a postmodern view of curriculum?*
5. *What contributions can postmodernism make to classroom practice?*
6. *What are the implications of both a modern and a postmodern view of curriculum for inservice and preservice teacher training?*

There are two contrasting paradigms within the field of curriculum, the modern and the postmodern. Within the modern paradigm, notions of what curriculum is or ought to be, are complicated by a host of influences (Klein, 1994). Definitions of the modern view have been influenced by: (1) public perceptions of what school should be like, (2) parental memories that are suggestive of what school experiences should be, (3) societal expectations for cultivating a productive adult citizenry, (4) standardized tests, (5) teacher accountability for student outcomes, (6) metaphors that describe the school as a factory, and (7) competing views of what knowledge or whose knowledge is most valuable.

At the heart of the postmodern paradigms are criticisms primarily leveled against the modernists. According to postmodernists, the modern view curriculum has (1) failed to ensure equal opportunity for all students irrespective of class and status; (2) promoted the knowledge and values of the dominant class; (3) become saturated in the political and economic practices of those who perform it (Apple, 1981); (4) suffered from an overreliance on the Tyler rationale; (5) suppressed the needs, identities, and humanity of students (Giroux, 1994); (6) silenced marginalized groups (Apple, 1990); and (7) disregarded the necessity for situated knowledge that acknowledges cultural pluralism, context, and locale. Taken as a whole this complex array of expectations may sorely compromise any degree of civility in a dialogue aimed at discerning what curriculum is or should be.

What practical implications might be culled from the postmodern critique? Having provided extensive critiques concerning how schools have failed, the postmodernists should be well positioned to offer practice-based suggestions that would be aligned with the aims they believe schools should strive to achieve. The postmodernists advocate for a curriculum that is emancipatory, liberating, and emergent. What experiences would comprise an emancipatory or liberating curriculum? What role would students exercise in the development of curriculum? Would curriculum become so dynamic that it would need to emerge concomitantly with the themes expressed in student-student interactions or student-teacher interactions? Would radical curriculum become the norm in our schools? Would any overarching framework, even if suggested by students themselves, be available to identify what students would learn?

Clearly any efforts to create postmodern curriculum require a reconceived or a new type of educator. For example, teachers would need to demonstrate a capacity for responding in novel ways. They would foster the active engagement of heterogeneous and diverse student populations via dynamic and enriching learning experiences. Blending the skills inherent to both a scientist and artist, they would be expected to simultaneously assess students' abilities and limitations and plan learning experiences aimed at manifesting their potentialities with ease.

The purpose of this chapter is to explore the major tenets of the modern and postmodern paradigms of curriculum, discuss their applicability for classroom practice, and propose a refined approach to curriculum development. In this chapter a brief description of the term "paradigm," is discussed. Next an overview of the modern view of curriculum, including a discussion of the limitations of this view, and a description of the contributions of the modern view for school practice are presented. This is followed by an overview of the postmodern view of curriculum, including a discussion of the limitations of this view and description of the contributions of the postmodern view for school practice. Next a summary of the modern/postmodern debate is discussed. Finally, a section devoted to moving beyond definitions is presented. Within this section, a series of questions, designed to guide curriculum development that is grounded in the modern paradigm but informed by the postmodern critique, are identified. I advocate for the modern paradigm and curriculum approaches that are accessible to educators, notwithstanding the contributions of the postmodernists. However, the reader is encouraged to consider each paradigm and analyze its utility for school practice.

WHAT IS A PARADIGM?

According to Worthen, Sanders, and Fitzpatrick (1997) a paradigm is considered to be a pattern or example. Also defined as a school of thought or philosophy, a paradigm is used to describe a constellation of worldviews held by individuals or groups that determine how they perceive and attempt to understand truth. Paradigms or worldviews are comprised of epistemological and ontological beliefs. "Epistemology is theory of knowledge or the study of nature of knowledge" (Worthen, Sanders, & Fitzpatrick, 1997, p. 69) as well as the limits and validity of associated with methods of inquiry. The practical application of epistemology is characterized by how individuals think knowledge or truth can be known, the limitations associated with ways of making inquiry into and presenting knowledge, and the inquirers' perception of their relationship with the object of inquiry. Ontology involves the systematic study of being. In practical terms, individuals' ontological beliefs determine how they think about reality and distinguish between what actually exists and what exists in thought. Understanding what a paradigm is and identifying what paradigmatic conception one ascribes to is crucial to comprehending the practical applications of various conceptions of curriculum for school practice. This information helps to clarify how individuals' paradigms influence their views of knowledge, methods of inquiry, and whether knowledge is verifiable or a belief that individuals hold.

Interpretative frameworks about the paradigms and related definitions of the field of curriculum are abundant in the literature (McNeil, 1996; Oliva, 1997; Ornstein & Hunkins, 1998; Schubert, 1986; Tanner & Tanner, 1995; Wiles & Bondi, 1998).[1] Conceptions of curriculum can be classified into modern (traditional and contemporary points of view) and postmodern paradigms (Ornstein & Hunkins, 1998).[2] A variety of definitions of the word curriculum (culled in part from Ornstein & Hunkins, 1998 and from Wiles & Bondi, 1998) attest to the wide range of beliefs that scholars hold about the purpose and function of curriculum (see Table 1.1).

THE MODERN VIEW OF CURRICULUM

The modern view of curriculum is comprised of traditionalist and contemporary conceptions. An overview of the definitions that follow illustrates that curriculum has been variously defined as a content or subject matter, a plan, experience, a system, and a field of study. The traditionalist's view of curriculum (comprised of the perennialist and essentialist movements) is grounded in the belief that curriculum content should be characterized by the inclusion of classical subjects and essential skills. In perennialism, the teacher's role is to

Table 1.1
A Framework for Defining Curriculum

Classification	Selected scholars who advocated this view
As a plan*	Tyler (1957), Taba (1962), Saylor, Alexander & Lewis (1981), Beauchamp (1981), Oliva (1997)
As content or subject matter*	Hutchins (1936), Bestor (1956), Phenix (1962), Oliva (1997)
As outcomes*	Popham & Baker (1970)
As a system*	Beauchamp (1981)
As experience*	Hall (1907), Charters (1923), Bobbit (1924), Counts (1932), Caswell & Campbell (1935), Dewey (1938), Rugg (1939), Smith, Stanley, & Shores (1957), Johnson (1970–71), Tanner & Tanner (1995), Doll (1996), Oliva (1997), Wiles & Bondi (1998)
As a field of study*	Beauchamp (1981), Schubert (1986), McNeil (1996)
As images or characterizations*	Schubert (1986)
As evolving, or nonplanned experiences**	Apple (1990), Aronowitz & Giroux (1991), Pinar (1992), Slattery (1995)

Notes: *Denotes modern view of curriculum.
 **Denotes postmodern view of curriculum.

help students learn permanent knowledge and think rationally. In essentialism, teachers guide students in mastering content based principles and facts and in becoming competent learners. Students are expected to be accepting of teachers' knowledge, never questioning their authority. Students' idiosyncratic interests are considered irrelevant to developing the curriculum.

Contemporary conceptions of curriculum (as characterized by progressivism and reconstructionism) emerged as a reaction against the extreme autocratic and directive teaching behaviors and lockstep curriculum that were evidenced by the traditionalists. Espousing the benefits of an interdisciplinary curriculum, the progessivists sought to integrate students' interests and to focus on present and future national and international issues (Ornstein & Hunkins, 1998). The progressivists promoted the development of lifelong learners, while reconstructionists encouraged students to acquire and use knowledge for the betterment of society and humankind.

The modernists advocate for a technocratic approach to curriculum making. In accord with their belief systems, curriculum was presumed to be comprised of identifiable components and procedures that are knowable and predetermined. The technocracy affiliated with the modern view of curriculum has been credited with promoting a sense of calmness by assuring that there are procedures to assure an orderly and efficient development and control of the curriculum (Hunkins & Hammill, 1994).

Traditionalists' Conceptions

Describing curriculum as subject matter, Hutchins (1936) claimed that "permanent studies (the rules of grammar, reading, rhetoric, logic, and mathematics) and great books of the Western World should comprise the curriculum" (p. 82). Similarly, Bestor (1956) stated that curriculum was "disciplined study in grammar, literature and writing, mathematics, science, history, and foreign language" (pp. 48–49). Stressing the importance of discipline-based inquiry, Phenix (1962) suggested that the determination of curriculum should consist of "knowledge from disciplines and a guided recapitulation of the process of inquiry" (p. 64). Illustrating the point that content may not be limited to solely textual matter transmitted in the classroom, Oliva (1997) reported that curriculum may be "a course of study," "a set of materials," or "that which is taught both inside and outside of the school and directed by the school" (p. 4).

Tyler (1957), Taba (1962), Saylor, Alexander, and Lewis (1981), Beauchamp (1981), and Oliva (1997) described curriculum as a plan. Tyler proposed that "curriculum is all of the learning of students which is planned by and directed by the school to attain its educational goals" (p. 79). Taba (1962) concurred that "curriculum is a plan for learning" (p. 11). Saylor et al. (1981) defined curriculum as a plan "for providing sets of learning opportunities for persons to be educated" (p. 9). Beauchamp (1981) suggested that curriculum is a substantive entity, or a thoughtfully developed plan to guide what is to be taught. Also describing curriculum as a plan, Oliva (1997) observed that "curriculum is everything that is planned by school personnel" (p. 4). Suggesting that "curriculum is all of the planned learning outcomes for which the school is responsible" (p. 48), Popham and Baker (1970) claimed that curriculum should be viewed as ends or terminal objectives.

Describing curriculum as a system, Beauchamp (1981) suggested that it consisted of three interactive components: personnel involved in curriculum making; organizational procedures necessary to produce, implement, evaluate, and modify a curriculum; and the maintenance required to keep a curriculum system functional. The notion of the curriculum as a system implies a governing of the cluster of relationships that guide humans in the process of curriculum development and use of the curriculum. As a system, curriculum is part of the total operations of schooling. The curriculum system provides a framework for individuals charged with the responsibility for making and overseeing the effectiveness of the curriculum, for deciding what shall be taught, and for selecting appropriate instructional strategies.

Summary of the Traditional View

The relationship between emergent definitions of what curriculum is and consensually agreed upon views of education has historical precedent. For example, the notion of curriculum as content or subject matter is rooted in the ideals of the classical humanists, such as Charles Elliot (McNeil, 1996), who favored the transmission of culture and traditional values. Interpretations of curriculum were closely aligned with the educational movement in which they emerged. The traditionalists' view of curriculum is grounded in the belief that reality can be known and transmitted to students by thoughtfully planning their learning experiences before they enter the classroom. Their movement is predicated upon the assumption that if experiences are comprised of carefully selected tasks that coincide with preestablished objectives, then students are more likely to attain specified educational outcomes. Learning experiences are to be selected and sequenced solely by the teacher without consideration of students' desires. The extent to which students attain desired outcomes can be directly assessed by behaviorally oriented measures such as tests and student products that highlight the degree to which objectives were mastered. According to the traditionalists, the teacher's role is exemplified by authoritative and directive behavior. The teacher is considered to be an expert about the subject matter or the content to be learned, or the final arbiter of knowledge.

Contemporary Conceptions

Progressivists have defined curriculum as experiences, or activities aimed at shaping student behavior, and as a field of study. Many progressivists believed that the socializing function of the school curriculum, or the process, rather than the product should predominate. For example, Caswell and Campbell (1935) believed that the curriculum was comprised of the experiences that students have under the school's guidance. Claiming that the curriculum was a sequence of potential school experiences, Smith, Stanley, and Shores (1957) stated that curriculum was "for the purpose of disciplining children and youth in group ways of thinking and acting" (p. 4). Johnson (1970–1971) suggested that "curriculum is concerned not with what students will do in the learning situation, but with what they will learn as a consequence of what they do. Curriculum is concerned with the results" (p. 25). Stressing the notion of confluence, the quality of interactions between students and teachers was viewed as vital to students' development in a progressive curriculum that integrated affective and cognitive domains (Ornstein & Hunkins, 1998).

The notion of curriculum as experience was also advocated by child-centered specialists who believed that the curriculum should be developed ac-

cording to the child's interests. Experts such as Hall (1907) and Dewey
(1938) suggested that curriculum be designed according to children's developmental and experiential needs. Using the information from child development literature to design a developmentally appropriate curriculum, Hall
recommended a pedocentric curriculum. Dewey (1916) believed that schools
should offer students the qualities that characterize education in a democratic
society: shared interests, freedom in interaction, participation, and social relationships. He advocated for a curriculum based on the needs and interests of
students, one that urged students to learn how to think, rather than a pre-
planned curriculum that stressed what to think. However, Dewey (1938) also
recognized the dynamism inherent in an actionable curriculum. He suggested
that teachers explore student reactions and interactions with learning experiences and use this information to design the curriculum in a way that was responsive to their learning needs. Constant change and reorganization of the
curriculum would be necessary to provide the "best possible consequences for
the further development of each student's experiences" (Posner, 1995, p. 51).
Along with promoting academic reasoning ability and social development,
Dewey recommended that curriculum also contribute to individuals' personal
development. Citing the relationship between student well-being and the
well-being of the nation, Dewey stressed the integral role that curriculum
could play in the development of healthy individuals who could work toward
changing society in healthy ways.

Schubert (1986) has characterized the curriculum as a set of images or characterizations. However he has argued that images connote a broader view than
that which is suggested by using labels. In harmony with that perspective, Schubert has maintained that curriculum can be viewed as subject matter, a program
of planned activities, intended learning objectives, cultural reproduction (a reflection of the culture of the local community or society), experiences, a set of
discrete tasks and concepts that require mastery, an agenda to facilitate social reconstruction, or an opportunity for individuals to reconceptualize their own
past and create their own destiny. In this last context, there is an assumption that
curriculum can offer individuals an opportunity to analyze their experiences and
construct their future. Schubert's characterizations of curriculum encompass a
variety of conceptions. These notions range from ideas rooted in the cult of efficiency and behaviorism to processes aimed at engaging students in self-
actualization and discovery of their own destiny. This latter conception has been
commended by the postmodernists (Pinar, 1992; Slattery, 1995).

The importance of content as a mechanism to help students acquire new
knowledge was suggested by Tanner and Tanner (1995), Doll (1996), Oliva
(1997), and Wiles and Bondi (1998). Tanner and Tanner (1995) stated that
currriculum is the "reconstruction of knowledge and experience that enables
the learner to grow in exercising intelligent control of subsequent knowledge
and experience" (p. 189). Similarly, Doll (1996) defined curriculum as "the
formal and informal content and processes by which learners gain knowledge

and understanding, develop skills, and alter attitudes, appreciations, and values under the auspices of that school" (p. 15). Oliva (1997) observed that "curriculum is everything that goes on within a school, including extra-class activities, guidance, and interpersonal relationships," " a series of experiences undergone by learners in school," or "that which an individual learner experiences as a result of schooling" (p. 4). Wiles and Bondi (1998) defined curriculum as "goals or sets of values, which are activated through a development process culminating in classroom experiences for students" (p. 10).

The reconstructionist's view of curriculum was advocated for by social efficiency experts and social reconstructionists. Social efficiency experts such as Bobbitt (1924) and Charters (1923) saw the curriculum as a tool to prepare adults for work in the industrial society. They stressed the identification of learning activities that were closely aligned with jobs, rather than the transmission of culture and classical subjects (McNeil, 1996). In distinct contrast to the ideals advocated by classical humanists and child-centered experts, others recommended that the curriculum be developed to address social agendas. Social reconstructionists such as Rugg (1939) and Counts (1932) envisioned the curriculum as a mechanism to bring about change and ameliorate the dilemmas of society. They believed that the curriculum should provide students with the knowledge necessary for examining justice and equality.

Beauchamp (1981), McNeil (1996), and Schubert (1986) suggested that curriculum should be viewed as a field of study. In this regard, curriculum was to be seen as a distinct and separate area of scholarship comprised of its own foundations, knowledge domains, research, principles, and specialists who interpret knowledge in the field.

Summary of the Contemporary View

The progressivists have embraced a school curriculum that would be humanistic and relevant to students' lives outside of the classroom. Correspondingly to these aims, learning experiences might be co-constructed and designed according to students' needs. Behaving in a more democratic manner, teachers would act as a facilitator or a guide and engage students as active learners. As a facilitator, the teacher was to guide students through processes, scientific inquiry, and problem-solving (Ornstein & Hunkins, 1998). Also advocating for a less authoritarian classroom environment, the reconstructionists viewed the teacher as an agent of change who would help students become aware of community-based, national, or international dilemmas that confronted humankind. Showing students how to use inquiry methods within the social sciences, among other skills and subjects, in order to examine the ways in which they can response proactively to dilemmas was considered to be one goal of the instruction.

Limitations of the Modern View

Owing primarily to their use of technicism, the modernists have been criticized on the grounds that they can not provide value-free information devoid of expressions that reveal dominant political or value commitments. The use of behavioral methodology to measure student outcomes arguably seeks to attain political power control, not truth (explanation). One of the major issues that modernists have to grapple with lies in the limitations associated with conclusions drawn from empirical research. Greene (1994) asserts that:

Too many researchers still find it difficult to confront the effects of technicism on their thinking or to face the problem of objectivity. The desire for precision and disinterestedness continues on, sometimes as a corrective against what is viewed as uncontained relativism and reliance on mere *opinion*. (p. 432)

Modernists have expended considerable energies in determining the effectiveness of the curriculum through measurable and observable ways. For example, they have used empirical methods to (1) measure student achievement, (2) determine if there is a cause-effect relationship between teaching behaviors and student outcomes, and (3) ascertain if there is a predictable relationship between teacher and student behaviors and student outcomes. However, some researchers have challenged both the inherent methodology and the defensibility of claims made by technocrats. One of the limitations associated with technicism lies in its inability to discern if the quality of research illuminates the social consequences associated with competing methodologies. Technocratic research varies in its ability to empirically predict consequences associated with assumptions underlying qualitative and quantitative methods of research. Second, knowledge claims that emanate from behavioral concepts may or may not be socially defensible.

Kendler (1993) advised empirical researchers to abandon their assumptions that reductionisitic or technocratic research can identify definitive principles that describe predictable human behavior. He cautioned those who believed that empirical methodology could be used solely to guide teaching and teacher education programs. Instead, he suggested that empiricists give up the notion that a gap between what is and what ought to be can be bridged only by empirical evidence. Agreeing with this point of view, Martin and Sugarman (1993) suggested that the research grounded in empirical techniques suffered from an overemphasis on its methodology. They asserted that empirical researchers have inadequately addressed the epistemological problems that confront assumptions underlying their work. They pointed out that empirical research fails to adequately address its own biases. Martin and Sugarman claimed that the empirical research on teaching (1) lacks an underlying theory that identifies specific variables, (2) provides an insufficient description of the characteristics of focal variables that are particularly worthy of empirical scrutiny, or (3) fails to explain why empirically based evidence is pragmatically unmanageable.

The selection of variables chosen for evaluation or research may be subject to bias. Consider for example, why summative measures of student achievement are more predominant than other, less tangible measures such as the quality of classroom life or the quality of teacher-student interactions that may

exert a significant influence on outcomes. Challenging educators to be clear about their intentions, Messick (1981) asked, "What evidence justifies the proposed test use in contrast to evidence supporting alternative proposals?" (p. 9). Resnick and Resnick (1985) raised a related issue and highlighted the political purpose of testing. They suggested that tests have been used for the purpose of public accountability, program evaluation, and institutional comparison.

Recognizing the potentially damaging impact of prepackaged curriculum, an insistence on attainment of educational outcomes, de-skilling of teachers, and trivializing learning into discrete and irrelevant tasks, Greene (1977) has also called attention to possibilities of what curriculum ought to be. While decrying the "anesthetic character of so many institutions in our culture, including schools" and rendering of students as "passive: gazers, not see-ers; hearers, not listeners" (p. 284), she claimed that "curriculum . . . ought to be a means for providing opportunities for the seizing of a range of meanings by persons open to the world, especially today" (p. 284).

How does the modern curriculum influence teacher and student roles? Highlighting the potential impediments to teaching embedded in a modern curriculum, Eisner (1990) wrote that:

Teachers unnecessarily constrained by routines or rules they have no control over are least likely to provide educationally liberating conditions for their students. Teachers who themselves cannot speculate and take risks are unlikely to make speculation and risk taking possible for students. (p. 63)

Moreover, the teacher's ability to implement creative and novel lesson plans may be severely constrained by external pressures to insure that students attain successful outcomes. Apple (1990) surmised that

curriculum determination at the level of the classroom, in teacher education, and elsewhere is being increasingly politicized, and is being more and more subject to legislative mandates, mandates from state departments of education, and so on. Test driven curricula, overly rationalized, and bureaucratized school experiences and planning models, atomized and reductive curricula, all of this is happening. This *has* often resulted in the de-skilling of teachers and curriculum workers, a separation of conception from execution as planning is done away from the local level, and has as well led to a severe intensification of educators' work as more and more has to be done with less and less time available to do it. (p. 382)

Pronouncing the injustices associated with modernism, Apple (1991), insisted that modern curriculum has done much to promote unequal power relationships, exalt the voice of the dominant class, and marginalize those without a political power base from creating their own visions of what school practice should be.

Contributions of the Modern View

What does the modern view of curriculum contribute to school practice?
The modernists ease the work of teachers by providing a framework for identifying specific objectives, selecting and organizing learning activities, and identifying concrete methods for evaluating the students' successful acquisition of
intended outcomes. There is little doubt that this process owes much to the
proliferation of packaged and pre-planned curriculum. The teacher's role in
curriculum development is minimized.

To thwart the perpetuation of the misperceptions that abound about the
field of curriculum we must be succinct and clear about how we use language.
The modern view of curriculum allows for planning experiences that has a distinct practical value for teachers. In my experience in working with educators
who study school curriculum, I have discovered that teachers need opportunities to develop an actionable platform for their ideas about curriculum. Simply
offering teachers textualized meanings of curricular concepts or lecturing
them about the important epochs in the field is insufficient for applicability in
the classroom.

How can we help teachers acquire a working knowledge of curriculum precepts and relate this information to practice-based situations? This can be accomplished by providing teachers with workshop activities or course-related
experiences in "school curriculum."[3] Portfolios, observations, and interviews,
for example, can be instrumental in helping teachers formulate new ways of
seeing how curriculum concepts are used in practice. Experiences for teachers
should be designed to (1) teach the basic principles of the curriculum knowledge base, (2) enhance understandings and application of the curriculum
knowledge base, (3) encourage the development of informed practitioners,
(4) help them visualize the connections between their idealized ways of teaching and their operational ways of teaching, (5) encourage their thinking about
the ways in which they have observed or practiced curriculum, and (6) offer
opportunities for engaging in a deliberate and personalized process of translating theory into practice.

Activities can be developed that encourage teachers to (1) construct and interpret their own knowledge about the field of curriculum, (2) analyze how
curriculum principles operate in their classroom, and (3) determine just what
essential curriculum knowledge is and how that knowledge can be used in
practice. A few examples follow. Students can learn much about the practical
application of curriculum by interviewing an administrator or curriculum specialist who oversees the effectiveness of the total school curriculum. Designing
a portfolio permits students to develop a "personalized" understanding of the
ways in which curriculum operates in educational settings and for seeing how
theory influences the actual practice of curriculum. Providing active learning
experiences rather than didactic teaching can promote student participation.
Developing learning activities that focus on how to redesign curriculum can
help teachers acquire the curriculum skills necessary to modifying the curricu-

lum. What type of learning experience might foster this last idea? Offering students experiences in curriculum design, an opportunity to write curriculum, teach various lessons, and formatively assess its effectiveness can help students discover the relationship between course conceptual material and practical application. Also creating learning experiences in which teachers have the opportunity to analyze classroom teaching and learning processes can facilitate their ability to develop more sophisticated ways of seeing and understanding classroom phenomena.

We can use supplementary journal articles that discuss teachers' use of curriculum in the classroom. How can articles that reveal the actual practice of curriculum facilitate student learning? When given opportunities to discuss readings that offer a synthesis of the current breadth of viewpoints in the field along with their own experiences, teachers often expand their recognition of the multiplicity of perspectives about issues in practice. Almost reflexively, they begin to appreciate the range of choices that they have in selecting an action. These experiences can illuminate how conceptual kinds of curricular knowledge can be applied to their own classroom practice. For example, these experiences might broaden their awareness of existing educational practice or strategies and lead to different kinds of actions and planning. Professors who teach courses in school curriculum, curriculum design, and evaluation can help teachers make sense of theoretical or conceptual constructs by translating abstract information into the language of practice. Moreover, we can exercise leadership by moving our conversations beyond the obvious, beyond mere criticism to a more proactive stance and a more hopeful vision of how modern and postmodernists can work together.

THE POSTMODERN VIEW OF CURRICULUM

Who are the postmodernists? The postmodernists are comprised by several voices who argue for a curriculum that is nonplanned, emergent, and evolving. The postmodernists are classified into several groups: Marxists, individuals with interests in individuals such as the feminist, phenomenological, and historical perspectives, and aesthetic critics. The Marxists offer an analysis of the political and economic underpinnings of curriculum. The feminists use autobiography, phenomenology, and psychoanalysis to portray women's experiences. The phenomenologists explore the meaning attached to a lived experience as construed by the person who has the experience and the meanings and significance perceived and received by society-at-large. The historians provide a critical synopsis of the field. The aesthetic critics call our attention to the division between the academic and so-called academic subjects, the marginalization of various subject content that has an aesthetic or nonempirical framework (see Lincoln, 1992).

Essentially, the postmodernist movement is based largely upon criticism of the field of curriculum. They claim that curriculum suffers from over-reliance on rendering quantifiable outcomes, technocracy, and bureaucracy and that curriculum serves an instrument to coerce, control, and oppress students' thinking (Ornstein & Hunkins, 1998). While it is true that Bobbitt's (1924) and Charters' (1923) ideas epitomize the technocratic and bureaucratic ideals associated with cultural hegemony, their view of the curriculum represents only one component of a much larger gestalt. Much of the postmodernists' critique is rooted in their extended criticism of the Tyler rationale (1949). The postmodernists criticize the Tyler rationale for its failure to address political aspects of the curriculum and discuss how curriculum research should be conducted about practical dilemmas in specific milieus (Schwab, 1970).

Apple (1986), Giroux (1994), Pinar (1988), and Slattery (1995) among others have criticized schools and the larger social structures committed to maintaining the hierarchies in schools. They have stressed that the modernists' conceptions of curriculum are a form of social legitimization (Lincoln, 1992). Apple has denounced the perpetuation of political and economic practices of a dominant majority who define what curriculum is. Pinar (1992) has condemned curriculum practices such as standardized testing that diminish teacher autonomy. Reducing students and teachers to automata is the result of the factory model, he asserted. Giroux (1981) has stressed the need for a curriculum that infuses a critical theoretical discussion about the quality and purpose of schooling and human life. He has asserted that the development of curriculum must be responsive to cultural pluralism and individual uniqueness. A new mode of curriculum is a necessity, he claimed, to abandon the pretense of being value-free and to create one that allows for knowledge to be problematic and situated in discourse that permits debate and communication. Giroux (1994) has also criticized modern curriculum for

selectively [offering] depictions of the larger world through representations that people struggle over to name what counts as knowledge, what counts as communities of learning, what social representations matter, and what visions of the future can be represented as legitimate. (p. 35)

However, Jencks (1992) declared that postmodernism is a hybridization and complexification of the modern curriculum and, as noted by Hunkins & Hammill (1994), a transformation, rather than an overturning of the Tyler/Taba tradition.

Postmodernists have decried the institutional frameworks that guide teaching and learning. Curriculum, they suggest should be reconceived in broader and more humanistic ways than are evidenced in the first part of the twentieth century (Lincoln, 1992). They have challenged the behavioral and empirical dimensions and what they perceive to be a politicized agenda supporting curriculum development. Briefly, postmodernists such as Giroux (1994), Pinar (1988), and Slattery (1995) claimed that the curriculum should be emancipatory, empowering, and liberating.

The notion of curriculum as evolving and nonplanned experiences has been suggested by several educators. Wiles and Bondi (1998) offer two definitions of postmodernism (Doll, 1993a; Friere, 1973) that seem to succinctly illustrate what this paradigm exemplifies. Doll (1993a) has suggested that postmodernism will result in

a new sense of educational order . . . culminating in a new concept of curriculum. The linear, sequential, easily quantifiable ordering system dominating education today could give way to a more complex, pluralistic, unpredictable system or network. Such a complex network will, like itself, always be in transition, in process. (p. 3)

In denouncing practices that emanate from the modern curriculum, Friere (1973) asserted that "the elite's values are superimposed on people. Education, as a practice of freedom, rejects the notion that knowledge is extended or transferred to students as if they were objects" (p. 96).

Emphasizing the emergent and dynamic nature of curriculum, Aronowitz and Giroux (1991) wrote that:

as we move into the 21st century, we find ourselves no longer constrained by modernist images of purpose and history. Elements of discontinuity, rapture, and difference (chaos) provide alternative sets of referents by which to understand modernity as well as challenge and modify it. (p. 115)

Illustrating the destabilizing impact of postmodernism and challenging universal meaning thought to reside in history, Aronowitz and Giroux (1991) observed that:

Postmodernism's refusal of grand narratives, its rejection of universal reason as a foundation for human affairs, its decentering of the humanist subject, its radical problematization of representation, and its celebration of plurality and the politics of racial, gender, and ethnic differences have sparked major debate among conservatives, liberals, and radicals in an increasing diverse number of fields. (p. 61)

Limitations of the Postmodern View

The postmodern interpretation of the modern view is shortsighted on several counts. First, the contention that Tyler (1949) advanced highly specific behavioral objectives is erroneous. In fact, Tyler (1949) suggested the use of broadly framed and generalizable objectives (Hlebowitsh, 1995). In a discussion about purposes of schools, Tyler (1968) identified two critical tasks that schools must undertake not because they "involve additions to the basic functions of purposes of the schools, but because they should be viewed as important tasks with purposes of their own" (p. 10). He cited the need for the curriculum to be responsive to disadvantaged students and to reach all "children whose backgrounds have given them little or no basis for school work" (p. 9). Tyler also claimed that it was imperative to provide "educational opportunities and to assure effective learning for youth from varied backgrounds of training, experience, and outlook" (p. 10). These statements reflect Tyler's recognition of the importance of developing curricula that would be responsive to the needs of individual students and society. Tyler's consideration of the context in which curriculum objectives were to be developed should serve to dispel any beliefs that are associated with a "content-neutral management model" (Hlebowitsh, 1995, p. 28).

The postmodernists' claim that modern views of curriculum have compressed "school experience into low-level group procedures" (Hlebowitsh, 1993, p. 19) represents a gross distortion of reality and a reductionist critique of the field. Furthermore, the postmodern critique is devoid of any discussion about how schools might work according to their ideological framework (Hlebowitsh, 1993, p. 45). Instead, as he has observed, their dialogue is centered on what is wrong and how schools do not work! As Hlebowitsh has so aptly noted, "A voice built on dissent, disapprobation, and consuming negativity is rarely able to supply its own plan for the construction of educative environments" (Hlebowitsh, 1993, p. 45). How can we talk about the aims of education without a sense of what we hope students will be able to do as a result of our work together? This is akin to trying to build a home without a blueprint or performing an appendectomy without the appropriate training.

Second, another limitation to the postmodern conception lies in its methodological integrity. Short (1987) suggested that the paradigmatic shifts away from a positivistic framework to other forms of inquiry that coalesced into dissemination of their perspective may have arisen from a necessity to:

work, publish, and discuss curriculum research in isolated enclaves somewhat protected from the interaction of tough critics of an approach or of its use in a particular study. While this isolationist tendency has gradually softened . . . there still remains what might be called a kind of irrational allegiance on the part of some persons to a particular method or particular interpretation of a methods long after a need to sharpen, or modify, or to abandon a method has become clear to others. (p. 7)

A more demeaning critique came from Tanner and Tanner (1981), who charged that aside from being atheoretical, the postmodernist movement represented poor scholarship and coalesced from individuals who were antiresearch.

According to Lincoln (1992), the premise upon which the postmodernists' viewpoint is grounded does and does not sustain critical analysis. On the one hand, impetus for the movement is based largely on specific unpalatable components of the Tyler (1949) rationale. Perhaps equally important to this discussion is recognition that the postmodernists' interpretation of Tyler's contributions to the field are at best very pejorative and rather extreme. Their interpretation of any theoretical conception of curriculum to the right of their own view would suggest that the entire modern view is comprised exclusively of Tyler's work. Furthermore, their failure to acknowledge that Tyler's ideas are not representative of simply one person's views is rather simplistic. His philosophical beliefs coincide with Dewey's (1916) view of education in a democratic society, that "the conception of education as a social process and function has no definite meaning until we define the kind of society we have in mind" (p. 97). Tyler's work is solidly aligned with Dewey's notion of the qualities that characterize a democratic education (shared interests, freedom in interaction, participation, and social relationships). Tyler's ideas are grounded in a clear understanding of the research that preceded the development of the *Rationale* and an awareness of the history of the field, but the postmodernist critique is not. Using this perspective, the postmodernists have missed or ignored other views of the curriculum, including those of other traditionalists and progressivists.

Third, their interpretation and analysis of history of curriculum development seems incomplete, despite the fact that their interests in political, social, aesthetic, economic, and cultural issues that exert significant influence upon curriculum design, implementation, and evaluation are worthy of serious consideration (Lincoln, 1992). They assert that reconceptualizing the field of curriculum is their priority. However, they either fail to acknowledge or simply lack an understanding of the historical mandates of the field, the current breadth of viewpoints in the field, and a commitment to a sense of unifying principles. When one considers this debate from this vantage point, the dilemma that the postmodernists present is drawn into sharper focus. While their emergent thrust is to reconceptualize curriculum, they propose to make sweeping changes to a field without acknowledging the historical framework of curriculum. To disown the field and insist on being considered a curricularist is antithetical to the role of a curricularist. Curricularists recognize that schools in a democratic society must commit to providing experiences that are both conserving and liberating. Learning must foster both the development of intellect by helping students learn about their histories and the fundamental tenets of subject areas and critical mindedness as exemplified in the ability to problem solve and think critically.

Fourth, it is equally quizzical that postmodernists impose impermeable boundaries and avert the possibility of a scholarly and collegial dialogue with modernists. They assume an imperialistic position by positing ideologies that defy characterization and explication of how their ideas might be applied to the school curriculum. Doll (1993b) suggested that attempts to define postmodernism, while perhaps still in its infancy, go against the very characterization of their movement to generate and open the field to novel conceptualizations. Despite the difficulties that arise when trying to delineate their agenda, I believe that their movement is not without its own agenda. Postmodernists demonstrate their own form of oppression and mechanisms for casting students into roles and characterizations that they might not understand or willingly select.

A more in-depth exploration of this interpretation may clarify this point. In a *Harvard Educational Review* article, Slattery (1995) suggested that "teachers must help students reinterpret their own lives and uncover new talents and creative insight" (p. 630). After reading this, many questions came to mind. What is the instructional value of such an activity? Why should we assume that students need or want to reinterpret their lives? If this idea is applicable to some groups of students, which type of student might benefit from this experience? Why is it the teacher's role to help student's reinterpret their lives? Should teachers be expected to serve as pseudo-therapists? At what point in their programs of professional development are teachers likely to receive such training? Are their professors trained to provide them with necessary knowledge and related experiences? Are we to assume that there is a direct correlation between these activities and healing students? What evidence suggests that all teachers possess the requisite instructional skills needed to successfully guide students' academic growth, let alone their personal inquiry? Perhaps more to the point, can the postmodernists provide an example of methodologies or strategies that teachers might use to help students reinterpret their lives? Also, the boundaries concerning what constitutes teaching and what is considered educational therapy appear to be inconsequential to many postmodernists.

The fifth difficulty associated with postmodernism is that it may suffer from an inability to offer persuasive knowledge claims or evidence of its overall effectiveness as a means to direct curriculum practice that society can trust. How can postmodern tenets be translated for use in teaching in the classroom? Consider the practicality and applicability of autobiographies and journals suggested by Pinar (1992) and Slattery (1995). The use of autobiographic narratives and personal journals have been mentioned as activities "to validate the lived experience and process of growth in each person in the schooling context" (Slattery, 1995, p. 630). How would the postmodernists respond to issues such as personal space, privacy, and appropriate types of professional expertise that might be violated by these activities? What about the student who does not want to write an autobiography? What about the intrusive nature of these learning activities? What about the appropriateness of teachers commenting on students' private reflection and inner musings? Is there a presumption that these activities are a viable substitute for teaching discipline-based knowledge?

Families might become outraged at use of a curriculum that encouraged revelation of family-related matters in a public forum. Students and parents might be averse to curriculum activities that fostered understandings but failed to provide immediate pay offs or measure progress in academic disciplines. Parents and politicians might balk at the notion of engaging students in discussions to talk about how they feel they could become empowered, as this could jeopardize the authoritative structures that oversee the function of schools. Some of their discussion about practical applications of the postmodern for curriculum development closely resemble long-standing practices or training outside the typical sphere of pre-service educators.

Doll (1989) suggested that learning experiences should be comprised of activities that create discomfort as a precursor to learning, yet offer students an opportunity to create their own alternatives. Isn't this similar to co-constructing the curriculum? To my way of thinking, creative teachers, regardless of their paradigmatic inclinations, will try to give students a modicum of choice when appropriate, if for no other reason than to encourage active participation in learning experiences. Doll suggested a two-tier hierarchical process of curriculum development in which students would be active in choosing homework assignments, methods of evaluation, and projects to be completed. Why are these suggestions purported to be aligned with postmodernism? Isn't this synonymous in part with allowing students to show what they know and have learned via self-selected forms of representation such as dramatic renditions, musical compositions, poetry, or other artistic media? Doll's third suggestion was to promote dialectical interaction to encourage mutual inquiry and the transaction of knowledge, rather than transmission. Certainly the thoughtful and skilled educator strives for this type of relationship with his/her students. What better way for students to become self-regulated and independent learners than through mutual inquiry? Surely this quality of teaching was not commensurate with the emergence of postmodernism! How do his suggestions differ from the practitioners who seek to offer students multiple perspectives of content-related knowledge? In what ways does his approach differ from that of the teacher who seeks to teach in ways that are responsive to students' diverse learning styles?

Pinar (1992) advocated for a curriculum that promotes intellectual freedom and social psychoanalysis. Intellectual freedom, he suggested, would permit exploration and contemplation of progressive forms of the arts, humanities, and social sciences. What he means by the term "progressive forms of the arts" seems to be left to the reader's discretion. He claimed, however, that although emergent learning might not be evaluated by standardized examinations, intelligence could be cultivated in fundamental ways, free of bureaucraticized frameworks. Social psychoanalysis would be purposeful in "[allowing] our labor and understandings to function as do those in psychoanalysis, to enlarge the perceptions and deepen the intelligence of the participants" (p. 234). In practical language, he suggested that teachers would have students realize "that intelligence and learning can lead to other worlds, not just the successful exploitation of this one" (p. 234).

Lofty and unconventional are ideals that Pinar has proposed, but perhaps of greater concern is how do we train teachers to become more psychologically oriented and more attuned to their inner selves? While I am not questioning the values embedded in his notions, I believe that the preparation of teachers often takes place in arenas that are completely devoid of such a psychoanalytical orientation. Moreover, the type of curriculum reform that Pinar suggests would necessitate that individuals analyze and process their reactions from an internal frame of reference, rather than expect the environment to be malleable in the service of fulfilling their innermost needs.

Sixth, despite their attacks on the hegemony of schools and larger social structures that preserve bureaucracy, postmodernists seem unwilling to provide an integrated theory of curriculum, a coherent program, or an exemplar of the practical application of critical pedagogy, claiming that such behavior is antithetical to their philosophical dispositions. What practical applications grounded in postmodernism can be offered to classroom teachers? Since most teachers are overly reliant upon textbooks, how can an undefined and unwritten postmodernist curriculum help them practice their ideals?

Questions loom concerning how postmodern ideology can be actualized into teaching and learning contexts. Superficial discussions or positing an imperial position does not absolve the postmodernists of an obligation to address these criticisms. The fact that postmodernists do not align themselves with either a pragmatic agenda or a critical position fails to achieve anything of substantive value for educators who are dealing with the reality of teaching diverse students (Contas, 1998).

Contributions of the Postmodern View

Apple (1990) has suggested that curriculum should be guided by a more cooperative and democratic work ethic. Problems of curriculum and teaching, he asserted, should involve those likely to be affected by school practice in deliberating and designing the objectives and ends that they believe schools should accomplish. Apple's suggestions for curriculum development are illustrated in part by the new democratic curriculum initiatives that coincide with the Carl D. Perkins Vocational Educational Act of 1984. One of the aims of this mandate is to integrate learning experiences with work opportunities for students with special needs and those who are otherwise educationally or economically disadvantaged.

Giroux (1994) recommended that we restructure the work that teachers do and begin to view teachers as public intellectuals.

As public individuals, teachers must bring to bear in their classrooms and other pedagogical sites, the courage, analytical tools, moral vision, time, and dedication that is necessary to return schools to their primary task: being places of critical education in the service of creating a public sphere of citizens who are able to exercise power over their own lives and especially over the conditions of knowledge acquisition. (p. 43)

Claiming that teachers bridge teaching to the operation of power outside the classroom, Giroux urged that teachers "close the gap between school and the real world" (p. 44), "expand the relevance of the curriculum to include the richness and diversity of the students. . . . decenter the curriculum" (p. 45). He stressed that "as public intellectuals, teachers need to make the issue of cultural difference a defining principle of curriculum development and research" (p. 45). He also asserted that we must develop an educational policy that "[moves] away from an assimilationist ethic and the profoundly Eurocentric fantasies of a common culture to one which links national identity to diverse traditions and histories" (p. 46).

In earlier work, Giroux (1990) claimed that understanding the meaning, authority, and subjectivity embedded in the construction of language is critical to the ways in which educators and students construct relationships with themselves, others, and the larger reality. Instrumental to this process is that educators broaden their own theoretical framework to include "new categories of analysis and by rethinking the actual purpose of teaching" (p. 368). He claimed that viewing curriculum as part of a larger "struggle between dominate and subordinate discourses has critical implications for how educators produce and 'read' curriculums, engage . . . students, and redefine critically their own role" (p. 368).

The postmodernist's reaction against extreme rationality inherent in the scientific movement has certainly opened up the field to novel ideas. They have called our attention to how politics, racism, class struggles, power, equality, equity, sexism, marginalized people, and aesthetics affect teaching and learning. They have aptly called attention to the dehumanizing and depersonalizing aspects of school life. Each of these variables deserves careful consideration when designing, implementing, and evaluating the curriculum. Claims that goals are inseparable from experiences that generate the goals and that curriculum needs to evolve contextually from students' experiences are unarguable (Hunkins & Hammill, 1994). The postmodernists' implicit admonition is that new metaphors are needed to guide notions of what curriculum development should be. They advocate for dismantling what they perceive is a non–student-centered, irrelevant, and lockstep curriculum comprised of discrete activities.

SUMMARY OF THE MODERN/POSTMODERN DEBATE

Scholars who affiliate themselves with the modern view have at times become embroiled in debates with postmodernists about which particular paradigms should guide curriculum development and inquiry. These debates center around issues of legitimacy, feasibility, utility, and application for classroom practice. For example, modern curriculum scholars have cited the lack of a unifying theory, coherent program, and practice-based exemplars as limitations of the postmodern perspective. In contrast, postmodernists have strongly criticized modern conceptions for oppressing classes of people, stultifying creativity, and limiting the development of students' potential.

Modern conceptions of curriculum are broadly perceived to have their etiology in the work of the Tyler (1949) rationale. However, when it is taken too literally, many educators have discounted the modern view, highlighting what they claim to be technocractic and reductionist limitations of this approach. Monocular interpretations of the modern perspective have generated substantial dialogue and research papers among curriculum scholars for decades.

The postmodernists have provided an eloquent body of literature in an attempt to expose how the curriculum operates to render unjust social ends. They claim that exposure is the first step in restoring schools to their appropriate role "in fostering empowerment, transcendence, and liberation" (Lincoln, 1992, p. 89). Their critique offers curricularists an opportunity to revisit the ways in which curriculum is viewed and practiced. However, as discussed earlier, I believe that it is a disservice to the lives we affect to remain embroiled in battles about which definition of curriculum is worth most. Instead, we can view the postmodernist's critique as an invitation to discuss paradigms, improve practice, and create new understandings.

The concerns that the postmodernists have articulated, as well as their vocal distaste for linearity, have prompted a reanalysis of the conceptualizations that govern notions of what curriculum is and should be. While the debates about which conception and definition is most appropriate to guide curriculum development, inquiry, and evaluation are remarkably similar to the paradigm debates in research methodologies,[4] I believe that paradigmatic conceptions of curriculum influence student outcomes to a much lesser degree than claimed. In my opinion, much of this esoteric discussion tends to become blather as it steers us further away from helping teachers broaden their ability to use alternative instructional strategies (Joyce & Weil, 1996) or modify the curriculum for the difficult to reach and difficult to teach student.

MOVING BEYOND DEFINITIONS

One avenue for moving beyond the issue of definitions requires an effort to focus on developing curriculum that reflects a synthesis of the modern, progressivist, and postmodernist views.[5] Such efforts might be shaped by offering a framework of questions to guide curriculum development. These guiding questions allow the curricularist to respond to the aims of education advocated by the traditionalist and progressivist and to incorporate the qualities of flexibility, dynamism, and responsiveness suggested by the postmodernists. Though the questions that follow are a synthesis of some of the concerns raised by the postmodernists, they are unequivocally grounded in the modernist view of curriculum.

Any framework designed to integrate the tenets posited by modern and postmodern paradigms will exemplify the challenges imposed by an intentional curriculum versus the taught curriculum. The ideas proposed hereafter may be instrumental in the development of the intentional curriculum. However, the real measure of success would ultimately be derived from their actual operationalization in the taught curriculum. While this topic will not be addressed in this chapter, there is little doubt that a different type of teacher and school culture will be needed to implement the suggested notions.

To plan and design a curriculum that is contextually responsive to students' learning styles, social-emotional characteristics, and cultural backgrounds and to plan activities that incorporate individuals' sensory modalities may be plausible, but if and how it becomes operationalized or taught will be a complicated endeavor. What skills and tools would be required of the average classroom teacher? Suffice it to say that operationalizing this type of curriculum would be no easy task. Teachers would need to be familiar and facile in their judicious use of curriculum strategies. They would need to think on their feet to adapt curriculum for students who may find classroom materials inaccessible. Teachers would need to be highly creative individuals, capable of thinking outside the scope of traditional or institutional expectations and able to use novel ways to engage the difficult-to-reach and the difficult-to-teach student. They would need to carefully analyze the issues that characterize students' emergent difficulties during learning and offer alternate representations of material to be learned. They would need both confidence and expertise in making curricular modifications. Associated with these skills, teachers would need to demonstrate empathic perceptual abilities, that is, the capacity to sense or feel what the student is experiencing so that they could respond appropriately to ameliorate learning dilemmas. Empathic perceptual ability would necessitate that teachers could objectify reality as it exists in actuality, not as a by-product of their own belief or expectation. Teachers would need to use the techniques inherent to various forms of methodological inquiry to formulate an understanding of what was happening in the here and now, devoid of their own prejudice or bias.

The school culture would need to invite teacher creativity rather than insist upon strict compliance with prepackaged curriculum. The culture would need to encourage and provide opportunities for teachers to engage in reconceptualizing the curriculum. Advisedly, school principals would need to exhibit the capacity to model such behaviors, identify areas of potential teacher growth, and create an environment that celebrates the pursuit of ongoing professional development.

The guiding questions presented here are designed to encourage educators to be reflective rather than reactionary and to look beyond the nature of cognitive factors that influence teaching and learning. These questions integrate the social, cultural, economic, political, phenomenological, aesthetic, moral, and ethical variables that influence the work done by both students and teacher and require an analysis of how learning and teaching are influenced by these factors in learning environments and the larger society. Representing a reconstructed view of curriculum development that emanates from a broadly conceived problem-focused approach, these questions are designed to stimulate a critical analysis of school curriculum for education in a democratic society.

BEHAR-HORENSTEIN'S QUESTIONS TO GUIDE CURRICULUM DEVELOPMENT

1. Does the purpose of the intentional curriculum reflect the needs of students in a democratic society?
2. Is the intentional curriculum relevant to life beyond the classroom?

3. Has the intentional curriculum been designed to coincide with students' learning needs? Is the curriculum developmentally appropriate?

4. Does the intentional curriculum design reflect the social, emotional, cognitive, cultural, economic, political, moral, ethical, phenomenological, and aesthetic needs of the students?

5. How will students' prior achievement and experiences be assessed and factored into the design of the intentional curriculum?

6. Is the intentional curriculum comprised of the current discipline-related knowledge base?

7. Is the intentional curriculum characterized by situated knowledge that acknowledges cultural pluralism as well as the identities and humanity of individuals?

8. Is the curriculum decontextualized, capable of redefinition in accord with the dynamism inherent to local milieu?

9. How should the intentional curriculum be organized to reflect the needs of students in a democratic society?

10. Does the curriculum exhibit flexibility? Is it dynamic, evolving, and emergent?

11. Is the intentional curriculum capable of accommodating play and creativity while simultaneously demonstrating rigor?

12. Does the curriculum empower students to use knowledge as a means to direct their own lives?

13. What learning experiences should be developed to coincide with teachers' instructional methodologies and students' thinking and learning styles?

14. What learning activities should be selected or designed to foster the growth of students' conceptual thinking, problem-solving behavior, and creativity?

15. What types of product and process-oriented assessments should be selected or constructed that coincide with students' learning experiences?

16. What types of self-selected representations are students able to use to demonstrate their acquisition or understanding of new knowledge?

CONCLUSION

As educators in the modern and postmodern camps continue to engage in esoteric and boundaryless debates about the "value" of a particular point of view, related issues have received little attention. For example, notably absent are discussions about how an understanding of the modern and postmodern tenets could be used to improve curriculum delivery or how modernists could respond to criticisms raised by the postmodernists. What insights are to be gained from the postmodern critique? How could their criticisms be used to strengthen the quality of classroom teaching or to develop a framework to guide curriculum development? In contrast, postmodernists might consider the benefits that frameworks and strategies grounded in the modern view of curriculum offer the practitioner. However, rather than summarily dismiss the modern view, I suggest that professors and practitioners explore how the modern view of curriculum can be refined. Thoughtful analysis of the postmodern critique may be helpful in improving curriculum delivery, promoting successful student achievement, and providing insight into alternative methods of implementing the curriculum. However, determining whether the curriculum can be enhanced by the ideals embraced by the modernists and postmodernists and evaluating the efficacy of their ideas will ultimately be left to the discretion of practitioners.

Case Study 1: Teacher Challenged by Student Diversity Issues

This year Jane Tungsten has been assigned to teach fourth-grade students at Lothgren Elementary School. Jane, who has been teaching for three years in the school system, learned in late August that several students who had been diagnosed with severe emotional problems would be mainstreamed into this year's class. As in the past, it is projected that this year's class will be comprised of a diverse student population, including at least four students who are highly gifted in mathematics and music and seven students who are considered at risk for academic failure due to high mobility.

Within the first month of the school year, Jane discovered that the state-adopted textbook series in mathematics was inaccessible to at least one-third of her students. Jane wants to rewrite portions of the curriculum and develop different learning activities to supplement those in the textbook. However, she has been told by her principal, Mr. Brishban, that he expects her students to demonstrate minimal attainment of the appropriate grade-level outcomes in mathematics or he cannot assure her that she will be invited to return to her position the following year.

Feeling the weight of Brishban's comments, Jane sits down and develops a list of issues that she believes are representative of her challenges. In one column she writes down all of the instructional components related to helping students attain successful outcomes, including the following: (1) selecting appropriate instructional strategies, (2) designing alternative learning experiences, (3) offering peer tutoring, (4) deciding how to address students' learning difficulties, (5) creating an engaging learning environment, (6) helping students cope with emotional issues, (7) deciding how to successfully mainstream the students with severe emotional problems, and (8) engaging families in their children's school activities. In the second column, she identifies some of the actions she can implement. For a third column, she plans to identify resources and support that would be helpful. Too tired to complete this last column, she closes her briefcase, leaves the classroom, and drives to a nearby coffeeshop.

FOLLOW-UP QUESTIONS

1. From the position of a modern curricularist, what are the relevant teacher and student issues that Jane should consider?

2. From the position of a postmodern curricularist, what are the relevant teacher and student issues that Jane should consider?

3. From the modernist position, what type of support or resources might be needed to help Jane ameliorate this situation?

4. From the postmodernist position, what type of support or resources might be needed to help Jane ameliorate this situation?

5. Assuming that you ascribe to tenets described by the modern curricularists, how would you approach Jane Tungsten's dilemmas?

6. Assuming that you ascribe to tenets described by the postmodern curricularists, how would you approach Jane Tungsten's dilemmas?

7. How could both the modernist and postmodern philosophies be used to address the issues confronting Jane?

NOTES

1. The purpose of this chapter is to present an overview of the paradigmatic movements in curriculum, not an exhaustive review. For additional information, see Pinar, Reynolds, Slattery, & Taubmann (1995), and Tanner & Tanner (1990).

2. Although Ornstein & Hunkins (1998) referred to the postmodernists as reconceptualists and subsumed this paradigm within reconstructionism, I suggest that postmodernism should be regarded as a movement distinct from reconstructionism.

3. I am referring to those courses that cover a broad range of topics related to generic curriculum concepts such as curriculum theory, curriculum planning and development, curriculum change, and curriculum evaluation (Johnston, 1994).

4. For further discussion of this point, see Behar-Horenstein & Morgan (1995).

5. Aronowitz and Giroux (1991) suggested that a combination of the best insights culled from modernism and postmodernism could be integrated to "deepen and extend" the practice of critical pedagogy (p. 117).

REFERENCES

Apple, M. W. (1981). On analyzing hegemony. In H. A. Giroux, A. N. Penna, & W. F. Pinar (Eds.), *Curriculum and instruction* (pp. 109–123). Berkeley, CA: McCutchan Publishers.

Apple, M. W. (1986). *Teachers and texts: A political economy of class and gender relations in education.* New York: Routledge & Kegan Paul.

Apple, M. W. (1990). The politics of official knowledge in the United States. *Journal of Curriculum Studies, 22*(4), 377–400.

Apple, M. W. (1991). The politics of curriculum and teaching. *National Association for Secondary School Principals, 75*(532), 39–50.

Aronowitz, S., & Giroux, H. A. (1991). *Postmodern education.* Westport, CT: Greenwood Publishing Group.

Beauchamp, G. (1981). *Curriculum theory* (4th ed.). Itasca, IL: Peacock.

Behar-Horenstein, L. S., & Morgan, R. R. (1995). Narrative research, teaching and teacher thinking: Perspectives and possibilities. *Peabody Journal of Education, 70*(2), 139–161.

Bestor, A. (1956). *The restoration of learning.* New York: Alfred A. Knopf.

Bobbitt, F. (1924). *How to make a curriculum.* New York: Houghton Mifflin.

Caswell, H. L., & Campbell, D. S. (1935). *Curriculum development.* New York: American Book Company.

Charters, W. W. (1923). *Curriculum construction.* New York: Macmillan.

Contas, M. A. (1998). The changing nature of educational research and a critique of postmodernism. *Educational Researcher, 27*(2), 26–33.

Counts, G. S. (1932). *Dare the school build a new social order?* New York: John Day.

Dewey, J. (1916). *Democracy and education.* New York: Macmillan.

Dewey, J. (1938). *Experience and education.* New York: Macmillan.

Doll, R. C. (1996). *Curriculum improvement: Decision making and process* (9th ed.). Needham Heights, MA: Allyn & Bacon.

Doll, W. E. (1989). Foundations for a postmodern curriculum. *Journal of Curriculum Studies, 21*(3), 243–253.

Doll, W. E. (1993a). *A post modern perspective on curriculum.* New York: Teachers College Press.

Doll, W. E. (1993b). Curriculum possibilities in a "post"-future. *Journal of Curriculum and Supervision, 8*(4), 277–292.

Eisner, E. W. (1990). Creative curriculum development: A developmental agenda. *Journal of Curriculum and Supervision, 6*(1), 62–73.

Friere, P. (1973). *Education for a critical consciousness.* New York: Seabury Press.

Giroux, H. A. (1981). Toward a new sociology of curriculum. In H. A. Giroux, A. N. Penna, & W. F. Pinar (Eds.), *Curriculum and instruction* (pp. 98–108). Berkeley, CA: McCutchan Publishers.

Giroux, H. A. (1990). Curriculum theory, textual authority, and the role of teachers as public intellectuals. *Journal of Curriculum and Supervision, 5*(4), 361–383.

Giroux, H. A. (1994). Teachers, public life, and curriculum reform. *Peabody Journal of Education, 69*(3), 35–47.

Greene, M. (1977). The artistic-aesthetic and curriculum. *Curriculum Inquiry, 6,* 283–296.

Greene, M. (1994). Epistemology and educational research: The influence of recent approaches to knowledge. *Review of Research in Education, 20,* 423–426.

Hall, G. S. (1907). *Aspects of child life and education.* Boston: Ginn and Company.

Hlebowitsh, P. S. (1995). Interpretations of the Tyler *Rationale*: A reply to Kliebard. *Journal of Curriculum Studies, 27*(1), 89–94.

Hlebowitsh, P. S. (1993). *Radical curriculum theory reconsidered: A historical approach.* New York: Teachers College Press.

Hunkins, F. P., & Hammill, P. A. (1994). Beyond Tyler and Taba: Reconceptualizing the curriculum process. *Peabody Journal of Education, 69*(3), 4–18.

Hutchins, R. M. (1936). *The higher learning in America.* New Haven, CT: Yale University Press.

Jencks, C. (Ed). (1992). *The post-modern reader.* New York: St. Martin's Press.

Johnson, M. (1970–1971). Appropriate research directions in curriculum and instruction. *Curriculum Theory Network, 6,* 24–37.

Johnston, S. (1994). Resolving questions of "why" and "how" about the study of curriculum in teacher education programmes. *Journal of Curriculum Studies, 26*(5), 525–540.

Joyce, B. R., & Weil, M. (1996). *Models of Teaching* (5th ed.). Boston: Allyn and Bacon.

Kendler, H. H. (1993). Psychology and the ethics of social psychology. *American Psychologist, 48*(10), 1046–1053.

Klein, M. F. (1994). The toll for curriculum reform. In A. C. Ornstein, and L. S. Behar (Eds.). *Peabody Journal of Education, 69*(3), 19–34.

Lincoln, Y. S. (1992). Curriculum studies and the traditions of inquiry: The humanistic tradition. In Philip W. Jackson (Ed.), *Handbook of research on curriculum*. New York: Macmillan.

Martin, J., & Sugarman, J. (1993). Beyond methodolatry: Two conceptions of relations between theory and research in research on teaching. *Educational Researcher, 22*(8), 17–24.

McNeil, J. D. (1996). *Curriculum: A comprehensive introduction* (5th ed.). New York: HarperCollins College Publishers.

Messick, S. (1981). Evidence and ethics in the evaluation of tests. *Educational Researcher, 10*(9), 9–20.

Oliva, P. F. (1997). *Developing the curriculum* (4th ed.). New York: Addison-Wesley, Longman.

Ornstein, A. C., & Hunkins, F. P. (1998). *Curriculum: Foundations, principles and issues* (3rd ed.). Needham Heights, MA: Allyn and Bacon.

Phenix, P. (1962). The disciplines in curriculum content. In A. Harry Passow (ed.), *Curriculum crossroads*. New York: Teachers College Press.

Pinar, W. F. (1988). The reconceptualization of curriculum studies, 1987: A personal retrospective. *Journal of Curriculum and Supervision, 3*(2), 157–167.

Pinar, W. F. (1992). Dreamt into existence by others: Curriculum theory and school reform. *Theory into Practice, 31*(3), 228–235.

Pinar, W. F., Reynolds, W. M., Slattery, P., & Taubmann, P. M. (1995). *Understanding curriculum: An introduction to the study of historical and contemporary curriculum discourses*. New York: Peter Lang Publishers.

Popham, W. J., & Baker, E. L. (1970). *Systematic instruction*. Englewood Cliffs, NJ: Prentice-Hall.

Posner, G. J. (1995). *Analyzing the curriculum* (2nd ed.). New York: McGraw-Hill.

Resnick, D., & Resnick, L. (1985). Standards, curriculum and performance: A historical and comparative perspective. *Educational Researcher, 14*(4) 5–20.

Rugg, H. O. (Ed.). (1939). *Democracy and the curriculum*. New York: Appleton-Century.

Saylor, J. G., Alexander, W. M., & Lewis, A. (1981). *Curriculum planning for better teaching and learning* (4th ed.). New York: Holt, Rinehart, & Winston.

Schubert, W. H. (1986). *Curriculum: Perspective, paradigm, and possibility*. New York: Macmillan.

Schwab, J. J. (1970). *The practical: A language for curriculum*. Washington, DC: National Educational Association.

Short, E. G. (1987). *Curriculum research in retrospect*. Paper delivered at the Society of the Study of Curriculum History, Washington, DC.

Slattery, P. S. (1995). A postmodern vision of time and learning: A response to the National Education Commission Report Prisoners of Time. *Harvard Educational Review, 65*(4), 612–633.

Smith, B. O., Stanley, W. O., & Shores, J. H. (1957). *Fundamentals of curriculum*. New York: World Book Company.

Taba, H. (1962). *Curriculum development: Theory and practice*. New York: Harcourt, Brace, Jovanovich.

Tanner, D., & Tanner, L. (1981). Emancipation from research: The reconceptualist prescription. In H. A. Giroux, A. N. Penna, & W. F. Pinar (Eds.), *Curriculum and instruction.* (pp. 382–391). Berkeley, CA: McCutchan Publishers.

Tanner, D., & Tanner, L. (1990). *History of the curriculum.* New York: Macmillan.

Tanner, D., & Tanner, L. (1995). *Curriculum development: Theory into practice* (3rd ed.). New York: Merrill.

Tyler, R. W. (1949). *Basic principles of curriculum and instruction.* Chicago: University of Chicago Press.

Tyler, R. W. (1957). The curriculum then and now. In *Proceedings of the 1950's conference on testing problems.* Princeton, NJ: Educational Testing Service.

Tyler, R. W. (1968). Purposes for our schools. *National Association of Secondary School Principals, 52*(332), 1–12.

Wiles, J., & Bondi, J. (1998). *Curriculum development: A guide to practice* (5th ed.). New York: Macmillan.

Worthen, B. R., Sanders, J. R., & Fitzpatrick, J. L. (1997). *Program evaluation: Alternative approaches and practical guidelines* (2nd ed.). White Plains, NY: Longman.

2

Shifting Paradigms: Implications for Curriculum Research and Practice

Edmund C. Short

GUIDING QUESTIONS

1. *How has the relationship between curriculum research and curriculum practice been understood in the past?*

2. *What attempts have been made to construe the domains of curriculum research, to match more directly the domains of curriculum practice?*

3. *How successful has this effort been in obtaining research that is able to inform curriculum practice?*

4. *What change in the way curriculum practice is construed has occurred in recent years?*

5. *What does this new understanding of curriculum practice suggest about what should be addressed by curriculum research if it is to be of value in conducting curriculum practice?*

6. *What exactly is the nature of the paradigm shift that is occurring in our understanding of the relationship between curriculum research and curriculum practice?*

For over thirty years I have been interested in what is known about the nature of curriculum and about curriculum decision-making. This interest manifested itself in 1973 in a study entitled, "Knowledge Production and Utilization in Curriculum" (Short, 1973), in which I explored the relationship between curriculum research and practice and reviewed the current state of affairs with respect to knowledge production, knowledge utilization, and their interrelationship within the field of curriculum. I have long since abandoned the knowledge-production-and-utilization paradigm that provided the framework and the ideology for that overview of what was known at that time about the relationship of curriculum practice to curriculum knowledge and of curriculum knowledge to curriculum practice. However, the issues involved in that study and my interest in them have persisted.

In 1991 I edited a book entitled, *Forms of Curriculum Inquiry*, that addressed the research side of this issue by describing and exhibiting multiple forms of inquiry that can yield curriculum knowledge. There is a kinship to be noted between the 1973 and the 1991 reports. The former identified disciplinary, conjunctive, technological, and practical forms of inquiry, while the latter presented seventeen forms of inquiry, from philosophical, historical, and scientific to ethnographic, narrative, and aesthetic; from phenomenological and hermeneutic to theoretical, normative, and critical; from evaluative, integrative, and deliberative to action research.

I included in that book a section on the relation of inquiry to practice in curriculum (pp. 7–10). A statement from that section highlights the differences between curriculum inquiry and curriculum practice as well as the ways in which they can be interrelated.

Practical curriculum activity involves problems of decision and action, judgment and enactment. Curriculum inquiry involves answering questions for which definite answers can be obtained; it attempts to answer particular questions and to provide knowledge or understanding about them. Curriculum practice is action-oriented rather than inquiry-oriented. Getting something done is the essence of curriculum practice. As in all fields of practical activity, curriculum practice involves deciding what should be done through various educative processes to bring about a desired state of affairs, and then acting upon that decision. Curriculum inquiry, on the other hand, is a highly disciplined intellectual activity in which some formally justified logic of procedure is employed to obtain a comfirmable answer to a researchable curriculum question that has been isolated for inquiry. . . . Curriculum practice is concerned with specifying, justifying, and enacting desired educative actions. . . . Curriculum inquiry is concerned with answering specific questions related to any of these domains of curriculum practice about which knowledge and understanding is sought. (p. 8)

I concluded with the pessimistic assertion that "it is not clear that the results of curriculum inquiry have deliberately and consistently been used in the doing of curriculum work" (p. 10) and attributed this circumstance to the fact that curriculum inquiries are only occasionally directed toward the problems of curriculum practice.

Personally I have not conducted empirical studies to find out the extent to which, or in just what ways, available curriculum knowledge is utilized in curriculum practice, although several researchers have looked into these questions (Connelly & Ben-Peretz, 1980; Connelly & Elbaz, 1980; Sanders & McCutcheon, 1986; Connelly & Clandinin, 1988, pp. 81–123; McCutcheon, 1988a; McCutcheon, 1988b; Ben-Peretz, 1990; Ross et al., 1992, pp. 3–18; Snyder et al., 1992, p. 418; Behar & George, 1994; McCutcheon, 1995, pp. 33–58; Cuban, 1998; Kelleher, 1998). More work along these lines clearly needs to be done, especially on how curriculum knowledge is used by teachers, curriculum committees, curriculum directors and supervisors, boards of education, educational reformers, and others.

CONFIGURING CURRICULUM RESEARCH AROUND DOMAINS OF CURRICULUM PRACTICE

Between the publications of these two reports in 1973 and in 1991, I began to recognize the importance of organizing what we know about curriculum and about curriculum decision-making. In an article entitled "Organizing What We Know about Curriculum" (Short, 1985), I urged scholars to take up the task of summarizing and synthesizing studies around practical domains of curriculum activity. Among domains suggested were curriculum policy-making, curriculum development and evaluation, curriculum change and enactment, and modes of curriculum decision-making. Although the results of individual studies might not provide worthy guidance for persons engaged in particular domains of curriculum activity, I argued that integration of research pertaining to particular domains of curriculum activity, if made accessible to curriculum practitioners, might prove more usable and trustworthy. In any case, it would be packaged in a form corresponding to the domains of curriculum activity in which it could most conveniently be used if it were considered to be relevant.

Major summaries of curriculum research have been published from the early 1960s to the present, with increasing frequency and quantity as time has passed. While many of these were explicitly organized around particular domains of curriculum activity, many were not. Of those published in *Review of Educational Research* between 1960 and 1978, 9 of 24 were not directly related to curriculum practice, according to my rough classification. Of the three published in *Review of Research in Education* between 1976 and 1992, all three were directly related to curriculum practice. In the 1960, 1969, 1982, and 1992 editions of *The Encyclopedia of Educational Research,* there were a total of 13 syntheses of curriculum research; 4 of these were not directly related to curriculum practice. In the 1992 *International Encyclopedia of Education,* 15 of 27 articles on curriculum knowledge were not directly related to curriculum practice. In the 1992 *Handbook of Research on Curriculum,* 13 of the 24 articles synthesizing curriculum research were not directly related to curriculum practice. These rough tallies suggest that, while a considerable amount of curriculum knowledge has been available in recent years for use by curriculum practitioners, quite a bit of it has not been organized around those practical activities in which they engage. Curriculum researchers should take note of this as they choose research topics or questions to study, and synthesizers of curriculum research should consider curriculum practitioners' activities as they conceptualize and formulate their summaries of research.

There are aspects of this concern with organizing what we know about curriculum and curriculum decision-making and with making it accessible to practitioners that I am less comfortable with in 2000 than I was in 1985; I shall return to this matter later in this chapter. But one of the difficulties in acting on my 1985 advice was that the domains of curriculum practice on which to focus curriculum research and around which to organize curriculum research knowledge are not self-evident. Indeed, the ones I posed (mentioned earlier) have not turned out to be ones consistently adopted either by curriculum researchers or by synthesizers of curriculum research. Nor has any other set of domains of curriculum practice gained such status. Perhaps they are too broad or global or too idiosyncratic to be useful to curriculum practitioners everywhere.

The real question is: What are the actual practical activities involved in curriculum work and in curriculum decision-making? What we have considered to be the domains of curriculum activities, if the literature is taken as our evidence, is a series of practical domains as conceptualized by researchers and synthesizers of research, whether they are actual domains of curriculum activity or not (Behar, 1994). I hasten to add that, no doubt, they thought them to be real ones, though they probably made no effort to substantiate them by looking at actual curriculum practice. In reality, we would have to have detailed studies of curriculum practice in order to identify common domains of curriculum activity with any degree of certainty. Such studies would not really settle the matter, because the domains would have to be named and related conceptually by the researchers, and in different studies different researchers would inevitably conceptualize them differently. Thus, the problem is not really an empirical problem but a conceptual one. And how are we to determine the best way or the right way to conceptualize domains of curriculum activity?

Before I move on to confront this dilemma, it may be of interest to survey the array of domains of practical curriculum activities that appear in the theoretical and research literature in curriculum. In a section of a 1985 book by Rosales-Dordelly and Short (1985, pp. 20–29; see also Short, 1993), we examined the scope and structure of curriculum knowledge and listed domains of curriculum activity recommended by five scholars between 1969 and 1984. Virtually no common domains were identified among these researchers and curriculum theorists. Recently, Ornstein and Hunkins (1998, pp. 16–20) again discussed this lack of consensus on domains of curriculum activity. They noted a number of additional sets of domains that have been recommended since 1985 by various curriculum scholars. They concluded that among these only two often-cited domains—curriculum development and curriculum design—contained significant curriculum knowledge for conducting practical curriculum activities. Still, there appears to be little consensus on what is meant by these categories; *development* and *design* are understood differently by different people. I am aware of an attempt made by one curriculum researcher to attach specific curriculum activities to particular domains of curriculum knowledge (Behar & Ornstein, 1994), but desirable as this may be, I am not sanguine about their wide adoption in the field of curriculum research or practice.

I now want to scan the array of particular domains of practical curriculum activities that have been either suggested or employed by curriculum researchers or curriculum synthesizers in the literature of recent years. The first group come from scholars wishing to set forth frameworks or guidelines for choosing research topics and/or questions for study related to curriculum practice. The second group come from scholars synthesizing curriculum research in encyclopedias or research handbooks.

Group One

Goodlad and Associates (1979) identified as one focus for curriculum inquiry the domain of curriculum decision-making processes, dividing that domain into several levels (societal, institutional, instructional, and personal). A second focus identified several substantive domains within which curricular decisions must be made (ideological, formal, perceived, operational, and experiential curricula). In each of these, various commonplaces might be studied or, across the substantive domains, discrepancies among them might be discovered. Commonplaces cited were goals and objectives, materials, content, learning activities, strategies, evaluation, grouping, time, and space. Data could be collected describing the substance of a domain, its decision-makers, its rationale, its priorities, attitudes toward it, its appropriateness, its comprehensiveness, its degree of individualization, and its barriers or facilitators. This set of practical domains and subcategories became the research framework employed by Goodlad and his associates in a nationwide study that culminated in the publication of *A Place Called School* and related volumes and reports. The proposed framework for practical curriculum inquiry was fully explicated in the 1979 book (pp. 43–76) and graphically represented in a matrix (p. 68).

Posner (1979) identified nine practical domains and several combinations of these domains that might become foci for curriculum research. The list of these is cast into a context-input–process-output model that is conceptualized as follows: context for planning/development, input for planning/development, process for planning/development, output for planning/development, context for teaching/learning, input for teaching/learning, process for teaching/learning, output for teaching/learning, and the integration of all these. Many kinds of research could contribute to any one of these domains.

Kimpston and Rogers (1986) identified four domains of practical curriculum planning: design, development, implementation, and evaluation. For each domain, they suggested particular presage, context, process, and outcome variables that could constitute independent or dependent variables in specific studies, depending upon the research question chosen. This framework is oriented largely toward hypothesis-testing kinds of research.

Posner (1989) proposed another set of practical curriculum domains for studies that included educational outcomes studies, studies of the curriculum development process, analyses of educational concepts and aims, studies of educational materials, studies of students, and studies of schools and classrooms. These were not conceptually tied together, since Posner's purpose was primarily to suggest possible research questions and research approaches appropriate to each domain.

Grove and Short (1991) presented an illustrative, but not exhaustive, list of practical domains for curriculum research when they addressed the kinds of theoretical studies that could be done on what they called curriculum components. The domains listed were curriculum development strategies, curriculum content selection and design, curriculum materials development, establishing educational objectives, defining curriculum, formulating and communicating curriculum plans and/or guides, and curriculum policy development.

Short (1991) divided curriculum practice into five kinds of practical activities: conceiving curriculum, justifying curriculum, expressing or communicating curriculum, enacting curriculum, and evaluating curriculum, which would permeate all the others.

Short (1993) suggested three broad domains of curriculum practice and inquiry: curriculum policy-making and evaluation, curriculum program development, and curriculum change and enactment. Each would have subdomains concerning precedents, processes, and prescriptions, within each of which several research questions could be formulated.

When we examine all seven of these sets of practical curriculum domains side by side, we can make a number of observations. They vary quite a bit from one another. A few domains appear somewhat frequently—development, decision-making, evaluation, objectives or outcomes, policy-making—sometimes with a unique twist, however, resulting from the larger framework of domains of which they are a part. Goodlad's is intended to describe curriculum practices through descriptive research techniques, some of which may be quantitative and some qualitative. Posner's earlier one is open to several different types of research approaches, but it is embedded in a systems framework that appears to be more suited to generating alternative research problems than to facilitating the focusing of results of research on practical curriculum activities. Kimpston and Rogers' framework is designed to facilitate the identification of hypothetic-deductive empirical questions and to produce scientific generalizations. Posner's second set of domains has face validity in terms of ordinary domains of practice, but he provides no argument for why the domains are divided up the way they are or for whether those suggested are all the possible ones. Grove and Short's list of domains, similarly, has considerable resonance with practice, but they admit the list is not fully inclusive, and so one is left to wonder what other domains there might be and why those listed are divided up the way they are. Short's first list is conceived somewhat differently from the rest as if to emphasize a wider scope of practical curriculum activities than most of the others. There would necessarily have to be subdomains within each of those identified, but Short's presentation is too brief and too sketchy to provide much help on what the subdomains might be. Short's second set of domains is somewhat more conventional, with just three broad categories (but each with three subcategories the same for each domain). They seem more suited to collating or summarizing related studies than to clearly differentiating practical curriculum activities on which research might be done.

Group Two

Now I turn to a second group of domains actually employed by scholars who have selected and grouped studies as they prepared summaries or syntheses of curriculum research for various encyclopedias or research handbooks where this sort of integrative work is usually published.

Schubert (1982) divided his coverage of the current state of curriculum research into eight domains of curriculum activity: purposes, content or learning experiences, organization, evaluation, and curriculum contexts (theory, change, policy, and hidden curriculum).

Posner (1984), in surveying the state of curriculum knowledge, dealt with two domains: curriculum content and curriculum development approaches.

Jenkins (1984) reviewed work under the following headings: policy-related curriculum research, curriculum analysis, curriculum design and implementation, and curriculum evaluation.

Goodlad (1984b) distinguished curriculum praxis from curriculum praxiology. Praxis refers to curriculum-building activity and praxiology to the study of curriculum-building activity. He identifies four commonplaces addressed in the models of praxis he reviewed: goals, learning activities, organization, and evaluation.

Hameyer (1984) wrote his synthesis of curriculum theory around curriculum processes, selecting and structuring curriculum content, and curriculum implementation.

Schubert and Schubert (1988) employed the construct of *paradigm* to order their review of curriculum research. Much of the article addresses the role of alternative paradigms in conducting research, but some reference is made to a paradigm's effect on one kind of practical activity, curriculum decision-making.

Connelly and Clandinin (1992) identified five practical curriculum preoccupations: curriculum development, curriculum evaluation, curriculum implementation, curriculum policy development, and curriculum policy analysis.

Hameyer (1994) covered domains similar to those in his 1984 article, but here he added one more: curriculum legitimation.

Goodlad (1994) reviewed knowledge of several curriculum commonplaces in his review of curriculum as a field of study.

None of the nine articles cited was more than ten pages in length. Some of the articles published in the journal *Review of Educational Research* and in the annual volume *Review of Research in Education* (mentioned earlier also as containing summaries of curriculum research) gave much lengthier treatments of their topics. But not until the publication of the 1,050–page *Handbook of Research on Curriculum* (Jackson, 1992) was there an attempt made to present exhaustive summaries of curriculum research, some as long as forty double-columned pages. The practical curriculum domains that were reflected in the titles of whole articles in the *Handbook* included the following: curriculum evaluation and assessment, curriculum policy, curriculum stability and change, organization of the curriculum, school organization and curriculum, teacher as curriculum-maker, curriculum implementation, textbooks in school and society, curriculum and pedagogy, cognition and curriculum, and curriculum differentiation. In most of these articles, research was organized around specific topics or subdomains within the broader domain reflected in the title.

What do we find when we examine the articles in group two, which reviewed and synthesized curriculum research? Is there evidence of convergence on particular domains of practical curriculum activities in these articles? Are the domains identified in this group similar to those identified in the first group, which looked at recommended guidelines for choosing practical topics or questions for research? While somewhat different conceptualizations of practical curriculum domains and subdomains were chosen by group-two scholars, there is some common usage of curriculum knowledge domains, such as curriculum purposes and goals, curriculum development processes, organization, evaluation, implementation, and policy development. Just as useful are others unique to particular writers: curriculum commonplaces, the hidden curriculum, curriculum legitimation, stability and change, textbooks, and curriculum differentiation. And compared with group one, these domains are not very different.

In surveying the literature in which practical curriculum domains have been put forth to assist in generating curriculum research studies and the literature in which they have been used to organize reviews of completed research, I don't wish to suggest that these lists of domains should become normative for future work. This brief survey was intended merely to provide evidence of how domains of practical curriculum activities have in fact been conceived and used in the literature and, incidentally, to provide background for later comments I wish to make about conceptual shifts that have gone on in curriculum research over recent years.

RECOGNIZING FLAWS IN THE APPLICATION-OF-RESEARCH PARADIGM

I now want to discuss more directly my earlier question: What are the constituent activities inherent in practical curriculum work and in curriculum decision-making as they are actually engaged in by those involved? I stated that if curriculum research is to be most useful and accessible, it should be attentive to the concerns that relate to practical curriculum activities and that research results should be organized and presented in the context of those practical curriculum activities. I have already said that empirical studies to determine what these activities may actually be cannot settle the question. Any effort toward identifying the most common domains of curriculum activities, even if they could be detected, would leave out certain activities that some people engage in and, if relevant knowledge about them were available, they might benefit from having that knowledge just as much as others might benefit from having knowledge related to the more common domains. Knowledge about central tendencies may be helpful, but it will not suffice for outliers. In addition, researchers attempting to deal with the question must face the dilemma of how they will conceptualize various curriculum activities or domains even before they seek to discover them. In truth, many different conceptualizations are possible, as we have seen in the rough survey of the curriculum research literature. Thus, providing a good match between curriculum research and practitioners' practical curriculum activities is clearly more problematic than it first appeared to be.

In addition to these difficulties that have to do with the seemingly commonsense matter of relating curriculum research to the domains of curriculum practice, there are more fundamental problems that have to do with the paradigm within which this approach is embedded. The knowlege-production-and-utilization paradigm is based on the assumption that knowledge produced through various forms of inquiry, even when it focuses on some aspect of curriculum practice, is to be used in curriculum practice by a process of applying the conclusions of the research in one or more domains of curriculum practice. If we mean by the phrase "applying research conclusions" that we can deduce from them what to do (what curriculum choices to make) in a particular situation, we are mistaken. Most research conclusions can inform our choices or make us see things differently, but they cannot, by inference, tell us what our choices should be (Dewey, 1929, pp. 19, 28, 42; Taylor, 1961, pp. 240–259). This erroneous assumption, held by many curriculum practitioners about the relation of curriculum research to curriculum practice, has been slow to disappear from the minds of curriculum practitioners and, to be honest, from the minds of many curriculum researchers as well. It has no doubt been perpetuated by a social science understanding of research.

For the last couple of decades, however, curriculum researchers have broadened their inquiries to include many more types of inquiry approaches where the application of research results seems less obvious than the way they might be used (Short, 1991; Pinar, et al., 1995). These newer studies indirectly inform curriculum practice in ways not yet clear to most curriculum specialists. Exploration of the epistemological issues inherent in this newer work has absorbed the attention of many curriculum researchers over the last few years (Walker, 1992), and they have failed to notice a shift in curriculum practitioners' understanding of their own practice. Interestingly, researchers studying teachers' knowledge of teaching and of related epistemological issues have acknowledged this shift more often than have those studying curriculum knowledge. (See Fenstermacher, 1986, pp. 16–37; Cochran-Smith & Lytle, 1993; Fenstermacher, 1994; Clandinin & Connelly, 1995, pp. 3–15.)

ACKNOWLEDGING A NEW CONCEPTUALIZATION OF CURRICULUM PRACTICE

What we are faced with, in actuality, is a new kind of situation in curriculum practice in which the knowledge that is most needed is not structural or general knowledge but situational and criterial knowledge. Curriculum practitioners know that they do not need to rely on the recommendations of outside authorities to make their curriculum decisions and that they do not need to turn to codified curriculum research which they merely apply to their own situation. (Most of it doesn't fit, and besides, as we have noted, one doesn't decide what to do in a given situation by applying general knowledge.) Knowledge production and utilization is the wrong model for practical curriculum decision-making and for much of curriculum research. Since Schwab (1970), curriculum practitioners have come to understand that their work is primarily to make choices among many possible competing curriculum options and to seek to make the best choices in given circumstances through a process of deliberation and good practical judgment. If research knowledge enters into this process, it is not in ways that determine choices or actions but that inform them.

The hard work of judging what choice is to be made on a given curriculum issue is situational. It depends on understanding the specific circumstances of a particular situation in which curriculum decisions are to be made. It depends on knowing what the ideal state of affairs is toward which the curriculum experiences to be chosen are to be directed. And it depends on presenting and assessing arguments for and against various options. It sounds more complex than simply turning to research for guidance, and it is. Those who have been persuaded by the work of Schwab and others (Reid, 1978, 1992; Walker, 1990, pp. 160–221) on deliberation and its centrality in curriculum decision-making have acquired a new understanding about curriculum practice that changes not only how they do curriculum work but also how research knowledge is employed in this deliberative process.

While not every curriculum decision-making setting has adopted this new conception of curriculum practice, it is one that has been acknowledged by more and more curriculum practitioners and curriculum theorists as representing what is actually involved in curriculum practice. Older models suggested that expert knowledge could determine facets of a curriculum program and, consequently, that reliance on research conclusions was the way to assure that appropriate decisions were made. In the new understanding of curriculum practice, there is no assurance that curriculum choices are going to be appropriate ones, except as persuasive arguments are mustered that compel one choice over another.

I will give a brief personal interpretation here of this new conception of curriculum practice, though fuller accounts elsewhere should be examined (Schwab, 1970, 1978a, 1978b, 1983; Reid, 1978, pp. 41–69, 1992; Walker, 1990, pp. 160–221; Harris, 1991; for additional background, see Raup et al., 1962; Dillon, 1994, pp. 3–24). The fundamental questions of what the curriculum should consist of; toward what ideals and purposes it should be directed; how it should be given educative form and substance; what situation-specific factors it has to take into account; and how it will be justified, enacted, and evaluated (and perhaps others) are all questions that are subject to deliberation. Many viewpoints and proposals for dealing with such questions are possible. To arrive at workable agreements on what the best response may be in each case, consideration must be given to the many possible options that can be generated, to the arguments both pro and con for each option, and ultimately, to the best of the options presented and the persuasiveness of the arguments for it.

This process of deliberation may go on at various levels (e. g., state, district, building, classroom) and is necessarily situational in orientation. Situational factors commensurate with the level at which the deliberation takes place will impinge upon the options and decisions that are possible and, therefore, should be thoroughly identified in each situation.

The elements or commonplaces on which substantive options are to be generated and choices made are also up for deliberation. They depend to a large extent upon the conception of curriculum adopted and its underlying assumptions as subscribed to by the deliberators. Conceptual and technical knowledge of alternative sets of commonplaces and conceptual frameworks may be consulted by curriculum deliberators as they attempt to come to agreement on these commonplaces.

In addition, criterial knowledge may be useful in coming to good judgments on what commonplaces to deal with, what options to consider, and what choices to adopt. The literature of curriculum theory provides such criterial knowledge for what counts as a sound curriculum as a whole—such things as coherence, balance, integrity, depth, breadth, relevance, continuity, variety, utility, significance, interest, comprehensiveness, and clarity (Schwab, 1970; Goodlad & Su, 1992; Beane, 1995).

The process of deliberation does not disregard research knowledge when it is deemed relevant. The role it plays is just different from the role it took under the earlier paradigm. Deliberation may require the conduct of situationally oriented research that is undertaken to discover something about unknown factors bearing on the particular situation that could affect a particular deliberation. It may require understanding of general knowledge from any one or from a number of disciplines or fields of inquiry. Consideration of critical social and political issues that impinge upon these judgments is consistent with, even morally required by, this notion of deliberation (Beyer, 1988). The important thing to note about the role of knowledge in curriculum deliberations is that all such knowledge, when identified as relevant to particular deliberations, functions in the background as particular choices are considered and weighed in the foreground. Another way of saying this is that knowledge informs the decisions but cannot prescribe or determine them. Schwab discussed this whole matter in his treatment of the arts of the eclectic, in which he employed the concept of *polyfocal conspectus* (perspective) (Schwab, 1978a). He implied that the more lenses or perspectives through which a problem is viewed the more likely deliberations will be able to settle upon the best solution. The role of knowledge is crucial in acquiring a polyfocal conspectus. All theoretical and practical knowledge should be held in view simultaneously while weighing choices and coming to decisions. This is in the nature of making practical judgments, curricular or otherwise.

A final point concerns the manner in which deliberation itself is conducted. Success in engaging in the deliberative process requires that all participants adhere to certain norms and expectations inherent in the process. These norms and expectations include such things as listening attentively to others' positions and arguments, accepting or rejecting them with carefully stated reasons and not with mindless acceptance or dismissal, compromising when persuaded of the flaws of one's own position or the merits of others' positions, high regard for the relevant facts, a commitment to criteria of acceptability of the end products of deliberation, and the like. This is not a process where dogmatic or uncooperative folks are likely to function well (Reid, 1978; Schwab, 1983; Walker, 1990, pp. 160–201).

Handy guidelines for making curriculum decisions within this new conception of curriculum practice are not yet being published with any frequency. The Henderson and Hawthorne (1995) volume is among the first, now in its second edition (1999). Curriculum theorists and adherents to this new conception of curriculum practice have not yet had time to devise many guidelines based on this conception or to critique or refine those that have appeared. My guess is that this is because of two difficulties they see in this task. One difficulty is that they may find it hard to express in a brief set of easy-to-understand procedures or guidelines all that needs to be taken into account in this new view of curriculum practice. Curriculum practitioners seem to want guidelines that are short and relatively simple, such as the long-used four-step process by Tyler (1949) or the somewhat more elaborate, but not too different, guidelines found in contemporary texts (Eisner, 1994; Glatthorn, 1994; Tanner & Tanner, 1995; Marsh & Willis, 1998; Oliva, 1997; Ornstein & Hunkins, 1998). The new guidelines might have to be longer and more complex and thus might not be too well received.

A second possible reason for the reluctance to recast practical guidelines for the new conception of curriculum practice is that the theorists may not be sure of how to specify the processes to be engaged in and the decisions to be made when the conceptualization of curriculum practice is so open. Nearly everything from curriculum commonplaces to various options to various arguments is virtually left to the judgment of the deliberative group; what is left to specify? Add to this the wealth of research knowledge and technical curriculum knowledge that might need to be brought to bear on this process, and one can begin to understand the difficulty of providing usable guidelines.

AN EVOLVING NEW PARADIGM FOR CURRICULUM RESEARCH AND INQUIRY

What may be lacking is a view of how this new conceptualization of curriculum practice should relate to curriculum research and inquiry—how curriculum research and practice inform each other. The earlier paradigm of knowledge production and utilization does not fit this new understanding of curriculum practice that centers on the deliberative process. Applying research knowledge within domains of curriculum practice is no longer appropriate in the context of deliberation, which focuses on what the best choice or course of action may be among many possible ones. What curriculum deliberators need to know is multifarious, even kaleidoscopic, while at the same time situationally oriented and situationally constrained.

One kind of knowledge appropriate to practical curriculum decision-making is knowledge of the situation itself. Questions like the following would need to be asked and answered: For whom is the curriculum intended? How can they be described in terms of their present capability, understanding, values, and aspirations? What ideals or expectations do the constituency supporting the curriculum hold? Do they expect to be actively or passively involved in making curriculum decisions? What institutional forums for curriculum deliberaton exist? How well do they function? Who will enact the decisions and how are they to be prepared for their task? How will the decisions be evaluated both during and following their enactment? Is there consensus on the desired criteria (goals, purposes, state of affairs) by which evaluative judgments of the decisions taken and the actions enacted will be made? How will subsequent changes be proposed and deliberated? What budgetary, time, and organizational constraints exist in the situation?

Another kind of knowledge appropriate to practical curriculum decision-making, no less fundamental in character than the kind just identified, is knowledge of what technical form or shape the sum total of curriculum decisions should take if the curriculum is to function truly as a curriculum. No single conceptualization of curriculum structure exists; there are many shapes it might take, so deliberate choice among them is necessary. Deliberators can either turn to the technical knowledge containing various models of curriculum components, structure, and rationale that reside in the conceptual and empirical literature of curriculum and choose among them, or they can construct some unique version for their own particular situation. Pragmatic knowledge of various options, their pros and cons as well as the formal technical knowledge of them, will be helpful in the deliberations over the form the curriculum will take.

Still another kind of knowledge that will enter into curriculum deliberations at the point of making practical curriculum decisions is relevant academic knowledge. Deliberators must be aware of pertinent general knowledge that may bear upon their choices, such as social and occupational trends, psychological aspects of learners and of the teaching/learning process, dominant and peripheral social norms and values, and extrasituational pressures (local, regional, national, global) that could affect curriculum content or the processes of education.

I could have included in the previous category knowledge about the current state of knowledge itself. This kind of knowledge needs to be highlighted separately for emphasis, however, it seems to me. Being up to date on what is known in various disciplines and fields of study is surely a prerequisite for deliberators to be able to wisely select or arrange such knowledge for inclusion at various stages of the curriculum. Related to this category, but really very different from it, is another category having to do with knowledge of available curriculum materials and other kinds of subject matter resources for use by students and teachers that contain selected representations of the formal knowledge.

Another kind of knowledge plays into curriculum decision-making. This is knowledge of certain political, ethical, philosophical, religious, gender, or other issues that can color the impact of curriculum if they are not given careful attention in curriculum deliberations. I am thinking here of sexism, ageism, racism, dogmatism, chauvinism, bullyism, multiculturalism, capitalism, and other similar stances often taken uncritically and incorporated into the curriculum. Much recent research deals with this kind of knowledge (Pinar et al., 1995; Sears & Carper, 1998).

There are probably several other kinds of knowledge that might be drawn on in the course of doing practical curriculum deliberation, but I will mention only one more. This is one I referred to earlier as criterial knowledge. Criterial knowledge, or knowledge of criteria, has to do with recognized standards of quality, integrity, or functionality. In practical curriculum work, deliberators must hold such standards in mind as they piece together or modify the array of particular choices that make up the entire curriculum. I identified some of these criteria that apply to the curriculum as a whole when I earlier discussed the deliberative conceptualization of curriculum practice, but other criteria can apply to specific elements of curriculum (various purposes, substances, designs, or pragmatic considerations) to assure the quality, integrity, or the functionality of the curriculum. A negative example might be when no one notices contradictory elements placed in different parts of the curriculum; this violates the criterion of consistency. Curriculum inquiry has produced some criterial knowledge applicable to certain aspects of curriculum, but much more knowledge of this type is needed.

I have already sketched out how in curriculum deliberation these various kinds of knowledge provide the givens with which deliberators must wrestle in both posing their preferred options and in defending their choices. This knowledge functions *eclectically* or *polyfocally*, as Schwab stated, or as I would describe it, it functions within an "if this, then that" model of reasoning, where causal connections are not sought, but plausible decisions or actions are devised and assessed within the parameters of the givens. Given certain desired states of affairs as the ideal and given a whole array of factual understandings and realities, then we are persuaded that a particular set of curriculum decisions and actions will enable students to reach the desired ideal. No assurances, but all things considered, it is a good bet for the reasons we give.

CONSIDERING HOW CURRICULUM PRACTICE AND CURRICULUM RESEARCH AND INQUIRY ARE RELATED IN THE NEW PARADIGM

It ought to go without saying, as a result of the view of curriculum practice articulated in this chapter and the way knowledge is used within this deliberative approach, that the work of curriculum researchers is quite different from that under the application-of-research paradigm. Much of the needed knowledge must be produced in-house by the deliberators about their own situation. We sometimes call this *situation analysis;* sometimes it takes the form of action research; at other times it is purely reflecting on and critiquing options presented and reasons given. Nobody outside the particular deliberative situation is going to need this particular knowledge, and it will seldom get published or disseminated elsewhere. Another large segment of the needed knowledge, however, is produced by curriculum researchers who seek more general and technical knowledge (both conceptual and criterial) that comes from ongoing study of curriculum practice. This would normally be published, and we need a lot more of it, especially in relation to various commonplaces. Still other scholars must keep up with the knowledge, skills, attitudes, and values that can become potential substance for somebody's curriculum. Someone else must keep up with the representations of this knowledge that are available in various kinds of curriculum materials and media, or participate in creating them, so that what is available may be catalogued, analyzed, and disseminated to potential users. This work has not usually attracted many researchers and compilers, but without this work being accomplished, curriculum deliberators can be overwhelmed in surveying and analyzing all these materials by themselves. Still other researchers can search the literature of the relevant academic and practical disciplines and fields of study and then summarize it in usable form for consideration by curriculum deliberators whenever they need to understand a particular type of general knowledge as it bears on their options and decisions. Finally, research needs to produce critical studies of important contemporary issues involving erroneously held beliefs and practices. These, then, if you will, are the new domains of curriculum knowledge that fit the domains of curriculum practice within the new paradigm.

What conceptualization of this new paradigm might represent this new relationship between deliberative curriculum decision-making and the concomitant kinds of curriculum research and inquiry spelled out in this chapter? I wish I had a good name for this new paradigm, but I don't. Something like Decision-oriented Curriculum Practice and Inquiry, or Practical Curriculum Deliberation and Inquiry, or Deliberative Curriculum Practice and Research? None of these captures the complete idea very well. In any case, the kinds of knowledge needed for deliberative curriculum practice entail a broader, and very different, set of domains of knowledge than those associated with the earlier paradigm. A good deal of the knowledge categorized within the new paradigm functions quite differently from that in the earlier one—a lot of it defining the problem and the context rather than suggesting decisions, actions, or solutions. It's a different world for both curriculum practitioners and curriculum researchers.

Case Study 2: The Role of Knowledge in Curriculum Decision-Making

Ralph Ryland leads a district school system team that is attempting to modify the curriculum in ways that will more adequately provide instruction in democratic, civic, and moral values. He has several members on his team who believe they should turn to the research literature on this topic to help them find solutions to their problem. Mr. Ryland is strongly in favor of drawing upon relevant research in making curriculum decisions, but the first explorations into the research literature on this topic turns up no definitive guidelines that seem to apply across the board to their need for answers locally. Momentarily discouraged, Mr. Ryland soon stumbles on a theoretical study of the relationship between curriculum research and curriculum practice that suggests that a paradigm shift has occurred in this matter and that most research that is appropriate for deliberating over what should be done in making local curriculum changes is situational in character—that is, the knowledge needed has to be generated within that particular situation and cannot be sought from the more general research literature.

Mr. Ryland quickly mounts a series of internal studies that his team thinks will generate situational knowledge helpful to them in making their decisions regarding the changes they might make in their curriculum related to democratic, civic, and moral values. These studies include: (1) a description of present curriculum efforts on this topic—what is taught and how effective it is; (2) a set of local criteria for what would count as adequate and successful outcomes of a curriculum change on this topic; (3) a projection of what programs exist elsewhere or could be designed locally that would fulfill their criteria for a good local curriculum effort on this topic; (4) a study of local political, religious, cultural, or community attitudes that will have to be taken into account in making these curriculum decisions; and (5) a study of the readiness and willingness of teachers, admininstrators, and the board of education to carry out changes that Mr. Ryland's team might recommend on this topic. Both Mr. Ryland and his team believe that they can make better decisions with the results of these local studies in hand.

FOLLOW-UP QUESTIONS

1. Consider the kind of knowledge that will be generated by each of the studies Mr. Ryland's team wishes to undertake. How will each kind of knowledge help them in making their curriculum decisions?

2. Though Mr. Ryland and his team seem to have subscribed to the paradigm shift that has occurred in the relationship between curriculum research and curriculum practice, what forms of traditional research knowledge might they still need to consult to inform their deliberations (in addition to the situational knowledge they will generate locally)?

3. If Mr. Ryland encounters resistance within his team to conducting and utilizing knowledge generated by these internal studies, what might he do to help them appreciate the value of this approach?

4. Do you think there might be any value in Mr. Ryland and his team publishing the results of each of their local studies, or would you favor their not trying to publish them and simply using the results internally in their local deliberations?

5. Is it fair to call the paradigm shift evidently embraced by Mr. Ryland and his team "modern" or "postmodern"?

REFERENCES

Beane, J. A. (Ed.). (1995). *Toward a coherent curriculum*. Alexandria, VA: Association for Supervision and Curriculum Development.

Behar, L. S. (1994). *The knowledge base of curriculum: An empirical analysis*. Lanham, MD: University Press of America.

Behar, L. S., & George, P. S. (1994). Teachers' use of curriculum knowledge. *Peabody Journal of Education, 69*, 48–69.

Behar, L. S., & Ornstein, A. C. (1994). Domains of curriculum knowledge: An empirical analysis. *High School Journal, 77*, 322–329.

Ben-Peretz, M. (1990). *The teacher-curriculum encounter: Freeing teachers from the tyranny of texts*. Albany: State University of New York Press.

Beyer, L. E. (1988). Curriculum deliberation. In T. Husen & T. N. Postlethwaite (Eds.), *International encyclopedia of education* (Supplement, Vol. 1, pp. 199–201). New York: Pergamon.

Clandinin, D. J., & Connelly, F. M. (1995). *Teachers' professional knowledge landscapes*. New York: Teachers College Press.

Cochran-Smith, M., & Lytle, S. L. (1993). *Inside outside: Teacher research and knowledge*. New York: Teachers College Press.

Connelly, F. M., & Ben-Peretz, M. (1980). Teachers' roles in the using and doing of curriculum research and curriculum development. *Journal of Curriculum Studies, 12*, 95–107.

Connelly, F. M., & Clandinin, D. J. (1988). *Teachers as curriculum planners*. New York: Teachers College Press.

Connelly, F. M., & Clandinin, D. J. (1992). Curriculum theory. In M. C. Alkin (Ed.), *Encyclopedia of educational research* (6th ed., pp. 287–292). New York: Macmillan.

Connelly, F. M., & Elbaz, F. (1980). Conceptual bases for curriculum thought: A teacher's perspective. In A. W. Foshay (Ed.), *Considered action for curriculum improvement* (pp. 95–119). Alexandria, VA: Association for Supervision and Curriculum Development.

Cuban, L. (1998). How schools change reforms: Redefining reform success and failure. *Teachers College Record, 99,* 453–477.

Dewey, J. (1929). *The source of a science of education.* New York: Liveright.

Dillon, J. T. (1994). *Deliberation in education and society.* Norwood, NJ: Ablex Publishing Company.

Eisner, E. W. (1994). *The educational imagination.* New York: Macmillan.

Fenstermacher, G. D. (1986). Philosophy of research on teaching: Three aspects. In M. C. Wittrock (Ed.), *Handbook of research on teaching* (3rd ed., pp. 37–49). New York: Macmillan.

Fenstermacher, G. D. (1994). The knower and the known: The nature of knowledge in research on teaching. In L. Darling-Hammond (Ed.), *Review of research in education, 20* (pp. 3–15). Washington, DC: American Educational Research Association.

Glatthorn, A. A. (1994). *Developing a quality curriculum.* Alexandria, VA: Association for Supervision and Curriculum Development.

Goodlad, J. I. (1984a). *A place called school.* New York: McGraw-Hill.

Goodlad, J. I. (1984b). Curriculum as a field of study. In T. Husen & T. N. Postlethwaite (Eds.), *International encyclopedia of education* (pp. 1141–1144). New York: Pergamon.

Goodlad, J. I. (1994). Curriculum as a field of study. In T. Husen & T. N. Postlethwaite (Eds.), *International encyclopedia of education* (2nd ed., pp. 1262–1266). New York: Pergamon.

Goodlad, J. I., & Associates. (1979). *Curriculum inquiry: The study of curriculum practice.* New York: McGraw-Hill.

Goodlad, J. I., & Su, Z. (1992). Organization of the curriculum. In P. W. Jackson (Ed.), *Handbook of research on curriculum* (pp. 327–344). New York: Macmillan.

Grove, R. W., & Short, E. C. (1991). Theoretical inquiry: Components and structure. In E. C. Short (Ed.), *Forms of curriculum inquiry* (pp. 211–224). Albany: State University of New York Press.

Hameyer, U. (1984). Curriculum theory. In T. Husen & T. N. Postlethwaite (Eds.), *International encyclopedia of education* (pp. 1265–1272). New York: Pergamon.

Hameyer, U. (1994). Curriculum theory. In T. Husen & T. N. Postlethwaite (Eds.), *International encyclopedia of education* (2nd ed., pp. 1348–1355). New York: Pergamon.

Harris, I. (1991). Deliberative inquiry: The arts of planning. In E. C. Short (Ed.), *Forms of curriculum inquiry* (pp. 285–307). Albany: State University of New York Press.

Henderson, J. G., & Hawthorne, R. D. (1995). *Transformative curriculum leadership.* Upper Saddle River, NJ: Prentice Hall.

Henderson, J. G., & Hawthorne, R. D. (1999). *Transformative curriculum leadership* (2nd ed.). Upper Saddle River, NJ: Prentice Hall.

Jackson, P. W. (1992). *Handbook of research on curriculum*. New York: Macmillan.

Jenkins, D. (1984). Curriculum research. In T. Husen & T. N. Postlethwaite (Eds.), *International encyclopedia of education* (pp. 1257–1263). New York: Pergamon.

Kelleher, R. D. (1998). *Teachers' life histories as curriculum context*. Unpublished doctoral dissertation, Georgia Southern University.

Kimpston, R. D., & Rogers, K. B. (1986). A framework for curriculum research. *Curriculum Inquiry, 16*, 463–474.

Marsh, C. J., & Willis, G. (1998). *Curriculum: Alternative approaches, ongoing issues*. Columbus, OH: Merrill.

McCutcheon, G.(1988a). Curriculum and the work of teachers. In L. E. Beyer & M. W. Apple (Eds.), *The curriculum: Problems, politics, and possibilities* (pp. 191–203). Albany: State University of New York Press.

McCutcheon, G. (1988b). Curriculum theory and practice: Considerations for the 1990s and beyond. *National Association of Secondary School Principals Bulletin, 72*, 33–42.

McCutcheon, G. (1995). *Developing the curriculum: Solo and group deliberation*. New York: Longman.

Oliva, P. F. (1997). *Developing the curriculum* (4th ed.). New York: Longman.

Ornstein, A. C., & Hunkins, F. P. (1998). *Curriculum: Foundations, principles, and issues* (3rd ed.). Boston: Allyn & Bacon.

Pinar, W. F., Reynolds, W. M., Slattery, P., & Taubman, P. M. (1995). *Understanding curriculum*. New York: Peter Lang.

Posner, G. J. (1979). Curiculum research: Domains of the field. *Journal of Curriculum Theorizing, 1*, 80–92.

Posner, G. J. (1984). Curriculum knowledge. In T. Husen & T. N. Postlethwaite (Eds.), *International encyclopedia of education* (pp. 1223–1227). New York: Pergamon.

Posner, G. J. (1989). Making sense of diversity: The current state of curriculum research. *Journal of Curriculum and Supervision, 4*, 340–361.

Raup, R. B., Axtelle, G. E., Benne, K. D., & Smith, B. O. (1962). *The improvement of practical intelligence* (Rev. ed., updated). New York: Bureau of Publications, Teachers College, Columbia University.

Reid, W. A. (1978). *Thinking about the curriculum: The nature and treatment of curriculum problems*. London: Routledge & Kegan Paul.

Reid, W. A. (1992). *The pursuit of curriculum: Schooling and the public interest*. Norwood, NJ: Ablex Publishing Company.

Rosales-Dordelly, C. L., & Short, E. C. (1985). *Curriculum professors' specialized knowledge*. Lanham, MD: University Press of America.

Ross, E. W., Cornell, J. W., & McCutcheon, G. (Ed.). (1992). *Teacher personal theorizing: Connecting curriculum practice, theory, and research*. Albany: State University of New York Press.

Sanders, D. P., & McCutcheon, G. (1986). The development of practical theories of teaching. *Journal of Curriculum and Supervision, 2*, 50–67.

Schubert, W. H. (1982). Curriculum research. In H. E. Mitzel (Ed.), *Encyclopedia of educational research* (5th ed., pp. 420–431). New York: Macmillan.

Schubert, W. H., & Schubert, A. L. (1988). Curriculum inquiries: Alternative paradigms. In T. Husen & T. N. Postlethwaite (Eds.), *International encyclopedia of education* (Supplement, Vol. 1, pp. 222–227). New York: Pergamon.

Schwab, J. J. (1970). *The practical: A language for curriculum.* Washington, DC: National Education Association. Reprinted in I. Westbury & N. J. Wilkof (Eds.) (1978), *Joseph J. Schwab: Selected essays* (pp. 287–321). Chicago: University of Chicago Press.

Schwab, J. J. (1978a). The practical: Arts of eclectic. In I. Westbury & N. J. Wilkof (Eds.), *J. J. Schwab: Selected essays* (pp. 322–364). Chicago: University of Chicago Press.

Schwab, J. J. (1978b). The practical: Translation into curriculum. In I. Westbury & N. J. Wilkof (Eds.), *J. J. Schwab: Selected essays* (pp. 365–383). Chicago: University of Chicago Press.

Schwab, J. J. (1983). The practical 4: Something for curriculum professors to do. *Curriculum Inquiry, 13,* 239–265.

Sears, J. T., & Carper, J. C. (Eds.). (1998). *Curriculum, religion, and public education: Conversations for an enlarging public square.* New York: Teachers College Press.

Short, E. C. (1973). Knowledge production and utilization in curriculum: A special case of the general phenomenon. *Review of Educational Research, 43,* 237–301.

Short, E. C. (1985). Organizing what we know about curriculum. *Curriculum Inquiry, 15,* 237–243.

Short, E. C. (1991). A research agenda: Setting priorities for curriculum research. *Journal of Curriculum and Supervision, 6,* 358–365.

Short, E. C. (1993). Three levels of questions addressed in the field of curriculum research and practice. *Journal of Curriculum and Supervision, 9,* 77–86.

Short, E. C. (Ed.). (1991). *Forms of curriculum inquiry.* Albany: State University of New York Press.

Snyder, J., Bolin, F., & Zumwalt, K. (1992). Curriculum implementation. In P. W. Jackson (Ed.), *Handbook of research on curriculum* (pp. 402–435). New York: Macmillan.

Tanner, D., & Tanner, L. N. (1995). *Curriculum development: Theory into practice.* New York: Macmillan.

Taylor, P. W. (1961). *Normative discourse.* Englewood Cliffs, NJ: Prentice-Hall.

Tyler, R. W. (1949). *Basic principles of curriculum and instruction.* Chicago: University of Chicago Press.

Walker, D. (1990). *Fundamentals of curriculum.* San Diego, CA: Harcourt Brace Jovanovich.

Walker, D. (1992). Methodological issues in curriculum research. In P. W. Jackson (Ed.), *Handbook of research on curriculum* (pp. 98–118). New York: Macmillan.

3

The Common Unity and the Progressive Restoration of the Curriculum Field

Peter S. Hlebowitsh

GUIDING QUESTIONS

1. *What are the general conceptual features of a so-called modernist view of the curriculum?*

2. *Why might it be important to understand the Latin derivation of the term for curriculum,* currere? *Use the meaning of the term* currere *as a metaphor to argue for or against the primacy of curriculum development in the work of the field.*

3. *What are the three fundamental factors discussed in the essay, and how did they emerge as a working framework for early progressive curricularists?*

4. *In what way can we consider curriculum development to be an inevitable outcome of all curriculum work?*

5. *Do you agree that the loss of design and curriculum development strategies could lead to the relativization of the public school mandate in school? Explain your position.*

6. *What are the four questions in the Tyler rationale? Explain how learning experiences are constructed through the employment of these four questions.*

A community of scholars in a field is renewed by its common history, its common basis of skills and its examination of commonly held problems. The expression of commonality does not eliminate debate or disagreement, but it does set a foundation for divergences. One might call this foundation the paradigm of a field, the loose framework of agreement that governs the work of scholarship. The development of a paradigm requires the hand of history and the continuing advancement of some center of intellectual gravity that encourages critical communication and progress. In the field of curriculum studies, the common unity has historically been forged by a commitment to the institution of public schooling, by a belief in developing curriculum-making ideas and by some agreement on the problem-solving process to be undertaken for school improvement (Tanner and Tanner, 1995).

Such a position has been viewed by some scholars as a modernist one (Pinar and others, 1995; Doll, 1993). Concerned with time and planning demands, the modernist conception of the curriculum does not shy away from establishing boundaries and controls in the learning experience or from limiting the possibilities of what youth will encounter in school in the interest of carrying out a social agenda believed to be vital to the sustenance of the society. The instruments of control include curriculum objectives, testing mechanisms, scheduling and planning techniques, models of instruction, and lesson planning—essentially everything traditionally associated with the act of curriculum development.

In recent years, this so-called modernist vision of the curriculum field has been challenged, even repudiated, by an emerging group of maverick scholars. As a result, a new curricularist has emerged in the field, prepared to void the historic basis of the field and replace it with a new manifesto. One, of course, might begin to describe this new curricularist in postmodern terms, as a scholar informed by a theoretical position that resonates with an exotic array of studies in hermeneutics, feminism, autobiography, aesthetics, deconstructionism, and eschatology. The mission of the new curricularist is not only to show that the historic or modernist vision of the field is misguided, but also to make it obvious that a new project is at hand.

William Pinar and others (1995) have tried to capture the new perspective in terms that point to a reconceptualization against a so-called traditional or modernist curriculum development outlook, one that presumably takes its legacy from the most managerial features of the field's early social efficiency movement. The problem, as they see it, revolves around the historic place that the act of curriculum development has had in the lives of American curricularists and in the lives of American school teachers and students. Believing that the function of curriculum development was tied to an administrative need to impose unreasonable control and authority on teachers and children, Pinar and others (1995) have proclaimed curriculum development to be no longer relevant to the work of the curriculum scholar. At the same time, they have argued that the work of the curricularist should move away from the regard that the earlier tradition placed on the institution of public schooling and move into more active theoretical realms unencumbered by practical institutional concerns.

One implication that follows from this way of looking at curriculum studies is the loss of a sense of common unity. As one gazes across the postmodern landscape of curriculum studies, one is confronted by a range of views so vast that any attempt to categorize it generally fails. This includes the attempt to categorize it as curriculum work. The postmodern rejection of the field has opened the gates to virtually all claimants. The very historical events and ideas that built the field are viewed as no more important (even less important) than any number of freewheeling ideas. This combination of rejecting the boundaries of the field and embracing alternativeness has put the curriculum field into a tailspin.

Today one is hard pressed to find any agreement on the kinds of questions that the curriculum community should be asking. The field has no common purpose, nor can any agreement be found on the nature of the history informing the field. Even the question of whether curriculum theory should be tied into school practice is up for debate. Questions that gave the field some coherence, such as what knowledge is most worthwhile, what learning and teaching patterns are most appropriate, and what evaluative mechanisms can best capture the effects of the curriculum experience, no longer hold sway.

Some might ask, why worry about such a phenomenon? Why not appreciate the place that each claimant has on the field of curriculum studies as a manifestation of a healthy variance in the field? The answer has less to do with what we might gain under such a condition than what we might lose. I still believe that the losses that accompany the effort to reconceptualize the field are truly losses. The case for the moribundity of the field, which has resulted in an effort to sweep away the so-called traditional curriculum development perspective of the field, has simply not been persuasive. As I will note, much of the argument has been ahistorical and stridently ideological.

In this essay, I will explain the historical, shall we say modernist, principles that have moved curriculum scholarship. This is work that is still very much with us today and very much a part of the daily school struggle to educate a generation of youth for enlightened participation in a democratic society. I will reiterate my case for the centrality of curriculum development and design in the work of curriculum scholarship and will raise questions about the validity of any reconceptualization in the field. I will argue throughout the essay that far from embracing the ideological criticisms against the so-called old modernist vision of the field (and in favor of the new one), curriculum scholars should focus their efforts on renewing the historical promise of the field and act in the interests of its restoration.

ORIGINS OF THE CURRICULUM FIELD AND THE PRIMACY OF PRACTICE

The definition of curriculum has long been identified with the Latin derivative *currere*, which is associated with the idea of running a racecourse. To use the metaphor in the context of schooling, we can imagine ourselves running through a course, completing the requirements of the race, and receiving some certificate of participation and completion, one that might also contain a judgment of and a reward for distinguished or meritorious participation. Along the way, professionally trained personnel assist the participants with the development of the skills needed to perform in the course, coaching and prodding their students to meet its demands, sometimes with success and sometimes not. Those personally staked in the race, including the parents and the community of the participants, make their own observations about the race and in most cases do their best to assist as well. The race, after all, is an ongoing one with no real end line, but with no with clear effects in the life destinies of the participants.

In the present-day form, the use of the term "course" has retained its place in the school. One takes a course or is enrolled in a course with a teacher, "running" through it according to the rules and regulations set down by the teacher or other curriculum determinants. A course of studies represents a set of conditions that identifies what students should learn and in what sequence, as well as ideas on how students will be evaluated for the purpose of certifying and designating meritorious and less-than-meritorious competence.

When one thinks about the school curriculum, one is immediately brought to the question of what course or course of action best embodies the societal or institutional desire to enlighten and inform the emerging generation of youth. What knowledge is most worthwhile for all youth? What behaviors are most desirable? What forms of experience produce the kinds of effects wanted in the education of all youth? How does one know such effects were secured? The school curriculum carries a societal agenda that points to a certain kind of school experience. Exactly what form this experience will take will depend on the curriculum decisions made.

The development of the field of curriculum studies was rooted in the very practical concerns implied by the term *currere*. Essentially, the field has been dedicated to determining how to design and implement a course of public school studies in relation to the development and realization of a societal mandate. In other words, the growth of curriculum studies in America was directly associated with a regard for actualizing the interests of the public domain in the education of all youth. The field was fashioned out of an effort to design "the course" for society, the actual sequence of events and experiences that had to be completed in order for a student to be competent in a certain range of skills, dispositions, attitudes, and knowledge believed to be appropriate for enlightened participation in society.

This ongoing struggle to meet practical demands yielded curriculum development frameworks centered on using the school for the maintenance and improvement of the public interest. Historically speaking, the field has been rife with practical proposals for school improvement. William Kilpatrick, for instance, articulated the Project Method; Jesse Newlon (1939b) tested "life situations" curricula in the Denver schools; Ralph Tyler formulated his famous rationale in the context of the Eight Year Study; Harold Rugg wrote a series of provocative social studies texts; and laboratory schools across the nation, often led by directors schooled in curriculum development, tested the practical vigor of various new ideas. Besides Dewey's laboratory school, there were the experimental schools described in the 26th Yearbook of the National Society for the Study of Education (1927), the descriptive accounts provided by Rugg and Shumaker (1928), by Dewey and his daughter, Evelyn (1915), and by the Lincoln School teacher units published by the Bureau of Publications at Teachers College. The vestiges of these early efforts are not reducible to the kinds of administrative/social efficiency traditions that the new curricularists seem only to see. Whole language instruction, cooperative learning, teacher-made units, interdisciplinary reform, teacher participation in curriculum development, teacher release time, general education, experimental schooling, civic learning, and the general perspective of placing the act of teaching and schooling in the context of the nature of the learner and the values of the society (to name only a very short list) are all, in some way, attributable to these early initiatives. Wraga (1996), in fact, has shown how some postmodern positions on education, when offering ideas on school practice, have done little more than appropriate practices historically situated in the work of progressive curricularists.

The formalized identification of the curriculum field and of the emerging curriculum expert can be traced to the early parts of the twentieth century. Interest in the growing development of the publicly supported school brought forth several thinkers who wanted to offer their own version of what might constitute a good public education. The absence of federal authority in the formation of school policy and practice opened the debate over to virtually all comers. Various thinkers freely offered their own versions of how the public school curriculum should be designed and operationalized. The questions were profound: What knowledge should the school privilege? What objectives should the school seek to attain? What pedagogical methods were most appropriate? These were the early queries that gave birth to a field dedicated to the development of the school curriculum.

One place to begin the examination of the school curriculum is with the early argument fashioned by traditional humanists who clamored for the centrality of the liberal arts in the education of all youth, arguing that life was in the subject matter of a few essential disciplines. Exposure to these disciplines, they asserted, exercised the mind and delivered the student to the vital Western culture of the human race. The curriculum, in turn, needed to be subject-centered and needed to be uniformly applied to all youth in order to ensure the appropriate measure of cultural and intellectual training in society. This was the essential message promoted in the Committee of Ten report (National Education Association, 1969) and in the work of mental disciplinarians, such as William Torrey Harris (1888) and Charles Elliot (1893). To Harris, certain subjects opened up to the wisdom of humanity: arithmetic and geography related to humanity's comprehension and quest over nature; history, literature, and language to humanity's comprehension of human life. These, in careful combination, were the windows that peered into life and that empowered individuals with the character and intellect they would need to conduct an intelligent life. Learning was in the subject matter.

Progressive child-centered advocates, largely working out of the nascent child study movement, countered this claim by arguing for the place of individualization in the curriculum. They contended that no one uniform framework of study, regardless of the nature of the subject matter that it embodied, could be appropriate for all children and that the life of the child (not the subject matter) was the key variable in the development of the school experience. This framed an early dualism that ensnared many curriculum thinkers. Advocates lined up on either side of the response to the question over whether the school should be subject-centered or child-centered.

Another response, however, emerged from a group that rejected the party-line loyalties that the dualism encouraged. This response essentially claimed that the school should be both child-centered and subject-centered and that another factor, attesting to the school's vital place in the development of democracy, had also to be considered. The debate between subject-centered and child-centered ideological positions faced some resolution in an antidote that combined both ingredients with a third one. Working out of the theoretical and school-based insight of John Dewey (1902), this early group of thinkers would lay claim to the idea that school formulations should be attuned to three fundamental factors: *(1) the nature of the learner, (2) the reflective consideration of the subject matter, and (3) the values and aims of the society.* The construction of this new trinity in educational thinking provided unique insight into the process of curriculum development because it insisted that school practice makes itself accountable to these three fundamental factors. Over time, the factors would evolve into a historical framework for guiding school practice (Tanner and Tanner, 1995).

THE PUBLIC SCHOOL MANDATE

As one of the leading voices of the new curriculum perspective, Pinar has taken the lead in criticizing the role of design and curriculum development in work of the curricularist. He is particularly averse to the application of procedural techniques and planning strategies in the curriculum. The result is the open rejection of what one might call conventional design considerations (objectives, evaluative mechanisms, and so forth). He says, in effect, that curriculum scholars should not have a program to offer because they cannot have a program to offer. From his point of view, the curriculum cannot be preordained or even fashioned with objectives, but must instead be brought to life by a self-affirmed and emancipated educator whose thinking is freed from the mechanical functions of curriculum practice. The purpose of curriculum theory is not to produce practical applications but to produce critical commentary that might inform the emergent judgments of individuals working in emergent situations. Practice, in this way, becomes an individualistic affair, an individual's personalized argument for action.

The loss of design, however, is indicative of the relativization of the public mandate in the school. Where the public interest converges with the mission of the school, the curriculum must prevail with an intervention. In an increasingly complex and pluralistic society, the public school in America has to give children an enlargening and amalgamating experience that purposely goes beyond (or even challenges) local traditions. This cannot be left to the individualistic expressions of teachers working in local school sites. A community-based vision for schooling only makes sense if it is accompanied by the wider purpose of building common political communities across parochial (community) lines. Such a function precisely underscores the importance of design. Design structures the larger experience. It tells us which knowledge is most worthwhile and which community traditions may or may not be worthy.

These decisions, moreover, require the articulation of some conception of what is to be done, when it is to be done, and how it is to be done. The intervention does not necessarily need to be overtly technical or prescriptive, but it does have to actualize a fundamental framework that makes a case for what is best for schooling in a democracy. The centrality of practical and deliberate judgments in the curriculum is underscored by the institutional character of the curriculum (Reid, 1994).

If we heed the call of the new curricularists, however, the theoretical focus of the field will move away from the public school and the institutional regard for public interest, in favor of more symbolic and individualistic theoretical pronouncements. But how can anyone be comfortable with a theoretical emphasis that contains no sharp sense of how to proceed with schooling in a democracy? The progressive branch of the curriculum field has always viewed schooling as operating within a miniature unit of democracy that was *deliberately and consciously* conceived to produce a comprehensive and enlargening social experience, where children learned about their differences and their commonalities, where vocational pursuits coexisted with academic ones, and where the ideals of tolerance and social mutuality were met by the needs for dissent and critical mindedness. The new curricularists, on the other hand, have left us with an embrace of alternativeness, a theoretical position that differs little from the free-market principles of conservative politics and capitalism. As the public school agenda continues to be ravaged by privatization arguments and by the appetites of various special interests, how does the postmodern/reconceptualist commitment to variety separate from the call of the marketplace?

THE INEVITABILITY OF CURRICULUM
DEVELOPMENT AND DESIGN

Paradoxically, the question of design never really escapes us, because it is impossible to conceive of any educational idea without eventually turning, one way or another, to design considerations. When one proclaims, in the language of the postmodern, a theoretical position advocating "liberatory" or "emancipatory" pedagogy, or a commitment to schooling that encourages, in the words of Slattery (1995, p. 94), "discovery learning, theological inquiry, autobiographical analysis, ecological sustainability, justice compassion and ecumenism," one immediately has to ask how such practices will be conducted? What will they be? How will they be organized? What latent effects might result from their application? One may abhor the notion of design and argue against the practicality of theory, but one cannot escape it (or forsake it) if there is any expectation of manifest effects in practice. This is another way of saying that the separation of curriculum theory from curriculum development is impossible because it results in denying the essential purpose of the theory.

This point is underscored by the fact that idiosyncratic curriculum planning strategies can sometimes be found even among those who argue against design. For instance, Kincheloe, Pinar, and Slattery (1994) have written about the development of interdisciplinary programs in southern studies. In this piece, they clearly stipulated various design considerations, including the need to deal with phenomenological and autobiographical elements. The authors argue for the *planning* of a curriculum around ideas of identity, politics, race, gender, and self. They want to be sure to bring certain objectives and certain knowledge to the forefront of the student's experience. When discussing race, for instance, they state that "European-Americans cannot hope to understand themselves unless they are knowledgeable and knowing of those they constructed as different, as other" (p. 432). They also make it clear that "class competition between poor Whites and Blacks needs to be unpacked, its racist elements expunged, and the possibility of class-based political collaborations needs to be elucidated" (p. 432). Moreover, we are told that "the African contribution to Christian evangelical worship needs to be acknowledged and reexperienced" (p. 432). These identified needs, dare I say objectives, are apparently required learning in the interdisciplinary unit. There are no expressed worries here about the dangers of imposition or the limitations that such factors might have on experience.

In another case of de facto design, Slattery and Daigle (1994) argued for the centrality of literature in the curriculum. "We believe," they state, "that literature might help us envision curriculum as a place of turmoil that is capable of nourishing our being in the midst of the frustration, violence, despair, and anguish of modern schooling" (p. 438). The authors further explain that "in recognizing curriculums as a place of turmoil and in deconstructing the anguish that catalyzes terror, there emerges support for a postmodern curriculum." Slattery and Daigle apparently feel that such a viewpoint is free from the limitations or ideological imperialism that they fear so much in the work of others. Nor are the authors bothered by the presumption that the school is full of despair and anguish. Here we have a confident proclamation of the kind of experience desired, if not required—one that palliates the despair of school life with literature and with postmodern commitments to emancipatory learning and self-reflection.

One might respond to these points by arguing that each curriculum description was an individualistic effort, not one that the authors would expect a teacher to follow and certainly not one that contained any sense on how to organize the curriculum. But the ideas offered by the authors were presumably offered in the interests of affecting practice. Why else offer them? The question is which position on design seems to have a greater hegemonic grip on the practical judgment of the teachers? The progressive view, which is often associated with Tyler, that insists on an accountability to the three fundamental factors within a problem-focused scheme, or the so-called postmodern position that advocates for highly ideologically driven learning experiences?

The ongoing historic struggle to identify workable curriculum development principles and to learn from various historical events related to the development of the school curriculum is a project anchored in the early development of the curriculum field. It is no less important today than it was at the turn of the century. Like it or not, it is not a matter that will simply go away. It is a matter, however, that will either be influenced by curricularists or not. In other words, someone will flex their muscles in attempting to exercise some authority or influence in the school curriculum. If the historical task of using curriculum development strategies to advance the interests of the institution of public schooling is to be viewed by the new curricularists as an anachronism, then one should understand that such a surrender of responsibility gives more influence to other determinants, often ones not bound by any regard for the nature of the learner or the widest values of society.

CURRICULUM OBJECTIVES AND THE SCHOOL EXPERIENCE

One of the initial tasks facing the work of the curricularist is to find a process that allows educators to balance their conceptions of school purpose, school content, and school organization with a variance of approved instructional and evaluative actions. To this end, Tyler conceived of school action as moving across a continuum of concerns that speaks to school purpose, the organization of experience, and the evaluation of experience. His basic questions are now famous (Tyler, 1949):

1. What educational purposes should the school seek to attain?
2. What educational experiences can be provided that are likely to attain these purposes?
3. How can these educational experiences be effectively organized?
4. How can we determine whether these purposes are being attained?

One critical portrayal of the rationale describes it as a lockstep managerial framework that projects the school experience in highly linear and atheoretical terms. Such a criticism, however, generally fails to appreciate the flexibility of the rationale in reacting to the educational situation in the school. The four questions are indeed described in a linear manner, but the rationale was con-

ceived as a document to be used for the development of the school curriculum, which means that it needs to be used in relation to some existing school condition. Therefore, one does not necessarily need to start with Question One. Many schools, in fact, are attracted to the idea of framing reform ideas around Question Four. An appropriate way to start with Question Four would inevitably lead to Question One and raise issues over whether the school's testing or evaluation strategies were comprehensive enough to provide data that attested to the fulfillment of all school purposes. Thus, if one purpose is to, say, learn to love mathematics, the school curriculum must design an evaluative mechanism that produces data on affective responses to mathematics teaching and learning. If another purpose is to socialize socially tolerant citizens capable of making intelligent choices, some mechanism has to be found to detect whether such a purpose is being fulfilled. This, of course, means that the data collection process goes beyond simple pencil and paper tests. Because of his early insistence on looking at evaluation as an evidence collection process tied to fundamental school purposes, Tyler could very well be considered one of the first advocates of portfolio assessment.

In most cases, the tendency of school leaders is to start with and focus on Questions Two and Three. Classroom instruction seems to be the one variable that the school is most keen on modifying. The traditional way to do this is to inservice teachers in an instructional model that stipulates a lesson design or lesson strategy that is presumably good for all teachers. We saw this occur in the 1980s on a grand scale during the heyday of the Madeline Hunter model. But in the Tyler rationale, the exercise of only one lesson strategy or instructional model would be viewed as a violation because no one strategy could effectively manage to be an appropriate instructional response to all school purposes. This is another way of saying that the Tyler rationale encourages instructional variance, a conclusion that is diametrically opposed to the assertion of procedural compulsion and hypermanaged instructional scripting that one could find in the criticism lodged against the rationale.

One of the main weapons in effecting instructional change through the rationale comes in the form of behavioral objectives. These objectives are, generally speaking, non–subject specific and representative of a set of skills that one desires to see in the behaviors of youth. They must be appropriate to the nature of the learner and the values and aims of the society. Tyler wanted broadly framed objectives with a generalizable tone that captured the spirit of what one wanted to accomplish without being too specific and too prescriptive. The following outline suggests some possibilities.

Behavioral Objectives

A. Social Skills and Social Values
    A 1. Positive attitudes toward self (the learner)
    A 2. Social democratic skills and attitudes (the learner in society)
    A 3. Intellectual and aesthetic values

B. Thinking Skills
    B 1. Engage in the analysis, synthesis, and evaluation of knowledge
    B 2. Apply scientific method to social thinking
    B 3. Understand cause-and-effect relationships
    B 4. Independent thinking
    B 5. Ability to analyze arguments and propaganda
    B 6. Evaluation of authenticity of information
    B 7. Ability to foresee the consequences of a proposed idea
    B 8. Ability to understand quantitative reasoning

C. Inquiry and Study Skills
    C 1. Ability to collect facts and data
    C 2. Skill in selecting dependable sources of data
    C 3. Ability to observe and listen attentively
    C 4. Ability to read critically
    C 5. Ability to discriminate between important and unimportant facts
    C 6. Ability to take notes, and read graphs, charts, tables, and maps
    C 7. Skills in outlining and summarizing
    C 8. Skills in effective planning and efficient use of time

D. Communicative Skills
    D 1. Skill in writing clearly and persuasively
    D 2. Skills in oral presentation
    D 3. Skills in debate and argumentation
    D 4. Skills in the preparation of charts, graphs, tables, and other non-verbal tools of communication

With the behavioral objectives in order, we could proceed to the step of identifying the subject matter. Often, the subject matter of the curriculum is already provided to the teacher in the form of state- or district-mandated decisions on content or in the form of a preidentified body of knowledge covered in a text or curriculum guide. But even in these cases, educators still have decisions to make about what to emphasize, how a chosen body of knowledge will be related to certain objectives, how the subject matter will be organized and sequenced, and what teaching strategies should be used to bring the important subject matter to light in the classroom. The choice of the content has to reflect confidence in the learn-ability and the age-appropriateness of the material. It also has to reflect an emerging pattern for the organization of the material, meaning that variously conceived problem-focused, interdisciplinary, or highly discipline-centered approaches might be used.With behavioral objectives in place and the content organized, one could begin to piece the two parts together and set the stage for a series of lessons that ensure that our objectives and our content will be covered. The convergence between what one teaches (the content) and the behavior that one wants to develop (the objectives) represents a point of birth for the lesson. It allows the teacher to say, "in lesson or lessons X, I am going to be sure to cover a certain range of content while also dedicating the lesson to the advancement of a certain range of behavioral objectives" (thinking, communication, inquiry, sociopersonal skills).

This thumbnail sketch of one way of operating the Tyler rationale should make it clear that the model allows for the exercise of teacher judgment. It is not a freewheeling affair and there certainly are boundaries, but the continuum that the rationale sets between educational purpose and the instructional and evaluative response to the purposes gives the curriculum a unity of design. The rationale does not script patterns of content organization, instructional or pedagogical or evaluative judgment, or even the articulation of school purpose. It does set philosophical parameters by maintaining that curriculum decisions be screened through the three fundamental processes, and it expects that there will be a basis of expected content and behavior in the education of youth.

THE RECONCEPTUALIZATION THAT NEVER WAS

As I suggested earlier, there is little question that something has happened to the curriculum field. In my view, most of the effect has not been good for the field. But good or bad, there is no persuasive evidence that the field has been reconceptualized in any meaningful way.

Some scholars like to point to the work of the social efficiency movement, particularly the work of John Franklin Bobbitt (1918), in making a case for the origins of the curriculum field. This is an important contention because the social efficiency position held to a functionalist view of society that placed the school in the role of sorting and slotting the student population in ways that were socially predestining and ultimately conforming to the socioeconomic status quo. Bobbitt's main curriculum technique, known as job analysis, promoted such an effect and provided an early example of an engineering or efficiency model for curriculum development. Few would deny the fact that Bobbitt's influence has been lasting in the sense that it led to a bureaucratized framework for curriculum design that assumed a prevailing factory or production model for schooling in America. Several scholars, including William Pinar, et al. (1995) and Michael Apple (1990), have accorded historic primacy to the social efficiency doctrine in the act of curriculum development and in the general historical development of the curriculum field. This turns out to be an important point because the very validity of the proclaimed reconceptualization of the curriculum studies field depends on making the case for the historic primacy of social efficiency thinking in the field.

What is ignored in this argument, however, is the fact that complaints about the overreaching effects of the social efficiency doctrine in the schools and in the curriculum field were well established long before any declared reconceptualization. In fact, arguably the best criticism ever written of social efficiency, particularly in relation to the work of Franklin Bobbitt, was written by Boyd Bode (1927), in his classic *Modern Educational Theories*. This was a criticism inspired by the progressive-experimentalist tradition in the field, the very same group of thinkers that was in alignment with the theoretical foundation forged by Dewey on the three fundamental factors (the learner, the society, and the subject matter). Far from being wedded to the doctrines of social efficiency, the field was active in its criticism of it.

The term *reconceptualization* is an important one to consider here because it connotes the reconceiving of an idea, which of course, demands that the original idea be completely and properly comprehended and understood. One does not want to reconceive an idea that has been originally misconceived. Such a process would likely lead to trouble.

Yet this is exactly what has occurred with the reconceptualization of the curriculum field. Elsewhere, I have offered a challenge to the new curricularists over their preferred portrayal of Tyler and other "traditional" scholars in the field (Hlebowitsh, 1993). I have argued that the Tyler Rationale is not a behavioristic construct that has taken its genes from the atomized curriculum that Franklin Bobbitt supported in earlier years (Hlebowitsh, 1992; 1995). The rationale itself is a progressive document that grows out of Dewey's work on reflective thinking and the educative process. I have also argued that the position taken on the idea of social control by many new curricularists has been constructed in an unbalanced manner that fails to reflect early progressive efforts to put children in control of their lives as opposed to putting them under control (Hlebowitsh, 1993).

These are particularly important points of contention because of the centrality of the Tyler rationale and the argument of social control in the process of proclaiming a reconceptualization in the curriculum field. A line has been drawn by the new curricularists between those who walk with Tyler and those who have walked away from Tyler. It has helped to create a field that is now largely in schism (Hlebowitsh, 1997). Many of us who have worked out of an experimentalist-progressive line continue to be labeled as traditionalists who are caught up in the task of designing oppressive environments for youth (Slattery, 1995). The labeling has even extended into portraying the work of progressive curricularists as the exercise of heterosexual male dominion over the classroom work of predominantly female teachers (Pinar, 1999). But if the so-called traditionalist curricularists were actually progressive liberals who took their framework from the early work of Dewey and if the history of the curriculum field does not fit into the argument of malevolent social control, then it very well might be time to reconceptualize the entire effort at reconceptualization or to restore the field to its common bases of understanding.

CONCLUSIONS

The time has come to find a common unity in the field of curriculum. Discussions between scholars working out of the postmodern or reconceptualized perspective and scholars working out of the modern or progressive one have not yielded any advancing ideas for the field. There is no mutuality of concern or insight that can serve as a basis for building a new consensus. And there will not be one any time soon. The problem is that the reconceptualization is an ideological criticism. But criticism is not theory, and criticism decrying practice has little to offer to those interested in practice.

The curriculum field is about the development of school experiences that advance the public mandate. It is a deliberative process that is set in a framework of historic questions about school purpose, instructional procedure, content organization, and evaluative design. The restoration of the historic basis of the field is now the best hope for saving the field.

Case Study 3: High School Curriculum Promotes Gender Bias

The following case description highlights a problem that calls for a curriculum remedy. After reading it, try to isolate the nature of the problem. Then describe the kind of data that you would like to collect to find out more about the problem.

Several teachers in your high school recently finished reading a research report that documents the incidence of gender bias in the American schools. They have noticed that many of the things mentioned in the report seem to also happen in your school. Boys, for instance, seem to get a lot more positive attention from teachers than do girls in the classroom. And the curriculum materials and testing mechanisms used in the school seem to favor the boys. You respond by telling your faculty that you will authorize a study of the problem in the school. You put together a team of faculty and university researchers to conduct a study. The team eventually files a report with the school board that contains four central conclusions. They are:

1. Boys in math and science classes are generally given more thought-provoking questions and more positive attention by teachers. They are also given more negative attention, including being punished more often and criticized more often. Differences in positive attention cannot be found between boys and girls in any other courses.

2. Boys drop out of the school at a slightly higher rate than girls and cite being "bored with school" as the main reason for dropping out.

3. Girls have less access to advanced placement work in math and science.

4. More girls than boys go to college, but very few choose math and science as continued disciplines of study.

5. The documented achievement of girls in the areas of reading and writing demonstrates that they have a considerable edge over boys.

You are asked by the school board to submit a plan for the revision of the high school curriculum in accordance with the report's findings.

FOLLOW-UP QUESTIONS

1. What might you study next?

2. What are some of the working hypotheses that might explain why the problem exists?

3. What might you need to know to verify or reject the hypotheses?

4. What curriculum response might you advocate if one of the hypotheses you formulated was confirmed?

5. Which of Tyler's four questions might be a good starting point for developing a curricular remedy to the problem?

6. How might the three factors play in this process? Describe the process you would use.

7. What curricular remedies might you consider testing?

NOTE

Selected sections of this chapter were adapted from Hlebowitsh, P.S. (1999) The Burdens of the New Curricularists. *Curriculum Inquiry, 29*(3), 343–354.

REFERENCES

Apple, M. (1990). *Ideology and curriculum*. New York: Routledge & Kegan Paul.

Bobbitt, J. F. (1918). *The curriculum*. Boston: Houghton-Mifflin.

Bode, B. (1927). *Modern educational theories*. New York: Macmillan.

Dewey, J. (1902). *The child and the curriculum*. Chicago: University of Chicago Press.

Dewey, J. (1916). *Democracy and education*. New York: Macmillan.

Dewey, J., & Dewey, E. (1915). *Schools of tomorrow*. E. P. Dutton and Co.

Doll, W. (1993). *A post-modern perspective on curriculum*. New York: Teachers College Press.

Eliot, C. (1893). Can school programs be shortened and enriched? *National Education Association Proceedings*. Washington, DC: National Education Association.

Harris, W. T. (1888). What shall the public schools teach? *The Forum, 4,* 573–581.

Hlebowitsh, P. S. (1992). Amid behavioral and behavioristic objectives: Reappraising appraisals of the Tyler Rationale. *Journal of Curriculum Studies, 24*(6), 533–547.

Hlebowitsh, P. S. (1993). *Radical curriculum theory reconsidered*. New York: Teachers College Press.

Hlebowitsh, P. S. (1995). Interpretations of the Tyler Rationale: A reply to Kliebard. *Journal of Curriculum Studies, 27*(1), 89–94.

Hlebowitsh, P. S. (1997). The search for the curriculum field. *Journal of Curriculum Studies, 29*(5), 507–511.

Kilpatrick, W. (1918). The project method. *Teachers College Record, 19*(4), 319–335.

Kincheloe, J., Pinar, W. F., & Slattery, P. (1994). A last dying chord? Toward cultural and educational renewal in the south. *Curriculum Inquiry, 24*(4), 407–436.

Kliebard, H. (1970). The Tyler Rationale. *School Review, 78*(2), 259–272.

Mayhew, K. C., & Edwards, A. C. (1936). *The Dewey school*. New York: Atherton Press.

National Education Association. (1969). *Report of the Committee of Ten on secondary school studies*. New York: Arno Press; originally published in 1893 by the U.S. Printing Office.

National Society for the Study of Education (1927). *Curriculum-making: Past and present*. Twenty-Sixth Yearbook. Part I. Bloomington, IL: Public School Publishing Co.

Newlon, J. H. (1939) *Education for democracy in our time*. New York: McGraw-Hill.

Pinar, W. F. (1988). *Contemporary curriculum discourses*. Scottsdale, AZ: Gorsuch, Scarsbrick Publishers.

Pinar, W. F. (1992). Dreamt into existence by others: Curriculum theory and school reform. *Theory into Practice, 31*(3), 228–235.

Pinar, W. F. (1999). Response to "Extracting Sun-Beams out of Cucumbers: The Retreat from Practice in Reconceptualized Curriculum Studies." *Educational Researcher, 28*(11):14–15.

Pinar, W. F., Reynolds, W. M., Slattery, P., & Taubman, P. M. (1995). *Understanding curriculum: An introduction to the study of historical and contemporary curriculum discourses*. New York: Peter Lang.

Reid, W. (1994). *Curriculum planning as deliberation*. (Rapport Nr. 11). Universitetet I Oslo, Oslo, Norway.

Rugg, H., & Shumaker, A. (1928). *The child-centered school*. New York: Word Book Co.

Slattery, P. (1995). *Curriculum development in the postmodern era*. Hamden, CT: Garland Press.

Slattery, P., & Daigle, K. (1994). Curriculum as a place of turmoil. *Curriculum Inquiry, 24*(4), 437–461.

Tanner, D., & Tanner, L. (1995). *Curriculum development*. New York: Macmillan.

Tyler, R. W. (1949). *Basic principles of curriculum and instruction*. Chicago: University of Chicago Press.

Wraga, W. G. (1996).Toward a theory for a new century. *Journal of Curriculum Studies, 28*(4), 463–474.

Supervision: Don't Discount the Value of the Modern

Jeffrey Glanz

GUIDING QUESTIONS

1. *Is "instructional leadership" synonymous with "supervision"?*
2. *What are the differences among premodern, modern, and postmodern conceptions of supervision?*
3. *Discuss how Mays' three approaches to supervision might be employed in practice?*
4. *Why does the author lament the "pedagogically correct" view that eschews the theory and practice of "supervision"?*
5. *Under what circumstances, if any, can a "supervisor" and "supervisee" become co-inquirers in the improvement of instruction?*
6. *What are some potential "dangers" of collegial relationships between teachers and supervisors?*

Postmodernists have criticized modern conceptions of supervision as bureau-cratic, hierarchical, and oppressive. According to a postmodernist view, super-vision stifles individual autonomy, especially that of the teacher. A postmodern supervisor seeks to unsettle conventional hierarchical power relationships, re-placing such relationships with "relational" ones (Waite, 1997). Anathema is the technicist mindset that imposes preconceived values or notions of "good" teaching through the employment of various supervisory strategies and tech-niques. For the postmodernist, "the hidden dangers" in "rational-technical thinking are that it reduces supervision to a rigidly defined set of behaviors and responses, and places the supervisor in a position to authoritatively diagnose teachers' pedagogical problems and impose particular solutions" (Holland,

1994, pp. 11–12). To the postmodern supervisor, the bureaucratic/technicist ontology, fueled by Cartesian dualism, must give way to more holistic, postmodern perspectives.

But what does postmodern supervision really mean? Examining the work of Eisner (1985), Smyth (1991), Garman (1986), Gordon (1992), and Waite (1995), it seems as if a postmodern supervisor would advocate that supervision be:

- collegial;
- non-evaluative; and
- non-directive.

Moreover, a postmodern view of supervision would seem to even eschew the term "supervision," which in and of itself connotes surveillance and control (Gordon, 1997; Sergiovanni, 1992). Postmodern interpretations clearly favor the term "instructional leadership," as Glickman (1992) explained several years ago:

Supervision is in such throes of change that not only is the historical understanding of the word becoming obsolete, but I've come to believe that if "instructional leadership" were substituted each time the word "supervision" appears in the text, and "instructional leader" substituted for "supervisor," little meaning would be lost and much might be gained. (p. 3)

Stephen Gordon (1997) concurs: "My argument is that while the primary goal should be a radical shift from control supervision to collegial supervision, changing the name of what we now call supervision, . . . will increase the chance" that the practice of supervision will change. He too advocates the term "instructional leadership."

I assert, however, that the postmodern proclivity to completely eschew expert supervision, evaluation, and judicious and intelligent use of directive supervision is misguided, potentially limiting, and yes, even dangerous. I will argue that collegial practices may not always be desirable and that directive supervision not only has its place in a supervisory program but serves to safeguard our democratic framework of schooling and provides practical guidelines for practitioners and suggestions for the training of future administrators.

THREE VIEWS OF SUPERVISION

Three eras in the evolution of supervision are apparent: the premodern, the modern, and the postmodern.

The Premodern

Earliest recorded instances of the word "supervision" established the process as entailing "general management, direction, control, and oversight"

(Grumet, 1979; Gwynn, 1961). An examination of early records from the Colonial period indicates that supervision was synonymous with "inspection." Parenthetically, those scholars who imply that early supervisory practices reflected democratic tendencies, at least as we understand democracy today, misread the evidence. Based on my historical investigations (Glanz, 1998), early supervisory practice was a far cry from democratic.

By the end of the nineteenth century, reformers concerned with undermining inefficiency and corruption transformed schools into streamlined, central administrative bureaucracies with superintendents as supervisors in charge (Elsbree, 1939; Gilland, 1935; Griffiths, 1966; Reller, 1935). Supervision, during this struggle, became an important tool by which the superintendent would legitimize his existence in the school system (Glanz, 1991). Supervision, therefore, was a function performed by superintendents to more efficiently administer schools.

Supervision as inspection became the dominant method of administering schools. Payne (1875), author of the first published textbook on supervision, stated emphatically that teachers must be "held responsible" for work performed in the classroom and that the supervisor, as expert inspector, would "oversee" and ensure "harmony and efficiency." A prominent superintendent, James M. Greenwood (1888), stated emphatically that "very much of my time is devoted to visiting schools and inspecting the work." Greenwood (1891), three years later, again illustrated his idea of how supervision should be performed. The skilled supervisor, said Greenwood, should simply walk into the classroom and "judge from a compound sensation of the disease at work among the inmates" (p. 227). A review of the literature of the period indicates that Greenwood's supervisory methods, which relied on inspection based on intuition rather than technical or scientific knowledge, were widely practiced.

Supervisors using inspectional practices did not favorably view the competency of most teachers. For instance, Balliet (1894), a superintendent from Massachusetts, insisted that there were only two types of teachers: the efficient and the inefficient. The only way to reform the schools, thought Balliet, was to "secure a competent superintendent; second, to let him 'reform' all the teachers who are incompetent and can be 'reformed'; thirdly, to bury the dead" (pp. 437–38). Characteristic of the remedies applied to improve teaching was this suggestion: "Weak teachers should place themselves in such a position in the room that every pupil's face may be seen without turning the head" (Fitzpatrick, 1893, p. 76). Teachers, for the most part, were seen by nineteenth-century supervisors as inept. As Bolin and Panaritis (1992) explained: "Teachers (mostly female and disenfranchised) were seen as a bedraggled troop—incompetent and backward in outlook" (p. 33).

The practice of supervision by inspection was indeed compatible with the emerging bureaucratic school system. The raison d'être of supervision in the premodern period was to achieve quality schooling by eradicating inefficiency and incompetence among the teaching force. Premodern supervision later gained legitimacy in the educational community through the application of the principles of scientific management, advanced first by Frederick Taylor (1911) and later translated into education by Franklin Bobbitt (1913). During this period, various elaborate rating forms were developed to produce efficient, competent teachers (Pajak, 1993b). Note that the improvement of instruction was less important than purging the schools of the inept.

In the premodern era, then, supervision was characterized in two ways: by "inspectional" practices, which reflected the "emergence of bureaucracy" in education, and by the "social efficiency" movement. The movement to alter supervisory theory and practice to more democratic and improvement foci would not occur until in the 1920s as a direct result of growing opposition to autocratic supervisory methods. This post-1920 period marks the beginning of what can be referred to as the "modern" era of supervision.

The Modern

Bureaucratic supervision, relying on inspectional methods and seeking efficiency above all else, dominated discourse in the field during the premodern era. This sort of supervision attracted much criticism from teachers and others (Rousmaniere, 1992). Representative of the nature of this opposition are comments made by Sallie Hill (1918), a teacher speaking before the Department of Classroom Teachers, decrying supervisory methods of rating. Hill charged in 1918:

There is no democracy in our schools. . . . Here let me say that I do not want to give the impression that we are sensitive. No person who has remained a teacher for ten years can be sensitive. She is either dead or has gone into some other business. . . . there are too many supervisors with big salaries and undue rating powers. (p. 506)

The movement to alter supervisory theory and practice to more democratic and improvement foci, while minimizing the evaluative function, occurred in the 1920s (e.g., Hosic, 1920; Barr & Burton, 1926, Burton, 1927; Ayer & Barr, 1928, Stone, 1929) as a direct result of growing opposition to autocratic supervisory methods. Consequently, supervisors tried to change their image as "snoopervisors" by adopting alternate methods of supervision. The following poem, quoted in part below, indicates the desired change of focus to more democratic methods in supervision:

> With keenly peering eyes and snooping nose,
> From room to room the Snoopervisor goes.
> He notes each slip, each fault with lofty frown,
> And on his rating card he writes it down;
> His duty done, when he has brought to light,
> The things the teachers do that are not right. . . .

> The supervisor enters quietly,
> "What do you need? How can I help today?
> John, let me show you. Mary, try this way."
> He aims to help, encourage and suggest,
> That teachers, pupils all may do their best. (Anonymous, 1929)

Influenced in large measure by John Dewey's (1929) theories of democratic *and* scientific thinking as well as by James Hosic's (1920) ideas of democratic supervision, supervisors attempted to apply scientific methods and cooperative problem-solving approaches to educational problems (Pajak, 1993a). Supervision, during this period, reflected efforts to employ democratic *and* scientific methods. Democratic supervision, in particular, implied that educators, including teachers, curriculum specialists, and supervisors would cooperate in order to improve instruction. Efforts by prominent superintendent Jesse Newlon reinforced democracy in supervision. In an article entitled "Reorganizing City School Supervision," Newlon (1923) asked: "How can the ends of supervision best be achieved?" He maintained that the school organization must be set up to "invite the participation of the teacher in the development of courses." The ends of supervision can be realized when teacher and supervisor work in a coordinated fashion. Newlon developed the idea of setting up "supervisory councils" to offer "genuine assistance" to teachers. In this way, he continued, "the teacher will be regarded as a fellow-worker rather than a mere cog in a big machine."

The idea that supervision can meet the diverse needs of a democratic society characterizes the modern conception of supervision from the 1920s through the 1980s. An examination of the publications devoted to instructional supervision indicates this modern democratic thrust is closely aligned with scientific thinking in order to facilitate instructional improvement (Holland, 1994; Pajak, 1993b). For the modern supervisor, cooperative, democratic, and scientific approaches to supervision are vital to support instructional improvement.

Various definitions (culled, in part, from Krey & Burke, 1989) and discussions of supervision during this era attest to the emphasis on cooperative, democratic, and scientific methods to improve instruction:

> The fact that he is invested for the time being with a good deal of delegated authority does not justify him in playing the autocrat. To do so is neither humane, wise, nor expedient . . . the democratic method is applicable to education, to educational supervision. (Hosic, 1920)

> If supervision were merely scientific management or inspection or bossing the job, then truly it would have but little in common with the art of teaching . . . in *modern* (emphasis added) school practice. (Editorial, 1921)

> The aim of supervision is the improvement of teaching. (Burton, 1922)

> The next step in supervision is scientific and expert supervision. (Oberholtzer, 1922)

Instructional supervision, therefore, has the large purpose of improving the quality of instruction, primarily by promoting the professional growth of all teachers. (Dunn, 1923)

Supervision is a cooperative undertaking in which both supervisor and teacher are to be mutually helpful and jointly responsible for the work in the classroom. (Nutt, 1928)

Supervision is a creative enterprise. It has for its objective the development of a group of professional workers who attack their problems scientifically. (Department of Superintendence, 1930)

Supervision is cooperative. All supervisory agents work toward common ends. (National Conference of Supervisors and Directors of Instruction, 1930)

Personally I think creative and democratic supervision are quite consistent with the scientific. (National Conference of Supervisors and Directors of Instruction, 1930)

Our times demand a new curriculum [and supervision] in which vitalized learning is directed toward the preservation of democracy. (*The Changing Curriculum*, 1937)

But the conditions which at one time partially justified the centralized, hierarchical scheme of administration and supervision no longer exist. (Featherstone, 1942)

Supervision can be objective and yet be human. Supervision can be creative and yet be thorough. . . . It can be co-operative and yet not shirk responsibilities. It can recognize the importance of individuals and yet retain instructional standards. It can give help and yet not be dictatorial. (Spears, 1953)

Supervision is teaching teachers on the job to improve instruction. (Bartky, 1953)

Supervision is cooperative, democratic, and helpful. (Burton & Brueckner, 1955)

Modern supervision helps the teacher to evaluate learning and in so doing makes it possible for the teacher to grow in ways which will stimulate learning. (Crosley, 1957)

Supervision is a process for stimulating teacher growth. (Hicks, 1960)

Action through wide participation of all concerned in the processes of inquiry and the judgement of outcomes [is the goal of supervision]. (Lucio & McNeil, 1962)

Modern supervision is positive, democratic action aimed at the improvement of classroom instruction through the continual growth of all concerned—the child, the teacher, the supervisor, the administrator, and the parent or other interested lay person. (Neagley & Evans, 1964)

Supervisory skills, based on a body of knowledge, theories, or propositions, in addition to human understandings, are needed to handle the practical and technical problems of education in the laboratory of the *modern* (emphasis added) school. It should be added that a necessary function of supervision is the continual study and development of new technical skills in order to discover better ways of defining purposes, predicting the outcome of proposals, managing situations, and assessing the consequences of actions. (Lucio & McNeil, 1969)

School supervision is instructional leadership. (Feyereisen, Fiorino, & Nowak, 1970)

Modern supervision is positive, dynamic, democratic action. (Neagley & Evans, 1970)

Clinical supervision may be defined as supervision focused upon the improvement of instruction by means of systematic cycles of planning, observation, and intensive intellectual analysis of actual teaching performances in the interest of rational modification. (Weller, 1971)

[Supervision] is planning for, observation, analysis and treatment of the teacher's classroom performance. (Mosher & Purpel, 1972)

Hindsight suggests that the profession went too far in its efforts to turn supervision into a helping function, a teaching function, a curricular function—anything, but the function it literally names, overseeing with a view to improving the quality of an operation. (Lewis & Miel, 1972)

Clinical supervision may therefore be defined as the rationale and practice designed to improve the teacher's classroom performance. It takes its principal data from the events of the classroom. The analysis of these data and the relationship between teacher and supervisor form the basis of the program, procedures, and strategies designed to improve the students' learning by improving the teacher's classroom behavior. (Cogan, 1973)

Instructional supervision is herein defined as: Behavior officially designated by the organization that directly affects teacher behavior in such a way as to facilitate pupil learning and achieve the goals of the organization. (Alfonso, Firth, & Neville, 1975)

Supervision is a major function of the school operation, not a task or a specific job or set of techniques. Supervision of instruction is directed toward both maintaining and improving the teaching-learning processes of the school. (Harris, 1975)

Supervision is conceived as a service to teachers. . . . Supervision is a means of offering to teachers specialized help in improving instruction. (Oliva, 1976)

A leadership function that bridges administration, curriculum, and teaching, and coordinates those school activities concerned with learning. (Wiles & Bondi, 1980).

[Clinical supervision] is that phase of instructional supervision which draws its data from first-hand observation of actual teaching events, and involves face-to-face (and other associated) interaction between the supervisor and the teacher in the analysis of teaching behaviors and activities for instructional improvement. (Goldhammer, Anderson, & Krajewski, 1980)

[Supervision] is an in-class support system designed to deliver assistance directly to the teacher . . . to bring about changes in classroom operation and teacher behavior. (Sergiovanni & Starratt, 1983)

Supervision is a process of facilitating the professional growth of a teacher. (Glatthorn, 1984)

Supervision refers to the school function that improves instruction through direct assistance to teachers, curriculum development, in-service training, group development, and action research. (Glickman, 1985)

We have defined supervisory leadership as the process of helping teachers to find the best possible methods to improve teaching and learning. Perhaps it is well to reemphasize that this does not mean telling them what to do but means sharing with them the problem-solving responsibility. (Tanner & Tanner, 1987)

Supervision is instructional leadership. (Krey & Burke, 1989)

We wish to promote an alternative model of supervision that is interactive rather than
directive, democratic rather than authoritarian, teacher-centered rather than
supervisor-centered. This supervisory style is called clinical supervision. (Acheson & Gall, 1997, although their first edition appeared in 1980)

As the various definitions and descriptions imply, supervision is of vital importance to promote instructional improvement. Modern conceptions of supervision promote professional growth of teachers, foster curriculum development, and support instruction.

Modernist supervision, if you will, provides assistance to teachers and direction for supervisors-in-training, whether through clinical practice (Goldhammer, 1969), developmental supervision (Glickman, 1985), cognitive coaching (Costa & Garmston, 1994), or group development and action research (Glickman, Gordon, & Ross-Gordon, 1995). Such task-oriented approaches, supported by the application of descriptive research methods and clinical practice, characterize supervision in the modern era. Informing practitioners that their school, in the postmodern vein, is viewed as indeterminate, nonlinear, cyclical, and contingent doesn't offer much solace for those who have to confront a multitude of social, psychological, and educational challenges daily. Teachers *want* constructive assistance from supervisors whom they perceive as trustworthy and skillful (Blumberg & Amidon, 1965; Blase & Kirby, 1992). If a supervisor can observe a teacher's classroom (see the case study at the end of this chapter) and accumulate practically verifiable information (e.g., data that indicates Teacher X is allowing girls less time to respond to questions than boys) so that the teacher can view his classroom from another perspective and consider alternate ways of doing things, then, I think, a modernist approach does have much to offer. Autocratic practices do not characterize the modern era as they did in premodern times (a point postmodernists tend to miss). As my personal experiences as a teacher and assistant principal for twenty years in the New York City public schools affirm, modern supervision can make a positive contribution to instructional improvement.

The Postmodern

Postmodernists or those with postmodern perspectives suggest that modernist views of supervision are overly technicist in orientation. As an alternative, they might suggest "dialogic supervision" (Waite, 1995) which advances collegial relationships between supervisors and teachers. Waite, for instance, advocates the "null technique," in which the supervisor becomes "witness to a teaching episode in order to enter into a dialogue with that teacher." (Waite, 1997). Dialogic supervision seeks to enhance the quality of the teacher-supervisor relationship by focusing more on the dialogue than the "data." This way, says Waite, "both the teacher and supervisor have a better chance of coming to the table on an equal footing." "Egalitarian reciprocity" is what

Waite suggests, while I maintain that such equality may not always be wise or even possible.

THREE WAYS OF DOING SUPERVISION

Too often, however, an either/or paradigm for viewing supervisory practice is adopted. Although in this chapter I urge that we consider the viability of "the modern," I do not advocate an abandonment of the postmodern viewpoint. As I will indicate at the conclusion of this chapter, I believe that a diversity of approaches to supervision should be accepted, both the modern and the postmodern.

Three approaches to supervision have been suggested by May (1989). These models of supervision may very well reflect the thinking and practice of supervision over the last fifty years. The three models of supervision articulated by May (1989) include the Applied Science Approach (which represents a modern conception of supervision); the Interpretive-Practical Approach; and the Critical-Emancipatory Approach (the latter two may represent a postmodern perspective, although some might argue that the former approach has modernist tendencies).

The Applied Science Approach

This approach to supervision relies on the empirical-analytical sciences and emphasizes technical aspects of the supervision process. At its most basic level, this applied science approach assumes that certain school personnel are in a better position to oversee the instructional process than others. In May's words, "This conception suggests that supervisors are experts and teachers are not [necessarily]. . . . This view of teaching and/or supervision carries several labels which embody a theme of control: directive, executive, behavioristic or positivist."

Using this approach implies that supervisors diagnose problems in the classroom after a series of close observations. Supervisors then prescribe a particular course of action, and teachers are expected to incorporate the suggested changes. Suggestions offered presumptively are drawn from a research base. Suggestions pertaining to technical classroom management skills and specific teaching strategies are common.

The applied science approach is technically oriented, hierarchical in its organizational structure, and most often associated with modern views of supervision. This prescriptive model is often called directive or evaluative supervision. This model, in my opinion, has its place in any supervisory program.

However, a modernist supervisor employing developmental supervision (Glickman, 1985) might not always need to assume such directive measures and yet can utilize this applied science approach. The supervisor may assume the role of research investigator by collecting data via Glickman, Gordon, and Ross-Gordon's (1995) "categorical frequency instruments" or Acheson and Gall's (1997) "selective verbatim" technique. Providing these data, without offering advice or suggesting specific courses of action, the "modern" supervi-

sor affords teachers the opportunity to reflect and view their classroom through "another set of eyes" (see case study at the end of this chapter).

The Interpretive-Practical Approach

The interpretive-practical approach is reflected in "person-centered" supervision. "Uniform answers to educational problems are viewed as impossible to apply because practical problems are seen to be context bound, situationally determined, and complex." The supervisor is not the overseer or prescriber but a guide, facilitator, or confidante. Relying on enhanced communication and shared understandings, this approach encourages interpersonal and collegial aspects in the supervision process. This model is often called consultative or collaborative supervision. Clinical supervision, embodying neo-progressivism, may, but does not always, characterize this approach (Hopkins & Moore, 1995).

Supervisors with a modernist bent, it should be noted, are also very concerned with the human relations element to supervision. Nearly every text quoted in "The Modern" section includes a chapter explicating the value of developing the human dimension of supervision. Being facilitative and concerned for people are very much modern notions. Yet, a modernist supervisor doesn't find evaluative supervision incompatible with the importance of nurturing the human enterprise. Supervision represents the process of supporting instructional services and thereby meeting the aims, goals, and objectives of the school organization. I am certain all of us who have school-age children want to be assured that teachers are held accountable and that high-quality instruction is a prime goal.

For the modern supervisor, however, the "collegial" element in this interpretive-practical approach may be somewhat problematic, as I will indicate later.

The Critical-Emancipatory Approach

May (1989) believes that this approach encourages reflective action on the part of both teachers and supervisors. Going beyond mere collaboration in the development of instructional goals, this approach challenges teachers to "examine the moral, ethical, and political dimensions embedded in everyday thinking and practice." Intending to raise teachers' consciousness and critical awareness of the sociopolitical contexts in which they work, emancipatory supervisors challenge teachers to take risks and construct knowledge for themselves (see, e.g., Bowers & Flinders, 1991; Waite, 1995).

These three models should not be viewed as evolutionary in the sense that one replaces the other as individuals make advancements in the supervision field. Rather, all three approaches, the technical, practical, and political, have viability and applicability for instructional improvement. As May (1989) argues, "each framework suggests a legitimate human interest." Myopic, biased, and inclined towards "pedagogically correct" practices (Lasley, 1993), educational supervision as a field needs to broaden its conception of supervision by including the modern.

IT'S NOT PEDAGOGICALLY CORRECT TO SAY "SUPERVISION"

Allow me to briefly argue why I think the postmodern conception is misguided when it eschews directive supervision and advocates only collegial relationships.

Sergiovanni (1992) hopes that a day will come when "supervision will no longer be needed." He and others like him who eschew the term "supervision" in favor of "instructional leadership" are not, I believe, disingenuous, but the penchant for substitute language, in general, is symptomatic of a more widespread trend to speak in euphemisms—sometimes referred to as jargon or educationese. Jerry Pulley (1994), a teacher educator at the University of Texas–Pan American, in a wonderful little article entitled "Doublespeak and Euphemisms in Education," maintains that our propensity for political correctness or what Lasley (1993) calls "pedagogical correctness" in this context, has beclouded our perspective so much so that our language has become confused and self-contradictory at best and "grossly deceptive" and evasive at worst.

To disparage modern conceptions of supervision because they rely on positivist social science approaches that attempt to accumulate practically verifiable information about the teaching-learning process offers little solace and doesn't provide much direction for practitioners in the field. Let's call "supervision" what it is and deal with it. Changing terminologies may be in Pulley's (1994) words "euphemistically correct," but it doesn't deal substantively with the underlying issues that beg for consideration and resolution (Hiser, 1994). As Pohly (1993) argues "some people suggest abandoning the term and substituting something more palatable, but that is a false solution because it fails to deal with the condition that produces the resistance" (p. 2).

Pedagogical correctness, as conceived by many postmodernists, "is characterized by a set of 'right' and often avant-garde beliefs about how, the curriculum [supervision], and schools should be structured" (Lasley, 1993, p. 77). The consequences of pedagogical correctness are both obvious and onerous. Cherishing certain practices in favor of others potentially limits practice because certain ways of doing supervision, for instance, are not considered relevant nor efficacious. Educators, according to Lasley (1993), "begin to think in terms of absolutes (a right or wrong way in all instances) rather than the efficacy of practice vis-à-vis a context" (p. 79). When supervisors or those concerned with supervision avoid particular methods because they may not be pedagogically correct, or fail to consider exceptions to practices that are mandated as pedagogically correct, instructional improvement is severely compromised.

Reluctance to offer directive methods of supervision is not only evident but illustrative of this penchant for "correctness." In preservice settings, for instance, there is much need for directive measures for many student teachers because of their lack of experience and low levels of confidence about teaching.

In a survey I conducted of forty student teachers in both urban and suburban settings in New Jersey, they often (65%) complained that their cooperating teacher and/or university supervisor were too nondirective and did not offer substantive comments after observing lessons. One student gave a typical response: "My professor is very nice and often praises me. Yet, sometimes I wish he'd offer more constructive criticisms. I can't be doing everything right!" (Glanz, 1996).

Studies done with preservice teachers support my observations and findings that student teachers prefer directive approaches over nondirective methods of supervision (Copeland, 1980; Copeland & Atkinson, 1978). Students in these studies reported that they had difficulty resolving instructional problems under nondirective approaches. Students preferred when cooperating teachers and university supervisors suggested concrete solutions and specific recommendations. Desrochers (1982) reported that student teachers considered supervisors more credible when they used a directive supervisory style. Although student teachers may prefer directive supervision, surveys of existing supervisory practices indicate that most supervisors use "collaborative and nondirective approaches" and "provide feedback that stimulates teachers' thinking rather than controls teachers' actions" (Glickman, 1990, p. 561).

Cooperating teachers ($N = 26$) and university supervisors ($N = 30$) in my study were asked whether they thought student teachers preferred directive or nondirective methods of supervision. University supervisors responded that they employed nondirective measures because, as one supervisor stated, "student teachers are so fragile and nervous that they need confidence-building and support." "I see myself as a facilitator, not an ogre," commented one university supervisor. Although cooperating teachers were more likely to employ directive measures, many were reluctant to offer other than cursory suggestions for improvement. When queried as to why more directive measures were not employed, cooperating teachers pointed out some of the following reasons: lack of time, wanting to remain collegial, lack of effectiveness, and too punitive. Admittedly, when asked whether they felt any pressure to be more nondirective than directive, few, if any, said they did. "I give the student what I think he or she needs," stated one cooperating teacher. Yet, I suspect that prevailing attitudes and theories do affect, sometimes unconsciously, the practice of supervision in schools.

Supervision for experienced teachers has been characterized as a "meaningless ritual" (Blumberg & Jonas, 1987). When supervisors or those concerned with supervision avoid engaging teachers in collaborative and meaningful discussions about instructional improvement and amid an impoverished school climate that is unresponsive to attempts at instructional improvement, then it is not surprising that supervision as such becomes perfunctory and unproductive. It is not that teachers do not see the need for reflection and improvement; to the contrary, most teachers welcome assistance and recommendations for improvement when offered intelligently and forthrightly.

Contrary to the widely held belief that inservice teachers do not want directive supervision, I believe that many of them welcome supervision that is constructive, direct, and intelligent. Teachers want one-to-one help. Teachers want feedback from, for example, an assistant principal who observes a lesson and conducts a post conference during which insights and suggestions for improvement are offered (Glanz, 1994). Under this scenario, both supervisor and supervisee can be co-inquirers. Often recommendations for improvement are not dictated but rather emerge amid a reflective, inductive dialogue between teacher and supervisor. The supervisor facilitates and guides the teacher to understand the complexities of classroom interaction. Although supervision can sometimes be threatening, particularly for nontenured faculty, it offers an opportunity to obtain valuable information about teaching and learning.

Pajak and Glickman (1984) conducted a study in which groups of inservice teachers were shown videotapes of simulated supervisor feedback in post-observation sessions. Teachers did not particularly favor supervisors who merely described their classroom observations without making any concrete suggestions. Most, if not all the teachers involved in the study preferred supervisors who after describing what they saw in the classroom made specific recommendations for improvement. As Glickman (1990) in summarizing this study states: "It can be surmised from these studies that teachers generally preferred descriptive feedback about their teaching, followed by discussion of interpretations and future goals, culminating in collaborative suggestions and decisions about future instructional actions" (p. 554).

Teachers want supervision of this sort. They want supervision that is well-informed, practical, and helpful, regardless of who offers it or what model is utilized (see, e.g., Blumberg & Jonas, 1987; Brandt, 1985; Whistler, 1984). Some of those who advocate a dissolution of supervision aren't cognizant or accepting of this premise. Relying on "pedagogically correct" approaches not only potentially limits viable options for improving instruction, but does little if anything to explain what supervisory practices may in fact contribute to our efforts in renewing schools. Whether called cognitive coaching, instructional leadership, facilitative practice, critical inquiry, or supervision, it's about working face to face with classroom teachers to refine teaching practice (Nolan, 1995).

The penchant for pedagogical correctness is quite obvious in regard to how educators view and discourse about supervision. According to current belief systems, supervision based on hierarchical roles is considered anathema. A perusal of various definitions, for example, in prominent textbooks on supervision (e.g., Krey & Burke, 1989; see also Holland, 1994), indicates an emphasis on "democratic and professional" processes of supervision and an avoidance of anything remotely referring to directive methods. Current thinking and action (i.e., discourse) in the field does not support bureaucratic authority, personal authority, professional-moral or technical-rational authority as being equally legitimate conceptions of supervision. Rather, supervision has been reconceptualized and redefined more narrowly, in the postmodernist sense (e.g., Sergiovanni & Starratt, 1993). Inclusivity and an acceptance of diverse ideas about theory and practice of supervision do not appear to dominate discourse on supervision.[1]

Collegial Relations: A Cautionary Note

Staunch advocates of teachers and principals, for example, as collaborative inquirers claim that traditional supervisory practice "values principal knowledge and essentially marginalizes teacher knowledge" (Reitzug, 1997, p. 342). Moreover, traditional supervision, according to this paradigm, "focuses instructional relationships in the school on a hierarchical principal-teacher dyad, thus isolating teachers from each other and severely restricting opportunities for educative discourse" (Reitzug, 1997, p. 343). Collegiality, in contrast, emphasizes autonomy, independence, equality of authority, sameness of rank, and self-governance (see e.g., Blase & Blase, 1998; Reitzug, 1997; Poole, 1994).

Collegiality, however, is "simply an inappropriate, even dangerous, paradigm for schools in modern democratic society" (Harris, 1997, p. 144). Ben Harris, in an essay entitled "Is a Collegial Relationship Possible between Supervisors and Teachers? No," affirms that:

Collegiality as a way of conceptualizing supervision in relation to the individual teacher is full of serious problems in common daily operations as well as problems of educational improvement and reform. If a superordinate goal shared by teachers, supervisors, students, parents, and the larger society can be clearly identified, it surely must be that of improving learning opportunities for all students. At the heart of any such goal-related activity is supervision of instruction. But this involves systematic efforts to improve curriculum, materials, teaching, support services, assessments, and leadership for instruction.

Collegial relationships combined with the teacher-centered realities of school life offer little promise of ensuring either minimum standards of educational quality or the reforms and restructuring urgently needed in a rapidly changing society. (p. 146)

Harris goes on to argue that supervisory leadership requires that minimum standards of quality be maintained by providing new teachers intensive mentoring and training beyond what is offered in preservice programs. "Ensuring that all children have access to teaching that promotes significant learning . . . is not a collegial responsibility," argues Harris. "Each teacher will hopefully do his or her best," continues Harris. Supervisors must be responsible "to ensure that every teachers' best efforts are good enough and to initiate supervisory interventions that are needed, securing the students' right to meaningful learning."

"When more dramatic improvements in teaching and learning are at stake, collegial relationships are even less practical" says Harris. Given the fact that teachers are busy and often overworked as they try to manage a classroom comprised of 30 or more students, and given the supervisor's very different, yet demanding routines, collegial relationships just don't make sense. Harris explains:

Supervisors are onlookers as experienced teachers, and they bring to the school and its teachers one or more unique perspectives and special professional skills. These supervisory perspectives derive from observing and analyzing many teachers at work, from knowing the broad scope and sequence of the curriculum, from responding to pressures from both within and outside the school, from seeing students' achievements as they progress through the system and across subject areas. Rarely can a classroom teacher have the same perspective on teaching and learning as that of a professional instructional supervisor. They work in different worlds in some ways. (pp. 147–148)

Admittedly, supervisors cannot be knowledgeable and expert in every specialty, so when teachers do possess unique skills their input and expertise should be acknowledged and utilized. "However, the responsibility for providing technical leadership for improving whole schools . . . must be heavily invested in a team of supervisory personnel. Such leadership, like good teaching, is very demanding and requires full-time professional attention" (p. 148).

Supervisors are specialists in curriculum, staff development, teaching methods, and instructional evaluation. These specialists must assume instructional leadership in order to ensure instructional quality. As Harris concludes, "to abdicate leadership for instructional change in exchange for collegiality could be an educational tragedy" (p. 150).

SUMMARY

I have indicated that "premodern" conceptions of supervision were bureaucratic and inspectional. Modern conceptions, by comparison, emphasized democratic supervisory practices relying on cooperative and scientific methods to improve instruction. I argued that the postmodern view, which emphasizes "pedagogically correct" practices and collegial relationships, is misguided.

Modern conceptions of supervision have a far greater positive impact on practice and implications for the training of future administrators than do postmodern views. Modern views of supervision, relying, in part, on a technical-rational view of the teaching-learning process, offers practitioners practical guidelines for instructional improvement (see case study at the end of the chapter). In contrast, some postmodernists who eschew directive supervision, in effect, limit alternative conceptions of supervision and are unappreciative of the needs among many prospective administrators who want concrete proposals and strategies. Such views are shortsighted because they fail to consider the exceptions to practices that are labeled "postmodernist." Admittedly, modernist conceptions with their reliance on the empirical-analytical sciences, emphasizing the technical aspects of the supervision process have marked limitations. Yet, postmodernist constructions can be equally limiting when they fail to consider a wide array of strategies, methodologies, and approaches aimed at improving instruction and promoting educational leadership as well as change.

A postmodern view, it seems to me, although embracing a more progressive paradigm for practice than evaluative supervision, should not dispel more traditional approaches (e.g., directive supervision) when warranted. Varied models of supervision, incorporating both postmodern and modern views, should always be welcomed and encouraged. Both administrators-in-training and practitioners will, then, be armed with varied modalities to enhance instructional improvement.

In this last section, I present a metaphor for supervision that, I believe, can help us recast and refocus our thinking about educational supervision that embraces both the modern and postmodern views (Glanz, 1997).

TOFU AS A METAPHOR FOR SUPERVISION

Supervision should be conceived as that process which utilizes a wide array of strategies, methodologies, and approaches aimed at improving instruction and promoting educational leadership as well as change. Those concerned with supervision may then work on curriculum development, staff development, schoolwide reform strategies, action research projects, and mentoring while, at the same time, they may utilize directive, collaborative, or empowering methods. Supervision is supervision regardless of the context in which it is practiced (e.g., preservice and/or inservice settings). Supervision as such does not become meaningless or lack purpose. Rather, supervision is pliable enough to meet a wide range of instructional needs. Remaining responsive to diverse demands would be the field's greatest asset. "Supervision as tofu" in this context becomes an apt metaphor.

"Tofu," translated into English as "bean curd," or "soybean curd," is an important product of the soybean used in China for more than 2000 years. Rich in proteins, vitamins, and minerals, low in calories and saturated fats, and entirely free of cholesterol, tofu appears to be the ideal food. Tofu is also unique because it has no taste. Tofu's remarkable quality is that it assumes the flavor of any other food with which it is placed. Tofu can be marinated, stir-fried, scrambled, baked, broiled, grilled, steamed, or barbecued. As Paino and Messinger (1991), authors of *The Tofu Book*, state: "It can hide in your cannelloni, taco, or stew, and—before your eyes—take on the flavor of those and many other foods" (p. 57). Once only found floating in vats in an Oriental grocery or health food store, tofu now is found in colorful packages on the shelves of many supermarkets.

Tofu's unique quality to remain almost incognito and yet to assume the flavor of its host dish without loss of its nutritional value can be a useful analogy for educational supervision. Supervision is tofu in the sense that it no longer must conform to prescribed or expected practices. Supervision is tofu in the sense that it is flexible enough to represent a wide array of instructional and reform strategies. Supervision is tofu in the sense that, although unseen at times, it remains a supporting service for teachers. As such, supervision as tofu retains its integrity yet remains responsive to diverse demands. Supervision as a function survives and flourishes because it is able to offer instructional assistance amid a rapidly changing and complex school system.

Supervision is also tofu because its knowledge base is broad, inclusive, and liberal. Supervision thus can function in a variety of settings with diverse groups of teachers, each possessing unique and varied needs. With supervision now broadly conceptualized and practiced, it is not limited to particular methodologies. Supervision can achieve conceptual clarity in this context because its practitioners no longer fear the use of "pedagogically incorrect" strategies when appropriate and warranted. "Directive," "differentiated," "transactional," and "transformational" supervision all find suitable justification within this more encompassing view of the field. Like other fields such as counseling (e.g., Williams, 1995) and religion (e.g., Pohly, 1993), supervision so practiced in schools becomes purposeful, relevant, and influential.

Supervision as tofu is diverse and versatile, yet uniform and substantial (like yin and yang). If diversity represents adaptability and flexibility in a range of settings and needs, then tofu is an apt metaphor to describe the work of supervision in schools. As tofu, unassuming yet nutritious, makes an ideal substitute for high-calorie foods, supervision as tofu also blends into the educational landscape to help provide needed services and assistance to teachers.

Case Study 4: Assessing Gender Influences in the Classroom

Ms. Georgina Urbay, a vice-principal in a suburban elementary school on the West Coast, just completed her master's degree at a local university. As a culminating project, she investigated gender influences on the quality of attention students receive in their class. Ms. Urbay was interested in learning whether gender biases existed in the classes she supervised. On previous occasions when she observed some of the newer teachers, her observations had focused either on the quantity of thought-provoking questions asked during a lesson or on identifying the nature of off-task behavior. She read about qualitative observation tools like the Wide Lens strategy. With this procedure, the observer makes brief notes of events as they occur in the classroom. These notes are usually made objectively and nonevaluatively. Rather than recording that "Susan was day-dreaming," Ms. Urbay might write "Susan was gazing out the rear window of the classroom." Ms. Urbay reserves the right to make interpretive observations as well, but includes her interpretive comments in brackets (see below).

Ms. Urbay speaks with Mr. Eric Jones, a second-year teacher, about her research into gender-related issues in the classroom and suggests that she is curious how gender might influence his teaching behavior. Mr. Jones invites Ms. Urbay into his classroom. She decides that rather than sitting in the back of the room as a detached observer, she would get a "better feel" for the classroom environment by participating to any extent possible in the lesson, at the same time as she was recording observations.

Ms. Urbay took the following notes during one segment of the lesson:

"5th grade class; 13 boys and 12 girls; self-contained classroom; Eric Jones, teacher; 9:45 A.M.; I enter as Mr. Jones tells class to take out their readers; As Mr. Jones gives instructions for silent reading, three students (2 male and 1 female) are out of their seats hanging their clothing in the rear classroom closet; The girl is talking; Mr. Jones tells her to be quiet and sit down; During silent reading students are reading quietly; After about 3 minutes a monitor enters classroom and teacher is recording daily attendance; Noise level in class rises; Monitor leaves room; Teacher walks back and forth as students get quiet; At 9:49 A.M., Mr. Jones asks a boy to tell the class what the story was about; Student responds; Class attentive; Mr. Jones asks a girl, 'Why do you think Billy in the story was so upset?'; Student responds; Teacher calls on a boy who also responds, albeit differently; Mr. Jones probes and asks boy to explain; Mr. Jones asks another thought-provoking question to a girl; Girl responds; Teacher asks another question to a boy and probes; . . . [10 minutes elapse and I note that it appears that Mr. Jones calls on boys and girls evenly, but that he consistently probes male responses, but rarely probes a female response, . . . curious, ask Mr. Jones about this!]; Time elapses; Teacher divides class into study groups; I join one of the groups with 2 boys and 1 girl; Teacher circulates; Students answer reading questions and discuss story; I ask them if they liked the story and to explain why or why not; Teacher requests attention from class; Mr. Jones continues asking many thought-provoking questions and follows the same pattern of probing more for boys than for girls; Interestingly, when the boy sitting to my right in the group was asked a question, he was probed, but the girl to my left was not; I could not discern any concern among the students."

FOLLOW-UP QUESTIONS

1. Describe the supervisory method utilized by Ms. Urbay.
2. What conclusions can you draw about Mr. Jones's teaching style and Ms. Urbay's supervision style?
3. Why would you consider this "modernist" approach to supervision useful or not useful?
4. How might a supervisor who advocates the interpretive-practical approach or the critical-emancipatory approach gain entry into Jones' room?
5. Since the author of this chapter also considered postmodern approaches viable, how could Ms. Urbay incorporate a "postmodern" approach to supervision?

NOTE

1. Recently, I was reviewing a manuscript that is likely to be published in one of the more widely read journals in the field in which the author(s) concluded, "Our student teachers need to know that our role is not to be judges and critics, or even models of expert teaching, but rather co-participants in the construction of narratives, the articulation of their commitments, and the shaping of their practices." I'm troubled by the apparent avoidance of anything remotely connoting directive methods of supervision because it potentially limits options. In disagreeing with the quoted author,

I believe that although there are times when the student teacher and supervisor can be "co-participants," student teachers, for the most part, need and want us to be constructive critics of their work. Also, see Stanulis Nevins (1994).

REFERENCES

Acheson, K. A., & Gall, M. D. (1997). *Techniques in the clinical supervision of teachers*. New York: Longman.

Alfonso, R. J., Firth, G. R., & Neville, R. F. (1975). *Instructional supervision: A behavior system*. Boston: Allyn and Bacon.

Anonymous. (1929). The snoopervisor, the whoopervisor, and the supervisor. *Playground and Recreation, 23*, 558.

Ayer, F. C., & Barr, A. C. (1928). *The organization of supervision: An analysis of the organization and administration of supervision in city school systems*. New York: D. Appleton and Company.

Balliet, T. M. (1894). Discussion of Anderson's paper. *NEA Proceedings*, 437–438.

Barr, A. S., & Burton, W. H. (1926). *The supervision of instruction: A general volume*. New York: D. Appleton-Century Company.

Bartky, J. A. (1953). *Supervision as human relations*. Boston: D. C. Heath.

Blase, J., & Blase, B. (1998). *Handbook of instructional leadership*. Thousand Oaks, CA: Corwin Press.

Blase, J., & Kirby, P. C. (1992). *Bringing out the best in teachers: What effective principals do*. Newbury Park, CA: Corwin Press.

Blumberg, A., & Amidon, E. (1965). Teacher perceptions of supervisor-teacher interaction. *Administrator's Notebook, 14*, 1–8.

Blumberg, A., & Jonas, R. S. (1987). The teacher's control over supervision. *Educational Leadership, 44*(8), 58–62.

Bobbitt, F. (1913). Some general principles of management applied to the problems of city-school systems. *Twelfth Yearbook of the National Society for the Study of Education, Part I, The supervision of city schools* (pp. 7–96). Chicago: The University of Chicago Press.

Bolin, F., & Panaritis, P. (1992). Searching for a common purpose: A perspective on the history of supervision. In C. D. Glickman (Ed.), *Supervision in transition* (pp. 30–43). Alexandria, VA: Association for Supervision and Curriculum Development.

Bowers, C. A., & Flinders, D. J. (1991). *Culturally responsive teaching and supervision*. New York: Teachers College Press.

Brandt, R. (1985). On teaching and supervising: A conversation with Madeline Hunter. *Educational Leadership, 42*, 61–66.

Burton, W. H. (1922). *Supervision and the improvement of teaching*. New York: D. Appleton.

Burton, W. H. (1927). *Supervision and the improvement of teaching*. New York: D. Appleton.

Burton, W. H., & Brueckner, L. J. (1955). *Supervision: A social process*. New York: Appleton-Century-Crofts.

The Changing Curriculum. (1937). Joint Committee on Curriculum. New York: D. Appleton-Century Company.

Cogan, M. L. (1973). *Clinical supervision*. Boston: Houghton Mifflin.

Copeland, W. D. (1980). Affective dispositions of teachers in training toward examples of supervisory behavior. *Journal of Educational Research, 74,* 37–42.

Copeland, W. D., & Atkinson, D. R. (1978). Student teachers' perceptions of directive and nondirective supervisory behavior. *Journal of Educational Research, 71,* 123–127.

Costa, A., & Garmston, R. (1994). *Cognitive coaching: Approaching renaissance schools.* Norwood, MA: Christopher-Gordon Publishers.

Crosley, M. (1957). *Supervision as co-operative action.* New York: Appleton-Century-Crofts.

Department of Superintendence (1930). *The superintendent surveys supervision.* Washington, DC: National Education Association.

Desrochers, C. G. (1982). *Relationships between supervisory directors and justification in the teacher-supervisor conference and teachers' perceptions of supervisor credibility.* Unpublished doctoral dissertation, University of California.

Dewey, J. (1929). *The sources of a science of education.* New York: Liveright.

Dunn, F. W. (1923). What is instructional supervision? *NEA Proceedings,* 763–768.

Editorial. (1921). What's in a name? *Journal of Educational Method, 1,* 85.

Eisner, E. W. (1985). *The educational imagination: On the design and evaluation of educational programs.* New York: Macmillan.

Elsbree, W. S. (1939). *American teacher: Evolution of a profession in a democracy.* New York: American Book Company.

Featherstone, W. B. (1942). Taking the super out of supervision. *Teachers College Record, 44,* 114–124.

Feyereisen, K. V., Fiorino, A. J., & Nowak, A. T. (1970). *Supervision and curriculum renewal.* New York: Appleton-Century-Crofts.

Fitzpatrick, F. A. (1893). How to improve the work of inefficient teachers. *NEA Proceedings,* 74–78.

Garman, N. B. (1986). Reflection, the heart of clinical supervision: A modern rationale for practice. *Journal of Curriculum and Supervision, 2*(1), 1–24.

Gilland, T. M. (1935). *The origin and development of the power and duties of the city school superintendent.* Chicago: University of Chicago Press.

Glanz, J. (1991). *Bureaucracy and professionalism: The evolution of public school supervision.* Rutherford, NJ: Fairleigh Dickinson University Press.

Glanz, J. (1994). Dilemmas of assistant principals in their supervisory role: Reflections of an assistant principal. *Journal of School Leadership, 4*(5), 577–593.

Glanz, J. (1996, April). *Pedagogical correctness in teacher education: Discourse about the role of supervision.* Paper presented at the annual meeting of the American Educational Research Association (AERA), New York City.

Glanz, J. (1997). The tao of supervision: Taoist insights into the theory and practice of educational supervision. *Journal of Curriculum and Supervision, 12,* 193–211.

Glanz, J. (1998). Histories, antecedents, and legacies: Constructing a history of school supervision. In G. R. Firth & E. Pajak (Eds.), *Handbook of Research on School Supervision* (pp. 39–79). New York: Macmillan.

Glatthorn, A. A. (1984). *Differentiated supervision.* Alexandria, VA: Association for Supervision and Curriculum Development.

Glickman, C. D. (1985). *Supervision of instruction: A developmental approach.* Boston: Allyn and Bacon.

Glickman, C. D. (1990). Supervision. In W. R. Houston (Ed.), *Handbook of research on teacher education* (pp. 549–566). New York: Macmillan.

Glickman, C. D. (1992). Introduction: Postmodernism and supervision. In C. D. Glickman (Ed.), *Supervision in transition* (pp. 30–43). Alexandria, VA: Association for Supervision and Curriculum Development.

Glickman, C. D., Gordon, S. P., & Ross-Gordon, J. M. (1995). *Supervision of instruction: A developmental approach.* Boston: Allyn and Bacon.

Goldhammer, R. (1969). *Clinical supervision: Special methods for the supervision of teachers.* New York: Holt, Rinehart, and Winston.

Goldhammer, R., Anderson, R. H., & Krajewski, R. J. (1980). *Clinical supervision* (2nd ed.). New York: Holt, Rinehart and Winston.

Gordon, S. P. (1992). Paradigms, transitions, and the new supervision. *Journal of Curriculum and Supervision, 8,* 62–76.

Gordon, S. P. (1997). Has the field of supervision evolved to a point that it should be called something else? Yes. In J. Glanz & R. F. Neville (Eds.), *Educational supervision: Perspectives, issues, and controversies* (pp. 114–123). Norwood, MA: Christopher-Gordon Publishers.

Greenwood, J. M. (1888). Efficient school supervision. *NEA Proceedings,* 519–521.

Greenwood, J. M. (1891). Discussion of Gove's paper. *NEA Proceedings,* 227.

Griffiths, D. E. (1966). *The school superintendent.* New York: Center for Applied Research in Education.

Grumet, M. (1979). Supervision and situation: A methodology of self-report for teacher education. *Journal of Curriculum Theorizing, 1,* 191–257.

Gwynn, J. M. (1961). *Theory and practice of supervision.* New York: Dodd, Mead and Company.

Harris, B. M. (1975). *Supervisory behavior in education.* Englewood Cliffs, NJ: Prentice-Hall.

Harris, B. M. (1997). Is a collegial relationship possible between supervisors and teachers? No. In J. Glanz & R. F. Neville (Eds.), *Educational supervision: Perspectives, issues, and controversies* (pp. 114–123). Norwood, MA: Christopher-Gordon Publishers.

Hicks, H. J. (1960). *Educational supervision in principle and practice.* New York: Ronald Press.

Hill, S. (1918). Defects of supervision and constructive suggestions thereon. *NEA Proceedings,* 347–350.

Hiser, D. (1994, May). Renaming versus change: Switching the label does nothing to rid us of prejudices we should shed. *Education Week, 13,* 33.

Holland, P. E. (1994). *What do we talk of when we talk of supervision?* Paper presented at the annual meeting of the Council of Professors of Instructional Supervision (COPIS).

Hopkins, W. S., & Moore, K. D. (1995). Clinical supervision: A neo-progressive approach. *Teacher Educator, 30,* 31–43.

Hosic, J. F. (1920). The democratization of supervision. *School and Society, 11,* 331–336.

Krey, R. D., & Burke, P. J. (1989). *A design for instructional supervision.* Springfield, IL: Charles C. Thomas.

Lasley, T. J. (1993). Rx for pedagogical correctness: Professional correctness. *The Clearing House, 67,* 77–79.

Lewis, A. J., & Miel, A. (1972). *Supervision for improved instruction: New challenges, new responses.* Belmont, CA: Wadsworth Publishing Company.

Lucio, W. H., & McNeil, J. D. (1962). *Supervision: A synthesis of thought and action.* New York: McGraw-Hill.

Lucio, W. H., & McNeil, J. D. (1969). *Supervision: A synthesis of thought and action* (2nd ed.). New York: McGraw-Hill.

May, W. T. (1989) Supervision and curriculum. In *Encyclopedia of education,* 728–730.

Mosher, R. L., & Purpel, D. E. (1972). *Supervision: The reluctant profession.* Boston: Houghton Mifflin.

National Conference of Supervisors and Directors of Instruction. (1930). *Current problems of supervisors, Third Yearbook.* New York: Teachers College, Columbia University.

Neagley, R. L., & Evans, N. D. (1964). *Handbook for effective supervision.* Englewood Cliffs, NJ: Prentice-Hall.

Neagley, R. L., & Evans, N. D. (1970). *Handbook for effective supervision of instruction.* Englewood Cliffs, NJ: Prentice-Hall.

Nevins Stanulis, R. (1994). Fading to a whisper: One mentor's story of sharing her wisdom without telling answers. *Journal of Teacher Education, 45,* 31–38.

Newlon, J. H. (1923). Attitude of the teacher toward supervision. *NEA Proceedings,* 546–549.

Nolan, J. F. (1995, April). Time for a name change? A response. *Instructional Supervision AERA/SIG Newsletter, 15,* 4.

Nutt, H. W. (1928). *Current problems in the supervision of instruction.* Richmond, VA: Johnson Publishing Company.

Oberholtzer, E. E. (1922). The next step in school supervision. *NEA Proceedings, 1441–1445.*

Oliva, P. F. (1976). *Supervision for today's schools.* New York: Thomas Y. Crowell.

Paino, J., & Messinger, L. (1991). *The tofu book: The new American cuisine.* New York: Avery Publishing.

Pajak, E. F. (1993a). *Approaches to clinical supervision: Alternatives for improving instruction.* Norwood, MA: Christopher Gordon Publishers.

Pajak, E. F. (1993b). Change and continuity in supervision and leadership. In G. Cawelti (Ed.), *Challenges and achievements of American education* (pp. 158–186). Alexandria, VA: Association for Supervision and Curriculum Development.

Pajak, E. F., & Glickman, C. D. (1984). *Teachers' discrimination between information and control in response to videotaped simulated supervisory conferences.* Paper presented at the annual meeting of the American Educational Research Association, New Orleans.

Payne, W. H. (1875). *Chapters on school supervision: A practical treatise on superintendency: Grading; arranging courses of study; the preparation and use of blanks, records and reports; examination for promotion, etc.* New York: Van Antwerp Bragg and Company.

Pohly, K. (1993). *Transforming the rough places: The ministry of supervision.* Dayton, OH: Whaleprints.

Poole, W. (1994). Removing the "super" from supervision. *Journal of Curriculum and Supervision, 9,* 284–309.

Pulley, J. L. (1994). Doublespeak and euphemisms in education. *The Clearing House, 67,* 271–273.

Reitzug, U. C. (1997). Images of principal instructional leadership: From supervision to collaborative inquiry. *Journal of Curriculum and Supervision, 12,* 324–343.

Reller, T. L. (1935). *The development of the city superintendency of schools in the United States.* Philadelphia: Author.

Rousmaniere, K. (1992). *City teachers: Teaching in New York City schools in the 1920s.* Unpublished doctoral dissertation, Columbia University.

Sergiovanni, T. J. (1992). Moral authority and the regeneration of supervision. In C. D. Glickman (Ed.), Supervision in transition (pp. 30–43). Alexandria, VA: Association for Supervision and Curriculum Development.

Sergiovanni, T. J., & Starratt, R. J. (1983). *Supervision: Human perspectives.* New York: McGraw-Hill.

Sergiovanni, T. J., & Starratt, R. J. (1993). *Supervision: A redefinition.* New York: McGraw-Hill.

Smyth, J. (1991). *Teachers as collaborative learners: Challenging dominant forms of supervision.* Philadelphia: Open University Press.

Spears, H. (1953). *Improving the supervision of instruction.* Englewood Cliffs, NJ: Prentice-Hall.

Stone, C. R. (1929). *Supervision of the elementary school.* Boston: Houghton-Mifflin Publishers.

Tanner, D., & Tanner, L. N. (1987). *Supervision in education: Problems and practices.* New York: Macmillan.

Taylor, F. W. (1910). *The principles of scientific management.* New York: Harper amd Brothers.

Waite, D. (1995). *Rethinking instructional supervision: Notes on its language and culture.* London: Falmer Press.

Waite, D. (1997, March). *Super(postmodern)vision.* Paper presented at the Annual Conference of the American Educational Research Association, Chicago.

Weller, R. H. (1971). *Verbal communication in instructional supervision.* New York: Teachers College Press.

Whistler, N. L. (1984). How teachers view their supervision. *Catalyst for Change, 14,* 26–29.

Wiles, J., & Bondi, J. (1980). *Supervision: A guide to practice.* Columbus, OH: Charles E. Merrill.

Williams, A. (1995). *Visual and active supervision: Roles, focus, technique.* New York: W. W. Norton & Company.

Supervisory Practices: Building a Constructivist Learning Community for Adults

Sally J. Zepeda

GUIDING QUESTIONS

1. *Can the tenets of the constructivist paradigm add to supervisory practices?*

2. *What lessons can be learned from the job-embedded literature and be transferred to supervision?*

3. *If the lessons learned from job-embedded staff development can be transferred to the field of supervision, what specific areas would need systematic research to ground its effectiveness?*

4. *How can practicing supervisors become constructivist leaders?*

5. *Can constructivist supervisory practices be developed in a school that is not a learning community? Implemented?*

6. *What mindset does an instructional leader need to develop in order to employ more growth-oriented types of supervision?*

The early models of instructional supervision (e.g., Cogan, 1973; Goldhammer, 1969) relied on the clinical processes of instructional planning through a pre-observation conference, an extended classroom observation, and a post-observation conference where the teacher and supervisor discussed the events of the classroom observation and developed follow-up plans. Simplistic as this was, and still is, the format of the clinical supervisory model employed in many schools has supplanted supervision with evaluation.

Schools, however, have changed dramatically since the first clinical models were developed. Schools are more complex; knowledge about teaching and learning for both students and adults has been systematically studied. Teacher preparation programs have changed, and research about staff development for inservice teachers has grounded new theories and practices. The teaching force has changed with regard to the proliferation of alternatively certified teachers (Chesley, Wood, & Zepeda, 1997), the greying of the profession, and early-retirement inducements. The situation is all the more compounded by high attrition rates of new teachers.

These complexities become even more exacerbated by hollow-sounding, sweeping, and indefinable reform initiatives such as restructuring, site-based management, and teacher empowerment. These reform strategies, offered under the broad umbrella of sweeping change, often signal thoughts of other initiatives such as school networks, partnerships, and democratic schools. The lexicon of schools becomes even more blurred by rhetoric about redefining roles for teachers and principals. The breakdown in implementing new school-based initiatives occurs when supervisory practices do not move forward as well. What supervisory practices are needed to promote professional growth? What type of leadership mindset is needed to enact more meaningful supervisory practices? These are some of the perennial questions that plague the field of supervision.

Viewed from a modernist perspective, supervision must be diverse enough to meet the needs of twenty-first century schools. As the needs of teachers change, supervisory practices designed to meet those needs must also change. Supervisors who are satisfied to maintain current knowledge at the expense of developing innovative strategies have already short-circuited the schools' potential to become a community of learners.

In this chapter, the author will explore supervisory practices that reflect modernist thinking about constructivism, adult learning theory, job-embedded learning, and the principles of learning communities. In essence, building a constructivist learning community is possible by judiciously applying modernist supervisory practices.

DEVELOPING MORE RESPONSIVE LEADERSHIP BY EXPLORING CONSTRUCTIVIST EPISTEMOLOGY

Providing for the professional betterment of teachers is a formidable task that requires sustained attention to their developmental needs, the needs of the organization, and the needs of the primary constituents—students. A tall order to be sure; however, not an impossibility if the site-level leadership is committed to discovering *which* practices provide *what* results. A beginning point is understanding the principles of constructivism and their relationship to supervisory practices.

In *The Constructivist Leader*, Lambert (1995) and her associates explore the nature of leadership from the perspective of the principal moving away from having "*to do things to or for others*" (p. 30, emphasis added by this author). Lambert asserts that constructivist leaders know that "adults in a

community can work together to construct meaning and knowledge" (p. 32). Constructivist theory places importance on the development of individual meanings, and as such, supervisory practices need to provide a mechanism for teachers to construct their own meanings about their classroom practices. Zepeda and Ponticell (1998) found that meanings derived from traditional supervisory practices were too often hollow: "It appeared to the teachers that supervisors invested little in the process; if it was meaningless to them, it was meaningless to the teachers" (p. 85). Walker and Lambert (1995) summarize the prevalent view of the uselessness of administratively driven supervision:

Teacher supervision may follow one of several patterns. Teachers may be closely supervised, with the principal setting job targets and fulfilling a quality control function; or supervision may be perfunctory, based on the assumption that everyone understands the standards and expectations and that teachers will perform their role as expected. In either instance, the principal is not seen as a facilitator of teacher growth, nor does the purpose of teacher supervision seem to be the professional development of the teaching staff. (pp. 5–10)

AN OVERVIEW OF CONSTRUCTIVIST THOUGHT

Historical foundation for the constructivist theory of learning is found in John Dewey's *Education and Experience*. Dewey (1938) advocated a paradigm shift from "learning from texts and teachers, [to] learning through experience" (pp. 19–20). Dewey also indicated that "there is no point in the philosophy of progressive education which is sounder than its emphasis upon the importance of the participation of the learner in the formation of purposes which direct his activities in the learning process" (p. 67).

Learning occurs when beliefs, theories, and perceptions are challenged through conversation and experience then adapted from new information. This new information or experience allows the learner to reinforce theories of practice and/or to create new practices (e.g., Dewey, 1938; Walker & Lambert, 1995).

To this end, knowledge is constructed by the learner in his/her environment. Socially constructed knowledge is conveyed by meanings made by the learner to others in the environment. Fosnot (1996) indicates that constructivism "is at once a theory of 'knowing' and a theory of 'coming to know' " (p. 167).

Vygotsky's zone of proximal development theory underscores that knowing is mediated and negotiated individually by the learner. The zone of proximal development keeps the learner stretching to construct new knowledge slightly above the level of his/her current knowledge (Curda & DeBacker, 1996). Brooks and Brooks (1993) believe that constructivists "help learners to internalize and reshape, or transform, new information" (p. 15). Because of this internalization and construction of new knowledge, "Deep understanding, not imitative behavior, [becomes] the goal" of learning (Brooks &

Brooks, 1993, p. 16). In a learning community that embraces the constructivist paradigm, interaction is encouraged, cooperation is valued, and learning is interdisciplinary (Brooks & Brooks, 1993).

CONSTRUCTIVISM AND SUPERVISION

Supervisory practices, if they are to help teachers grow, need to be adjusted to fit the complex nature of teaching and learning. Reformers and reform movements have been calling for a more professional view of teaching and learning for the adults who comprise the learning community. For example, the National Commission on Teaching and America's Future brought forth the challenge: America will provide all students with what should be their educational birthright: access to competent, caring, and qualified teachers. The supervision of the teaching force, however, now comes into play; constructivist supervision, if properly applied, can promote ongoing growth. Darling-Hammond (1996) believes that, "If students have an inalienable right to be taught by a qualified teacher, teachers have a right to be supervised by a highly qualified principal" (p. 198).

Constructivist supervisors would provide (1) time to interact with others, (2) time for reflection, and (3) needed resources. These elements are needed so teachers can have multiple opportunities to transfer information and to construct a deeper understanding of their own practices and those of others.

The constructivist playing field would support:

- differentiated forms of supervision (e.g., peer coaching, mentoring, and portfolio development);
- an environment rich with dialogue;
- autonomous relationships so teachers can negotiate their own learning based upon what makes sense to them;
- activities extending reflection; and
- self-analysis of practice.

Supervision would be long-term and continuous throughout the year. Currently, most supervision is conducted as a "one-shot" affair. This type of supervision is separate and discrete, lacking unity of purpose. Supervision should assist in building a cooperative learning environment. The supervisor's role is not the focal point of the learning process for adults. Rather, the supervisor would coordinate efforts to ensure unity.

Constructivist supervisory practices would mirror Honebein's (1996) goals of constructivist learning environments:

- provide experience with the knowledge construction process;
- provide experience in and appreciation for multiple perspectives;
- embed learning in realistic and relevant contexts;

- encourage ownership and voice in the learning process;
- embed learning in social experience;
- encourage the use of multiple modes of representation; and
- encourage self-awareness in the knowledge of construction process. (p. 11)

Brookfield's (1986) discussion of facilitators of adult learning has great promise for supervisors of instruction in the K-12 arena. According to Brookfield (1986) "Facilitators . . . see themselves as resources for learning, rather than as didactic instructors who have all the answers" (p. 63). From such a relationship, the supervisor and teacher will be able to focus on what is important and co-design supervision as a collaborative process. The success of collaboration is dependent upon building trusting and respectful relationships (Zepeda & Ponticell, 1998).

ADULT LEARNING

What can the field of supervision gain by examining the principles of adult learning from a constructivist paradigm? First and foremost, adult learning theory and the constructivist paradigm stress the importance of acknowledging prior experiences, constructing knowledge, and applying knowledge to new situations. Zemke and Zemke (1995) conclude from their studies that:

- adults tend to prefer self-direction as they mature;
- adults' experiences are a rich resource for learning. Adults learn more effectively through experiential techniques such as discussion or problem-solving than they do through more passive techniques such as listening;
- adults are aware of specific learning needs generated by real-life events; and
- adults are competency-based learners, meaning that they want to learn a skill or acquire knowledge that they can apply pragmatically to their immediate circumstances. (p. 32)

Teachers need continuous learning opportunities as they:

have been asked to assume new responsibilities and adopt new practices that are substantially different from traditional notions about what it means to be a teacher. Under these circumstances, teachers need time to be learners themselves—a truth that is rarely factored . . . and is quite likely an important variable in the dismal track record of educational change efforts over the past 30 years. (Adelman, Walking Eagle, & Hargreaves, 1997, p. 2)

Adults need to feel a sense of belonging and safety. Without a quality learning relationship between teachers and supervisors, professional and/or personal growth is not likely to be forthcoming. Open discussion is critical in developing a learning environment. McCall (1997) indicates, "Underlying all others is a basic assumption that adult learning is best achieved in dialogue" (p. 12). Lambert (1995) and her associates report that "Administrators admitted that changes are often unsuccessful because preliminary dialogue is rushed" (p. 35). Wheatley (1992, as cited in Lambert, 1995) believes that "individuals generate information in their interactions with each other, information that becomes a feedback spiral enriching and creating additional information" (p. 32).

Effective supervisors find time to speak with each teacher individually throughout the year. Discussion focuses on the developmental needs and the types of supervisory strategies needed for the individual teacher's professional growth. By formulating learning objectives, both the teacher and the supervisor can make assessments regarding goal attainment. Some objectives might be easily obtained over a relatively short period of time; others might take longer.

Learning activities need to be sequenced so adults can build on prior experiences. Adults need time to practice new skills and get "friendly" feedback from those who can be supportive (e.g., supervisors and peers). Job-embedded activities need to allow the teacher to put new skills to use in a timely fashion.

The adult learner needs to be involved in self-analysis and evaluation: is growth being experienced as a result of a variety of supervisory practices? Assessment leads to modifications of instructional practices and the supervisory strategies being needed to implement these practices. Supervision, along with staff development activities, should have a unified thread that weaves through both organizational and personal learning goals.

LEARNING COMMUNITIES: ESSENTIAL TO THE CONSTRUCTIVIST PARADIGM

School leaders need to begin reconceptualizing the ways adults work with one another so that they can "act wisely and feel deeply, within an environment that challenges the individual to look beyond her/himself and [to] experience the value of interdependence" (O'Reilly & Latimer, 1990, p. 1). To this end, "principals must intimately be involved in the instructional life of their schools. Through that involvement, they can provide the leadership essential to the school's success as a learning center" (Ackerman, Donaldson, & van der Bogert, 1996, pp. 31–32). The role of the principal in a learning community needs to change *from* telling teachers how to teach *to* facilitating the processes by which teachers can discover knowledge about themselves and their practices (Zepeda, 1999).

By examining the school as a learning community, the nature of supervision can be better defined and then operationalized. A community of learning is comprised of members who can:

- share ideas and learn from one another;
- support one another through more collaborative practices (e.g., peer coaching, mentoring, and other processes that promote sustained growth);

- accept divergent points of view and agree to "disagree" with one another in non-judgmental ways; and

- enter into dialogue with one another, critically reflecting on issues that matter most to the school.

These processes resonate with the principles of adult learning—interpersonal sensitivity, collaboration, self-analysis, and autonomy.

Creating a learning community is a difficult venture, because of the complex and fragmented ways in which schools are organized. For example, members of a school's learning community are divided by departments, grade levels, and specialty groups such as special education and gifted and talented. Brookfield (1986) indicates that "When adults teach and learn in one another's company, they find themselves engaging in a challenging, passionate, and creative activity" (p. 1). An inclusive environment fosters individual and group self-analysis and processes that promote shared inquiry. Community members can create knowledge while constantly assessing beliefs, assumptions, values, and experiences.

Forest (1998) indicates, "There are no real shortcuts to building community thoroughly from the ground up and maintaining it vigilantly over time. Basic to this understanding is a realization that community grows from within. It can be fostered from without—indeed it must be to survive—but it cannot be imposed" (p. 291).

Glickman (1993) posits that America's schools are the only institution "designed and funded as the agent of the larger society in protecting the core values of its citizens: democracy" (p. 8). Darling-Hammond (1997) states: "In order to create a cohesive community . . . school people must have the occasion to engage in democratic discourse about the real stuff of teaching and learning" (p. 336). Democratic forms of supervision include open-ended opportunities for teachers to explore their teaching practices with the support of supervisors and colleagues. Democratic discourse in this context would include more meaningful post-observation conferences. Bellon and Bellon (1982) describe lesson reconstruction, a strategy in which the supervisor and the teacher reconstruct classroom events. The supervisor's notes provide only the broad framework; the teacher takes the lead in talking about the lesson.

Teachers who can direct their energies toward professional growth are more likely to be invested in the process of discovering meaningfulness in their work as they envision newly found and constructed knowledge. Effective supervisory practices can only enhance this process. Building relationships with teachers must become center stage; otherwise, learning and community-building will be stifled.

SUPERVISORY LEADERSHIP

Principals who are able to develop learning communities have a leadership style that holds all who comprise the community in equal esteem. Effective principals are secure in their leadership approaches; they can be both leaders and followers: "This more dynamic sharing feature makes leadership a community endeavor" (Crow, Matthews, & McCleary, 1996, p. 31). Foster (1989, cited by Crow and his colleagues, 1996), indicates:

The idea that leadership occurs within a community suggests that ultimately leadership resides in the community itself. . . . Leadership, then, is not a function of position but rather represents a conjunction of ideas where leadership is shared and transferred between leaders and followers, each only a temporary designation. . . . Leaders and followers become interchangeable. (pp. 31–32)

O'Neil's (1998) discussion of the constructivist classroom centers primarily on students. However, learning communities promote growth in *all* its members:

The key tenet of constructivist theory . . . is that people learn by actively constructing knowledge, weighing new information against their previous understanding, thinking about and working through discrepancies (on their own and with others), and coming to a new understanding. (O'Neil, 1998, p. 51)

Teachers have tremendous insights about teaching and learning. The daily process of recognizing insights and acting on the knowledge gained from them is job-embedded learning.

EMBEDDING CONSTRUCTIVISM IN SUPERVISORY PRACTICES

The complex nature of schools mirrors the needs of teachers. For this reason, no one supervision strategy can adequately address all needs exhibited by all teachers. The goal of all supervisory processes is growth. Staff developers have discovered that learning that is job-embedded is extremely effective; it is custom designed for the user (Wood & Killian, 1998). Supervision, like other forms of professional development, needs the same "tailor-made approach" for assisting teachers with their growth.

Pajak (1993) offers several options for embedding supervision into teachers' workdays. These include collegial supervision (peer coaching and cognitive coaching), self-directed supervision, informal supervision, and inquiry-based supervision (action research). These techniques underscore the belief that teachers are professionals who take responsibility for their own learning.

Sergiovanni and Starratt (1997) believe that teachers must be equal partners in the supervisory process:

Successful informal supervision requires that certain expectations be accepted by teachers. Otherwise, it [informal supervisory practices] will likely be viewed as . . . informal surveillance. . . . If teachers are to invite supervisors into their classrooms as equal partners in teaching and learning, teachers must, in turn, be invited into the process of supervision as equal partners. (p. 258)

With more reciprocal approaches coupled with mutual respect, teachers, as well as supervisors, are more likely to embrace formative learning.

Many roles assumed by teachers, who practice informal, job-embedded forms of supervision, have been identified: coach, consultant, guide, and mentor. These roles require the collapse of the traditional hierarchical roles of supervisor (e.g., master and inspector) that signal deficit thinking as the primary intent of supervision.

ATTRIBUTES OF JOB-EMBEDDED LEARNING: SUPERVISORY APPLICATIONS

Wood and Killian (1998) define job-embedded learning as "learning that occurs as teachers and administrators engage in their daily work activities" (p. 52). Among their findings is the conclusion that schools need to:

Restructure supervision and teacher evaluation so that they support teacher learning and the achievement of personal, professional, and school achievement goals . . . both supervision and teacher evaluation should be modified to focus on school and/or personal improvement goals rather than the district and state required observation forms. (p. 54)

Through job-embedded supervision, the work of teachers and principals can become more collaborative and can serve to flatten traditional boundaries that pit administrators against teachers (e.g., Blumberg, 1980). Job-embedded supervision:

- encourages reflection through processes such as peer coaching and auto-supervision;
- increases transfer of newly-learned skills;
- promotes collegiality;
- links the work of teachers to one another—reduces isolation;
- makes supervision more relevant to each teacher;
- facilitates the ongoing refinement of practice; and
- assists in the development of a common lexicon so mutual meanings can emerge.

Reflection is serious thought concerning any issue pertaining to professional practice. Supervisory practices, if they are to have lasting impact, need to promote self-analysis and the construction of knowledge based on listening to one's own voice—through dialogue, discussion with peers, feedback, and reflection. Without reflection and the ability to interact with peers, supervision is ritualistic.

When learning is job-embedded, transfer of new skills into practice is embedded as well. In the traditional clinical supervision model, there exists down time between observation and feedback, which is usually offered in a post-observation conference. This down time can interrupt the transfer of new skills into teaching practice. When supervision is embedded, new skills are implemented *during* the supervisory process, not *after*. Moreover, new skills can become a part of the teacher's practice *as they are being learned*.

Supervision that takes place between equals promotes collegiality. The work of the school is accomplished most efficiently when all members of the learning community work together as a team (Calabrese & Zepeda, 1997). A collegial atmosphere also assists in meeting teachers' need for social interaction and helps to eliminate isolation.

In his landmark study, Lortie (1975) identified isolation as one of the most common problems faced by new teachers. The "cubicle nature" of schools enhances the distant feeling too prevalent among educators. Classrooms and class periods confine teachers. This feeling of isolation has been compared to treading water over one's head without a life preserver (Ganser, 1997). Supervision that is conducted by teachers, for teachers, unites faculty.

Adults seek learning opportunities that are relevant to their current situation (Dalellew & Martinez, 1988). Supervision that is a part of the individual teacher's daily practice meets this need. Often, after an inservice or teacher observation (formative or summative), teachers return to their classrooms and leave at the door what they have learned. Lost is the opportunity for the teacher to contextualize skills within the complexities of the classroom. Teachers need time to conceptualize what a practice or application of a technique will look and sound like.

Supervision is most helpful when feedback is continuous and supportive to the efforts of the teacher. Feedback that comes from a variety sources is more valid than from a single source (e.g., only the administrator assigned to evaluate the teacher). More important is the dialogue and interaction *of the moment* that occurs between professionals. Without this type of open-ended discussion, supervision remains hollow.

Feedback needs to be built on mutual trust and respect, which can be difficult to build between teachers and administrators. "Sustained, substantive, and structured collegial interactions enhance mutuality and support risk taking" (Ponticell, 1995, p. 17). If teachers believe they can achieve a valued outcome that is relevant to their teaching situation, they will sustain the effort and energy required to practice a new instructional technique. If teachers do not believe success is possible, they easily give up what they have learned or blame results on factors other than themselves.

WANTED: SUPERVISORS WITH CAPACITY BUILDING

Supervisory strategies, for the most part, lack the glue that promotes holistic growth for teachers. The supervisor can forward the growth of the school by working with teachers in ways that help them enlarge views and practices beyond individual classrooms. Supervisors who purposefully promote growth-oriented practices assist the school in building capacity as a learning community.

With administrative responsibility steadily increasing, it is understandable how supervisory practices have succumbed to the less important role of legally binding and state mandated evaluation processes. Supervision is often neglected in order to find time in the school year to comply with statutes while swimming upstream daily to keep the school running on an even keel. This neglect is wrought with tensions.

These tensions are worth facing; they must be resolved so the principal can actively involve teachers in the processes of supervision. Supervisory practices that promote professional development need to be at center stage in the learning community, with all members assuming equal responsibility to grow. If principals do not rise to the occasion, supervision will continually fail to meet teacher's needs.

The effective supervisor is able to recognize the developmental ranges of his/her teachers. From a supervisory perspective, needs differ between novice and veteran teachers.

Novices need supervisory experiences that:

- introduce them to the supervisory process employed by the building and/or district;
- engage them in overall goal setting; and
- include supervisory process such as pre-observation conferences, observations, and post-observation conferences that begin early and continue throughout the year.

Veteran teachers need supervisory experiences that:

- acknowledge them as professional career teachers who have experiences to draw upon as they reflect upon their practice;
- allow them to develop their own plans for learning and experimentation;
- signal to them that risk-taking is part of the learning process;
- enable professional sense-making; and
- encourage self-assessment and reflection. (Zepeda & Ponticell, 1995)

As learning becomes even more central to supervision, teachers will have an expanded role in developing, designing, and facilitating their own learning. Ponticell (1995) claims that "teachers are more willing to look at and change classroom practices when they are instrumental in designing and taking charge of their own professional growth activities" (p. 17).

WHERE DO WE GO FROM HERE?

For the most part, current supervisory practices are not necessarily meeting the needs of teachers. What is wrong? Nothing! The real issues surrounding the diminishing impact of supervision deal primarily with:

1. the infrequency of meaningful dialogue between teachers and supervisors;
2. the legal mandates regarding formative supervision versus summative evaluation;
3. insular environments that discourage discourse about professional development among peers situated in a caring, learning community;
4. the lack of understanding about how adults learn, and a closed mind to assessing multiple perspectives on daily practice offered by both supervisors and peers;
5. the lack of leadership by teachers due to the frenetic pace of their workdays and the lack of opportunity; and
6. the lack of job-embedded supervisory practices that can enhance the traditional models of supervision.

In *The Prince*, Machiavelli stated, "There is nothing more difficult to take in hand, more perilous to conduct, or more uncertain of its success, than to take the lead in the introduction of a new order of things."

The book *Fusion Leadership: Unlocking the Subtle Forces That Change People and Organizations*, by Daft and Lengel (1998), defines leadership for change through the terms "fusion" and "fission." Although Daft and Lengel's work is primarily intended for the corporate sector, school leaders might think of how the principles of fusion and fission could be applied to the school setting.

Daft and Lengel compare the negative energy produced by top-down, traditional hierarchical leadership to the fission of an atomic explosion. Fission is divisive; its potential rests in its ability to destroy from the inside out. With fission leadership, barriers are built which promote isolation. Members of the organization compete against one another; attempts at collaboration are stifled.

Traditional supervision, as practiced in most schools, bears a strong resemblance to fission leadership. Teachers and administrators are members of two competing teams: the judged and the judge. In such a hostile environment, potential for growth is thwarted. Out of necessity, the need for survival supplants learning. This form of supervision resembles "premodern" conceptions of supervision.

In sharp contrast, fusion leadership, a modernist paradigm, builds partnerships, joins parts of an organization into a cohesive unit by eliminating boundaries. Fusion leadership promotes a "common ground and a sense of community based on what people share—vision, norms, and outcomes" (p. 15). Through true fusion, "The team image that emerges is different from any of the individual visions, yet it reflects the deeper needs of each member" (p. 16).

Collaborative supervision promotes a common vision for all members of the school community. Barriers created by traditional hierarchies no longer divide teachers from administrators. Through fusion leadership, growth and learning are nurtured. Teachers can risk innovation in their classrooms. A common vision for individual and organizational growth can emerge. "Superfusion" must replace "snoopervision."

Case Study 5: Ethical and Political Challenges of Supervision

Ms. Quest, Mr. Newman, and Mrs. Constance teach mathematics at Polya Tech High School, in an urban setting in the Midwest. Newman is a recent college graduate; Quest has six years teaching experience at a small, rural school system and is new to Polya Tech; and Constance has 25 years teaching experience, most of it at Polya Tech. Last week, Dr. Rita Bell, assistant principal, conducted her first observations of all three teachers. During the weekly faculty meeting, Quest and Constance began discussing their recent observations. To their surprise, they discovered that the narrative portion of the observation instruments were nearly identical, but the criteria identified for improvement were different for each teacher.

Two days later, Newman found his observation report in his mailbox. Distraught, he sought out Constance to discuss the comments on the observation instrument. Mrs. Constance discovered that, although the criteria identified for improvement on Newman's report were different from hers or Quest's, all three narratives were strikingly similar. At Constance's suggestion, the two teachers conferred with Quest. Upon detailed examination of Quest's form, another trend was observed. The same "suggestion for improvement" had been written to address three seemingly unrelated criteria: classroom management, explains purpose, and content area knowledge. Constance, Quest, and Newman decided to bring this discovery to the attention of their other colleagues in the mathematics department. This tightly knit group was supportive and listened intently. After the meeting, several people commented on the similarities found within their forms as well, although different assistant principals observed them.

The department asked for a meeting with Dr. Bell. Constance approached Bell to schedule a meeting to discuss this issue. Bell responded, "I evaluate teachers; teachers do not evaluate me!" Bell refused to meet with the department as a group, but she reluctantly agreed to meet with each teacher individually if they wanted to make appointments. After several teachers met with Bell, the department requested a formal meeting with the principal, Mrs. Baker, and the building union representative. Mrs. Baker listened intently, agreed to meet with the department, and asked if she should contact the union rep. After Constance left Baker's office, she asked Dr. Bell to come to her office. Bell entered Baker's office and shut the door.

FOLLOW-UP QUESTIONS

1. Describe the political dynamics associated with supervision at Polya Tech.

2. From a modernist perspective, what supervisory practices might Dr. Bell use to meet the individual needs of Constance, Newman, and Quest?

3. Identify the ethical and moral issues surrounding supervision in this case. If you were Mrs. Baker, how would you work with Dr. Bell? The members of the mathematics department? The other assistant principals?

4. Develop a plan to evaluate the situation at Polya Tech. Who should be involved in this evaluation?

5. How might job-embedded approaches to supervision be used to meet the individual needs of Constance, Newman, and Quest?

6. Apply the principals of "fusion" and "fission" to the leadership issues in this case.

7. What would it take to move the teachers and administrators at Polya Tech toward creating a learning community?

REFERENCES

Ackerman, R. H., Donaldson, G. A., & van der Bogert, R. (1996). *Making sense as a school leader: Persisting questions, creative opportunities.* San Francisco, CA: Jossey-Bass Publishers.

Adelman, N. E., Walking Eagle, K. P., & Hargreaves, A. (1997). Framing the cases: Time for change. In N. E. Adelman, K. P. Walking Eagle, & A. Hargreaves (Eds.), *Racing with the clock: Making time for teaching and learning in school reform* (pp. 1–7). New York: Teachers College Press.

Bellon, J. J., & Bellon, E. C. (1982). *Classroom supervision and instructional improvement: A synergistic process.* Dubuque, IA: Kendall/Hunt Publishing Company.

Blumberg, A. (1980). *Supervisors and teachers: A private cold war.* Berkeley, CA: McCutchan Publishing Corporation.

Brookfield, S. D. (1986). *Understanding and facilitating adult learning.* San Francisco, CA: Jossey-Bass.

Brooks, J. G., & Brooks, M. G. (1993). *In search of understanding: The case for the constructivist classroom.* Alexandria, VA: Association for Supervision and Curriculum Development.

Calabrese, R. L., & Zepeda, S. J. (1997). *The reflective supervisor.* Larchmont, NY: Eye on Education.

Chesley, L. S., Wood, F., & Zepeda, S. J. (1997). Induction: Meeting the needs of the alternatively certified teacher. *Journal of Staff Development, 18*(1), 28–32.

Cogan, M. L. (1973). *Clinical supervision.* Boston: Houghton Mifflin.

Crow, G. M., Matthews, L. J., & McCleary, L. E. (1996). *Leadership: A relevant and realistic role for principals.* Larchmont, NY: Eye on Education.

Curda, L. K., & DeBacker, T. D. (1996). *The theory behind Vygotsky's zone of proximal development.* Paper presented at the University of Oklahoma, Norman.

Daft, R. L., & Lengel, R. H. (1998). *Fusion leadership: Unlocking the subtle forces that change people and organizations.* San Francisco, CA: Berret-Koehler Publishers.

Dalellew, T., & Martinez, Y. (1988). Andragogy and development: A search for the meaning of staff development. *Journal of Staff Development, 9*(3), 28–31.

Darling-Hammond, L. (1996). What matters most: A competent teacher for every child. *Phi Delta Kappan, 78*(3), 193–200.

Darling-Hammond, L. (1997). *The right to learn: A blueprint for creating schools that work.* San Francisco: Jossey-Bass Publishers.

Dewey, J. (1938). *Education and experience.* New York: Collier Macmillan Publishers.

Forest, L. (1998). Cooperative learning communities: Expanding from classroom cocoon to global connections. In C. M. Brody & N. Davidson (Eds.), *Professional development for cooperative learning: Issues and approaches* (pp. 228–307). Albany: State University of New York Press.

Fosnot, C. (1996). *Constructivism: Theory, perspectives, and practice.* New York: Teachers College Press.

Ganser, T. (1997). Similes for beginning teachers. *Kappa Delta Pi Record, 33*(3) 106–108.

Glickman, C. D. (1993). *Renewing America's schools.* San Francisco: Jossey-Bass Publishers.

Goldhammer, R. (1969). *Clinical supervision: Special methods for the supervision of teachers.* New York: Holt, Rinehart, Winston.

Honebein, P. (1996). Seven goals for the design of constructivist learning environments. In B. Wilson (Ed.), *Constructivist learning environments* (pp. 17–24). New Jersey: Educational Technology Publications.

Lambert, L. (1995). Toward a theory of constructivist leadership. In L. Lambert, D. Walker, D. Zimmerman, J. Cooper, M. Lambert, M. E. Gardner, & P. J. Ford-Slack (Eds.), *The constructivist leader* (pp. 28–51). New York: Teachers College Press.

Lortie, D. C. (1975). *Schoolteacher: A sociological study.* Chicago: University of Chicago Press.

McCall, J. (1997). *The principal as steward.* Larchmont, NY: Eye on Education.

O'Neil, J. (1998). Constructivism-Wanted: Deep understanding. In J. O'Neil & S. Willis (Eds.), *Transforming classroom practice* (pp. 49–70). Alexandria, VA: Association for Supervision and Curriculum Development.

O'Reilly, G., & Latimer, M. (1990). *Who teaches, who principals, who learns?* Victoria, BC, Canada: Canadian Society for Studies in Education (ERIC Document Reproduction Services No. ED 324 770).

Pajak, E. (1993). *Approaches to clinical supervision: Alternatives for improving instruction.* Norwood, MA: Christopher Gordon Publishers.

Ponticell, J. A. (1995). Promoting teacher professionalism through collegiality. *Journal of Staff Development, 16*(3), 13–18.

Sergiovanni, T. J., & Starratt, R. J. (1997). *Supervision: A redefinition* (6th ed.). Boston: McGraw-Hill.

Walker, D., & Lambert, L. (1995). Learning and leading theory: A century in the making. In L. Lambert, D. Walker, D. Zimmerman, J. Cooper, M. Lambert, M. E. Gardner, & P. J. Ford-Slack (Eds.), *The constructivist leader* (pp. 28–51). New York: Teachers College Press.

Wood, F. H., & Killian, J. (1998). Job-embedded learning makes the difference in school improvement. *Journal of Staff Development, 19*(1), 52–54.

Zemke, R., & Zemke, S. (1995). Adult learning: What do we know for sure? *Training, 32*(6), 31–40.

Zepeda, S. J. (1999). *Staff development: Practices that promote leadership in learning communities.* Larchmont, NY: Eye on Education.

Zepeda, S. J., & Ponticell, J. A. (1995). The supervisory continuum: A developmental approach. *National Association of Secondary School Principals Practitioner, 22*(1), 1–4.

Zepeda, S. J., & Ponticell, J. A. (1998). At cross-purposes: What do teachers need, want, and get from supervision? *Journal of Curriculum and Supervision, 14*(1), 68–87.

6

Collaborative Supervision: Implications for Supervision Research and Inquiry

Martha N. Ovando

GUIDING QUESTIONS

1. *What are the contributions of scientific methods and cooperative problem-solving approaches to educational problems?*
2. *What does "collaborative supervision" mean to you?*
3. *What is the difference, if any, among the following terms: "cooperation," "collegiality," and "collaboration"?*
4. *How does the author distinguish among these three terms?*
5. *According to the author, what would collaborative supervision "look like" in a school?*
6. *What factors are essential for collaborative supervision to become a reality in schools?*

A retrospective glance at the evolution of supervision reminds us that the ideals of a democratic society and the contributions of scientific thinking are reflected in the development of modern supervisory paradigms. On the other hand, postmodernist interpretations of supervision argue against the application of scientific methods and cooperative problem-solving approaches to educational problems and question scientific knowledge as the most appropriate source of expertise, as well as the use of technical and rational evidence. These two supervision perspectives appear to be contradictory at first; however, a closer look at their underlying assumptions and propositions reveals that they are not mutually exclusive but complementary.

Modern supervision "implies that educators, including teachers, curriculum specialists, and supervisors would cooperate in order to improve instruction" (Glanz, 1997a, p. 5). The notion of teacher participation in supervision was recognized and reinforced as early as the 1900s. Specifically, Newlon (1923) affirmed that by creating "supervisory councils," teachers could "be regarded as fellow-workers." Currently, scientific thinking and cooperative problem-solving continue to be valued for the purpose of enhancing teaching and learning (Holland, 1994; Pajak, 1993a). Further, supervision is viewed as "engaging teachers, face to face, in an effort to improve instruction with information, techniques, and skills that are likely to have beneficial effects on student learning" (Glanz, 1997b, p. 125).

Modern supervision advances the idea that this perspective relies on cooperative, democratic, and scientific methods to enhance instruction and schooling (Franseth, 1955; Glickman, Gordon, & Ross-Gordon, 1998; Harris, 1985; Mosher & Purpel, 1972; Neagley & Evans, 1964; Scott & Simpson, 1930; Spears, 1953; Wiles & Bondi, 1996), which can have profound effects on modern supervision paradigms and knowledge in the field of supervision. Therefore, the purpose of this chapter is to heighten our awareness of the implications of a supervisory paradigm that embraces and emphasizes the characteristics of modern supervision mentioned. To this end, a collaborative supervision perspective is presented providing an account of its conceptualization, characteristics, process, benefits, and implications to promulgate future research and inquiry into the field of supervision impact and the practice of supervision in school-based settings.

MODERN SUPERVISION BACKGROUND

The modern perspective of supervision emphasizes a collaborative focus for the purpose of enhancing teaching and learning. This collaborative focus has evolved from a traditional collegial perspective, often times confused with congeniality, to a more democratic and inclusive perspective. As Kosmoski (1997) affirms, "Supervisors who utilize the democratic style give teachers more responsibility for their own actions and involve teachers in the decision-making process. The collegial and collaborative nature of the relationship between the teacher and the supervisor is emphasized" (pp. 20–21).

For instance, by the 1920s, supervision was perceived as a cooperative undertaking in which both supervisor and teacher were to be mutually helpful and jointly responsible for the work in the classroom (Nutt, 1928). Later, the Department of Superintendence defined supervision by focusing on the teacher's role in the classroom, when it stated that "Supervision has for its object the development of a group of professional workers who attack their problems scientifically, free from the control of tradition and actuated in the spirit of inquiry" (Commission on Supervision, 1930, p. 4).

By the 1930s supervision was considered as a creative endeavor attempting to unify democratic and scientific supervisory practices. As Scott and Simpson (1930) then affirmed, "Supervision is creative when objective standards, built upon the findings of research and the best in educational theory and practice, are applied subjectively with the human element in mind" (p. 346).

During the 1940s, group processes were emphasized, giving attention to "member interactions related to group effectiveness" (Harris, 1998, p. 8). Further, "promoting democracy among students and faculty was considered central to the purposes of supervision in education" (Pajak, 1993b, p. 4).

By the 1950s, supervision objectives and human dimensions were highlighted. As Spears (1953) affirmed, supervision was thought to "be creative and yet be thorough. . . . It can be cooperative and yet not shirk responsibilities. It can recognize the importance of individuals and yet retain instructional standards. It can give help and yet not be dictatorial" (p. 16). Similarly, Franseth (1955) believed that supervision was most effective when a climate of acceptance, support, and understanding was present and when a scientific approach was utilized in addressing problems. Supervision was also defined as "primarily aimed at studying and improving co-operatively all factors which affect growth and development" (Burton & Brueckner, 1955, p. 11). Supporting the cooperative and democratic nature of modern supervision, Burton and Bruekner (1955) also affirmed that supervision was cooperative, democratic, and helpful.

During the 1960s, supervision was generally seen as leadership that encouraged a continuous involvement of all personnel in a cooperative attempt to achieve the most effective school program (Franseth, 1961) and as action through wide participation of all concerned in the process of inquiry and the judgment of outcomes, which was the goal of supervision (Lucio & McNeil, 1962). Further, modern supervision was perceived as positive, democratic action aimed at the improvement of classroom instruction through the continual growth of all concerned—the child, the teacher, the supervisor, the administrator, and the parent or other interested person (Neagley & Evans, 1964).

By the 1970s, supervision included planning for observation, analysis, and treatment of the teacher's classroom performance (Mosher & Purpel, 1972), giving emphasis to the need to gather classroom-based information. Supervision generated data from the events of the classroom by applying systematic descriptive techniques in order to mirror the teaching behaviors considered. The analysis of these data and the relationship between teacher and supervisor formed the basis of the program, procedures, and strategies designed to improve students' learning by improving the teacher's classroom behavior (Cogan, 1973).

By the 1980s, instructional supervision emphasized the use of data from firsthand observation of actual teaching events and involved face-to-face (and other associated) interaction between the supervisor and the teacher in the analysis of teaching behaviors and activities for instructional improvement (Goldhammer, Anderson, & Krajewski, 1980). Similarly, cooperative professional development as a supervisory option was conceived as "a moderately formalized process by which two or more teachers agreed to work together for

their own professional growth, usually by observing each other's classes, giving each other feedback about the observation, and discussing shared professional concerns" (Glatthorn, 1984, p. 39). Supervision was also promoted as an alternative model that is interactive rather than directive, democratic rather than authoritarian, teacher-centered rather than supervisor-centered (Acheson & Gall, 1992).

More recently, Glanz (1997a) affirmed that "if a supervisor can observe a teacher's classroom and accumulate practically verifiable information (e.g., data that indicates Teacher X is allowing girls less time to respond to questions as compared to boys) so that teacher can view his classroom from another perspective and consider alternate ways of doing things, then I think, a modernist approach does have much to offer" (p. 9). Similarly, Kosmoski (1997) asserts that modern "educational supervision became a partnership between the supervisor and the teacher. Supervisors recognized the need for teacher involvement, ownership, and collaboration to successfully improve instruction and student success"(p. 11).

COLLABORATIVE SUPERVISION

Most of the definitions and perspectives of modern supervision emphasize the need for a productive working relationship as an essential component of processes aimed at enhancing teaching and learning, the need for a democratic process that involves not only the teacher and the supervisors but other education professionals as well, and the need for observational data that can generate meaningful information about the events of classroom instruction. A supervisory perspective that has incorporated these characteristics and that has been field tested, to some extent, is collaborative supervision.

For the purpose of this discussion, collaborative supervision is defined as "a process by which people with diverse expertise (teachers, principals, supervisors, and others) work jointly with equal status and shared commitment in order to achieve mutually beneficial instructional goals" (Harris & Ovando, 1992, p. 13). This supervision reinforces "collaborative supervisor-teacher interaction and problem solving, mutual trust, and feedback that is neither evaluative nor judgmental" (Hosack-Curlin, 1989, p. 46). While concepts of collaboration have not always been reflected in common practice, trends appear to be discernible. Collaboration in this context is positioned at a higher level than collegiality and cooperation; therefore, it must be differentiated.

Collegiality, on one hand, is a basic relationship among colleagues reflecting positive relationships that characterize the human relations approach (Sergiovanni & Starratt, 1998). As Harris (1997) argues, a collegial relationship is "a misguided paradigm for defining teacher-supervisor relationships because its origins, current university applications, and underlying concepts are not appropriate to the mission, purposes, and organizational contexts of public elementary and secondary schools" (p. 145). Further, Harris (1997) notes that the following factors support his argument:

1. Collegiality, as a set of concepts and practices with an ancient heritage of church and university traditions, is simply an inappropriate, even dangerous, paradigm for schools in modern democratic society.

2. Practical realities involving the urgent and differentiated roles, responsibilities, and priorities of teachers and supervisors are serious deterrents to collegiality becoming the genuine basis for effective professional relationships.

3. Alternative relationships are necessary to accomplish the mutual professional goals of teachers and supervisors. These alternatives call for collaborative and team relationships that are at odds with many underlying assumptions and traditions of collegiality. (p. 144)

Cooperation, in turn, occurs when people "act or work with another or others" (*Webster's Ninth New Collegiate Dictionary*, 1987, p. 288). For example, when "two individuals or organizations reach some mutual agreement, but their work together does not progress beyond this level" (Hord, 1986, p. 23), when "an individual provides assistance or resources for the achievement of predetermined goals" (Harris & Ovando, 1992, p. 13), or when "supervisors and teachers can maintain positive professional relationships and work together toward the common purpose of instructional improvement whether the supervisor uses controlling directive, informational directive, collaborative, or non-directive behaviors, provided the supervisor selects and effectively implements the correct approach" (Glickman, Gordon, & Ross-Gordon, 1998, p. 175). Cooperation, therefore, should not be confused with collaboration.

Collaboration, on the other hand, means "to work jointly with others or together esp. in an intellectual endeavor" (*Webster's Ninth New Collegiate Dictionary*, 1987, p. 259). More specifically, collaboration means "participation by equals in making instructional decisions. Its outcome is a mutual plan of action" (Glickman, Gordon, & Ross-Gordon, 1998, p. 175). It is further viewed "as the essential modus operandi characterizing all aspects of supervisory practice at all levels, student to school board and beyond" (Harris & Ovando, 1992, p. 12). Finally, as Appley and Winder's (1977) early definition suggests, "collaboration [is seen] as a relational system" in which:

1. Individuals in a group share mutual aspirations and common conceptual framework;

2. The interactions among individuals are characterized by "justice as fairness"; and

3. These aspirations and conceptualizations are characterized by each individual's consciousness of his or her motives toward the other; by caring or concern for the other; and by commitment to work with the other over time provided that this commitment is a matter of choice. (p. 281)

Collaborative supervision commonly implies joint efforts, commonality of goals, shared decision-making and responsibilities, and mutuality of respect and interests. In this context, collaboration is a much more sophisticated level of participation than either collegiality or cooperation. Our aim in supervision should not be to merely "cooperate" (all participants in a school organization should cooperate) or maintain "collegial" relationships (after all, supervisors and teachers are colleagues in only the loosest sense of the word), but rather to achieve "collaboration" (collaboration represents supervision's highest ideal).

Collaborative Supervision Characteristics

Previous literature addressing interorganizational relationships highlights salient features of collaboration that might have implications for supervision. For instance, contrasting collaboration and cooperation, Hord (1986) suggests ten collaboration qualities. These include: (1) needs and interests (clear understanding of the mutual gain and shared interests between entities before joining any collaborative endeavor); (2) time (setting the necessary time for mutual activities and decisions); (3) energy (the need to reach out and an action-orientation on the part of the collaborating individuals); (4) communication (continuous sharing of information through meetings and other interaction arrangements); (5) resources (sharing the different human, material, and financial resources needed for the mutually expected outcomes and rewards); (6) organizational factors (individuals' commitment to collaborate and to actually work jointly); (7) control (flexibility that allows risk taking and giving up personal control); (8) perceptions (understanding of individuals' perspectives and willingness to see other's point of view); (9) leadership (setting an example of strong support and encouragement of a collaborative attitude); and (10) personal traits (individuals' persistence and willingness to share).

Collaboration is essential not only in interorganizational relationships but also in all facets of education, in general, and more specifically in instructional supervision; therefore, it requires a new way of thinking. As Garman (1982) recognized, collaboration requires the kind and quality of a supervisor's and teacher's involvement that will lead to instructional development and to the creation of an "educational alliance." Further, others affirm that a collaborative process "legitimates teachers' practical understanding and their definition of problems for both research and professional development" (Lieberman, 1986, p. 31). Thus, to be effective, collaborative supervision must reflect essential process characteristics (Harris & Ovando, 1992). These characteristics are:

- *Mutual respect* based on recognition of shared and differentiated responsibilities and expertise.
- *Tolerance* for differing values, perceptions, and interpretations of reality, problems, and options.
- *Acceptance* of the need and capability for continuing development of all persons, including self.
- *Commitment* to sincere efforts toward consensus on goals and actions in pursuit of the ideal for the common good.
- *Courage* in challenging, influencing, and expressing disagreement without seeking to control, dominate, or manipulate.

- *Sharing* of information related to joint efforts in an open and honest mode.
- *Adherence* to laws, regulations, guidelines, and ground rules that apply.
- *Respect* for the wisdom of the profession based on theory, research, and practitioners' collective experience.
- *Differentiation of responsibilities* for deciding and acting, reflecting trust and rationality.
- *Teaming* as the central mode of organization for action as well as an attitude stressing We rather than You or I.

Further, supervisors who wish to use a collaborative supervision approach need to keep in mind that "collaboration is both an attitude and repertoire of behaviors. Unless teachers have the attitude that they are equal, collaborative behaviors can be used to undermine true equality" (Glickman, Gordon, & Ross-Gordon, 1998, p. 175). While these characteristics and considerations illustrate the level of intensity and demands on those who desire to engage in collaborative supervision, some have been successful in incorporating at least one of these features into other specific supervisory approaches. For instance, Glatthorn (1984) affirms that the cooperative professional development option "can take many forms from modest programs of two or three exchanges of observations to very ambitious and comprehensive projects in which teams of teachers collaborate in several aspects of the instructional function" (p. 40). This option emphasizes mutual respect, acceptance of need, and courage to challenge each other.

Another approach that reflects collaborative characteristics presented here is known as "peer supervision." According to Heller (1989), supervision "is a process by which persons with the same or different rank within an organization help each other for their mutual benefit. The process is not one of checking up on or evaluating one another. Rather, it is a helping relationship that provides mutual support. When this process involves individuals at the same rank within an organization, it is called peer supervision" (p. 7). Later on, peer supervision was confirmed as "a process of professional guidance, help and growth" (James, Heller, & Ellis, 1992, p. 100). The mission statement of peer supervision conceptualized by James and his associates (1992) reads:

We believe in a supervision process that leads to professional growth and enhances learning. Staff members will use their colleagues and the services of the community. We believe that growth occurs by taking risks within a supportive, professional network. The supervision process is collaborative but not evaluative. (p. 104)

Previous studies focusing on collaborative supervision concluded that "teachers' perceptions in general do support an open, collaborative relationship for the purpose of achieving quality teaching for successful learning" (Ovando & Harris, 1993, p. 309) reinforcing the value of the collaborative process characteristics presented here. Further, a field testing project, which attempted to "document actual outcomes of a collaborative process aimed at enhancing teaching and learning" (Ovando, 1995, p. 147), confirmed that both teachers and supervisors may benefit from a collaborative process, provided that formative evaluations were a critical ingredient of the process.

Therefore, a collaborative process should reflect features associated with formative assessments. As Harris and Ovando (1992) note, "When formative purposes are reinforced by collaborative processes in both words and actions, a truly developmental process emerges that has powerful effects for improving instruction" (p. 15). Formative evaluation can be distinguished from summative processes by at least eight design features within a collaborative perspective.

1. Expectations are jointly developed but focus on individual needs.
2. Evaluator is a group of professionals with diverse expertise, including teachers.
3. Data used are objective, multivariate, multisource, and mutually selected with diagnostic utility.
4. Time frame is continuous, flexible, and jointly scheduled with a logical sequence for short- and long-term goals.
5. Analysis and processes are diagnostic, involving teachers and others, interpretations are linked to development plans.
6. Processes overall are interactive and reflective, involving sharing a full shared range of processes and decisions.
7. Resource requirements are moderately costly in direct outlays but are morale building and developmentally substantial.
8. Follow-on is mutually agreed upon objectives and activities for growth. (Harris & Ovando, 1992, p. 15)

An important attribute of formative evaluation within a collaborative approach is the use of classroom-based data, usually gathered through a variety of observation techniques that, used in combination with other postmodern approaches, could yield enriched accounts of classroom events. More specifically, Glickman, Gordon, and Ross-Gordon (1998) affirm that "a formative observation instrument used to describe what is occurring in a classroom (consistent with what teacher and supervisor agreed to focus on and later discuss) is a means for professional growth and instructional improvement" (p. 244).

While an extensive review of the different observation techniques is beyond this discourse, it seems relevant to point out that most supervision paradigms, whether modern or postmodern, call for data gathering that reflects actual classroom events. As Krajewski (1993) puts it, "the supervisor collects data requested by the teacher in a manner agreed to by both supervisor and teacher. Observing is both a science and art, and there are various technologies available for gathering data" (p. 106). Consequently, an important skill for those in supervisory roles is "to gather data related to teacher behavior and student achievement that was agreed upon during the planning conference" (Costa & Garmston, 1993, p. 52).

The supervisory literature suggests that a number of observation and data gathering technologies hold promise to describe classroom teaching and learning events. Some examples include Flanders' Interaction Analysis Category System-FIAC (Amidon & Flanders, 1967; Flanders, 1970), Discipline and Group Management in Classrooms (Kounin, 1977), DeTEK- Developmental Teacher Evaluation Kit (Harris & Hill, 1982), selective verbatim (Acheson & Gall, 1992), wide lens, seating chart observational records, checklist and timeline coding (Kosmoski, 1997), categorical frequency instruments, visual diagramming, and performance indicator instruments (Glickman, Gordon, & Ross-Gordon, 1998). While these data-gathering devices are useful, expert opinion suggests that additional qualitative observations have potential for "a supervisor to provide a broad and complex recording of classroom life" (Glickman, Gordon, & Ross-Gordon, 1998, p. 254). Some examples include detached open-ended narrative, participant open-ended observations, focus questionnaire observations and educational criticism (Glickman, Gordon & Ross-Gordon, 1998). Moreover, data from classroom observations need to be confirmed with additional sources of information. According to Sergiovanni and Starratt (1998), using additional sources may include

interviews with teachers, examples of student work, photo essays, data descriptions of teacher-student interaction patterns, movement flowcharts, case studies of students, and analysis of books read by students, student performance exhibits, a folio of tests, and homework assignments and other assignments given by the teacher. In supplying multiple sources of information about his or her teaching, the teacher must become a partner in the process. (p. 226)

Given the wide variety of observation techniques, the challenge for teachers and supervisors is on the shared decision-making to select the most appropriate format. Every observation format has specific purposes and requires a certain skill level. Therefore,

choosing what to observe—the student responses, teacher-student interaction, teacher question and reinforcement, lesson pacing, teacher centeredness and body language, student interactions, and social climate—how to observe—video, audio, interaction analysis, typescripts, coding by systematic observation systems—and when to observe—linking behaviors and data variables, selecting sequences and interaction patterns—are all keys to observation process and therefore to success of the remaining components of the observation cycle. (Krajewski, 1993, p. 107)

While that discussion focused on the clinical domain of collaborative supervision, it is relevant to point out that the attributes of this paradigm are widely recognized in the field and applied to all aspects of education. For instance, educational endeavors addressing curriculum development, planning, staff development, program evaluation, instructional innovations, and educational change illustrate a collaborative philosophy by which educators and professionals from other fields jointly plan, implement and evaluate educational improvements, recognizing that the demands for change in education can not be met by "isolated individuals" (Harris, 1985, p. 144).

Process

A process that has potential for mutual reflection and problem solving and for significantly affecting teaching and learning needs to follow "a systematic collaborative supervision model" (Ovando, 1995, p. 147). Such a model must assure "voluntary participation and focus on formative, not summative evaluation" (Harris & Ovando, 1992, p. 15) of professionals with diverse experience, expertise, and background for the purpose of achieving mutually agreed-upon goals. This process is based on the Harris (1989) Flowchart of the Teaching Improvement Process. This process includes joint planning and scheduling, information-gathering, processing and summarizing, analyzing and reflecting, and designing improvement. Furthermore, a follow-on component was added to reflect the continuous support provided as teachers and supervisors introduce changes (see Figure 6.1). Moreover, this process needs to be "interactive and reflective, involving sharing a full range of processes and decisions" (Hopfengardener & Leahy, 1988, p. 48) and ultimately it should lead to enhanced teaching and learning.

Benefits

Given its nature, collaborative supervision has implicit advantages for all involved. For instance, Glanz (1997a) suggests that "modern conceptions of supervision have a far greater positive impact on practice and implications for the training of future administrators" (p. 16). Similarly, early attempts to incorporate some of the collaborative process characteristics illustrate that, in peer-assisted endeavors, commitment is increased and teachers perceive that they have the ability to engage in a process that promises to improve professional performance (Withall & Wood, 1979). Brophy (1979) also found that teachers who work together can expand their learning about their own teaching. Similarly, James, Heller, and Ellis (1992) found that "a major benefit of a [peer supervision] program is its influence on the climate of the school. It creates a spirit of cooperation and collaboration among staff members. It is a springboard to open discussion on education and helps educators generate ideas for curriculum projects, professional development and school improvement" (p. 110). Further, "the most significant value of peer assistance is to the students. Peer assistance improves instruction because teachers are looking at what they are doing and analyzing it with a peer" (James, Heller, & Ellis, 1992, p. 110).

In cooperative professional development, a supervisory option within a differentiated approach, it has been concluded that teachers may benefit from useful feedback provided to one another "without extensive training and without the use of complex forms— and cooperative professional development is

Figure 6.1

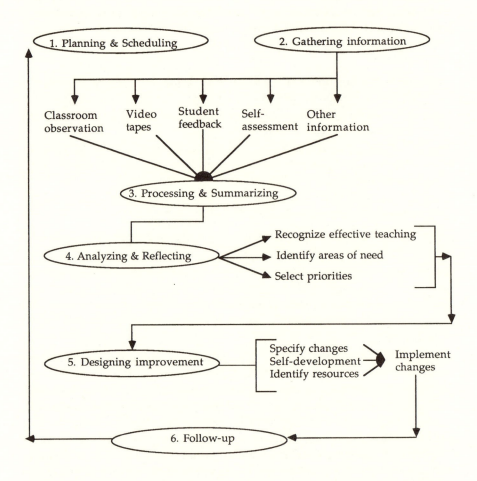

structured to make such feedback occur more regularly and more systematically" (Glatthorn, 1984, p. 43). Similarly, previous researchers report that cooperative arrangements "can improve the attitudes and professional
interdependence of . . . teachers who received it. . . . The favorable effects of
collegial supervision were strongest in the communication adequacy" (Nelson, Schwartz, & Schmuck, 1974) of those involved in the process.

More specifically, the collaborative supervision perspective presented here
may yield important benefits for teachers and supervisors. For instance, the
outcomes of a field-based project of the systematic collaborative model focus
of this chapter suggest "that teachers introduced positive changes in the classroom and that collaborative supervisors gained specific field based learning"
(Ovando, 1995, p. 144). Further, teachers' instructional changes lead to im-

proved student behavior, to better teacher-student interactions, and to increased student success.

In addition, collaborative supervisor benefits included reinforcement of knowledge and skills associated with supervisory practice. Furthermore, collaborative supervisors reported learning that:

Professional dialogue requires clear and open communication as well as respect for teachers' professional expertise.

Supervisory styles should be adapted to meet the needs of individual teachers, whether beginner or experienced.

Observation protocols need to fit the specific teaching-learning situation and the needs of the teacher; therefore, a variety of observation guides or instruments should be available.

Trust and positive attitude are essential for teachers to be positive, receptive, reflective, and responsive to suggestions.

Positive feedback is fundamental in a collaborative teacher-supervisor relationship to reinforce teachers' quality performance.

Mutual respect is critical in a collaborative teacher-supervisor relationship. Respect for each others' strength and expertise should always be present.

Teacher's commitment is an essential ingredient for working in a collaborative mode. Teachers who are open and willing to learn about teaching and learning will participate and are usually dedicated to improve what they do in the classroom.

Supervisory models must be selected carefully. They need to match both teacher's and supervisor's beliefs and experience as well as the specific school culture.

Instructional leadership is a critical component of supervisors' professional background. Knowledge, skills, and attitudes associated with the teaching and learning process are essential to work with teachers. (Ovando, 1995, pp. 151–152)

Further, it has been concluded that when a collaborative supervision process is completed, positive changes in student behaviors and supervision may result. By working together, the supervisor and teacher have opportunities to meet regularly, to focus on personal reflection, and to plan and refine their thinking processes. In the end, these experiences and activities enhance the teacher's classroom performance and the instructional supervisor's effectiveness as well (Ovando, 1995).

While limited, the benefits of collaborative supervision just described illustrate that this perspective has potential to enhance teaching and learning. However, it is important to highlight some of the factors that might influence the desirable continuity of a collaborative supervision that is essential to achieve success for all. According to Glatthorn (1984), the attitude of the administrator, the attitude of teacher associations, the prevailing school climate, the extent to which the program was monitored, and the resources available could strongly influence a collaborative process.

Similarly, James, Heller, and Ellis (1992) suggest that the survival of a supervision program with a collaborative emphasis depends on factors such as voluntary participation, administrative support, teacher and administrator involvement, clear communication and definitions of supervision and evaluation, and facilitator commitment. Others found that mutual agreement on the main focus of the observations and the evidence of student achievement may also influence the collaborative cycles (Perkins, 1998). More recently, it has been suggested that "meaningful interactions about professional practices apparently lead to increased trust within relationships and stimulate both mentors and mentees to critically examine their work and to improve their teaching" (Arredondo & Ruzinski, 1998, p. 324).

In addition to the preceding factors, it appears from the supervisory literature that a number of issues remain, such as whether or not a collaborative supervision perspective is truly democratic, whether or not the context of schooling dictates the nature of a supervisory approach, whether or not teachers' perspectives on supervision are congruent with the spirit of collaborative supervision, whether or not there is one best way of structuring a collaborative approach, and even whether a collaborative perspective truly leads to increased student success. These and other issues imply the need for additional research that could highlight the real contributions of a collaborative supervision paradigm.

IMPLICATIONS FOR RESEARCH

Collaborative supervision appears to have incorporated critical components of the modern supervision perspective to some extent. Given its definition, process characteristics, systemic process, and benefits, it may be inferred that by mutually diagnosing, planning, implementing, and assessing teaching and learning improvements, education professionals, including supervisors and teachers who use this approach, could indeed enhance student success. However, the factors and issues presented illustrate the need for additional research.

Few studies focusing on early cooperative arrangements offer some encouraging insights and useful guidelines for supervision practitioners (Glatthorn, 1990); however, we must realize that determining the true potential and contributions of collaborative supervision as a modern practice requires further study. As noted elsewhere, while understanding how teachers may benefit from a collaborative project is important, other questions associated with classroom instruction effectiveness must be the focus of further inquiry (Ovando, 1995). Furthermore, as Zepeda and Ponticell (1998) suggest, "Given the breadth and length of discourse among scholars and policy makers regarding the supervision of teachers, the field of supervision should not be satisfied. . . . Far more research is needed from many contexts examining teachers' perspectives on supervision" (p. 71). Supporting the need to pay closer attention to context, Sergiovanni and Starratt (1998) recommend an "understanding of the various contexts of the learner" (p. 101) as well. Consequently, there is a need to focus our attention on teaching contexts because:

These contexts involve those kinds of long-standing and deeply personal influences on the self-perception, the expressive style, the language, social perspectives, and the sense of family and group belonging of the learner. The students' race, ethnic identification, social class, gender and family background, therefore, are major influences on basic attitudes toward schools, toward authority, toward the so-called mainstream culture, and toward the traditional academic tasks of classroom learning. (Sergiovanni & Starratt, 1998, pp. 101–102)

While collaborative supervision appears to offer teachers "freedom to address topics and concerns in an open and supportive environment" (Ovando, 1995, p. 153), further inquiry is needed to determine when a collaborative supervision approach is more constructive. Glickman, Gordon, and Ross-Gordon (1998), for instance, suggest that "there are circumstances in which a supervisor definitely should use collaborative behaviors" (p. 174). Thus, future research should go beyond the study of collaborative skills and attempt to determine when and in which kinds of school settings and environments a collaborative supervision approach would be most appropriate. Research is also needed to investigate the effect of the collaborative supervision process on teacher and supervisor effectiveness. Zepeda and Ponticell (1998) observe that future research should also focus on the "conduct of supervision" and the "perspectives of teachers and supervisors engaged in the conduct of those processes" (p. 87). Finally, it is imperative that research go beyond investigating the attitudes, perspectives, and preferences of those involved in collaborative supervision processes. Additional insight is needed regarding comprehensive collaborative supervision improvements of student outcomes, which should be the main purpose of education. Consequently, collaborative endeavors resulting from school and community relationships, which might include not only teachers and supervisors but also community leaders, nurses, social workers, journalists, and others, should also be examined.

Greater understanding of modern supervision practices will illuminate their true contributions to the education of all students. In addition, we will be in a better position to see how modern and postmodern perspectives complement each other rather than contradict each other. From a Taoist perspective, according to Glanz (1997c), "conflicting theories or proposals for supervision should be welcomed, not resisted. By accepting a diversity of views to inform practice, a balance of centeredness can be attained" (p. 205). Supervision in this context "can be conceived as a function that uses a wide array of strategies, methodologies, and approaches aimed to improve instruction and to promote educational leadership as well as change" (Glanz, 1997c, p. 207), which in turn should lead to excellence and equity for all students.

Case Study 6: Supervisor Challenged by an Experienced Teacher

Ms. Perfect is an experienced math teacher. She has been teaching math and science at different grade levels for the last thirteen years. This year, she is teaching fifth-grade enriched math. She uses teaching strategies such as problem-solving in groups, questioning strategies, and manipulatives. Her philosophy is that all students, regardless of age or ability, need to work with manipulatives. She has received excellent reviews on her prior appraisal period and has been nominated for the Teacher of the Year Award.

Ms. Perfect is really an excellent teacher. She has a wonderful rapport with her students, she is knowledgeable of many teaching strategies, and she is truly creative in her approach. She was nominated for the Teacher of the Year Award by three different administrators. At the beginning of the school year, she told her supervisor that she did not know what he could do to help her, given her experience and expertise, but agreed to engage in a supervisory process. After some clarifications and agreements they decided to give it a try.

The supervisor and Ms. Perfect decided to go for a cup of coffee, since he had missed his morning coffee. Ms. Perfect informed the supervisor that she was interested in focusing on "pacing for instruction" and the "types of questions she asked during class." They agreed that the observational data collected would be processed by the supervisor and later analyzed by both of them.

The supervisor was delayed on his way to Ms. Perfect's class; however, when he arrived he was able to collect information on the two concerns the teacher had. He immediately realized that she was indeed an excellent teacher. She had a wonderful rapport with the students, she was knowledgeable of different teaching strategies, and she was truly creative in her teaching. However, there was a problem with student participation. After completing a fifty-minute observation, the supervisor left a note on Ms. Perfect's desk thanking her for allowing him to observe her class and telling her that he enjoyed the lesson.

During the reflection session Ms. Perfect asked if the supervisor had any suggestions, expecting none. To Ms. Perfect's surprise, the supervisor indicated that in a number of instances she did not recognize individual students and that perhaps she needed to provide more individual reinforcement. The supervisor also gave her the number of times she called only on certain students. He said: "Three of the students were called on more than seven times while five out of the twenty-one students did not answer one question."

Ms. Perfect thanked the supervisor for his "perceptions" of the lesson, but asked him why he was so late for the observation. She said, "I knew something important happened, but you might have sent a note or called. You, in fact, missed parts of the lesson in which I did solicit participation of other students." She informed him that she had to leave his office because of a prior appointment.

FOLLOW-UP QUESTIONS

1. To what extent does this case reflect the process characteristics of collaborative supervision?

2. Describe the next steps you would take to assist this teacher following a collaborative approach.

3. In what way(s) does this case illustrate the features of modernist supervision?

4. What follow-up activities would you propose and how would you work with the teacher to enhance student participation in this class?

5. How would you proceed to use collaborative supervision to work with a first year teacher?

6. How would you proceed to involve other professionals in a collaborative process to enhance student learning?

REFERENCES

Acheson, K. A., & Gall, M. D. (1992). *Techniques in the clinical supervision of teachers* (3rd. ed.). New York: Longman.

Amidon, E., & Flanders, N. (1967). Interaction analysis as a feedback system. In E. Amidon & J. Hough (Eds.), *Interaction analysis: Theory, research, and application* (pp. 122–124). Reading, MA: Addison-Wesley.

Appley, D. E., & Winder, A. E. (1977). An evolving definition of collaboration and some implications for the world of work. *Journal of Applied Behavioral Science, 13*(3), 279–290.

Arredondo, D. E. & Ruzinski, T. T. (1998). Using structured interactions in conference and journals to promote cognitive development among mentors and mentees. *Journal of Curriculum and Supervision, 13*(4), 300–327.

Brophy, J. E. (1979). *Using observations to improve your teaching.* East Lansing, MI: Institute for Research on Teaching.

Burton, W. H., & Brueckner, L. J. (1955). *Supervision: A social process.* New York: Appleton-Century-Crofts.

Cogan, M. L. (1973). *Clinical supervision.* New York: Longman.

Commission on Supervision, Department of Superintendence, NEA (1930). *The superintendent surveys supervision. Eighth Year Book of the Department of Superintendence.* Washington, DC: National Education Association.

Costa, A. L., & Garmston, R. J. (1993). *Cognitive coaching: A foundation for renaissance schools.* Norwood, MA: Christopher-Gordon Publishers.

Flanders, N. (1970). *Analyzing teaching behavior.* Reading, MA: Addison-Wesley.

Franseth, J. (1955). *Supervision in rural schools* (Bulletin 1955 No. 11). Washington, DC: U.S. Department of Health, Education and Welfare, Office of Education.

Franseth, J. (1961). *Supervision as leadership.* Evanston, IL: Row, Peterson.

Garman, N. B. (1982). The clinical approach to supervision. In T. J. Sergiovanni (Ed.), *Supervision of teaching* (pp. 35–52). Alexandria, VA: Association for Supervision and Curriculum Development.

Glanz, J. (1997a, March). *Supervision: Don't discount the value of the modern.* Symposium conducted at the Annual Conference of the American Educational Research Association, Chicago, IL.

Glanz, J. (1997b). Has the field of supervision evolved to a point that it should be called something else? No. In Glanz, J., & Neville, R. (Eds.), *Educational supervision: Perspectives, issues, and controversies* (pp. 124–133). Norwood, MA: Christopher-Gordon Publishers.

Glanz, J. (1997c). The tao of supervision: Taoist insights into the theory and practice of educational supervision. *Journal of Curriculum and Supervision, 12*(3), 193–210.

Glatthorn, A. A. (1984). *Differentiated supervision.* Alexandria, VA: Association for Supervision and Curriculum Development.

Glatthorn, A. A. (1990). *Supervisory leadership: Introduction to instructional supervision.* Glenview, IL: Scott, Foresman/Little, Brown Higher Education.

Glickman, C. D., Gordon, S. P. & Ross-Gordon, J. M. (1998). *Supervision of instruction: A developmental approach.* Boston: Allyn and Bacon.

Goldhammer, R., Anderson, R. H., & Krajewski, R. J. (1980). *Clinical supervision* (2nd ed.). New York: Holt, Rinehart and Winston.

Harris, B. M. (1985). *Supervisory behavior in education.* Englewood Cliffs, NJ: Prentice-Hall.

Harris, B. M. (1989). *In-service education for staff development.* Boston: Allyn & Bacon.

Harris, B. M. (1997). Is a collegial relationship possible between supervisors and teachers? No. In J. Glanz & R. F. Neville (Eds.), *Educational supervision: Perspectives, issues, and controversies* (pp. 144–150). Norwood, MA: Christopher-Gordon Publishers.

Harris, B. M. (1998). Paradigms and parameters of supervision in education. In G. R. Firth & E. F. Pajak (Eds.), *Handbook of research on school supervision* (pp. 1–34). New York: Simon & Schuster Macmillan.

Harris, B. M., & Hill, J. (1982). *Developmental teacher evaluation kit.* Austin, TX: Southwest Educational Development Lab.

Harris, B. M., & Ovando, M. N. (1992). Collaborative supervision and the developmental evaluation of teaching. *Journal of School Administrators Association of New York State, 23*(1), 12–18.

Heller, D. D. (1989). *Peer supervision: A way to professionalizing teaching.* Bloomington, IN: Phi Delta Kappa Educational Foundation.

Holland, P. E. (1994, November). *What do we talk about when we talk of supervision?* Paper presented at the Annual Meeting of the Council of Professors of Instructional Supervision.

Hopfengardener, J. D., & Leahy, P. E. (1988). Providing collegial support for experienced teachers. *Journal of Staff Development, 9*(2), 45–51.

Hord, S. M. (1986). A synthesis of research on organizational collaboration. *Educational Leadership, 43*(5), 22–26.

Hosack-Curlin, K. (1989). *Mastering coaching and supervision.* El Segundo, CA: TIP Publications.

James, S., Heller, D., & Ellis, W. (1992). Peer assistance in a small district: Widham, southeast Vermont. In C. D. Glickman (Ed.), *Supervision in transition* (pp. 97–112). Alexandria, VA: Association for Supervision and Curriculum Development.

Kounin, J. (1977). *Discipline and group management in classrooms.* New York: Holt, Rinehart & Winston.

Kosmoski, G. J. (1997). *Supervision.* Mequon, WI: Stylex Publishing Co.

Krajewski, R. J. (1993). The observation cycle: A methodology for coaching and problem solving. In R. H. Anderson & K. J. Snyder (Eds.), *Clinical supervi-*

sion: Coaching for higher performance (pp. 99–112). Lancaster, PA: Technomic Publishing.

Lieberman, A. (1986). Collaborative research: Working with, not working on. *Educational Leadership*, *43*(5), 28–32.

Lucio, W. H., & McNeil, J. D. (1962). *Supervision: A synthesis of thought and action.* New York: McGraw-Hill.

Mosher, R. L., & Purpel, D. E. (1972). *Supervision: The reluctant profession.* Boston: Houghton Mifflin.

Neagley, R. L., & Evans, N. D. (1964). *Handbook for effective supervision.* Englewood Cliffs, NJ: Prentice-Hall.

Nelson, J. J., Schwartz, M., & Schmuck, R. (1974). *Collegial supervision: A sub-study of organization development in multi-unit schools.* Bethesda, MD: ERIC Document Reproduction Service, ED 166–174.

Newlon, J. H. (1923). Attitude of the teacher toward supervision. *NEA Proceedings*, 546–549.

Nutt, H. W. (1928). *Current problems in the supervision of instruction.* Richmond, VA: Johnson Publishing Company.

Ovando, M. N. (1995) Enhancing teaching and learning through collaborative supervision. *People and Education*, *3*(2), 144–155.

Ovando, M. N., & Harris, B. M. (1993). Teachers' perceptions of the post-observation conference: Implications for formative evaluation. *Journal of Personnel Evaluation in Education*, *7*, 301–310.

Pajak, E. (1993a). Change and continuity in supervision and leadership. In G. Cawelti (Ed.), *Challenges and achievements of American education* (pp. 158–186). Alexandria, VA: Association for Supervision and Curriculum Development.

Pajak, E. (1993b). *Approaches to clinical supervision: Alternatives for improving instruction.* Norwood, MA: Christopher Gordon Publishers.

Perkins, S. J. (1998). On becoming a peer coach: Practices, identities, and beliefs of experienced coaches. *Journal of Curriculum and Supervision*, *13*(3), 237–254.

Scott, Z. E., & Simpson, I. J. (1930). Creative supervision. *In the superintendent surveys supervision. Eighth Yearbook of the Department of Superintendence.* Washington, DC: National Education Association.

Sergiovanni, J., & Starratt, R. J. (1998). *Supervision: A redefinition.* Boston, MA: McGraw-Hill.

Spears, H. (1953). *Improving the supervision of instruction.* Englewood Cliffs, NJ: Prentice-Hall.

Webster's Ninth New Collegiate Dictionary. (1987). Philippines: Merriam-Webster.

Wiles, J., & Bondi, J. (1996). *Supervision: A guide to practice.* Englewood Cliffs, NJ: Prentice-Hall.

Withall, H., & Wood, F. H. (1979). Taking the threat out of classroom observation and feedback. *Journal of Teacher Education*, *30*, 55–58.

Zepeda, S. J., & Ponticell, J. A. (1998). At cross-purpose: What do teachers need, want and get from supervision? *Journal of Curriculum and Supervision*, *14*(1), 68–87.

PART II

POSTMODERN CONCEPTIONS
OF CURRICULUM
AND SUPERVISION

Introduction

In Part II, postmodern curriculum and supervision scholars charge that dominant representations advocated by modernist thinking are contraindicated for maximizing students' learning experiences. They proclaim that postmodernist perspectives offer new lenses through which problems may be viewed as possibilities for reconstruction rather than ills that require symptom relief. Several authors suggest that a synthesis of paradigmatic principles may invite partnerships, communication, and practices that are more humane, equitable, and inclusive. Summoning a call to action to heal the inequities and injustices prevalent in school-based curriculum and supervisory practice, these authors urge the initiation of collegial dialogue. They criticize the organizational structures that mitigate against teacher innovation and that seek to impose sanction or criticism. Instead they espouse understanding classroom and organizational dilemmas and embrace problem-solving, analysis, and authentic dialogue as mechanisms to formulate a reconceptualized view of the work that educators do.

In the first chapter of Part II, Patrick Slattery describes the impact of postmodernism on teaching, research, and representation of curriculum phenomena. Although postmodern theory is beyond definition, he helps readers understand the complexities of this paradigm and how it can be applied to school-based practice. He claims that postmodernism offers a wider and less restrictive way to view the practice of curriculum, one that transcends the boundaries accessible in the modern paradigm. Challenging the authority of modernist tenets that have governed curriculum practice and educational research, Slattery asserts that postmodernism welcomes exposure to the indeterminacy, paradox, and chaos endemic to contemporary classrooms. He argues that students should be permitted to deconstruct, reconceptualize, and define their own educational experiences without the strictures imposed by modernist practice.

Next, James Henderson proposes that critical curriculum theorizing can transform curriculum and teaching practices. Claiming that practice grounded in the modernist rationales can be authoritarian, irrational, unethical, and even unwise, he advocates for curriculum practice that is deliberative, interpretative, and contemplative. He recommends that scholars and practitioners engage in civil dialogue about diverse educational perspectives to formulate visionary and consensually developed curriculum practice. Critical to this aim is the dissolution of hierarchical frameworks that preclude teacher enactment and innovation. Henderson asserts that scholars and practitioners must continually question the relationship between knowledge and power and be willing to dismantle and replace educational practices that impede efforts to enact democracy as a moral way of living. He urges educators to initiate processes necessary to the practice of transformative curriculum leadership.

In Chapter 9, Geneva Gay and Pamula Hart asseverate that postmodernist and multicultural educators are committed to nullifying the modernist practices that seek to promote exclusion, dominance, and marginalization. Suggesting that there is a strong parallel between the goals of postmodernism and multicultural education, they assert that pedagogical actions central to their goals should be an integral part of both teachers' professional development and school-based curriculum practice. To demonstrate how principles of postmodernism can be enacted, they describe seven principles, along with corollary multicultural interpretations and possibilities for teaching-learning activities. Using an interactive format, readers will become engaged in the analysis and deliberation of the practical applications offered. Implementing these ideas, Gay and Hart argue, will require fundamental changes in what constitutes teacher competence, instructional facilitation, and responsiveness to cultural diversity. They claim that authentic movement towards achieving academic equality and social justice for ethnically diverse students will occur when educators are willing to endure the discomfort associated with confronting the inequities prevalent in teacher education programs and school classrooms.

In the next chapter, Duncan Waite and Margarida Ramires Fernandes explore how characteristics of interactions influence the nature of supervision. They assert that the conditions of postmodernity have deepened our understanding of context and the interactional processes between supervisors and teachers. However, they encourage readers to examine both the facilitating and the debilitating aspects of postmodernity. Following an identification of the hallmarks of postmodernism, they describe how postmodernism may affect the nature of supervision. They advocate for the use of the dialogic approach to supervision, in which communication is a negotiated process, mutual critique is invited, and teachers and supervisors work as partners. Waite and Fernandes urge the implementation of supervisory practices that are more inclusive, democratic, and egalitarian.

In Chapter 11, Pat Holland and Maryalice Obermiller suggest that a postmodern approach to supervision must become a contextually based activity that provides pragmatic rather than prescriptive conversations, as well as in-the-moment deliberation and reflection-in-action. Using practice-based scenarios in instructional technology, they describe how concepts of postmodern theory have been enacted to catalyze teachers' professional development and student engagement. Holland and Obermiller depict how supervisory practice guided by postmodernist thinking acknowledges multiple realities of all participants, promotes egalitarian relationships, and preserves the synergy inherent to collective inquiry, while dignifying the individuality of participants.

In the final chapter of Part II, while opposing the modernist claim that truth can be objectified, Edward Pajak and Karen Evans assert that postmodernism offers a more inclusive perspective from which to consider supervision. Many postmodernists have helped to redefine conceptions of leadership, and a broadened view that emphasizes the importance of equity and open communication. However, they also point out that postmodernism provides little practical guidance to assist supervisors in the process of change and inquiry. Using Habermas's theory of communicative action, they illustrate how tenets of modern and postmodernism can be joined together. After identifying the virtues and vices associated with each paradigm, Pajak and Evans suggest that postmodernist thinking can help to cultivate the kind of collaborative and constructive dialogue that is needed in solving contemporary educational issues. They demonstrate how viewing the teacher within the organizational system rather than within the classroom can result in improvement of classroom practices.

7

Postmodernism as a Challenge to Dominant Representations of Curriculum

Patrick Slattery

GUIDING QUESTIONS

1. *What are some of the various interpretations of postmodernism?*
2. *Can there be a postmodern curriculum in the schools?*
3. *How can graduate students use postmodern theory in their research?*
4. *Why do modern critics have such a negative reaction to postmodernism?*
5. *What are some of the positive contributions of postmodern theory?*
6. *After reading this chapter, how has your thinking about curriculum and schooling changed?*
7. *Finally, can the world survive without a postmodern vision?*

This chapter explores postmodern theory and its influence on contemporary curriculum discourses in the university and in schools. Postmodernism challenges dominant modern conceptions of curriculum and supports the emergence of alternative forms of teaching, research, and data representation. There is no singular or simple definition of postmodernism. There are many postmodernisms: literary deconstruction, poststructuralism, postmodern art, eliminative postmodernism, and constructive postmodernism, among others. Some would contend that postmodernism is more of a mood or attitude rather than a cohesive set of principles and practices. I would agree with this analysis. The attempt to define postmodern curriculum theory is difficult, some would say impossible. However, I believe that it is possible to describe and understand many features of postmodern theory and apply these ideas to curriculum. All graduate students and teachers must have some familiarity with emerging postmodern theories because these theories have captured the attention of many educators and researchers in the past fifteen years, greatly influencing curriculum philosophies and practices. Postmodern theories must be engaged, if for no other reason than to develop intelligent and thoughtful critiques of postmodern practices. However, I hope that this chapter will convince you that postmodernism has much to offer the educational community and the global society. In the upheaval and conflict of the modern world, postmodernism may offer a fresh way to look at our sociopolitical, economic, ethical, religious, psychological, ecological and educational dilemmas.

POSTMODERNISM AND DECONSTRUCTION

There has been a postmodern movement in art, architecture, philosophy, science, literature, and education in recent years. Some would say that it started in the 1960s—that it has emphasized eclecticism, parody, irony, indeterminacy, ambiguity, complexity, multiculturalism, and multiple forms of understanding the world and texts. One famous postmodern writer, Jean-François Lyotard, stated that postmodernism is an incredulity toward metanarratives (Lyotard, 1984). In other words, any theory that attempts to provide a universal, all-encompassing narrative of the way that the world works, people should behave, texts should be interpreted, governments should be structured, schools should be organized, or art should be produced must be examined, questioned, and deconstructed. Let's explore this important concept of deconstruction.

Contemporary approaches to research in the reconceptualized curriculum field[1] utilize postmodern theories and multiple forms of representation in order to challenge status-quo social arrangements that are destructive and unjust. Thus, many postmodernists foreground cultural studies, autobiography, arts-based inquiry, critical pedagogies, radical democracy, anti-racism, feminisims, and ecology—among other issues. Postmodern curriculum research and teaching challenges singular interpretations of data and singular methodologies for curricular organization, thus encouraging an informed eclecticism in the teaching and research process. This is done for a variety of reasons. Some postmodern theorists seek to expose the contradictions, limitations and self-serving ideologies found within hegemonic social structures[2] and universalizing metanarratives derived exclusively from propositional language and statistics. This is accomplished by deconstruction—a strategy for reading texts and data that exposes internal contradictions and power relations—or hermeneutics—the art and process of interpretation of texts—or poststructural analysis—a philosophical commentary that exposes both the political consequences and linguistic difficulties of clear expression by decentering the authority of texts (Lather, 1991; Marshall, 1992; Pinar, Reynolds, Slattery & Taubman, 1995; Sarup, 1989).

In short, what we see in postmodern theory is an attempt to expose contradictions and prejudices that are found in every written text and human artifact. There is no text that contains the whole truth and nothing but the truth. Various history books present different interpretations of the same historical events. Catholics and Protestants argue over which books to include in the Christian Bible—not to mention the addition of other gospels by the Gnostics and the Book of Mormon by the Latter-Day Saints church. Even within various religious denominations there are schisms because people interpret sacred books differently.

Various works of art have been either praised or censured depending on the aesthetic sensibilities of the critic, curator, or government official. Impressionism, for example, was scoffed at by art "experts" in the nineteenth century but sold for millions of dollars in the twentieth century. There is no agreement about historical, religious, athletic, musical, artistic, or educational interpretations, practices, and styles—and there never will be. In the 1960s the backward high-jump style was banned by the International Olympic Committee only to become the standard in the 1970s—the Fosbury Flop. Jackie Robinson broke the color barrier in major league baseball under protest by many in the white establishment, but his success paved the way for integration of sports. Igor Stravinsky's first production of "The Rite of Spring" in Paris in 1913 was halted by an audience riot; the music was unsettling to the sophisticated connoisseurs. By the 1930s Stravinsky was hailed as a musical genius, and "The Rite of Spring" was used by Disney in the cartoon animation "Fantasia." Elvis Presley, The Beatles, Kurt Cobain, Marilyn Manson, Ice T, Rage Against the Machine: the list of controversial musicians whose work was critiqued or banned by authorities and later appreciated is endless. In education the philosophy of John Dewey, Maria Montessori, and others has been maligned and later revered. Oscar Romero, Martin Luther King, Jr., and Dietrich Bonhoeffer were all assassinated. Rosa Parks was imprisoned. Helen Keller was belittled for being politically naive and then sentimentalized and trivialized. Visionaries and prophets are often rejected by their contemporary societies. For postmodernists, metanarratives that attempt universalization are foolhardy, dangerous, and unjust—in part because they silence the voices of opposition, creativity, change, and prophecy.

Modern systems from the Enlightenment to Marxism to Newtonian physics have sought and promoted absolute and universal truth and natural laws. Postmodernism does not deny truth, but rather holds that there are many truths and shifting conceptions of truth, beauty, goodness, and knowledge. Postmodernism does not seek to destroy truth, only to deconstruct modern notions of metanarratives that attempt to explain a universal and unalterable truth for all people in all circumstances. This is a brief introduction to the important notion of deconstruction, which is a central feature of many postmodern theories.

DEFINING POSTMODERNISM

Just as the world has entered a new millennium, American education enters a new era. Educators are uncertain what to call it, but almost everyone agrees that, like the world, education has changed and continues to change at an accelerating rate. While modernism continues to exert its influence on social and educational practices, a new impulse has developed. Some call it "postmodernism" or "the postmodern condition." What complicates the term, beside its assimilation of the word "modernism," is that postmodernism has yet to replace modernism but now exists concurrently alongside it.

Understanding the failures of the medieval ways of seeing the world, modernist thinkers sought new methods to understand and control the outside environment. In due time, Cartesian science became a foundation for this new impulse, as science set out to make sense of complex phenomena by reducing them to their constituent parts before analyzing them in detail. Following this scientific orientation, an analogous socioeconomic feature of modernism came into being: capitalism with its insistent faith in the benefits of science and technology, its doctrine of progress, its cult of reason, and its logic of organization that would culminate in an authoritarian empirical science and an assemblyline mentality in the twentieth century.

Postmodernism, then, has something to do with questioning these modernist tenets and with the establishment of a new paradigm—that is to say, a new way of seeing the world. More specifically, postmodern observers analyze those social assumptions previously shielded by the modernist ethos. They admit previously inadmissible evidence, derived from new questions asked by previously excluded voices; they challenge hierarchical structures of knowledge and power that promote "experts" above the "masses," and they seek new ways of knowing that transcend empirically verified facts and "reasonable" linear arguments deployed in a quest for certainty (Slattery, 1995; Best and Kellner, 1997).

When it is based on a critical democratic system of meaning concerned with analyzing knowledge for the purpose of understanding oneself and one's relation to society, naming and then changing social situations that impede the development of egalitarian communities committed to economic and social justice, and understanding how world views and self-concepts come to be constructed, postmodernism provides a powerful tool for progressive social and educational change (Giroux, 1991; Kincheloe, 1991).

To understand the nature of education as it takes place in both schools and cultural sites, we must understand the nature and effects of the postmodern condition. First of all, be careful to avoid confusing postmodernism as a social critique with postmodernism as a social condition ("hyperreality" is a familiar synonym for "the postmodern condition"). To describe the emerging new era I use the postmodern critique to isolate the special features of the postmodern social condition. The postmodern critique and the postmodern condition may be closely connected, and in the attempt to distinguish them, many educators get lost in the landscape. Modernists fail to understand that they no longer tell their stories from an omniscient perspective, but being human, they must now tell human stories from a particular social and historical vantage point. Reason was undermined; it was usurped by those in power who spoke with the authority of a disembodied science unrestrained by self-analysis (Giroux, 1991).

POSTMODERN PARADIGMS

Exploring postmodern paradigms offers an opportunity for scholars to provide new visions to address the tragedies of recent history that have not been ameliorated in the modern era—the Holocaust, slavery, genocide, environmental degradation, racism, apartheid, homophobia, nuclear destruction, political and religious inquisitions and persecution, child labor abuses, colonialism, vulgar materialism, economic class warfare, and other absurdities of the modern era.[3] Many scholars contend that postmodern visions not only deconstruct the logic and philosophies that have contributed to worldviews that foster a climate for these tragedies but also provide an alternative to such destruction. Some go further and insist that the postmodern vision of curriculum research and classroom practices can influence changes that will lead to justice. As we explore possible postmodern alternatives, we must constantly be reminded of Derrida's (1972) clarification, "I was quite explicit about the fact that nothing of what I have said had a destructive meaning. [Deconstruction] has nothing to do with destruction. [I]t is simply a question of . . . being alert to the implications, to the historical sedimentation in the language we use—and that is not destruction" (p. 271). I agree. We must be vigilant in our efforts to deconstruct all texts—including postmodern texts themselves—because there are ambiguities, internal contradiction, and prejudice within every narrative and text.

Another concern of postmodernists is the way that intolerance and tyranny are perpetuated in the name of reason and certainty, and they seek to redress unjust power arrangements and maximize democratic participation (Harroway, 1997; Pinar, 1997). Constructive postmodernists seek to create a just, caring, and ecologically sustainable culture in the aftermath of modernity and deconstruction (Bowers, 1997; Griffin, 1988; Orr, 1992). Some postmodern scholars foreground liberatory ethics—following from liberation theology—to challenge the complicity of social and economic arrangements in sustaining status-quo power arrangements (McLaren, 1997). Finally, moderate postmodernists combine modern and postmodern discourses and interpret the postmodern primarily as a modality of the modern rather than a radical rupture or paradigm shift (Harvey, 1989; Rorty, 1991). While the variety of postmodernisms confounds critics, as I said at the outset, there remains no concise or singular definition of postmodern research. However, postmodernism does provide a powerful tool for progressive social and educational change when it is tied to a critical democratic system of meaning, the identification of injustice, action to challenge hegemonic social structures, and appreciation of multicultural worldviews.

MULTIPLE UNDERSTANDINGS

Postmodernism is itself understood in multiple ways. Poststructuralism and deconstruction, as associated with names such as Derrida, Deleuze, Foucault, Guattari, Jameson, Lacan, and Kristeva, open the possibility of criticizing the theories, institutions, and practices that are culpable in the brutalization of contemporary life. Critical and cultural theorists such as Anyon, Apple, Carlson, Fine, Giroux, hooks, Kincheloe, McLaren, Steinberg, and West utilize postmodern theories to promote antiracist, antihomophobic, and liberatory social and educational practices. The poststructural and feminist perspectives of Britzman, M. A. Doll, Ellsworth, Grumet, Lather, Noddings, Pagano, Pinar, and Sears foreground gender in the postmodern dialogues. In contrast to Lyotard, who critiques the notion of grand narratives, constructive postmodernists such as Griffin, Kung, W. E. Doll, and Jencks create a narrative that interfaces with emerging ecumenical and liberation theologies to construct a just, caring, and ecologically sustainable culture in the emerging historical epoch. In the postmodern spirit, some researchers utilize an eclectic mix of these and other theories to propose a radically new vision of art, music, literature, philosophy, and education. Critics who attempt to universalize or harmonize all postmodern theories are operating within the modern obsession with control and reason.

Postmodernism is a complex set of reactions to modern philosophy and its presuppositions rather than any consensus on substantive doctrines. Thus, it is impossible to universalize postmodern curriculum practices for research and schooling. However, postmodernism does typically challenge foundationalism, essentialism, and realism. For Rorty (1989) the presuppositions to be set aside are foundationalist assumptions shared by sixteenth- to eighteenth-century philosophers. For Nietzsche, Heidegger, Foucault, and Derrida, the presuppositions to be set aside are as old as metaphysics and Plato. Some, such as Lyotard (1992) and Griffin (1988), have even suggested that postmodern philosophy preceded modern philosophy in the sense that the presuppositions of philosophical modernism emerged out of a disposition whose antecedent beliefs are postmodern. For Lyotard this might include a sense of the interconnectedness of the universe rather than the fragmentation of information into fields of study. Lyotard (1984) explains:

Didactics does not simply consist in the transmission of information; and competence, even when defined as a performance skill, does not simply reduce to having a good memory for data or having easy access to a computer. It is a commonplace that what is of utmost importance is the capacity to actualize the relaxant data for solving a problem "here and now," and to organize the data into an efficient strategy. As long as the game is not a game of perfect information, the advantage will be with the player who has knowledge and can obtain information. By definition, this is the case of a student in a learning situation. But in games of perfect information, the best performativity cannot exist in obtaining perfect information in this way. It comes rather from arranging the data in a new way in what constitutes a "move" properly speaking. This new arrangement is usually achieved by connecting together series of data that were previously held to be independent. This capacity to articulate what used to be separate can be called imagination. (p. 51–52)

Here Maxine Greene's (1995) conclusion that the principles and the contexts of education have to be chosen by living human beings against their own life-worlds and in the light of their lives with others, "by persons able to call, to say, to sing, and—using their imaginations, tapping their courage—to transform" (p. 198) is affirmed. Constructive postmodernism seeks such transformation.

While the postmodern movement in education and philosophy certainly has affinities with opposition to the spectator theory of knowledge that emerged in Europe before the term "postmodern" became common-place—such as Dewey's early opposition to positivism, Wittgenstein's insistence on the language-game character of representation, and Sellars critique of "the myth of the given"—current postmodern thought moves beyond such opposition. Griffin's (1988) *The Reenchantment of Science* and Greene's (1995) *Releasing the Imagination* both provide examples of such a transformation. I argue along with Lyotard (1984) that modern movements—in society and in curriculum research—are efforts to return to terror:

It must be clear that it is our business not to supply reality but to invent allusions to the conceivable which cannot be presented. . . . We have paid a high enough price for the nostalgia of the whole and the one, for the reconciliation of the sensible, of the transparent and the communicable experience. We can hear the mutterings for a desire for a return of terror. . . . let us wage war on totality. (pp. 81–82)

The postmodern curriculum, in Lyotard's spirit, wages war on totality of representation that reduces learning to information transmission, disciplinary structures, grand narratives, and concepts of "reason" that continue to foster the bifurcations that perpetuate racism, patriarchy, environmental degradation, homophobia, colonialism, and classism. The postmodern curriculum refuses to be bound by rigid modern bifurcations and the divisive linear logic that follows.

POSTMODERN DISCOURSES

The concepts of the death of the author (Derrida, 1976, 1981) and the death of the subject (Foucault, 1972a, 1972b, 1975, 1977) foreground self-deception and the limitations and contradictions of truth statements by individuals, thus revealing a "fictional self" capable of many complex meanings rather than an "authentic self" capable—in the Enlightenment sense—of being wholly knowable and rational. In other words, we never fully "know" ourselves because we are always in the process of learning and are continually influenced by many complicated factors that we are not even consciously aware of. Thus, the idea of a singular author or a cohesive individual is impossible because we are all made up of a complex interrelationship of many people and ideas.

Postmodernism repudiates depth models of psychology that provide a body of disciplinary knowledge to explain the world while assuming to remain detached and objective—thus, we cannot escape our context and speak with absolute certainty.

It rejects grand narratives or universal explanations of history that propose to have the whole story and final solution because there are many different versions of any event, depending on who is telling the story and from what vantage point (Lyotard, 1984).

Postmodernism points to illusion of the transparency of language, where words are merely signs always pointing with precision to the signified object (Foucault, 1983). Thus, the possibility of linguistic certainty is eliminated because ambiguity and uncertainty will always be present as words have many interpretations and nuances.

It sees a communication and media revolution in which the distinction between reality and the word or image which portrays it breaks down into a condition of hyperreality and signs—"simulacra"—which come to replace reality (Baudrillard, 1988).

The impossibility of any final meaning to any idea arises because words have no fixed or stable relationship to the concepts or things that they are meant to signify—the meaning of words can only be described by more words—meaning is endlessly deferred (Derrida, 1976).

The effects of power on the objects it represents (Ellsworth, 1997; Rouse, 1987) is associated with "Identity Politics"—movements that represent the empowerment and civil rights agenda of groups marginalized by their racial, gender, sexual, physical, and other identities—and "Queer Theory"—philosophies that investigate notions of identity by "refusing normal practices and the practice of normalcy," by "exploring those things that education either dismisses or cannot bear to know," and by "imagining a sociality unhinged from the dominant conceptual order" (Britzman, 1995). Queer Theory can be understood as protesting the idea of "normal" behavior, emphasizing instead diverse forms of individual and social identity.

Postmodernism considers the failure of pure reason to understand the world (Pinar, 1997) along with the importance of intuition, emotion, arts, and spirituality in understanding complex issues.

It looks to the de-centering of the Western logos and with it the dethroning of the "first world" so that multicultural global communities are validated along with Western cultures (Banks and Banks, 1997).

It foresees the end of a belief in progress as a natural and neutral panacea that assumes that things are always getting better as a result of technology or communication (Bauman, 1992; Lyotard, 1992).

It sees a celebration of difference and multiplicity, leading to a revolutionary multiculturalism that unites critique and action in liberatory practices (Giroux, 1997; McLaren, 1997) and affirms diversity from an antiracist position (Nieto, 1996) as we move toward equity in both the process and outcomes of education (Gay, 1994).

This brief introduction to some of the postmodern concepts may seem difficult. However, remember that any new idea is often challenging. Think of great musicians, sports figures, educators, scientists, religious leaders, and inventors, like those introduced earlier, whose creative work was ridiculed or rejected because it challenged long-held beliefs and practices. Just as Copernicus and Galileo provided a new perspective on the position of the Earth in the universe over five hundred years ago, twentieth-century space exploration and photographs of the Earth from space have provided a stunning perspective of the relation of human life to the cosmos. The Italian religious and political leaders who silenced and excommunicated Galileo did not stop the emergence of the modern cosmology, so why should we expect negative reactions to silence the emerging postmodern worldview?

RESEARCH REPRESENTATION

Now that we have looked closely at various postmodern discourses, let's examine the implications for curriculum and research in the schools and university.[4] As many universities explore alternative forms of research and data representation in both undergraduate and graduate education programs, a number of important questions are raised about the nature of educational research by postmodern inquiry. Ellis (1997) contends that the "crisis of representation provoked by postmodernism challenges some of our most venerable notions about scientific knowledge and truth" (p. 115), which in turn results in a loss of faith in the theory of language as a clear and concise economy of writing on which scientific inquiry has been based. Ellis explains that the postmodern critique undermines any social science research devoid of intuition and emotions and questions the usefulness of rigid disciplinary boundaries that separate the humanities, social sciences, natural sciences, and the arts. Eisner (1997) recently presented the "promise and perils" of alternative forms of representation, particularly as related to arts-based research:

One of the basic questions scholars are now raising is how we perform the magical feat of transforming the contents of our consciousness into a public form that others can understand. The assumption that the language of the social sciences—propositional language and number—are the exclusive agents of meaning is becoming increasingly problematic, and as a result, we are exploring the potential of other forms of representation for illuminating the educational worlds we wish to understand. . . . The concept of alternative forms of data representation presents an image that acknowledges the variety of ways through which our experience is coded. (p. 4)

I support Eisner's critique of the hegemony of propositional language and number in educational research—as well as McLeod's (1987) insistence that word, number, image, gesture, and sound are all equally valid forms of research representation and Lawrence-Lightfoot and Davis's (1997) development of "portraiture" as an alternative method of inquiry blending aesthetics, narrative, and empiricism in order to capture the complexity, dynamics, and subtlety of experience and school life. These multiple approaches to educational research in the realm of the visual, literary, psychoanalytic, musical, and theatrical arenas must be encouraged and legitimated not just in the academy but also in research practices in classrooms and in schools. Traditional social science research in both quantitative and qualitative varieties is no more or less rigorous, insightful, or useful than informed eclectic postmodern alternatives. Novellas, plays, musical compositions, film documentaries, narratives, allegories, paradigm parables, portraitures, readers theater, art installations, or multimedia projects can be valid forms of research and data representation (Diamond and Mullen, 1999). Their validity is reflected partly in what Eisner (1994) calls "structural corroboration"— the interpretation of data corroborated by the way in which all artifacts support one another consensually—and "referential adequacy"—a phenomenological experience of the object of study in a new, more adequate way (pp. 236–242).

However, postmodern theories provide additional ways to understand and validate contemporary curriculum research. Lather (1991, 1997), for example, contends that validity refers to how we are able to improve the lives of those we study. Lawrence-Lightfoot (1983) and Lawrence-Lightfoot and Davis (1997) remind us that validity in art is not based on replication and generalizability, but rather demands the idiosyncratic, anecdotal, and autobiographical. Kincheloe (1991) even suggests that "validity is probably an inappropriate word in the non-positivistic context" (p. 135), preferring to assess the trustworthiness of postmodern educational research by examining the credibility of portrayals of constructed realities.[5] Kincheloe (1991) writes:

Our goal in research is not merely to validate the statistical relationship of variables, but it is to understand, to make intelligible, and to preserve the cohesiveness of the phenomenon being studied. . . . This process may better be accomplished by portraying patterns rather than by discovering causes. As a result, a researcher may be more concerned with choosing a language where signification and the concern with meaning take precedence over statistical significance. (p. 133)

Kincheloe conceives of critical postmodern research as more emotionally empathetic and artistic with an emphasis on participant reflection.

Richardson (1994) argues that the debates about contemporary educational research and multiple forms of data representation emerge from postmodern theory:

The core of postmodernism is the doubt that any method or theory, discourse or genre, tradition or novelty, has a universal and general claim as the "right" or privileged form of authoritative knowledge. Postmodernism suspects all truth claims of masking and serving particular interests in local, cultural and political struggles. . . . No method has a privileged status. The superiority of [social] science over literature—or from another vantage point literature over [social] science research—is challenged. (p. 517)

While considerable attention has been given to debates about the merit of quantitative versus qualitative research methods, postmodern inquiry challenges the superiority of any methodology and exposes the contradictions in traditional methods of identifying issues for inquiry, selecting modes of analysis, and inscribing data into transmittable form. Postmodernism situates the researcher and the research subject in a historical and social context where knowledge is co-produced between the two, with results that are always contingent, tentative, and open to further interpretation. Since there are multiple ways of knowing and interpreting data, discovering a universal transcendent truth outside of a specific context—or for that matter a replicable and final solution to any research question—is impossible. Postmodernism resists the positivist urge for universal and unalterable objectivity, contending instead that we come to understanding through experiences that *evoke* rather than simply *represent* and *replicate*.

Jipson and Paley (1997) write, "As forms of this newer kind of practice continue to erupt in multiple ways, in multiple locations, for multiple reasons, inside and outside the grids of defined research categories, the sphere of scholarly inquiry has become an extraordinary animated site for a diverse and experimental analytic production by a number of thinkers not hesitant to situate inquiry in a vaster epistemological space" (p. 3). Tierney and Lincoln (1997) contend that we must provide such multiple forms of data representation for multiple audiences because "multiple texts, directed toward research, policy, social change efforts, or public intellectual needs . . . may better represent both the complexity of the lives we study, and the lives we lead as academics and private persons" (p. xi). They conclude that "how we present our work, and to whom, is more up for grabs today than at any other time in this century" (p. vii). Postmodern curriculum discourses contribute to our understanding of the multiplicity, complexity, and ongoing paradigm struggle in education.

Some scholars argue that the bifurcation of progressive education versus postmodern education only makes sense within the framework of modern dualisms. For example, Carlson (1995) reconceptualizes the terms "progress" and "progressivism" from a postmodern perspective:

A new democratic discourse can only be built by constructing some provisional notion of directionality in social development, and thus some idea of progress. Of course, such an idea of progress cannot be grounded on a linear, monolithic, or overly predetermined sense of direction. Rather, progress in a postmodern sense must be consistent with the notion of "bricolage," the path laid down by walking [as in the open-ended anthropological research of Claude Levi-Strauss]. (pp. 337–338)

Carlson concludes, along with many postmodern theorists, that democratic progressivism in education will have to live with certain tensions, ambiguities, chaos, and contradictions that are not fully resolvable. Working comfortably within ambiguity and complexity rather than lusting after certainty and reason is a postmodern response to questions of progress and justice.[6]

CURRICULUM IMPLICATIONS

The general field of curriculum, the field interested in school subjects, the relationship between school subjects, and the relationship between the curriculum and the world, is no longer preoccupied with development—writing behavioral objectives, evaluating with standardized tests, proposing universal school reform practices, and so on. "The field today is preoccupied with *understanding*. To understand curriculum does not mean that many of us do not want to change curriculum, both theoretically and institutionally; we do want change. However, many degrees of complexity have entered our conception of what it means to do curriculum research. In general, we are no longer technicians" (Pinar, et al., 1995, p. 6, emphasis in original).[7] Postmodern curriculum research, as exemplified here, does not have a direct application to school subjects or a causal relationship with schooling practices. Rather, postmodernism contributes to school reform by reconceptualizing the very nature of the debate and allowing educators to challenge assumptions and envision alternative possibilities for change. Direct classroom applications emerge from within a specific *context* rather than from the imposition of universal principals.[8]

As an example, consider the curricular reform initiative of block scheduling. I have served as a consultant for many school districts investigating scheduling alternatives, and I attempt to help educators understand that changing a time schedule does not directly correlate with curricular improvement. Some teachers and students flourish in the new block schedule, others languish. Experiences of time are complex and diverse. Unlike time management experts who present school districts with universal methods of organizing instruction, as well as expensive software and training guides for implementing block scheduling, my goal is to help educators explore the philosophy of time and multiple scheduling alternatives within the context of their local community. We must investigate the philosophical nature of time and visions of time and space before attempting to impose a comprehensive scheduling reform in schools. However, too often educators attempt to reform before they reflect. I have witnessed many schools in turmoil after quickly adopting a block schedule only to encounter unexpected—and sometimes unresolvable—conflicts after implementation of the program. This results from the modernist assumption that a universal solution to the question of time and space allocation actually exists.[9]

Postmodern discourses can empower educators to explore and envision the complexity and ambiguity of schools and society and their interrelationship. This creates an approach to research and representation called "a general economy of writing" by Bataille (1991). He explores open-ended questions and the "excesses of energy" produced by inquiry. Thus, ambiguity and uncertainty become integral to the research process. Bataille challenges the model of an "efficient economy of writing" in modern scientific inquiry, because it destroys the possibility of meaning making.

POSTMODERN IMPLICATIONS FOR CURRICULUM

As noted in the poststructural concept of "the death of the subject," the cohesive, unified identity of an individual that is fully capable of self-presence is an illusion of modern rational thinking and the scientism of modern psychology. Descartes' *Cogito* continues to be undermined as postmodern psychology investigates the nature of language and human existence. Sarup (1989) contends that the autonomous subject has been dispersed into a range of plural, polymorphous, subject-positions inscribed in language, thus emphasizing diverse forms of individual and social identity. Bakhtin (1993) locates "self" within the dialogue between self and others, creating a relationship of simultaneity in difference. Wang (1997) explains, "The self, while distinguishable to itself, is always seen in relation to others and to the world of lived experience. At the same time, for Bakhtin, the sense of self is not only relational, but unfixable. . . . self is engaged in its continuous becoming and transforming" (p. 20). Usher and Edwards (1994) present the postmodern case when they contend that the idea of self-presence as perfect representation is replaced by the "decentered subject, where the subject of consciousness, the reasoning, thinking, transparent subject, is displaced by the opaque subject of the unconscious" (p. 57).

What might this mean for educational research and classroom practices in the university and in K–12 schooling? Usher and Edwards (1994) offer this insight:

[I]t is impossible to be a teacher without also being a learner, that in order to be a teacher it is first necessary to abandon the position of the "one who knows," recognising both one's own lack of knowledge and of self-transparence and mastery and that one's own learning is never, and never will be, complete. (p. 80)

It follows here that the distinction between teachers and students is never so clear-cut as it is conventionally assumed, particularly in schools. Postmodern theorists such as Usher and Edwards contend that psychoanalysis provides the means to reconceptualize this aspect of authority in the teacher-student relationship. However, this deconstruction does not imply an advocacy of chaos in the classroom without any structure or a move to destruction. On the contrary, it means the discovery of limits, ambiguity, contrasts, multiplicity, irony, layers of interpretations, uncertainty, and shades of differences. Teachers and students must therefore continue the learning process indefinitely and defer final explanations. Usher and Edwards (1994) explain:

It is important to stress that what we are talking about here is not the humanistic conception of "lifelong learning" as the continual adaptation to the needs of the existing
socio-economic order. Nor is it merely a restatement of the notion of learner centeredness. . . . Rather it is an argument for teachers to continually question the ground upon
which they stand, to question their own ready implication in the discourse of mastery.
For this, teachers need to be trained to analyse what is repressed in order to foreground
the affects, release the emotions [and imagination], and broaden the sense of fulfillment. The pupils would then be allowed to extend their analysis to their environment.
To create the space they live in rather than just fit in with the set rules. Literally. To
paint. To build. To co-operate. To participate. The limit then would be the analysis of
the transference. (p. 80)

Here Usher and Edwards address the critiques of postmodernism directly.
They admit that postmodern theories resonate with certain strands of progressive education but without its teleology of emancipated free expression and its
containment within the overall framework of modernist educational theory
and practice. They write that psychoanalysis in the Lacanian mode, then, is itself radically self-subversive and a process that does not simply examine its own
ground but systematically cuts the ground away from itself.

What I propose is that the very concept of expertise, like Lyotard's grand
narratives, Usher and Edwards' all-knowing teacher, and Eisner's hegemony
of propositional language and number in educational research must all be vig-
orously challenged. In order for this to occur, autobiographical, psychoanalytic, phenomenological, aesthetic, and multicultural perspectives must be
foregrounded. Thus, postmodern researchers explore new lines of inquiry in
this vein, aware of the necessity of deconstructing both traditional methodologies and postmodern inquiry itself. These are uncharted territories. Postmodern curriculum research is therefore often dismissed as nonconformist,
unverifiable, unreliable, or simply incomprehensible.

As postmodern curriculum discourses move to expand research practices,
alternative forms of representation such as phenomenological narratives, arts-
based experiences, and autobiographical excavations are being utilized. Jipson
and Paley (1997) describe this current research climate:

Increasingly, this production has pushed beyond conventional formulations and has
linked the construction of research knowledge to alternate models of representation including performance art, personal conversation, nonobjective artistic practice, asigni-
fying presentation, journal entry, dream narrative, deep subjectivity, and fictional
production. . . . It is about efforts to re-create structures and disclosures of knowledge
that are responsive to, but unconstrained by, the weight of traditional research protocols. (p. 3)

CONCLUSION

The postmodern curriculum is challenging the modernist assumptions
about the meaning and validity of educational research, as well as traditional

teaching and learning practices. As students are allowed to deconstruct and re-conceptualize education within the postmodern paradigm, they carry this capacity for complexity back into their schools and classrooms—no longer fearful that the chaos, paradox, and indeterminancy they experience must be suppressed or erased. As more and more educators are empowered to explore alternative forms of representation within a postmodern context, reconceptualization will continue to characterize our schools and research communities. With Tierney and Lincoln (1997), I concur that research philosophies and methodologies are dramatically changing in the postmodern era and are more inconclusive than at any time in this century.

Case Study 7: Resisting Traditional Approaches to Curriculum Implementation

A graduate student in one of my classes who studied the concepts of curriculum presented in this chapter appreciated my perspective, but she could not imagine implementing a postmodern classroom. Her principal demanded daily lesson plans with specific outcomes outlined in the curriculum guide. The district administered proficiency tests in math, reading, science, and English. Her tenure depended on how well her students performed on these tests, and her pay scale followed a merit system that rewarded compliance with the traditional program. She resented the environment the system created, but she saw no realistic chance to deviate. Additionally, her students behaved so disruptively and their participation was so sporadic that she doubted they would accept a contextual and experiential curriculum. In short, she considered postmodern curriculum philosophy too idealistic and impractical. But for her final course project she explored the possibilities. Since the district did not test social studies and since most teachers skipped the thirty-minute social studies block to spend more time on the "important" subjects, she decided to experiment with her relatively safe social studies curriculum. She videotaped her lessons for a two-week unit on deserts. Instead of writing lesson plans in advance with specific objectives and evaluation requirements, she introduced the lesson with this simple statement: "Today we begin our next unit in social studies. Our topic is deserts." Bored and distracted faces appeared on the video. A few took notes. Most sat silently waiting for instructions. Then she dropped her bombshell: "I do not know very much about deserts. I have never been to a desert. We are going to have to figure out how to learn about deserts together." Immediately, one student raised his hand. "I went to a desert in California last summer." He described his trip enthusiastically, but he struggled to remember the name of the desert. Another student suggested that they look at a map and find its name. The class moved to the map. Another student pointed to Africa and said that her father once went hunting on a safari. "What's a safari?" another student asked. The class consulted to the dictionary to find the answer. Over the next few days, the students decided to divide themselves into groups to investigate deserts. One group selected animals of the deserts. They made a small-scale model of a desert and a safari. Another group made maps of the various deserts of the world. Other groups investigated plant life, human habitation, and survival. The teacher reported that she had never seen such enthusiasm for a unit of study in her career. Students who formerly presented severe behavior problems emerged as group leaders. Another group of students went to the library every day at recess to find more information about their topics. She became convinced of the power of the postmodern ideas and reconceptualized curriculum when she completed this experimental project. The maps and models of deserts were displayed in the corridor and caught the attention of other teachers. I suspect that she will find ways to resist a steady dose of the traditional approach to curriculum and instruction in the future. Is this an example of postmodern curriculum? I do not know. However, it was one teacher's attempt at implementing the things she had learned in her graduate class on postmodern theory. She began to shift her way of viewing curriculum as she deconstructed the modern curriculum in her school district.

FOLLOW-UP QUESTIONS

1. Do you have any beliefs that you consider to be absolutely true? What should be done about people who hold a different view than yours?

2. Some people believe that their religious text contains the absolute truth. Should there be only one Bible with only one interpretation for all Americans? For all human beings? And if so, which one? Can we affirm and celebrate the diversity of religious beliefs, political philosophies, sexual orientations, ethnic customs, racial heritages, and linguistic patterns in the world? What does postmodern theory teach us that can allow us to affirm diversity without splintering into warring factions?

3. Can the same be said for historical interpretation, teaching methods, and curriculum philosophies? Is there a metanarrative that applies to teaching and learning? Or are there multiple styles, approaches, methods, techniques, and outcomes?

4. What distinguishes postmodern theories from progressive education, social reconstruction, and critical pedagogy?

5. How might postmodern theory influence your school and classroom? What changes in your teaching could you make in order to move toward a postmodern vision? Was the fourth-grade teacher in the case study above actually moving toward a postmodern vision?

NOTES

1. See chapter four of William F. Pinar, William M. Reynolds, Patrick Slattery, & Peter M. Taubman, *Understanding curriculum: An introduction to the study of historical and contemporary curriculum discourses* (New York: Peter Lang Publishers, 1995) for a review of the reconceptualization of the curriculum field from 1970 to 1979.

2. I use the term hegemony here to mean ideological social control imposed on the general population either by force or psychological manipulation by power elites in business, the media, government or other institutions.

3. A good example of this phenomenon is the censoring of the Enola Gay exhibit at the Smithsonian Air and Space Museum in Washington, DC in 1995. See Martin Harwit, *An Exhibit Denied: Lobbying the History of the Enola Gay* (New York: Copernicus, 1996) and John Weaver, Patrick Slattery, & Toby Daspit, "Museums and Memory: Toward a Critical Understanding of the Politics of Space and Time" (*JCT: The Journal of Curriculum Theorizing*, 1998, *14*(4), forthcoming).

4. At this point you may want to revisit the discussion "Defining Postmodernism" in this chapter that set the stage for this discussion.

5. Kincheloe offers two dimensions of critical postmodern validity in *Teachers as Researchers: Qualitative Inquiry as a Path to Empowerment* (New York: Falmer Press, 1991). The first is Credibility of Portrayals of Constructed Realities. "Critical researchers reject the positivistic notion of internal validity which is based on the assumption that a tangible, knowable reality exists and research descriptions accurately portray that reality. The world is not explicable in terms of simplistic cause-effect relationships. The universe can be viewed from multiple perspectives which are constructions of the human mind. There is no absolute benchmark to which we can turn for certainty and comfort—we award credibility only when the constructions are plausible to those who constructed them" (p. 136). The second is Anticipatory Accommodation. "Here critical constructivist researchers reject the positivistic notion of external validity. The ability to make pristine generalizations from one research study to another again accepts a one-dimensional, cause-effect universe. Time or context factors are irrelevant in the positivistic context. If we accept a Piagetian notion of cognitive constructivism, we begin to see that in everyday situations humans don't make generalizations in this positivistic way. Piaget's notion of accommodation seems appropriate in this context as it asserts that humans reshape cognitive structures to accommodate unique aspects of what is being perceived in new contexts. We learn from our comparisons of different contexts. Researchers will always have to decide whether a research generalization is relevant to a particular student, whether the generalization needs to be fine tuned to accommodate the student's uniqueness, or whether the generalization is irrelevant to certain students in certain classrooms" (pp. 135–136). Kincheloe concludes that the notion of validity is transcended because the way we compare our action research to other groups is more in terms of a heuristic (a means of furthering investigation, questioning our practice) rather than in terms of mathematical probability. And what is ultimately the purpose of reconceptualizing the notion of validity? Kincheloe, like other postmodern theorists, turns to the notion of power. The hegemony of number and propositional language in positivist research creates a dominant ideology that blocks our recognition of exceptions and attempts to modify the assimilated understandings of the world of education. Postmodern research is necessary, I contend, in order to challenge modern ideologies and offer different ways of understanding education.

6. See Patrick Slattery and Marla Morris, "Simone de Beauvoir's Ethics and Postmodern Ambiguity: The Assertion of Freedom in the Face of the Absurd" (*Educational Theory*, *49*(1) 21–36) for a detailed analysis of postmodern ambiguity as related to notions of freedom and justice.

7. My commitment to justice and improvement in schooling and society inspires my work as a teacher and researcher. I often use the phrase "just, caring, and ecologically sustainable" to describe my vision of educational communities. I believe that understanding more so than prescriptive problem-solving in the modernist tradition will effect such change. This is true despite the ranting of recent critics like Constas and McCarty, who contend that postmodernists are more interested in maintaining the pretense of avant-garde theorizing than in promoting the value of practical change in education.

8. See Joe L. Kincheloe, Shirley R. Steinberg, & Patrick Slattery, *Contextualizing Teaching* (New York: Longman Publishing, 2000) for an analysis of the postmodern emphasis on context in teaching and research.

9. See Patrick Slattery "Postmodern visions of time and learning: A response to the national education commission report Prisoner of Time" (*Harvard Educational Review*, 65(4), 612–633) for a detailed review of this issue.

REFERENCES

Bakhtin, M. (1993). *Toward a philosophy of the act.* (Holquist, M., & Liapunov, V., Eds.). Austin, TX: University of Texas Press.

Banks, J. A., & Banks, C.A.M. (1997). *Multicultural education: Issues and perspectives* (3rd ed.). Boston: Allyn and Bacon.

Bataille, G. (1991). *The accursed share*, vol. 1. New York: Zone Books.

Baudrillard, J. (1988). *Selected works* (M. Poster, ed.). Cambridge: Polity Press.

Bauman, Z. (1992). *Intimations of postmodernity*. London: Routledge.

Best, S., & Kellner, D. (1997). *The postmodern turn*. New York: Guilford Press.

Bowers, C. A. (1997). *The culture of denial: Why the environmental movement needs a strategy for reforming universities and public schools*. Albany: State University of New York Press.

Britzman, D. P. (1995). "Is there a queer pedagogy? Or, stop reading straight." *Educational Theory*, 45(2), 151–165.

Carlson, D. (1995). Making progress: Progressive education in the postmodern. *Educational Theory*, 45(3), 337–357.

Derrida, J. (1972). Discussion: Structure, sign and play in the discourse of the human sciences. In R. Macksey & E. Donato (Eds.), *The structuralist controversy* (pp. 247–272). Baltimore, MD: Johns Hopkins University Press.

Derrida, J. (1976). *Of grammatology*. Baltimore: Johns Hopkins University Press.

Derrida, J. (1981). *Positions*. Chicago: University of Chicago Press.

Diamond, C.T.P., & Mullen, C. A. (Eds.). (1999). *The postmodern educator: Arts-based inquiries and teacher development*. New York: Peter Lang.

Eisner, E. W. (1994). *The educational imagination: On the design and evaluation of school programs* (3rd ed.). New York: Macmillan.

Eisner, E. W. (1997). The promise and perils of alternative forms of data representation. *Educational Researcher, 26*(6), 4–10.

Ellis, C. (1997). Evocative autoethnography: Writing emotionally about our lives. In W. G. Tierney and Y. S. Lincoln (Eds.), *Representation and the Text* (pp. 115–142). Albany: State University of New York Press.

Ellsworth, E. (1997). *Teaching position: Difference, pedagogy, and the power of address*. New York: Teachers College Press.

Foucault, M. (1972a). *Power/knowledge*. New York: Pantheon.

Foucault, M. (1972b). *The archaeology of knowledge*. New York: Pantheon.

Foucault, M. (1975). *Discipline and punish*. New York: Pantheon.

Foucault, M. (1977). *Language, counter-memory, practice*. Ithaca, NY: Cornell University Press.

Foucault, M. (1983). *This is not a pipe* (J. Harkness, trans.). Berkeley: University of California Press.

Gay, G. (1994). *At the essence of learning: Multicultural education*. West Lafayette, IN: Kappa Delta Pi.

Giroux, H. A. (1997). *Pedagogy and the politics of hope: Theory, culture, and schooling*. Boulder, CO: Westview Press.

Giroux, H. A. (Ed.). (1991). *Postmodernism, feminism, and cultural politics: Redrawing educational boundaries.* Albany: State University of New York Press.

Greene, M. (1995). *Releasing the imagination.* New York: Teachers College Press.

Griffin, D. R. (1988). *The reenchantment of science: Postmodern proposals.* Albany: State University of New York.

Harroway, D. (1997). *Modest_ witness @ second_ millennium.femaleMan_ meet_ oncomouse TM: Feminism and technoscience.* New York: Routledge.

Harvey, D. (1989). *The condition of postmodernity.* Oxford: Blackwell.

Jipson, J., & Paley, N. (Eds.). (1997). *Daredevil research: Re-creating analytic practice.* New York: Peter Lang.

Kincheloe, J. L. (1991). *Teachers as researchers: Qualitative inquiry as a path to empowerment.* New York: Falmer Press.

Lather, P. (1991). *Getting smart: Feminist research and pedagogy with/in the postmodern.* New York: Routledge.

Lather, P., & Smithies, C. (1997). *Troubling the angels: Women living with HIV/AIDS.* Boulder, CO: Westview/HarperCollins.

Lawrence-Lightfoot, S. (1983). *The good high school: Portraits of character and culture.* New York: Basic Books.

Lawrence-Lightfoot, S., & Davis, J. H. (1997). *The art and science of portraiture.* San Francisco: Jossey-Bass.

Lyotard, J.-F. (1984). *The postmodern condition: A report on knowledge.* (G. Bennington and B. Massumi, trans.). Minneapolis: University of Minnesota Press.

Lyotard, J.-F. (1992). *The postmodern explained to children: Correspondences 1982–1984.* London: Turnaround.

Marshall, B. K. (1992). *Teaching the postmodern.* London: Routledge.

McLaren, P. (1997). *Revolutionary multiculturalism: Pedagogy of dissent for the new millennium.* Boulder, CO: Westview Press.

McLeod, J. (1987). The arts and education. In J. Simpson (Ed.), *Education and the arts.* Edmonton, Alberta: Fine Arts Council, Alberta Teachers' Association.

Nieto, S. (1996). *Affirming diversity: The socio-political context of multicultural education.* New York: Longman.

Orr, D. W. (1992). *Ecological literacy: Education and the transition to a postmodern world.* Albany: State University of New York Press.

Pinar, W. F. (1997). Regimes of reason and the male narrative voice. In W. G. Tierney and Y. S. Lincoln (Eds.), *Representation and the text* (pp. 81–113). Albany: State University of New York Press.

Pinar, W. F., Reynolds, W. M., Slattery, P., & Taubman, P. M. (1995). *Understanding curriculum: An introduction to the study of historical and contemporary curriculum discourses.* New York: Peter Lang.

Richardson, L. (1994). Writing: A method of inquiry. In N. K. Denzin and Y. S. Lincoln (Eds.), *Handbook of qualitative research* (pp. 516–529). Thousand Oaks, CA: Sage.

Rorty, R. (1989). *Contingency, irony, and solidarity.* Cambridge: Cambridge University Press.

Rorty, R. (1991). *Objectivity, relativism, and truth.* Cambridge: Cambridge University Press.

Rouse, J. (1987). *Knowledge + power: Toward a political philosophy of science.* Ithaca, NY: Cornell University Press.

Sarup, M. (1989). *An introductory guide to post-structuralism and post-modernism*. Athens: University of Georgia Press.

Slattery, P. (1995). *Curriculum development in the postmodern era*. New York: Garland.

Tierney, W. G., & Lincoln, Y. S. (Eds.). (1997). *Representation and the text*. Albany: State University of New York Press.

Usher, R., & Edwards, R. (1994). *Postmodernism and education*. New York: Routledge.

Wang, H. (1997). Curriculum as polyphonic authoring: A pedagogy through the "loophole." *JCT: Journal of Curriculum Theorizing, 13*(4), 20–24.

8

Informing Curriculum and Teaching Transformation through Postmodern Studies

James G. Henderson

GUIDING QUESTIONS

1. *What is the balanced perspective of affirmative postmodernism?*
2. *What are the deliberative, interpretive, and contemplative dimensions of curriculum understanding?*
3. *What is descriptive, skeptical, and reconciliative work in postmodern studies, and how does this work inform curriculum understanding?*
4. *What is James Macdonald's perspective on curriculum studies?*
5. *What eight curriculum fundamentals are central to the consideration of systemic educational reform?*
6. *Can you briefly summarize this chapter's illustrative premodern, modern, and postmodern interpretations of these eight curriculum fundamentals?*
7. *What is transformative curriculum leadership practice?*
8. *What is transformative curriculum leadership praxis?*

INTRODUCTION: AFFIRMATIVE POSTMODERNISM

As one who engages in curriculum scholarship, I write from the perspective of affirmative postmodernism, which is well-summarized by Rosenau (1992): "Affirmative post-modernists frequently employ terms such as oppression, exploitation, domination, liberation, freedom, insubordination, and resistance—all of which imply judgment or at least a normative frame of reference in which some definitive preferences are expressed" (p. 136). As an affirmative postmodernist, I am critical of all antimodern positions. I feel fortunate to be born in a culture that has been deeply influenced by the "Enlightenment" projects of Rene Descartes, John Locke, Thomas Hobbes, and many other "modernists." I feel thankful that I live in a society that has, in part, been structured by a Constitution that has its genesis in the "Age of Reason." However, I am not completely satisfied with the critical heritage of Enlightenment. I want to retheorize the critical spirit of that era and encourage a curriculum and teaching transformation that is informed by this theoretical work. I agree with Palmer's (1998) balanced assessment of the modern era:

I have not forgotten that objectivism originated, in part, to save us from the evils of reckless subjectivity. The victims of the Black Death would have benefited from the objective knowledge that their suffering was caused by fleas from infected rats, not by offenses against God. The countless women burned at the stake because someone called them witches bear mute testimony to the cruelties that subjectivity can breed. Objectivism set out to put truth on firmer ground than the whims of princes and priests, and for that we can be grateful. But history is full of ironies, and one of them is the way objectivism has bred new versions of the same evils it tried to correct (p. 52).

Let's acknowledge the advances in human emancipation fostered by Enlightenment reason, but let's also get on with our emancipatory efforts (Whitson, 1991). Much more liberatory work needs to be done.

Within the limited pages of this chapter, I can only provide the broad parameters of my critical curriculum theorizing and its implications for curriculum and teaching transformation. As a curriculum scholar whose work is informed by postmodern studies, I recognize that I am writing from a particular epistemological standpoint—not from a "God's eye" view of reality (Flax, 1995). Therefore, I will begin by briefly explaining how I got started on my critical journey. As an undergraduate, I studied a great deal of French literature and philosophy. I still remember reading Descartes' (1969) philosophy and feeling deeply disturbed by his rational epistemology. At the time I couldn't say why; but as the years unfolded, I began to understand my discomfort. I was experiencing my own attempts at living a "rational" life as too narrow, and I was increasingly perceiving the "rationality" of the political and educational leaders who were impacting my life as dangerously flawed. I felt confused on how best to free myself to live a good and deeply satisfying life; and I felt the elders of my "tribe" were unhelpful and even harmful. Whether it was President Lyndon Johnson's explanations of why Indochina should be a killing field for Americans, Vietnamese, and others or my first school principal's argument that I comply with the school district's instructional goals, I found their rationales deeply authoritarian, irrational, unethical, and unwise.

I felt something was wrong with "modern" reason and, at first intuitively, I set out on a journey to examine alternative ways of living a "reasonable" life. I must leave out the many personal details of this journey and focus instead on the current results of my inquiries. Over the years, I have gravitated to a particular philosophical referent for the "good" life: *Human wisdom is cultivated by a robust deliberative, interpretative, and contemplative understanding.* In the context of curriculum theorizing, I agree with Pinar, Reynolds, Slattery, and Taubman (1995) that "curriculum" guided by artifacts of modern reasoning, such as the Tyler Rationale (Tyler, 1949), is seriously limited and dehumanizing. I believe that curriculum needs to be understood in terms of its multifaceted deliberative, interpretive, and contemplative dimensions. Pinar and associates (1995) write: "And you thought curriculum was what the district office required you to teach, or what the state education department published in scope and sequence guides, or, if you are yet to teach, a list of books you were to read. As you know now, curriculum incorporates those literal and institutional meanings, but it is by no means limited to them" (p. 847).

Curriculum Understanding

Space provides me with only a limited opportunity to discuss the interrelated deliberative, interpretive, and contemplative dimensions of curriculum understanding. I begin with curriculum deliberation, which has been insightfully discussed by a host of scholars, including Dewey (1922), Schwab (1969, 1971), Walker (1971), and Reid (1978). Drawing on this literature tradition, McCutcheon (1995) describes curriculum deliberation as a collaboration over educational means and ends in a context of conflicting ideological interests and in light of diverse possible outcomes and moral consequences. She writes: "A deliberative approach is a decision-making process in which people, individually or in groups, conceive a problem, create and weigh likely alternative solutions to it, envision the probable results of each alternative, and select or develop the best course of action" (McCutcheon, 1995, p. 4). McCutcheon (1999) analyzes several case studies of curriculum deliberation and provides the following recommendations for curriculum leaders:

- Carefully consider group dynamics and composition.
- Establish settings that encourage thoughtful deliberation.
- Allow for sufficient deliberative time.
- Foster inclusive dialogue.
- Maintain a problem-solving task orientation.
- Actively facilitate communication. (pp. 44–45)

Curriculum interpretation is elucidated by the tradition of philosophical hermeneutics. Smith (1991) provides a concise account of this tradition:

The hermeneutic imagination constantly asks for what is at work in particular ways of speaking and acting in order to facilitate an ever-deepening appreciation of that wholeness and integrity of the world which must be present for thought and action to be possible at all. . . . The hermeneutic modus has more the character of conversation than, say, of analysis and the trumpeting of truth claims. When one is engaged in a good conversation, there is a certain quality of self-forgetfulness as one gives oneself over to the conversation itself, so that the truth that is realized in the conversation is never the possession of any one of the speakers or camps, but rather is something that all concerned realize they share in together. (pp. 197–198)

Pinar and associates (1995) signal the hermeneutic features of their curriculum understanding when they write: "Curriculum is an extraordinarily complicated conversation" (p. 848).

Robust curriculum interpretation occurs whenever educational stakeholders with diverse perspectives engage in a civil discourse that touches on both the letter and the spirit of their respective points of view. Sears (1998) provides a vivid example of this civil curriculum discourse as a group of educators, representing a broad range of ideological positions, discuss a set of controversial educational issues. The refreshing openness and civility of their educational dialogue is nicely captured by one of the religious conservatives in the group: "Because a fundamental tenet of Christianity is salvation by genuine, voluntary belief in Jesus Christ, one of the conclusions that a true biblical fundamentalist must come to is that he has no right—ever—to impose by force his beliefs onto another person even if it might seem the expedient thing to do. A true historical fundamentalist is a person who believes in the exchange of ideas through persuasion, not pressure" (Sears, 1998, p. 46).

Curriculum deliberation and interpretation are deepened by contemplative inquiries, for this latter form of disciplined understanding helps educational stakeholders become attuned to the broad moral visions that underlie their deliberative and interpretive work. Curriculum contemplation addresses the normative side of educational thinking and feeling—the consideration of what Dewey (1938/1963) characterizes as an "end in view." Eisner (1994) describes curriculum norms as "images of educational virtue" (p. 35); and he notes that without careful normative inquiry, education lacks a "rudder" (p. 35). Curriculum contemplation can result in many forms of visionary consensus-building, including school mission statements. Sergiovanni (1992) argues that grassroots curriculum contemplation, what he terms the building of an educational "covenant," is central to wise educational leadership:

When purpose, social contract, and local school autonomy become the basis of schooling, two important things happen. The school is transformed from an organization to a covenantal community, and the basis of authority changes, from an emphasis on bureaucratic and psychological authority to moral authority. To put it another way, the school changes from a secular organization to a sacred organization, from a mere instrument designed to achieve certain ends to a virtuous enterprise. (p. 102)

Relevant Postmodern Cultural Study

My views on the deliberative, interpretive, and contemplative dimensions of curriculum understanding have been informed by *descriptive, skeptical,* and *reconciliative* work in postmodern studies. The descriptive work helps clarify the value of curriculum deliberation, the skeptical work offers insight into the art and politics of curriculum interpretation, and the reconciliative work illuminates curriculum contemplation.

Hargreaves (1994) announces the descriptive purpose of his postmodern analysis by distinguishing between postmodernity and postmodernism:

My prime concern in this book is with *postmodernity*, not *postmodernism*. *Postmodernism* is an aesthetic, cultural and intellectual phenomenon. It encompasses a particular set of styles, practices and cultural forms in literature, music, architecture, philosophy and broader intellectual discourse—pastiche, collage, deconstruction, absence of linearity, mixture of periods and styles and the like. *Postmodernity*, by contrast, is a social condition. It comprises particular patterns of social, economic, political and cultural relations. From this standpoint, postmodernism is part of the broader phenomenon of postmodernity. It is a component and a consequence of the postmodern social condition. In many ways, postmodernism is an *effect* of postmodernity. (p. 38)

Applying his general descriptive analysis of postmodernity to the study of teachers' occupational setting, Hargreaves (1994) concludes that teachers' work in the future must become grounded in authentic deliberation and collaboration. He writes: "Processes of inquiry, analysis, information gathering and other aspects of learning how-to-learn in an engaged and critical way become more important as goals and methods for teachers and schools in the postmodern world" (p. 57). Teachers must become the sources, not the targets of curriculum deliberation (Sirotnik, 1989). The managerial binary, *curriculum development/instructional implementation*, must be deconstructed, replaced by an emphasis on teacher enactment: "From the enactment perspective, curriculum is viewed as the educational experiences jointly created by student and teacher. The externally created curricular materials and programmed instructional strategies . . . are seen as tools for students and teacher to use as they construct the enacted experience in the classroom" (Snyder, Bolin, and Zumwalt, 1992, p. 418). In a word, educators must begin to practice sophisticated forms of curriculum deliberation both in and outside the classroom. If they don't, there will increasingly be a "disconnect" between their rationalized work settings and the emerging postmodern society around them (Hargreaves, 1994). Modern public schooling will increasingly lose its justification, to be replaced by voucher programs and other educational alternatives (Mathews, 1996).

The *skeptical* work in postmodern studies emerge in analyses of the relationship between knowledge and power. Flax (1995) writes that: "Without power, there can be no practice; yet, in practice, power and . . . right do not always converge. The problem, then, is to discover knowledge which will enable us to exercise power appropriately" (p. 147). Slattery (1995) clearly documents how we have entered an historical era where many philosophers and other people are questioning the value of living by universal principles. He notes that this skepticism is clearly articulated in the work of the French cultural critic, Jean Francois Lyotard:

Integral to postmodernism is the critique of reason, totality, universal principles, and metanarratives. . . . [T]his critique is clearly articulated in the work of Jean Francois Lyotard. In the text *The Postmodern Condition*, Lyotard (1984) challenges Enlightenment notions of totality and argues that postmodernism is inseparable from an incredulity toward metanarratives. What are these metanarratives? For Lyotard, they are unified historical narratives and overarching philosophies of history. Examples would be the Enlightenment concept of the gradual but steady progress of reason and freedom . . . and Karl Marx's drama of the forward march of human productivity and class conflict resulting in proletarian revolution. The postmodern era will reject these and other modern metanarratives because their . . . theories propose that knowledge, truth, and justice exist independent of contingent, historical practices. (pp. 36–37)

As Flax (1995) notes, there are a variety of reasons why postmodern skepticism has so much credence today—at least in academic circles. She points out that Western political-economic dominance is under challenge by Japan and other countries, by nationalist and anticolonialist movements in the Third World, by the women's movement, and by antiracist critics. A central topic in these diverse critical challenges is the interrogation of "eurocentrism," a broad term that refers to the way European countries, and European-influenced countries such as the United States, have dominated global policies and practices in the modern era. Harding (1998) defines eurocentrism:

Central among the presuppositions of eurocentric discourses are that peoples of European descent, their institutions, practices, and favored conceptual schemes, express the unique heights of human development. Moreover, peoples of European descent and their civilization are presumed to be fundamentally self-generated, owing little or nothing to the institutions, practices, conceptual schemes, or peoples of other parts of the world. These assumptions have organized in different ways in the last several hundred years—but especially since the eighteenth century—economic, political, historical, legal, geographical, archeological, sociological, linguistic, anthropological, psychological, pedagogical, literary, art historical, philosophical, biological, medical, and technological institutions and their practices. (p. 14)

Postmodernists want to question eurocentrism because of the ways in which these "institutions, practices, and favored conceptual schemes" overtly and covertly undermine personal and social justice.

Postmodern skepticism is deeply "reflexive" in the sense that this line of critical questioning acknowledges that not only all human knowledge can be questioned, but even the critical questions themselves can be challenged. Lawson (1985) writes:

The post-modern predicament is indeed one of crisis, a crisis of our truths, our values, our most cherished beliefs. A crisis that owes *reflexivity* its origin, its necessity, and its force. Reflexivity, as a turning back on oneself, a form of self-awareness, has been part of philosophy from its inception, but reflexive questions have been given their special force in consequence of [the deep metanarrative questioning of our current era]. . . . Our concepts are no longer regarded as transparent—either in reflecting the world or conveying ideas. As a result all our claims about language and the world—and implicitly all our claims in general—are reflexive in a manner which cannot be avoided. (p. 9)

Concerning the reflexivity that lies at the heart of postmodern skepticism, Harding (1998) writes that postmodernists must "acknowledge for [themselves] . . . the same critical standards [they propose] for everyone else's knowledge systems" (pp. 20–21). They must also recognize that their criticisms are also only standpoints—that no one can escape from, or transcend, the historically and culturally "situated" nature of human knowing (Anderson, Reder, and Simon, 1996).

If educators continually question the relationship between knowledge and power, if they continually engage in postmodern skepticism with its embedded reflexivity, how do they function without paralyzing themselves or becoming moral relativists? Flax (1995) writes that people who practice this type of criticism are required to "grow up" and realize that there are no final guarantees for anything that humans do (p. 163). She adds that this is done through "a sense of tolerance, empathy, friendly concern, and even benign indifference." (p. 163). She states that postmodernists reject big-picture fantasies and utopias and, instead, work with a deep sense of humility and a healthy dose of irony. Slattery (1995) writes that curriculum stakeholders who engage in postmodern skepticism are willing to celebrate "the diverse and complex understandings within each unique context" (p. 243). They are willing to alter modern educational structures as necessary, and they tackle fundamental issues of educational service without becoming sidetracked by institutional maintenance concerns. They seek opportunities for curriculum debate that focuses on "the development of autobiographical, aesthetic, intuitive, and . . . [visionary] experience" (Slattery, 1995, p. 257). They want to discuss "the socio-cultural and sociopolitical relations emerging from an understanding of the individual in relation to knowledge, other learners, the world, and ultimately the self" (Slattery, 1995, p. 257).

The *reconciliative* work in postmodern studies can be found in the many calls for a renewed moral feeling—for a reintegration of important subjective and objective features of moral purpose. This line of analysis criticizes the hierarchical compartmentalization of human knowing that occurred during the Enlightenment era. Palmer (1998) criticizes the end result of this epistemological balkanization in higher education: "Any way of knowing that requires subjective involvement between the knower and the known is regarded as primitive, unreliable, and even dangerous. The intuitive is derided as irrational, true feeling is dismissed as sentimental, the imagination is seen as chaotic and unruly, and storytelling is labeled as personal and pointless. That is why music, art, and dance are at the bottom of the academic pecking order and the 'hard' sciences are at the top" (p. 52). In a similar vein, Eisner (1994) notes

the negative impact of modern epistemology on pre K-12 public educational policy:

The tendency to separate the cognitive from the affective is reflected in our separation of the mind from the body, of thinking from feeling, and the way we have dichotomized the work of the head from the work of the hand. What might seem at first to be abstract distinctions that have little bearing upon the real world in which we live turn out to shape not only our conception of mind but our educational policies as well. Students who are good with their hands might be regarded as talented, but seldom as intelligent. Those who are emotive, sensitive, or imaginative might have aptitudes for the arts, but the really "bright" go into mathematics or the sciences. In some states those who are considered intelligent, as defined by their IQ, receive state funds to enhance their educational development. Those who are merely "talented" do not. Such distinctions in policy and in theory do not, in my view, do justice either to the children or to the society. (pp. 23–24)

Postmodern commentators who address the negative consequences of modern rationality argue that the reconciliation of human cognition, emotion, and spirituality would open the door for a deeper, loving embrace of life in its diverse and interrelated manifestations. Their arguments generally occur in two interrelated steps. They first note the crises of the Enlightenment heritage and then offer solutions based on an integration of humanity's premodern mythic and modern rational capacities (Hatab, 1990). They call for a reenchantment of the world in ways that would not resurface premodern superstition, dogmatism, and tribalism. Kesson (1999) writes:

In modernity, humans have supposedly overcome their earlier reliance on myth, magic, and superstition as organizing principles, as well as their "embeddedness" in nature. The world, as historian Morris Berman (1981) and others have pointed out, has now become "disenchanted." We have become fully conscious human beings (the story goes), employing reason, logic, empiricism, and abstract thinking to gain power and control over the forces of nature. (p. 87)

Kesson (1999) then notes that the price of this modern Faustian bargain has been personal alienation, social anomie, environmental destruction, patriarchal oppression, and colonialist exploitation. Her solution is to incorporate mythopoetic ideas and activities into educational practices. She wants teachers to validate their students' emotions, creative capacities, and sacred sense of selves.

Borgmann (1992) argues that humanity is at an important historical crossroads. Either people begin to reconstruct a renewed sense of communal purpose based on an inclusive understanding of human diversity and passion, or they will increasingly experience the ills of a "hypermodernism" characterized by a stressful life of information overload, technical narrowness, materialistic compulsion, cultural kitsch, and restless faddism. Borgmann (1992) describes the endpoint of a hypermodern knowing:

At length it will lead to a disconnected, disembodied, and disoriented sort of life. The human substance will be diminished through a simultaneous diffusion and individuation of the person. Hyperintelligence allows us to diffuse our attention and action over ever more voluminous spaces. At the same time, we are shrinking to a source of instructions and finally to a point of arbitrary desires. Hyperintelligence is neither a total nor an unavoidable overlay on the real world and human intelligence. It is obviously growing and thickening, suffocating reality and rendering humanity less mindful and intelligent. (pp. 108–109)

Based on this cultural critique, Borgmann argues for a "patient vigor for a common order centered on communal celebrations" (p. 116). He wants people to engage their minds and bodies in ways that center their lives, and he wants people to undertake these personally meaningful activities in a social context of public ritual and ceremony. Borgmann's solution resonates with Greene's (1988) affirmation of people's capacity to engage in responsible and authentic self-direction. Greene (1988) characterizes this capacity as the "positive freedom" of democratic societies, which "comes into being when individuals come together in a particular way, when they are authentically present to one another (without masks, pretenses, badges of office), when they have a project they can mutually pursue" (p. 16).

Curriculum and Teaching Practice

My curriculum study interests have led me to embrace a particular perspective on curriculum and teaching practice. I see curriculum and teaching as the opportunity to enact *democracy as a moral way of living*. Macdonald (1975) creates an analogy that can be adapted to my point of view: "[In light of] Dewey's comment that educational philosophy was the essence of all philosophy because it was 'the study of how to have a world,' curriculum theory . . . might be said to be the essence of educational theory because it is the study of how to have a learning environment" (p. 12). To extend Macdonald's analogy into the realm of educational practice: If curriculum theorizing is "the study of how to have a learning environment," then curriculum and teaching practices are the enactment of this learning environment. Drawing on my curriculum study work, which I have briefly presented in this chapter, I understand *democracy as a moral way of living* as the daily practice of a robust deliberation, interpretation, and contemplation. This is the learning environment that interests me.

Over the years, I have learned to introduce this learning environment perspective in three inquiry steps: (1) examining systemic curriculum and teaching reform in the context of specific premodern, modern, and postmodern paradigm shifts; (2) studying the possibility of initiating a particular transformative curriculum leadership (TCL) practice; and (3) considering ways of deepening this TCL practice into a praxis—critically informed reform practice. I turn now to a brief explanation of each of these inquiry steps.

SYSTEMIC CURRICULUM AND TEACHING REFORM
AND PARADIGM SHIFTS

Sarason (1990) argues that educational reform inevitably fails unless systemic change efforts are undertaken. Reformers must approach education as a complex system with many interrelated components. They can't develop new program designs, new teaching practices, new forms of assessment, or other educational matters without considering the interrelationship of all aspects of curriculum and teaching practice. They must think about educational change in ecological terms (Eisner, 1992), or else their efforts will be short-lived and faddish in nature—the proverbial "pendulum swing" of educational reform. I use Sarason's argument as an important organizer in a *Fundamentals of Curriculum* graduate course that I regularly teach. I invite students to study the basics of curriculum, the way a naturalist would study a particular ecological niche. They are asked to think about the interrelationships between eight facets of comprehensive curriculum and teaching work: educational philosophizing (ideological positioning), program designing, classroom planning, teaching, evaluating, organizing instruction, enacting power relations, and continuing professional development.

Upon completing this general "ecological" study of curriculum fundamentals, I then ask the graduate students to think about systemic educational reform across three distinctive "paradigmatic" frames of reference: premodern, modern, and postmodern. The *premodern* frame of reference focuses on: (1) the dissemination of knowledge through religious expertise; (2) homogeneous social and cultural values; and (3) small, authoritarian community school operations. The *modern* frame of reference focuses on: (1) the dissemination of knowledge through scientific expertise; (2) heterogeneous social and cultural values in a homogeneous "melting pot" context; and (3) large, rationally managed school operations. The *postmodern* frame of reference focuses on: (1) co-constructing knowledge through collaborative inquiry; (2) heterogeneous social and cultural values in a multicultural educational context; and (3) small, diversified community school operations.

The guide for this examination of three particular, systemic paradigmatic shifts is the 3×8 matrix in Table 8.1. The suspension periods (. . .) in the table refer to the possible "language game" (Wittgenstein, 1953) amplification of any cell in the matrix. For example, "true belief" in the matrix's first cell could be expanded to include "born-again Christian" convictions; "rational efficiency" in the second cell could be supplemented with a discussion of effective school behaviors, including the establishment of pupil performance goals; and "reflective dialogue" could be amplified by a discussion of participatory democracy and civil discourse.

When introducing these three "paradigms" of curriculum and teaching practice to graduate students, I point out that the study of the *postmodern* frame of reference must also include an examination of the *premodern* frame of reference for two important reasons. First of all, the serious consideration of

Table 8.1
Three Curriculum and Teaching Paradigms

Fundamentals of Comprehensive Practice and Systemic Reform	"Premodern" Frame	"Modern" Frame	"Postmodern" Frame
Educational Philosophizing (Ideological Positioning)	True Belief; Parental Control; Family Values; Ethnic Identity; Authoritarian Rule; Subjectivism . . .	Rational Efficiency; Work Diversification; Comprehensive School Settings; Scientific, Objective Rationality . . .	Reflective Dialogue with Diverse Others; Inquiry-based Collaboration; Multiliterate Rationality . . .
Program Designing	Maximize Respect for and Rule of Authority . . .	Maximize Test Achievement; Achieve Efficient and Fair Student Sorting . . .	Foster Multi-intelligent Expression Encourage Equity, Pluralism and Civility . . .
Classroom Planning	Classical Authoratative Texts	Subject Specialization (Math & Science Dominated) . . .	Curriculum Integration . . .
Teaching	Text-Centered . . .	Test-Centered . . .	Thinking-Centered (Constructivist) . . .
Evaluating	Memory Examinations . . .	Standardized Achievement Tests . . .	Public Exhibits and Defenses of Expressive Outcomes . . .
Organizing Instruction	Small: Homogeneous Communities . . .	Bureaucratic Specialization . . .	Small: Heterogeneous Communities . . .
Enacting Power Relations	Communal; Tribal; Authoritarian; Power-over . . .	Highly Structured; Diversified Roles; Power-over . . .	Collaborative; Dia-logical; Power-with . . .
Continuing Professional Development	Study of Great Ideas; Classics, Biblical Subjects . . .	Study of Efficient Techniques, Cybernetics . . .	Study of Curriculum Deliberation, Interpretation, Contemplation . . .

any "postmodern" understanding of education is, in part, based on a critique of the modern, rationally managed twentieth-century school. To entertain this critique opens the door for premodern as well as postmodern deliberations, interpretations and contemplations. Second, as illustrated in Table 8.1, there are some interesting conceptual and political parallels between particular premodern and postmodern frames of reference. For example, as I have noted earlier in this chapter, many postmodern cultural study projects incorporate premodern concerns about moral and mythopoetic knowing. Sears (1998) writes:

Postmodernism, then, is best understood by its relationship to the concept of modernism—itself born pointing its finger at the limitations of spirituality, prayer, and faith in the unseen. As metaphysical oversoul, modernism sought to improve humankind's ability to confront problems. Rooted in the realization that medieval beliefs were no longer adequate to deal with practical problems, modernism has its intellectual foundation in Enlightenment figures, such as Descartes, Bacon, and Newton, who invited a timid peasantry to understand, predict, and control their physical environment. Wedding nascent capitalism, rugged individualism, and democratic liberalism, modernism via science and technology displaced feudal lords with industrial barons and temple priests with laboratory scientists. Postmodernism shares with premoderns its distrust of modernist claims of scholarly objectivity and scientific truth and their resulting predispositions toward state control or planning and the inevitability of social or technological progress. (p. 52)

INITIATING A PARTICULAR TRANSFORMATIVE CURRICULUM LEADERSHIP PRACTICE

The next step in my work with graduate students is to ask them to consider the possibility of becoming a "transformative curriculum leader" (Henderson and Hawthorne, 1995, 2000). This leader is defined as a curriculum stakeholder (student, teacher, parent, administrator, local community resident, or other) who collaboratively undertakes a systemic, postmodern educational reform based on the following interpretations of the above eight curriculum basics:

- *Educational Philosophizing*: Students are educated to become people who can think for themselves, who can engage life imaginatively and fully as lifelong learners, and who can embrace democracy as a vibrant way of living.

- *Program Designing*: Curriculum stakeholders create a guiding, open-ended blueprint for the enactment of the above sophisticated education. This blueprint includes a platform of curricular beliefs, programmatic articulations, teaching-learning scenarios, and assessment plans.

- *Classroom Planning*: With due respect for diverse teaching styles as well as diverse student learning styles, teachers collaboratively plan specific teaching-learning contexts (courses, units, lessons, and so on) with their peers and/or with their students.

- *Teaching*: Teachers enact the specific teaching-learning transactions. This work requires a professional artistry that can be cultivated through continuing reflective inquiries.

- *Evaluating*: Curriculum stakeholders collaboratively deliberate over who establishes assessment policies, what will be the primary focus of the assessment activities, how the data gathering and analysis will occur, what criteria will be used to judge the data, and who participates in the assessment activities. Evaluative activities are enacted in accordance with these deliberations.

- *Organizing Instruction*: Curriculum stakeholders collaboratively deliberate over the organizational structures in which the teaching-learning transactions are embedded. Based on these deliberations, they enact specific organizational development activities.

- *Enacting Power Relations*: Curriculum stakeholders work to establish personal trust and power sharing interactions.

- *Continuing Professional Development*: Teachers are held accountable for their continuing creative, caring, critical, contemplative, and collegial reflective inquiries. Transformative curriculum leaders establish and sustain professional support groups while initiating and reviewing specific reform projects.

Those graduate students who express an interest in TCL work are then asked to create an action research plan and, if politically feasible, to enact this plan in their work setting. This action research work is usually quite delicate and requires a certain amount of progressive local administrative and university-based support (Hackney and Henderson, 1999).

TURNING TRANSFORMATIVE CURRICULUM LEADERSHIP PRACTICE INTO A PRAXIS

The final step in my work with graduate students is to encourage the enactment of a TCL *praxis*, which is defined as a critically informed practice. This complex professional development step requires students to question their TCL practices in light of critical curriculum theorizing and, in reciprocal fashion, to interrogate their theoretical studies in light of their practical TCL experiences. As Seigfried (1996) notes, "realigning theory with praxis" (p. 21) is a central feature of the emancipatory work of the "classical" American pragmatic philosophers, a group that includes Charles Sanders Peirce, William James, Josiah Royce, John Dewey, and George Herbert Mead. This work requires both a *critical knowledge* of the root causes of human oppression, exploitation, and domination—the term "critical" is derived from the Greek *krisis*, referring to a judgment as to what constitutes the source of a disease—and *progressive* action to ameliorate and/or eradicate these root causes.

Pinar and associates (1995) present a wide range of curriculum theory projects that can serve this critical pragmatic purpose. Their book is organized around emancipatory work on the political, racial, gender, phenomenological, poststructural, autobiographical, aesthetic, theological, institutional, and international subtexts of curriculum practice. They celebrate the multitextual understanding that results from this comprehensive curriculum study:

Thanks to political scholarship we are clear that we must see the curriculum as an ideological document in the reproduction of power. . . . To understand curriculum politically leads us to racial and gender investigations (and they lead back to politics), as both sets of representations function to distribute knowledge and power differentially. Phenomenological, aesthetic, autobiographical and theological experience both expresses political privilege and undermines it. International understandings of curriculum help us to bracket the taken-for-granted, and the intertextual understanding of curriculum that the reconceptualized field offers can lead us to ask, with greater complexity and sophistication, the traditional curriculum questions: what knowledge is of most worth? What do we make of the world we have been given, and how shall we remake ourselves to give birth to a new social order? (p. 866)

Henderson and Kesson (1999) provide concrete guidance on how transformative curriculum leaders can tap into this rich, multidimensional tradition of curriculum theorizing. After providing an overview of transformative curriculum reform guided by democratic ideals, this edited book introduces four curriculum theory projects that foster TCL praxis. Each project provides specific guidance on how a particular form of "emancipatory" curriculum theorizing can inform day-to-day democratic curriculum work. The first project addresses *curriculum deliberation* and focuses on how to free educational stakeholders from top-down, rational management mandates through on-the-site collaborative decision-making. The second project addresses *reflexive systems* and focuses on how to free educational stakeholders from the limited, linear rationality of bureaucratic planning and control (an artifact of the modernist paradigm in education) through "interpretive" systems thinking informed by chaos, complexity, and narrative theorizing. The third project addresses *democratic cultural criticism* and focuses on how educational stakeholders can challenge unjust and dominating power structures. The fourth project addresses *educational mythopoetics* and focuses on how educational stakeholders can free themselves from the alienating and disenchanting effects of modern technical and bureaucratic life. Collectively, these four projects address the three liberatory dimensions of curriculum *understanding* that have been discussed in this chapter: deliberation, interpretation, and contemplation.

CONCLUDING CASE STUDY

I end this chapter by presenting a brief case study that is designed to foster the three inquiry steps I have just presented. Again, these three steps are: (1) examining systemic curriculum and teaching reform in the context of specific premodern, modern, and postmodern paradigm shifts; (2) studying the possibility of initiating a particular TCL practice; and (3) considering ways of deepening this TCL practice into a praxis. After presenting this case, I conclude with a set of five questions that encourage an application of the case study to the work of systemic curriculum and teaching reform.

Case Study 8: Assuming the Transformative Curriculum
Leadership Challenge

Karen McCleary is beginning her second year as principal at Candle Elementary School. Karen is excited about her position, not so much because she finds administrative work enjoyable but because she has the opportunity to encourage fundamental curriculum and teaching reform.

Karen agreed to take the Candle principalship for two important reasons. She has fifteen years of teaching experience in the school district, serving as teacher union president for four of these years. In this latter capacity, she established a good working relationship with the district's administrative team, especially the superintendent. She was able to work on a variety of progressive projects, establishing a good political base for educational reform work. However, she felt limited in her presidential role because she lacked the positional authority to help bring about deep-seated systemic reform. She wanted to dive deeper into the challenges of educational change. While taking graduate education courses for her administrative certificate, Karen had decided to pursue a Ph.D. in Curriculum and Instruction at a local university. As part of her doctoral studies, which she has not yet completed, she studied ways to foster a particular postmodern curriculum and teaching transformation. She wanted to begin to integrate this theoretical work into her daily practices.

As Karen is driving to Candle for the first day of the new school year, she reflects on the three steps of effecting curriculum and teaching transformation. She thinks about the best way to introduce the concept of postmodern systemic reform to the variety of curriculum stakeholders at Candle. Reflecting on her teacher union activities, she knows that educational reform work always creates "allies" and "enemies"; and she wonders which introductory approach will generate the most political mileage. She thinks about the specific challenges of transformative curriculum leadership reform and wonders if she can find some highly committed risk takers on the faculty and in the community. If she can find such individuals, she hopes that she will be able to support their initial reform work and also encourage a deeper understanding of their emancipatory efforts.

As Karen pulls into the school parking lot, she feels a little anxious. Will she find some support for her reform agenda? Will she move too fast and thus alienate some of the premodern and modern conservatives on her faculty and in her community? Will she display the necessary persistence and sense of humor for this difficult reform work? As these questions flash though her mind, she gets a sinking feeling; but then she reminds herself that she experiences this reform work as a moral calling. This inspires her to meet the new school year with hope, and she walks into the school building in this frame of mind.

FOLLOW-UP QUESTIONS

1. Based on your own experiences, what recommendations might you offer Karen McCleary on how to introduce the concept of postmodern systemic reform to the variety of curriculum stakeholders at Candle?

2. Can you identify potential transformative curriculum leaders in your work setting? If so, what criteria did you use to identify these people? Do you think Karen should consider your criteria?

3. How do you understand transformative curriculum leadership praxis? Based on this understanding, what advice might you offer Karen on ways she could encourage emancipatory insight into transformative curriculum leadership work?

4. Can you identify premodern and modern conservatives in your work setting? If so, what advice might you offer Karen on how to work with these people?

5. If Karen begins to feel overwhelmed by the challenges of transformative curriculum leadership reform, could you offer any words or insights that might reinspire her "moral calling?"

REFERENCES

Anderson, J. R., Reder, L. M., & Simon, H. A. (1996). Situated learning and education. *Educational Researcher, 25*(4), 5–11.

Berman, M. (1981). *The reenchantment of the world.* New York: Basic Books.

Borgmann, A. (1992). *Crossing the postmodern divide.* Chicago: University of Chicago Press.

Descartes, R. (1969). *The philosophical works of Descartes* (E. S. Haldane & G.R.T. Ross, trans., 2 vols.). Cambridge: Cambridge University Press.

Dewey, J. (1922). *Human nature and conduct.* New York: Henry Holt.

Dewey, J. (1963). *Experience and education.* New York: Macmillan (original work published 1938).

Eisner, E. W. (1992). Educational reform and the ecology of schooling. *Teachers College Record, 93*(4), 610–627.

Eisner, E. W. (1994). *The educational imagination: On the design and evaluation of school programs* (3rd ed.). New York: Macmillan.

Flax, J. (1995). Responsibility without grounds. In R. F. Goodman & W. R. Fisher (Eds.), *Rethinking knowledge: Reflections across the disciplines* (pp. 147–167). Albany: State University of New York Press.

Greene, M. (1988). *The dialectic of freedom.* New York: Teachers College Press.

Hackney, C. E., & Henderson, J. G. (1999). Educating school leaders for inquiry-based democratic learning communities. *Educational Horizons, 77*(2), 67–73.

Harding, S. (1998). *Is science multi-cultural: Postcolonialisms, feminisms, and epistemologies.* Bloomington: Indiana University Press.

Hargreaves, A. (1994). *Changing teachers, changing times: Teachers' work and culture in the postmodern age.* New York: Teachers College Press.

Hatab, L. J. (1990). *Myth and philosophy: A contest of truths.* La Salle, IL: Open Court.

Henderson, J. G., & Hawthorne, R. D. (1995). *Transformative curriculum leadership* (1st ed.). Upper Saddle River, NJ: Merrill/Prentice Hall.

Henderson, J. G., & Hawthorne, R. D. (forthcoming). *Transformative curriculum leadership* (2nd ed.). Upper Saddle River, NJ: Merrill/Prentice Hall.

Henderson, J. G., & Kesson, K. R. (Eds.). (1999). *Understanding democratic curriculum leadership.* New York: Teachers College Press.

Kesson, K. R. (1999). Toward a curriculum of mythopoetic meaning. In J. G. Henderson & K. R. Kesson (Eds.), *Understanding democratic curriculum leadership* (pp. 84–105). New York: Teachers College Press.

Lawson, H. (1985). *Reflexivity: The post-modern predicament.* La Salle, IL: Open Court.

Lyotard, J. F. (1984). *The postmodern condition: A report on knowledge* (G. Bennington & B. Massouri, trans.). Minneapolis: University of Minnesota Press.

Macdonald, J. B. (1975). Curriculum theory. In W. Pinar (Ed.), *Curriculum theorizing: The reconceptualists* (pp. 5–13). Berkeley, CA: McCutchan.

Mathews, D. (1996). *Is there a public for public schools?* Dayton, OH: Kettering Foundation Press.

McCutcheon, G. (1995). *Developing the curriculum: Solo and group deliberation.* White Plains, NY: Longman.

McCutcheon, G. (1999). Deliberation to develop school curricula. In J. G. Henderson & K. R. Kesson (Eds.), *Understanding democratic curriculum leadership* (pp. 33–46). New York: Teachers College Press.

Palmer, P. J. (1998). *The courage to teach: Exploring the inner landscape of a teacher's life.* San Francisco: Jossey-Bass.

Pinar, W. F., Reynolds, W. M., Slattery, P., & Taubman, P. M. (1995). *Understanding curriculum: An introduction to the study of historical and contemporary curriculum discourses.* New York: Peter Lang.

Reid, W. (1978). *Thinking about the curriculum.* London: Routledge & Kegan Paul.

Rosenau, P. M. (1992). *Post-modernism and the social sciences: Insights, inroads, and intrusions.* Princeton, NJ: Princeton University Press.

Sarason, S. (1990). *The predictable failure of educational reform.* San Francisco: Jossey-Bass.

Schwab, J. J. (1969). The practical: A language for curriculum. *School Review, 78,* 1–23.

Schwab, J. J. (1971). The practical: Arts of eclectic. *School Review, 79,* 493–542.

Sears, J. T. (1998). Crossing boundaries and becoming the other: Voices across borders. In J. T. Sears (Ed.), *Curriculum, religion, and public education: Conversations for an enlarging public square* (pp. 36–58). New York: Teachers College Press.

Seigfried, C. H. (1996). *Pragmatism and feminism: Reweaving the social fabric.* Chicago: University of Chicago Press.

Sergiovanni, T. (1992). *Moral leadership: Getting to the heart of school improvement.* San Francisco: Jossey-Bass.

Sirotnik, K. A. (1989). The school as the center of change. In T. J. Sergiovanni & J. H. Moore (Eds.), *Schooling for tomorrow: Directing reforms to issues that count* (pp. 89–113). Boston: Allyn & Bacon.

Slattery, P. (1995). *Curriculum development in the postmodern era.* New York: Garland Publishers.

Smith, D. G. (1991). Hermeneutic inquiry: The hermeneutic imagination and the pedagogic text. In E. C. Short (Ed.), *Forms of curriculum inquiry* (pp. 187–209). Albany: State University of New York Press.

Snyder, J., Bolin, F., & Zumwalt, K. (1992). Curriculum implementation. In P. W. Jackson (Ed.), *Handbook of research on curriculum* (pp. 402–435). New York: Macmillan.

Tyler, R. W. (1949). *Basic principles of curriculum and instruction.* Chicago: University of Chicago Press.

Walker, D. F. (1971). A naturalistic model for curriculum development. *School Review, 80*(1), 51–59.

Whitson, J. A. (1991). Post-structuralist pedagogy as counter-hegemonic praxis (Can we find the baby in the bathwater?). *Education and Society, 9*(1), 73–86.

Wittgenstein, L. (1953). *Philosophical investigations* (G.E.M. Anscombe, trans.). NewYork: Macmillan.

9

Postmodern Visions in Multicultural Education Preparation and Practice

Geneva Gay and Pamula Hart

GUIDING QUESTIONS

1. *As a preservice education student, classroom teacher, or school administrator, describe your own guiding principles of education. As you read this chapter, determine how the tenets of postmodern and multicultural education discussed reflect or challenge your principles.*

2. *How does multicultural education operationalize the conceptual principles of postmodernism?*

3. *In what ways do the postmodern principles challenge current beliefs and assumptions about objectivity and universality of curriculum content, the perspectives from which it is presented, and the impact it has on an ethnically diverse student population?*

4. *How does the student population influence and ultimately shape postmodern and multicultural classroom premises and priorities?*

5. *How does embracing the ideology of multicultural education challenge and even alter current pedagogical practices, student-teacher relationships, and the roles they play in classroom interactions?*

6. *What are the long-term societal goals of multicultural education? How do they differ from the current ones?*

The United States, and all of its attendant institutions, are on the cusp of radical change. These institutions, including government, the family, the economy, and schools, are searching for new terrains of imagination, thought, and action accompanied by reflection on and analysis of what currently exists as well. Rightfully so, because the progress imperative originates in the need to be better than we are and in recognition that present creations are merely imperfect experimentations of future possibilities.

Paulo Freire (1980) provides a compelling description of the transition period in social time and texture between the end of modernity and the advent of postmodernity. He contends that a society moving from one epoch to another needs a flexible, critical spirit to "perceive the marked contradictions which occur in society as emerging values in search of affirmation and fulfillment clash with earlier values seeking self-preservation. The time of epochal transition constitutes an historical-cultural 'tidal wave' " (p. 7). As contradictions between ways of knowing, being, behaving, and valuing of the dawning past and the emerging future intensify, the magnitude and emotions of this "tidal wave" also increase. The resulting disequilibrium signals a time for crafting new sociopolitical decisions and directions.

Tensions between yesterday's standards and tomorrow's challenges are being played out graphically in all levels and dimensions of the educational enterprise. Kindergarten through college are profoundly affected, as well as educational purposes and visions, curricular designs, instructional practices, policy-making, accountability standards, and the performance appraisal of both students and educators. Issues related to ethnic and cultural diversity hold a prominent place in these struggles. The origins of many of the present-day challenges provoked by diversity can be traced back to the formative years of the creation of U.S. society. Peoples, perspectives, and experiences that did not derive from European origins were ignored, denigrated, or rejected. As a result, a social order, educational system, and political practices grounded in the exclusion, domination, and marginalization of large segments of the ethnic, racial, and cultural mixtures of the nation's population have emerged. Postmodern and multicultural educators are committed to nullifying these biases and counteracting their effects. They intend to do this by (1) exposing the inequities and negative consequences of European American social, political, cultural, economic, and educational domination, and (2) reconstructing society, schools, and educational programs so that they are more representative of genuine social realities, cultural and demographic diversities, and imagined possibilities.

Multicultural education has a similar mission, and therefore can be seen as an ideological analogue of and a methodological tool for putting postmodern ideals into pedagogical practice (Gay, 1995). Sleeter and McLaren (1995a) explain that multicultural education and critical pedagogy (the instructional formation of postmodernist ideology) bring to bear upon the educational process "insurgent, resistant, and insurrectional modes of interpretation and classroom practices which set out to imperil the familiar, to contest the legitimizing norms of mainstream cultural life, and to render problematic the common discursive frames and regimes upon which 'proper' behavior, comportment, and social interaction are premised" (p. 7). In this sense, both multicultural and postmodern education are transformative, even revolutionary.

These assertions are developed in further detail in this chapter, with specific emphasis on the professional preparation of K-12 teachers and their practice in classrooms with students. In its broadest reach, this is a grand scheme, and far exceeds the space limitations here. Of necessity we have limited the scope of our focus and content and have been rather cautious in amplifying them. Three key contentions permeate the discussions provided. First, strong ideological and ethical parallels exist between postmodern and multicultural educational thought. Second, abstract and theoretical ideas have greater personal meaning and pedagogical value when they are accompanied by illustrations for practical application. Third, pedagogical actions that exemplify tenets of multicultural education and postmodernism should be as much a part of the lived experience of teachers' professional preparation as their classroom practice with K-12 students.

Seven postmodern education principles are presented, along with corollary multicultural interpretations and teaching-learning possibilities. These are multiple sources of knowledge and ways of knowing; community; holistic teaching and learning; emancipation and empowerment; shifting centers and crossing borders; resistance and struggle; and becoming. They serve four simultaneous functions—as guiding premises, characteristic traits, learning objectives, and methodological strategies—for designing and implementing multicultural curriculum and instruction. We decided to focus on principles instead of traditional subjects, disciplines, or content because they offer greater opportunities for innovative teaching, are more conducive to new-age social and educational demands, and transcend conventional curricular structures. Throughout these discussions we view curriculum as the learning experiences in which students engage, and instruction as the ways these experiences are facilitated by teachers. This fluid and dynamic conception of curriculum is congruent with postmodernist and multicultural education visions.

In an effort to model some of the messages of postmodernism, we have attempted to make the content of this chapter somewhat interactive. Two techniques are used to do this. We encourage the readers to join with us as co-constructors of meaning. We do this by shifting the magnitude and depth of the suggested instructional strategies, going from being very detailed and specific to sketchy and general. The intent is to increase the level of involvement of the readers in creating their own instructional strategies as they progress through the chapter. The first four principles discussed have the most practice possibilities. For the other three we have provided explanations of what they mean and fewer implementation techniques. We encourage the readers to elaborate on these and develop their own practical applications. Hopefully, the detailed strategies will inform and serve as models for the readers in generating other instructional strategies. Throughout the chapter we also frequently invite, challenge, and prompt the readers to be reflective. This seemed a reasonable course to take since reflection and knowledge construction are central tenets of postmodern and multicultural education. This is also consistent with our belief that teacher education should include much more active and participatory learning.

COMMUNITY

Community building is both a method and goal of postmodern teaching and learning. Contrary to the notion that success results from individual initiative, the reverse is closer to "truth." Both individual and collective life are, in fact, interdependent enterprises. No one creates or lives life alone! People do better at achieving qualitative lives when they collaborate, interact, and communicate with each other. Thus, postmodernism replaces individualism with communalism as the "normative center" in which the potential of human life is realized. In multicultural education teacher preparation and classroom practice is expressed in two equally important ways: First, in using many different kinds of cooperative, mutual aid and reciprocal learning structures and tasks; second, in accepting "community" as a value to be practiced habitually, not just a functional expediency, an occasional relief from regular classroom routines, or a passing vogue. It also means teaching students skills for how to be members of groups, to demonstrate caring, to assist others in their efforts to become better, and to share individual resources for the benefit of collective quality.

Working collaboratively and cooperatively is a challenging task. One way to begin to develop the skills it requires and to provide opportunities for prospective teachers to practice them is using jigsaw learning activities. In addition to their community building facility, these activities enable students to learn a large amount of information expeditiously.

Jigsaw activities have at least three stages or "rounds." In the first round, "home-based expert groups" are organized, and initial assignments are explained. In organizing the small groups it is important to keep the membership to a manageable number (4–5 is ideal) and equal, or as close as possible, so that none will be unfairly advantaged or disadvantaged based on size. The use of small groups increases community-building and multicultural education learning possibilities if the membership in the groups is ethnically, racially, linguistically, and gender diverse. Different techniques should be used to maximize student participation in the decision-making about how groups are organized and tasks assigned. Once organized, inform the groups that they are responsible for extrapolating specific ideas, factual information, trends, and representations from their assigned readings. After the members of the expert groups have completed the readings individually, ask them to discuss their "findings" with each other to answer questions, reach consensus about key ideas, facts, and themes, and ensure that *each* group member is comfortable with the consensus decisions.

During the second round of the jigsaw process the expert groups disband and form new groups. These are composed of one member from each of the expert groups. They share the consensus information of their home-based groups with representatives from other groups, answer questions, and harvest the insights, opinions, or explanations this information provokes. After all the home-based group representatives have shared their information, they return to their original groups. This return signals the third round of the jigsaw. The home-based group members now share what they learned from each of the other groups. They may conclude the learning experience by creating a composite statement about the overall topic or issue of discussion to share with the entire class. It should include information and insights collected within and across groups and can be presented in some creative format, using media, art, performance, symbolic images, and various writing genres. Whatever the format, the emphasis is on "composite and collaborate presentation," which requires consensus, cooperation, shared responsibilities, and power negotiations —in other words, behaviors and skills fundamental to community building.

Pre-service teachers should complement their jigsaw learning experiences by acquiring some knowledge and skills about group dynamics and how these, in turn, can be conveyed to their students in K-12 classrooms. This is important because knowing how to work in and facilitate group dynamics are essential to effective jigsaw instruction. To expedite this level of learning, preservice education students and their instructors should explore the following questions:

- How can jigsaw tasks be structured so that students who are weak readers or reluctant participants in discussions can be fully engaged in the different levels of small group exchanges?

- How can jigsaw activities be designed and implemented so that students who prefer to work independently will understand the importance of working on a team and will participate seriously in the process?

- How can jigsaw tasks be designed and implemented so that both academically strong and weak students make comparable quality contributions to the process and feel comfortable, confident, and capable in doing so?

Ensuring high academic quality as well as developing caring relationships and genuine community are embedded in these questions and the answers they demand.

Conducting collaborative case study analyses is another way for preservice teachers to learn principles and skills of community building. Sometimes preservice teachers are expected to learn about "different" students by developing observational profiles of them. Often they will collect information by "shadowing" the targeted individual within the confines of school. A variation of this activity that focuses as well on sharing resources, responsibilities, and benefits; developing human connections and caring; and working cooperatively (components of community-building) is having teacher education students work in teams on this assignment and compiling more comprehensive, multi-site "shadowing" of the individual of concern. To broaden the scope and depth of their information, the teams should observe their targeted student in a variety of settings, situations, and interactions both within and outside of the school community. The teams of "researchers" should try to construct a holistic view of the students they are observing by:

- obtaining and analyzing actual school records for the current and previous years.
- canvassing the community where the targeted individual lives
- speaking to the student's caregivers
- shadowing the student in social and recreational situations
- observing the student in academic setting

The logic of these tasks is that information accumulated by a team is more comprehensive, rich, and dependable than that acquired by a single individual. Observations of students in a variety of places and times, as well as in their naturalistic settings, generates more accurate and authentic knowledge than can be obtained in school settings only. This broader knowledge base helps teachers to better understand their students, and this heightened comprehension will improve their teaching success. Gathering such an extensive amount of information could be an overwhelming task for one person. Collaborative case study analyses relieve this burden and give each member of the "research team" opportunities to make essential contributions to the overall project, to bring unique perspectives about the child's life, and to help make better-*informed* decisions about how to best serve the educational needs of the students they teach.

HOLISTIC TEACHING AND LEARNING

Emphases in U.S. education tend to be compartmentalized, with the greatest attention given to cognitive ventures. The assumption seems to be that teaching and learning can be organized into discrete, mutually exclusive categories, and educators must focus on one versus the others. For example, many teachers think there is no place for values, morality, and cultural diversity in teaching math and science. Others believe that art is not intellectual and that physical education deals only with the performance of rote behaviors. In fact, these are artificial divisions that can, in the final analysis, interfere with more than facilitate genuine learning, that is, the mastery of knowledge and skills that are significant and comprehensive.

Postmodernism resists all type of educational fragmentation and related linear and hierarchical rankings of knowledge. Instead, it emphasizes a dialectic, dynamic holism among different kinds of learning—the idea being that the complex, multifarious nature of human capability requires multidimensional and multi-tiered complementary instructional approaches for its maximum facilitation. In other words, the intellectual knowledge with which schools are most preoccupied is never exclusively intellectual. It includes emotional, physical, social, and ethical aspects as well. Of necessity, then, quality teaching must deal with different types of learning—affective, social, emotional, political, cognitive, moral—in concert with each other. Therefore, questions about whether education is, or should be, about some of these but not others are non-issues; it is, unavoidably, all of them.

Multicultural education argues similarly that learning about and for cultural diversity has multiple dimensions, which must be addressed simultaneously. Teaching factual information about atrocities committed against ethnic groups and catalog listings of ethnic contributions is insufficient. Students also need to know the psychological, political, and economic contexts and consequences of these, as well as many other aspects of ethnic groups' histories, lives, cultures, and experiences. No single disciplinary perspective, methodology, or content is sufficient to accomplish these tasks; instead, insights and analyses drawn from many different areas of study are necessary. On the whole, elementary teachers have more experience with holistic teaching and learning than their high school and college counterparts. Their generalist preparation and self-contained classroom structures are more amenable to this approach to teaching than the subject and area specializations of high schools and colleges. Therefore, the suggestion we offer for how to translate this principle to multicultural practice is intended for the latter.

The catalyst for the activity is *Huckleberry Finn*. Heated controversy continues to surface around this novel's negative language and portrayal of the African American adult character as inferior, powerless, and subservient to the European American youth character. While critics claim the book is racist and should be removed from the curriculum, proponents argue it is a "classic" piece of good literature. The oppositional claims are reasoned from historical and sociological standpoints, while the advocacy arguments hinge on the literary merits of the book. Holistic analysis of it will provide a better understanding of its literary value, as well as its political, cultural, sociolinguistic, and historical messages, meanings, and symbolism.

By today's standards *Huckleberry Finn* is an intolerable, negative example for some proponents of racial equality and social justice, including multiculturalists and postmodernists. When it was first written it was considered quite liberal and progressive. It was intended to demonstrate how personal relationships could override the social, racial, and political conventions of the time period in which it was written. The characterizations, situations, and language used to establish the settings for the issues and relationships that are played out in the story are time-bound and reflect prevailing norms. Interdisciplinary, contextual analyses will help students understand why and how *Huckleberry Finn* reflects a specific author's cultural orientations and ideological perspectives, as well as a particular sociopolitical period in time, rather than being a universal and timeless example of "good literature."

Similar approaches should be applied in the study of other literary renderings (fictional novels, autobiographies, narratives, poems, musical lyrics, folkloric musings, etc.) of racial issues, situations, and events of different ethnic groups in both historical and commentary times. Some of these are the forced removal of Native Americans from the southeastern states to the Great Plains; the economic discrimination imposed upon Irish immigrants in the nineteenth century; the racial persecution of Italian Americans during the "Red Scare" period of the early 1920s; the internment of Japanese Americans during World War II; the Civil Rights Movement of the 1960s and the 1970s; affirmative action reversals of the 1990s; and negative portrayals of different ethnic groups in mass media. Commercial, educational, and public broadcasting films and videos should complement written materials as sources of knowledge on these dilemmas. For example, *Birth of a Nation*, *Ethnic Notions*, *Something Strong Within*, and *Skin Deep* convey powerful messages about the creation, dissemination, and effect of racial images that are far beyond the capability of print materials.

These analyses should lead students to two key conclusions: (1) Social, civic, and racial issues are multidimensional, complex, and frequently multiethnic; and (2) "good literature" is a relative concept, and never merely literary; invariably, it transmits political messages, social values, and constructed images. Literary works and visual media, like all other sources of knowledge, reflect the personal biases, experiences, perspectives, and intentions of the authors and prompt different responses in different people at different times. We would be remiss if we did not acknowledge the necessity of including multiple perspectives of various ethnic groups in and across various time periods in these analyses.

MULTIPLE SOURCES OF KNOWLEDGE AND WAYS OF KNOWING

Both postmodernism and multicultural education argue that no one ideology (set of beliefs and values), epistemology (nature of knowledge and ways of knowing), or ontology (reality) is preeminent and prevalent in all times and circumstances. There is no cultural unanimity or consensus across all ethnic and social groups. The Association for the Accreditation of Colleges of Teacher Education endorsed this position in its 1973 policy statement on multicultural education. The title of the document carried the message "No One Model American." According to Huebner (1975), what is taught in schools is actually about human temporality rather than universality. Macdonald (1975) argues that, invariably, school curricula are designed to reflect and serve the interests of some people more than others. More recently, Darder (1995) explicated the underlining message of these viewpoints for multicultural teacher preparation and classroom instruction. She believes the essence of the multicultural education struggle is creating a more authentic United States—one that is comprised of "multiple cultures, multiple histories, multiple regions, multiple realities, multiple identities, multiple ways of living, surviving, and being human" (1995, p. 320).

Various scholars have demonstrated that knowledge, like virtually every other human endeavor, is not monolithic or static. For example, Gardner

(1993) identifies seven different types of intelligences, and Banks (1996) describes five types of knowledges. It is now common practice for educators to talk about different literacies (social, vocational, scientific, computer, reading, environmental, multicultural, etc.) and different types of literacies within given categories. Thus, reading literacy includes word meanings, textual analysis, comprehension, decoding, and interpretation. Human development encompasses mental, moral, social, physical, psychological, and cultural dimensions. Multicultural knowledge embraces a wide range of facts, feelings, opinions, experiences, beliefs, attitudes, historical memories, scholarly analyses, and literary artifacts about different ethnic diversity.

Giroux (1993) believes that teaching should have a more critical character and perceive knowledge as a tentative, constantly changing, social and cultural creation. All knowledge claims should be examined critically to determine their sources, purposes, how they empower and privilege some "realities" but ignore or denigrate others. In other words, critical pedagogy teaches students how to interrogate master narratives so that the fallacy of objective reality, universal truth, and knowledge as transcendent of culture, social context, time, and intentionality can be unveiled and transformed. One practical translation of this idea is rethinking some common "stock-in-trade" assumptions about ethnic, racial, and cultural diversity in the United States. For example, the assumption that mainstream U.S. culture is a European American creation is erroneous because, in fact, it is a composite of contributions and influences from many different ethnic groups. Another way to begin deconstructing the fallacy of incontestable claims of truth is to expose to critical view the many oxymoronic contradictions embedded in U.S. dominant cultural traditions, such as waging war to guarantee peace; destroying in order to build; progress being contingent upon conquest; and in order to have winners, there must be some losers. To pursue this "deconstruction" further, teachers and their students should identify other presumed truths and oxymorons (especially about power and privilege), examine how they are portrayed and transmitted in schools and society, and consider ways they can be reformed. From these analyses emerges yet another level of knowing, exemplifying the notion that knowledge is a social phenomenon that is being continually created.

Students from different ethnic groups and cultural backgrounds bring useful "raw data" and "experiential expertise" to the learning encounter. These personal stories, or autobiographies, are significant sources of knowledge for multicultural curriculum and instruction. The challenge for teachers is how to access and use them to facilitate learning for culturally diverse students. It raises a more specific question for further pedagogical thought and action. That is, how can the personal stories of diverse students' lives be used to teach mathematical, literary, scientific, sociological, economic, and other academic concepts and skills?

The most natural way to use autobiography in teaching is to give students the opportunity to tell about themselves. This can be accomplished on multiple levels. Classroom display of "Stars of the Week" is a simple way to provide a window into the lives of elementary students. Although there are many unique way of organizing such displays, there are some constant elements. Children write short captions, bring special objects such as photographs, stuffed animals, or trophies to class and, most important, share their displays publicly with the entire class. Another variation is to post baby pictures of the students or childhood pictures of parents and have "Who's Who" competitions, with the owners of the photographs giving anonymous tips about the identity.

More sophisticated ways of accomplishing the same goal of "self-creation" is to give students the opportunity to write short stories about themselves. This can be done in primary grades as well as in high school and teacher education programs. In its most simplistic form, primary children are given prompts or sentence starters, in which to respond. An example is, "The people I live with are____." For older students, this activity can be modified to focus on specific topics or aspects of their lives. Short autobiographical narratives also can focus on influential people in the students' lives, significant obstacles they have had to overcome, and how their culture, race, gender, and ethnicity influence their daily experiences. Personal timelines and longer narratives, with illustrations and references to significant social and political events, are other ways for students to "construct themselves" by sharing self-selected aspects of their personal lives in media and means of their own choosing.

Unfortunately, too many teachers know too little about their students' lives outside of school or the rich cultural and experiential knowledge they bring to classroom and are unable to capitalize on the potential of autobiography as a pedagogical technique. This situation needs to be remedied before students' personal experiences can be incorporated into school curricula. They can start by getting to know the communities where their students live, through personal and practical exposure. This can be a daunting task. Most pre- and in-service teachers do not live or socialize in the communities in which they teach and therefore do not understand what their "culture" looks, feels, or sounds like. As a way to bridge this gap, teachers should *spend purposeful and focused* time in their students' communities. This means engaging in some kind of intentional activities instead of merely taking quick "drive throughs" or general "field trips." These experiences might include repeated walk-abouts within different ethnic communities; visits to various religious institutions, playgrounds, recreational centers, local businesses, and places of entertainment; notations of diverse types of architecture and housing; observations of where people gather, for what purposes, and how they spend their recreational time; looking at posters, billboards, street art, and other types of advertising; talking to parents and other community residents; watching children at play in different locations; identifying community power brokers and how they demonstrate their authority/influence; and engaging in community service projects. They help to situate students outside of school, which, in turn, provides greater insights into how they construct meaning within school learning situations. These experiences should be preceded by some guided discussions and conceptual framing about ethnic cultures and communities and be followed by analytical and reflective debriefing.

Ethnic group cultures are dynamic diverse entities. As such, they offer a wide variety of knowledges to be learned, as well as require many knowledges to be understood. Both defy unidimensional analyses. Instead, multiple sources of information, perspectives, techniques, and interpretations must be employed. This plurality should not discourage making teacher preparation and classroom instruction multiculturally inclusive. Rather, it should be seen as magnifying the need, underscoring the significance, and indicating the richness of the benefits to be had by studying ethnic and cultural diversity.

Attending effectively to these many different kinds of knowledge in teacher preparation and classroom instruction requires strategies that incorporate multiple perspectives, comparative analyses, interdisciplinary teaching, and integrated curricular designs. For example, pre- and inservice teachers may improve their understanding about the nature of knowledge, culture, and diversity by applying them to schools. Many of them do not realize that schools, colleges, and universities have cultures of their own, which largely reflect that of mainstream U.S. society. Therefore, the first step in developing multicultural competence is for preservice teachers to examine what is meant by school culture, identify its salient characteristics, determine how they were created, and analyze the influences they have on students from different ethnic, racial, and social groups. This learning can be facilitated by students in "foundations" education courses creating a working definition of culture that includes specific values, behaviors, and beliefs. As the students share their thoughts, have the class listen for common features across the definitions. Then, discuss the results, and respond to questions such as:

- How do your conceptions of culture apply to schools?
- Why did similar ideas emerge when the individuals in class represent different personal, ethnic, racial, social, and educational backgrounds and experiences?
- How did you learn about this culture? Was it explicitly or implicitly taught to you? Did this happen as an adult or as a child?
- Think about the students you are currently working with, or desire to teach. Do you think they are aware of these characteristics? Why or why not? How do you know? How did *they* learn?
- Are there any students you believe who do not know school culture? What indication do they give to support your beliefs? Are there any observable ethnic, racial, and religious patterns?

Culture is often seen as something that ethnic, racial, and religious minority groups have, but majority European Americans do not have. Many teachers have shared these misconceptions (Spindler & Spindler, 1994). The following activities are designed to challenge them. Have students bring five items to class that reflect their personal cultures, and explain the significance of each. Debrief the sharing experiences with follow-up questions such as:

- What processes did you go through to choose these items?
- Explain the ease or difficulty you encountered in doing this task?
- Did any common items and themes emerge as individuals shared their cultural bags?
- How do these items reflect our working definition of culture?
- Should we refine our definition of culture as a result of this activity? If so how?
- Has this activity changed your ideas about your own and others' cultures? If so, in what ways? If not, why?

A learning activity for middle and high school, college, and teacher education students on multiple sources of knowledge might begin with the question, "What are the various ways we attain knowledge? From the lists the students generate, ask if some of these sources are more valid or important than others, and what makes them so. After these discussions, introduce a news story from a major daily paper (*New York Times, Washington Post, Seattle Times, Chicago Tribune*) or from television. It should be a story that focuses on a specific ethnic community or on an individual or event within that community. Share a copy with all the participants and have them read or listen for major facts, important people, and the way in which these people are characterized; think about from whose perspective the story is written; and determine what clues led them to their answers, such as photographs or other visual images, descriptive language, evaluative statements, and background information. Share another version of the same story from a local ethnic community newspaper. Using the same questions posed earlier, have the students discern similarities and differences between the text, tone, content, perspectives, background, characterizations, and reader responses. Discuss possible reasons why the same story was reported in different ways and prompted very different responses. After these discussions are completed, review the concept of multiple perspectives. Introduce Banks' (1996; 1997) model of knowledge construction, which provides an overview of the ways knowledge is created, disseminated, and used with different ethnic and social groups in schools.

Another powerful way to introduce the concept of multiple perspectives in elementary classrooms is by reading different story books on the same event, like *The Three Little Pigs* and *The True Story of the Three Little Pigs*, or *Little Red Riding Hood* and *Flossie & the Fox* (McKissack, 1986). Older students might use presentations on the same issue made in different genre, such as a novel and a movie, or a painting and a scholarly research. An example of the latter is Tom Feeling's (1995) artistic rendition of the "Middle Passage," John Hope Franklin's and Alfred Moss's (1994) historical analysis of it, Charles Johnson's (1990) novel about it, and Lerone Bennett's (1975) interpretation of the Africans' transformative response to it. By comparing these variations on the same stories, students can begin to realize that situations differ depending on who is telling the story and which medium they use for the telling.

This teaching technique that begins in reading can be readily extended to social studies. First, select a particular event or period in history for analysis, such as the Harlem Renaissance, immigration of various Asian ethnic groups, the relationships between Native Americans and Quakers, or the unionization movement among Mexican American farm workers. Second, have the students determine the major individuals, groups, and issues involved in the event, using many different sources of information, including textbooks, trade books, personal narratives, newspaper accounts, and scholarly reports. As an entire class or in small groups, the students read each source, focusing on four or five main themes, such as identifying (1) what positions are taken in the various sources and why, (2) beliefs about who or what started the conflict, (3) what different groups did to solve the problem, (4) how the conflict was finally solved, and (5) how the resolution affected the different groups involved. After these questions have been answered, the students should analyze the diversity of responses and explain reasons for it. They also should be challenged to determine which of the perspectives and sources are "the real truth." If they respond by interrogating what is "real truth" and by whose standards, then they will come to understand that truth and knowledge have multiple valid meanings.

SHIFTING CENTERS AND CROSSING BORDERS

Individuals living in postmodern multicultural societies must have a wide repertoire of skills in cultural diversity. This is so because they need to participate in many different spheres of living, master different kinds of learnings, and interact with people from a broad spectrum of social, ethnic, racial, cultural, and linguistic backgrounds. The protection or security people once derived from living with people very similar to themselves, in relatively isolated ethnic enclaves, will no longer suffice. The world will be wide open for exploration. In order to capitalize on opportunities this openness offers and deal with the challenges it poses, individuals will have to cross many different borders of being and create new "centers" to ground themselves in heretofore unknown or unaccepted realities.

These border crossings and shifting centers are numerous and continuously unfolding. Crossing one border reveals yet others to be surmounted. For example, we may come to abandon the archaic policies and practices of "English only" and realize that linguistic pluralism is enriching, not diminishing to individuals and U.S. society. Having crossed this border we may then decide that Spanish is the most logical choice for a second national language. After living with this decision for a while, the country may take yet another enlightening step by recognizing the value of studying additional languages. As the various borders are crossed, linguistic centers (that is, core values, beliefs, and practices) shift as well, from monolingualism to bilingualism to multilingualism.

Other critical borders to be crossed and centers to be reconfigured in postmodern and multicultural education are located in race, class, gender, and culture. Among these are confronting one's anxieties about ethnically diverse groups and speaking out against racial prejudices even when it involves opposing friends and family. Mainstream European Americans need to experience being minorities, and ethnic minorities need to experience being the majority. Exchange programs abroad and among schools or classes in different ethnic communities and pen and e-mail pal relationships offer great opportunities for these kind of border crossings. The feelings of elation are beyond description for African Americans, on their first ventures to Caribbean and African nations, at being a part of the overwhelming majority and seeing people like themselves in a wide range of prestigious positions of power, authority, and privilege. Conversely, Europeans Americans who spend a significant amount of time in these cultural environments talk about how happy they are to be home again upon their return. Deep admiration is due international students and new immigrants in the United States for the myriad borders they have to cross repeatedly, how often they have to reconstitute their stabilizing centers, and the courage and strength it must take for them to live and learn in the midst of unfamiliar cultural practices. In addition, these border crossings demand other important skills such as cross-cultural services, perspective taking, participatory action learning in different ethnic communities and institutions, and interethnic communication and interracial relations.

EMANCIPATION AND EMPOWERMENT

These principles mean being freed from the undue constraining forces of contemporary conventions of all kinds—personal, social, intellectual, political, and cultural. Prevailing rules of order, etiquette, and education in the United States place great faith in and expend much effort toward getting people to conform to some externally determined notions about how and what they are supposed to be, whether that is citizen, adult, worker, student, teacher, or educated person. Tenets of behaviorism and vocationalism permeate these priorities. This explains why critical and postmodern theory see the primary effects of school as personal reductionism and social reproduction. That is to say, the educational process largely perpetuate the existing social order and power relationships, rather than refining, reforming, or transforming them. Schools assume that an identifiable and immutable fund of knowledge exists that is to be transmitted, that students should learn mostly by memorizing and regurgitating information, and that the purpose in life is for individuals to find their niche in and adjust to the status quo. Consequently, those students who arrive at school already advantaged by conventional standards of power, privilege, and mainstream status (middle or upper class, English language dominant, White, and European American male) are reaffirmed throughout the educational process. Likewise, most of those who begin school as underprivileged,

powerless, and marginalized (poor, limited English proficient, ethnics of color) continue to be so throughout schooling and life beyond.

Postmodern education is committed to breaking these confining, predestined-like chains of convention, beginning with the idea that lockstep replications of status quo orientations do not have to be. They can be broken, transcended, and transformed. This liberation begins with students actively confronting and engaging with learning stimuli, massaging them, seeking new insights, developing confidence in their own abilities, trying out new possibilities, developing competence, and actively seeking new levels of capabilities. The emancipation promoted by postmodernism is both intellectual and personal, social and political.

Within the parameters of multicultural education, postmodern notions of emancipation mean being free of the psychological stress and intellectual doubts resulting from impositions of racial and cultural inferiority. Steele (1997) and Steele and Aronson (1995) provide a compelling case about the negative effects the threat of racial prejudice can have on the intellectual performance of students. Removing this threat and developing cultural knowledge, positive ethnic self-concepts, and acknowledging cultural contributions of ethnic groups are affirming to the personal worth and capability of ethnically diverse students. There is something very uplifting and rejuvenating about seeing the contributions of one's own ethnic group honored in curriculum content and instructional materials. These images and information also penetrate the shroud of cultural hegemony and expose the fallacies of racial inferiority. They unleash the emotional and mental energies and efforts previously consumed by many students of color in protecting their beleagued psyches to be redirected toward intellectual pursuits. Slattery (1995) suggests that addressing issues of ethnic self-identity and dignity in school curricula improves school performance, develops compassion toward others, and promotes social justice. Consequently, knowledge of and pride in one's own ethnicity is psychologically, academically, and socially liberating (Cross, 1991; Gay, 1994).

The confidence and efficacy engendered by this competence are the bedrock of personal empowerment. Knowledge of and respect for others' ethnicity extends this liberation to a social level. Freedom from cultural, racial, and ethnic bias makes other ways of living and being more accessible, so that individuals can enrich, enliven, and expand their human potentialities. This enrichment and expansion constitute another dimension of postmodern emancipation and empowerment in educating teachers as well as students. For instance, teachers are better empowered to implement liberatory education if they are consciously aware of and understand the cultural underpinnings of their own thoughts and behaviors; are racially, ethnically, and culturally unbiased; know and appreciate the culture and ethnicity of their students; and act deliberately and competently to incorporate ethnic and cultural diversity into the contents, contexts, and processes of their teaching.

BECOMING

Improving the quality of living for individuals, groups, and societies is strongly emphasized by postmodernists and multiculturalists. It entails more than stable employment, and is not restricted to reaching some specific end point in time or a destination called "success," where individuals rest on their laurels and enjoy the cumulative fruits of their labors. Postmodern notions of quality living are more dynamic and fluid and are grounded in psychoemotional well-being, ethical behavior, and establishing caring connections with others. They see this as something that is continually unfolding and emerging. Life is something like an experiment, with a virtually infinite supply of generative hypotheses to be tested and possibilities to be explored. Thus, people need to be in a perpetual state of becoming better. These ideas are not as fanciful or narcissistic as they might at first appear. Critical self-reflection and the importance of human connectedness provide the needed grounding and balance. Since people in a postmodern society are always crossing borders, acquiring new knowledge, and encountering different peoples and experiences, corollary changes must occur in how they live their individual and collective lives in the present and the future.

For multicultural education, teaching for becoming engages students in analyzing how their current lives came to be as they are and how they can be reconstructed. This involves both marginal and mainstream groups exploring the effects of marginalization, power, and exploitation on their own and each others' lives; their sense of ethnic identity, pride, and affiliation; feelings of efficacy; and actions for self-determination. Case studies of ethnically diverse individuals and groups in the act of transforming their lives are valuable tools to use in these learning experiences. They exemplify the power of the processes of becoming and provide possible models for students to emulate. They also demonstrate that to be in control of one's own social creation is the ultimate goal of liberation—the hope of all individuals, ethnic groups, and societies.

To move the principle of becoming from conceptualizations to implementation, review and reflect on some of the practice possibilities suggested earlier in the chapter. Do any of these suggest directions for action? What other shifts in the philosophical orientations, curriculum designs, and instructional styles will have to occur for education for becoming to be actualized? What kinds of obstacles will teachers have to overcome? Is the concept feasible for classroom practice in grades K-12, as well as teacher education?

RESISTANCE AND STRUGGLE

Postmodern and multicultural visions are not easily or quickly accomplished, nor is the journey toward them always harmonious and consensual. Overcoming racism, political imperialism, economic inequities, psychological abuse, academic underachievement, and cultural hegemony often are not conducive to gentle and congenial remedies. They are too deeply entrenched into the fabric of society to bow to quick and easy solutions. Furthermore, too many people are at various levels of consciousness, competence, commitment, and engagement with these issues for conflict to be avoided. Whether through policies, programs, effects, or personal experience, encounters between victims and victimizers are inherently conflictual. These tensions also can play out within individuals and groups who both victimize and are victimized. A case in point is men of color who suffer from racism, while simultaneously being sexist toward female members of their own ethnic groups. The most public of these struggles occur as champions of the status quo trying to protect their position and privilege collide with forces of social transformation. Even within the social transformation camp, where postmodernism and multicultural education reside, struggle ensues as different advocates search for complementary (if not, common) language, directions, and strategies to give practical meanings to their causes, which incorporate their various perspectives.

Gaining and sustaining a momentum for multicultural reform is fraught with struggle. It is positioned in such dilemmas as: Is it better to align one's cultural diversity reform efforts with proponents and kindred spirits, or to invest them in persuading the skeptics and counterbalancing the opponents? Should multicultural education stand alone or be incorporated into other areas of study? Should reformers seek compromise positions or insist upon achieving their ideals? How much can one negotiate ideological principles and related practices within endangering their internal integrity? Consequently, resistance and struggle in postmodern and multicultural education are always two-directional, one resisting opposition from "current norms" and the other seeking ways to exemplify new directions in learning and living.

Even welcomed change is not easily accomplished. It simultaneously entices and intimidates. Given this, more progress can be made in promoting multicultural education by teaching K-12 students and preservice teachers about the nature of change, the value of struggle, various ways in which opposition to it is expressed, and how to resist this opposition. These skills are imperative in the professional development of educators because their multicultural advocacy is likely to be questioned, challenged, and resisted by someone at some point in time. One viable response is learning how to circumvent tendencies to relegate multicultural education to marginal status in curricula by incorporating elements of culture and diversity into the heart of high-status subjects (such as reading, math, and science) and skills.

Accomplishing these tasks is both a challenge and an invitation, a politically expedient and pedagogically sound maneuver that entails masterful border crossings, shifting of academic centers, and transformative activism. Instructional programs and practices cannot be merely replicative or transmissive; they must be regenerative and creative since U.S. society and schools are far from their potential in embracing ethnic, racial, and cultural diversity. The experiment with social, academic, and political democracy is flawed and far from incomplete, as evident by continuing inequities in power, privilege, and resource distributions among diverse groups. Postmodern education is directed toward creating a new social order in which these no longer exist. This goal is symbolized in the multicultural agenda by its commitment to combating all forms of oppression and promoting personal, political, and cultural efficacy and empowerment among ethnically diverse individuals and collectives. To accomplish these goals a wide variety of pedagogical action strategies are endorsed, which range from recognizing the sources, character, and effects of oppressive practices to acquiring counterbalancing knowledge, to developing strategies of resistance, to obtaining economic and political power for promoting social justice.

CONCLUSION

Implementing the ideas and actions suggested above requires some fundamental changes in how teacher education and K-12 classroom instruction are conceived, structured, and enacted. The kind of changes needed are the reverse of those symbolized by many long-held notions about teaching competence, facilitating instruction, and promoting cultural diversity in school settings. Among these are believing that good teaching anywhere is good teaching everywhere; being color-blind and seeing no differences; and treating all students the same regardless of their race, class, ethnicity, or gender. U.S. educators profess belief in "individualized instruction" and "variable rates of learning" for K-12 students while simultaneously denying these prerogatives to participants in teacher education programs.

These contradictions send conflicting messages about what counts most in the educational enterprise regarding both content and process. Indeed, having teacher education students learn by actually doing multicultural curriculum and instruction throughout the duration and across the various dimensions of their preparation programs would be a radical step forward. These kinds of changes are mandated by postmodern and multicultural concerns about the redistribution of educational power and privilege, achievement of academic and political equity, the social construction of knowledge, reflective analysis, and students being more actively engaged and centered in their own learning.

Another message that comes through clearly from the preceding discussion is that issues of ethnic and cultural diversity need to be confronted deliberately and directly in both teacher education and K-12 classrooms. Inequities cannot be identified, understood, and corrected if we shy away from their harshness and brutality, pretend they do not exist, or hope that they will go away if they are not mentioned. Achieving a more egalitarian and just society and better quality educational opportunities and outcomes for ethnically diverse students means that we must endure the discomfort and pain associated with confronting inequities. Change of any significance emerges from struggle. Thus, struggle is a characteristic feature of postmodern, multicultural social and educational transformation. This is a reality that should be modeled by teacher educators, and the skills it requires should be taught to students in both professional preparation and K-12 classrooms. The measure of their success in facilitating this transformation is not in any one specific artifact or particular action, but in the quality of the journey they take toward accomplishing academic equality and social justice for ethnically, racially, and culturally diverse students.

Case Study 9: Curriculum Activity Inspires Students to Display Multiple Perspectives

This sixth-grade class in "Issues and Perspectives" is taught by a team of four teachers, one each from language arts, social studies, fine arts, and career development. The students have been examining the topic, "Messages Images Tell" and have just completed an assignment of "Personal Images of the United States," in which they created visual representations of their perceptions of the country. Their products are now on display around the room, and an exploration of them is about to begin. The range, variety, and richness of the images are breathtaking—there's a 24″ × 36″ of a biracial, multiethnic student in class, with the caption "I am what America is and has the Potential to Be"; there is a drawing of a multigenerational Native American family bowed down from carrying a model of the United States on their backs; a drawing of many different people, all wearing various sets of numbers; there is a poster of eight naked babies from different ethnic groups; a collage showing teaming buildings of steel that seem to grow out of garbage dumps; yet another picture shows individuals in silhouette looking at a map of the United States from the four cardinal directions—there's nothing on the inside of the map but big question marks; and there are many, many other images as well.

The classroom is alive with energy, excitement, anticipation, and freeflowing conversation. The students can hardly wait for the structured dialogue to begin. The teacher appeals to them to wait until he dispenses with some administrative tasks. Once these are completed, he announces, "Let us begin." This invitation is met with a barrage of thoughts, opinions, feelings, interpretations, comparisons, speculations, and throughout it all, pride, critique, discovery, insight, celebration of accomplishment.

In the midst of these exuberant exchanges, the school principal enters the room. With an air of exasperation, she wants to know, "What's going on here?" From her posture and persona it is obvious that she is making reference to the level of conversation as well as the display of images. One student in a far corner of the room, who has been rather reluctant to speak out in class, is the first to respond, asking of the principal, "Why? You got a problem with it?" Others quickly chime in, with a surprising approach to answering the principal's queries. One asks, "What do you think is going on?" Another questions, "What do you see?" A third wants to know, "What do you feel about what you see?" The principal seems puzzled by these questioning responses. She again looks around the room at the images, then back at the students and the teacher, before returning her eyes once again to the displays. The thought crosses her mind, "Is this the same class my predecessor said never did anything constructive? Why would he have ever thought that?"

The teaching team member who had the primary responsibility for facilitating the class dialogue on the images simply sat and listened to the students query the principal. He smiled rather coyly, with pleasure and pride in what was happening. He himself had been in the place of the students and the principal not too long ago. Graphic memories flashed through his mind of a learning encounter he had experienced in his teacher education program during a unit on "The Children We Teach" that was similar in design and purpose to the one on "Messages Images Tell" he was now teaching.

FOLLOW-UP QUESTIONS

1. How does the culture (structure, participation, roles, ambiance, etc.) of this classroom reflect the postmodern and multicultural education principles discussed in this chapter?

2. In what ways do the focus and content of the course, "Issues and Perspectives" embody the core elements of multicultural education discussed in the chapter?

3. What underlying values or assumptions do the four classroom teachers have about the relationship between multicultural education and student achievement and empowerment?

4. What kinds of groundwork, modeling, and preparation would classroom teachers need to provide for their students to create this postmodernist, multicultural classroom climate and its learning experiences?

5. Recognizing that multiple layers of multicultural education are incorporated in this course, which component(s) would be the most realistic to begin the implementation process? Explain why.

6. If you, as a classroom teacher or building administrator, wanted to emulate this case study or aspects of it, what systemic changes or supportive structures would you have to put in place? Provide an explanation for each of your suggestion.

7. Continue to develop the story line through several additional discourse sequences of the case study (such as what the principal, students, and teacher will say and do next), based on your understanding of the multicultural practices and postmodern principles discussed in the chapter. You might even project yourself into the case classroom by assuming the role of a visitor to this class and asking some questions or making observations of your own.

REFERENCES

Banks, J. A. (1997). *Educating citizens in a multicultural society.* New York: Teachers College Press, Columbia University.

Banks, J. A. (Ed). (1996). *Multicultural education, transformative knowledge, and action.* New York: Teachers College Press, Columbia University.

Bennett, L., Jr. (1975). *The shaping of Black America.* Chicago: Johnson Publishing Company.

Cross, W. E., III (1991). *Shades of black: Diversity in African American identity.* Philadelphia: Temple University Press.

Darder, A. (1995). Buscando America: The contribution of critical Latino educators to the academic development and empowerment of Latino students in the U.S. In C. E. Sleeter & P. L. McLaren (Eds.), *Multicultural education, critical pedagogy, and the politics of difference* (pp. 319–345). Albany: State University of New York Press.

Feelings, T. (1995). *The middle passage*. New York: Dial Books.

Franklin, J. H., & Moss, A. A., Jr. (1994). *From slavery to freedom: A history of Negro Americans* (7th ed.). New York: Alfred A. Knopf.

Freire, P. (1980). *Education for critical consciousness*. New York: Continuum.

Gardner, H. (1993). *Frames of mind: The theory of multiple intelligences*. New York: Basic Books.

Gay, G. (1994). *At the essence of learning: Multicultural education*. West Lafayette, IN: Kappa Delta Pi.

Gay, G. (1995). Mirror images on common issues: Parallels between multicultural education and critical pedagogy. In C. E. Sleeter & P. L. McLaren (Eds.), *Multicultural education, critical pedagogy, and the politics of difference* (pp. 155–189). Albany: State University of New York Press.

Giroux, H. A. (1993). *Border crossings: Cultural workers and the politics of education*. New York: Routledge.

Huebner, D. (1975). Curriculum as concern for man's temporality. In W. Pinar (Ed.), *Curriculum theorizing: The reconceptualists* (pp. 237–250). Berkeley, CA: McCutchan.

Johnson, C. R. (1990). *Middle passage*. New York: Atheneum.

Macdonald, J. B. (1975). Curriculum and human interests. In W. Pinar (Ed.), *Curriculum theorizing: The reconceptualists* (pp. 283–294). Berkeley, CA: McCutchan.

McKissack, P. C. (1986). *Flossie & the fox*. New York: Dial Books for Young Readers.

Slattery, P. (1995). *Curriculum development in the postmodern era*. New York: Garland.

Sleeter, C. E., & McLaren, P. L. (1995a). Introduction: Exploring connections to build a critical multiculturalism. In C. E. Sleeter & P. L. McLaren (Eds.), *Multicultural education, critical pedagogy, and the politics of difference* (pp. 5–32). Albany: State University of New York Press.

Sleeter, C. E., & McLaren, P. L. (Eds.). (1995b). *Multicultural education, critical pedagogy, and the politics of difference*. Albany: State University of New York Press.

Spindler, G., & Spindler, L. (Eds.). (1994). *Pathways to cultural awareness: Cultural therapy with teachers and students*. Thousand Oaks, CA: Corwin Press.

Steele, C. M. (1997). A threat in the air: How stereotypes shape intellectual identity and performance. *American Psychologist, 52*(6), 613–629.

Steele, C. M., & Aronson, J. (1995). Stereotype threat and the intellectual test performance of African Americans. *Journal of Personality and Social Psychology, 69*, 797–811.

10

Complicity in Supervision: Another Postmodern Moment

Duncan Waite and
Margarida Ramires Fernandes

GUIDING QUESTIONS

1. *What are the implications of looking at supervision as an isolated and decontextualized task?*

2. *Why is it unacceptable in the postmodern age to look at supervision as an isolated and decontextualized task?*

3. *The authors cite some paradoxes and contradictions of the postmodern age. What are they? Can you name others?*

4. *What do the authors mean by "Everyone is a member of multiple communities, simultaneously"? What implications does this have for schooling and for supervision?*

5. *What benefits can a dialogic approach have for the supervisor and the supervisee?*

Supervision is an interactive, relational process. Whatever else it is, supervision is a process involving people. This must be the case, unless supervision is wholly an abstraction. Supervision is a process carried out by real human actors. As such, supervision, like other interactive processes, is subject to certain interactional "rules" (ethnomethodologically speaking, of course) and rituals. Elsewhere (e.g., Waite, 1995a), one of the authors of this chapter has sketched out an initial take on some of the interactional rules and rituals particular to supervision, through empirically grounded analysis of the lived world of supervisors and teachers. In this chapter, we'll be more figurative, more global, and interpretative in looking at supervision. That is, we'll take a step back and ruminate a bit.

SOME CHARACTERISTICS OF INTERACTION
APPLICABLE TO SUPERVISORY PROCESSES

What are the characteristics of interaction? Which of these have relevance for supervision in schools?

Interpersonal interaction involves interpersonal communication, some but not all of which is done face to face. In face-to-face interaction, temporal and contextual considerations are involved. This is true of all supervision interactions—supervision conferences, curriculum development sessions, staff/professional development, or what have you.

Western, modern ideas of face-to-face interaction include communication, generally verbal communication, between individuals. A postmodern and/or a poststructuralist sensibility (and we maintain that there are differences) would trouble both the modern conception of the individual and the modern notion of communication.

Let's start with the individual. Is there really such a thing? This probably seems like a silly question to most readers. "Of course, there is such a thing as an individual," those readers are apt to say. But is there, really?

That the question seems silly is an indication of our general, collective notions of personhood, the deep structure of our culturally conditioned way of thinking. Other cultures don't see individuals when they see people. But, in the United States especially, where notions of "rugged individualism" are part of the very fabric of our collective identity, the individual is often seen as the basic component of society. George Herbert Mead (1934) saw it differently, as did Mikhail Bakhtin (1981) and others.

For Mead (1934), the society precedes/predates the individual (if, indeed, "individual" is the proper term at all). Think of it, there was a society long before any of us was born. We are born into a family of some sort, which lives in a certain place—a town, a farm, a city, or a suburb, which itself has a history (a genealogy). The various members of this family, whether in a single-parent household or a more traditional nuclear family, have different social relationships, are parts of different social networks or webs of relationships. This family, these people, have certain characteristics (most socially constructed), such as ethnicity and socioeconomic status.

As we grow up, we are socialized. This socialization, though having numerous nonverbal components (kinesic, tactile, visual, olfactory, and so on), is carried out primarily, according to Mead (1934), through symbols, the most preeminent of which is language. Even the physical trappings of our world become socially constituted; our responses to them are socially constructed (Blumer, 1972) and mediated through language.

What are the implications of looking at people as individuals? First, if the person alone is responsible and a teacher, he or she is solely responsible for his or her teaching and the learning of his or her students. We can almost hear the snickering of the reader, who is saying, "Why, of course, the teacher is responsible for the learning of his or her students! It's insane to think otherwise."

Here in the West (and, forgive us, for we know this is a geocentric term, but we employ it here out of convention), we have built our system of assessment, evaluation, and sanction upon this (taken-for-granted and indefensible) premise. Under our system of assessment and evaluation, there exist such things as "failing" teachers. The state of North Carolina, for example, has in place a system of naming, blaming, and shaming, whereby teachers whose classes fail to perform to established levels of "achievement" on end-of-the-year tests are put at risk of losing their jobs (and principals whose schools likewise "fail" are at risk also). This all makes some kind of sense if and only if the teacher alone is responsible for the performance of his or her students on these tests (see Apple, 1998; Hargreaves, 1998). But, let's stop and think about this a moment.

Individualism, one of the major motifs of U.S./Western society, permits this type of blaming of the individual. It permits others, especially those in positions of power vis-à-vis a solitary teacher, to shirk responsibility for that teacher and his or her "performance" in the classroom. This view of individualism absolves state and national legislatures from accepting responsibility for the education of citizens. All they need do is crank up the it's-the-teachers'-fault publicity machine, do some teacher bashing, and they get off cheaply. Imagine how much would need to be invested in education if local communities and state and national governments really took the responsibility/obligation of educating their citizens seriously? But we digress.

People, teachers and supervisors, do not come to supervision without baggage, without an already formed and forming identity—a biography, a set of experiences, beliefs, attitudes, ideolect, propriospect (Goodenough, 1981), and so on.[1] These personal and cultural attributes affect communication in all instances and are pertinent to discussions of supervision. The work of the present authors in Dialogic Supervision (Waite, 1995a), based on the work of Mikhail Bakhtin (1981), takes this position and begins, only begins, to apply it to supervision. Others, in other fields, have recognized that interactions are sociohistorical events (e.g., Hall, 1995).

Supervisory interactions take place within a context, and contexts are multifaceted, multilayered, and dynamic (Cicourel, 1992). Contexts influence, perhaps are the primary determinants of, just *who* is communicating and *what* is being communicated. A particular context helps define the "individual," the person, and others' perceptions of him or her and his or her actions. The contexts within which supervisory interactions occur are influenced by postmodernity—some to a greater extent, some to a lesser extent. Supervision and supervisory interactions also contribute to the postmodernity of contexts. The influences are mutual, back and forth, never one way.

On a grand scale, at the global or macro level, contexts that influence supervision and supervisory interactions are postmodern contexts. Postmodernity is characterized by spatial displacement and temporal intensification. Intensification (Apple, 1998; Hargreaves, 1991) leaves little time for relaxation or for keeping up with one's field, reduces opportunities for interaction with colleagues, creates chronic work overload (fostering dependency on outside experts), and encourages cutting corners, among its other effects. Under conditions of postmodernity, what Giddens (1990) calls a "radicalized modernity," relationships suffer. Without romanticizing the past, a moment's reflection on the changes that have occurred from then to now should make clear the radical differences between past and present. Think, for instance, of demographic trends, divorce, for example, and the nature of the family (Goldscheider & Waite, 1991). By all accounts, the "blended family" is becoming more predominant on the American scene. Increasingly, children must negotiate two homes and two sets of parents and stepparents and, in some cases, stepsiblings and half-siblings. In the past, of course, the predominant family structure was the nuclear family.

Communities have undergone similar, drastic changes. Again, without romanticizing the past and our conceptions of it, we readily recognize that the world around us, our communities especially, have changed and are changing ever and ever more rapidly. "Community" has recently become a catchphrase in educational discourse. More and more authors have issued a call for community (e.g., Sergiovanni & Starratt, 1997). Yet, how similar is this call to community to calls for a return to family values, for example? Are we wishing for something that never really was? Are we overromanticizing what communities are, can be, and can do? What are the possibilities of/for community, by whatever definition, within contexts of the postmodern?

In the first place, no community, no organization or institution is a totalized whole. People, our students and our fellow faculty, are always members of "multiple" communities; and this fact seems to have escaped the notice of many of the current authors who call for community. Communities have geographical boundaries, at least in conventional notions of the term. Communities are shaped, even defined, by the relationships which comprise them. In the traditional community, these relationships were primarily determined by the geographical locale. People, except the few who were either wealthy enough or daring enough to venture out, grew up within a well-defined set of relationships, generally kin, neighbors and known fellow townspeople. This is definitely not the case today, and probably could not be the case even in our schools.

Another aspect of community, one often not considered in others' musings on the concept, is that communities have a temporal dimension. These two primary factors or dimensions can, to be a bit essentialistic, define a community. Who is here now? Even in traditional communities people died and others were born. These people moved in and out of their community in these ways, not in a spatial sense, but in a temporal sense ("gone but not forgotten"?).

Today, the spatial, the temporal, and the interactional combine to make (modern and/or postmodern) communities fluid and dynamic, hardly stable enough to hold still long enough to constitute a "community" in the conventional sense of the word. People move. Children enter a school and are gone again so soon that school records have trouble keeping up with them. Teachers come and go.

In a transition-filled environment—a school, a neighborhood, a town, or a city—people are reluctant to form attachments. You notice this in large urban environments especially. The people you meet in such environments are just so many faces, nameless and seemingly not members of the web of relationships that bind us one to another. (In the American South it is still customary to ask new acquaintances where they are from, who their mother and father are, and what church they go to. This, we've come to understand, is a way for strangers to begin to become familiar, to establish references of familiarity.) Some schools, especially large high schools, are in many ways similar to these large urban environments.

These contexts, both micro and macro, affect the nature of the person, the "individual," engaged in interpersonal communication, the concept with which we began this chapter. We trust that in what we've written to this point, we've troubled the notion of what constitutes a person, the personal in interpersonal communication. What of communication?

In simpler, earlier conceptions of communication the models held there to be a sender, a receiver, and a message. But these models are as mistaken as they are oversimplified. First, as intimated above, communication takes place in a particular context, and contexts are dynamic and multilayered. It's commonplace to hear someone say his or her remarks were taken out of context. Messages cannot be decoded (correctly) without reference to, understanding of, the contexts surrounding them. So, the first "layer" of context of a spoken or written message is the immediately surrounding words. In a conversation or dialogue, one must have access to the preceding utterance, be it of the same or another speaker, to make sense of what was said and to respond accordingly. (This is due to the relevancy principle in conversation, which, loosely stated, ethnomethodologically, is that someone's spoken contribution is held to be accountable by the other speakers present on grounds of relevance to the topic and the immediately preceding utterance; if not so relevant, either the speaker must do more interactional work to make it so relevant—i.e., "Remember when you said that . . . ," or the other speakers will sanction the one who wishes to make a nonrelevant comment or will disregard that speaker's contribution, which, by the way, they may do anyway, but on other interactional/personal grounds.) Those who do analysis of transcripts of conversation know that it is important in order to understand what was said and how it was interpreted by those co-present to know what followed the particular message portion under consideration, something not available to a speaker at the moment of his or her contribution to a discussion, but something available to the analyst working from a transcript. Why is this so? Simply because meaning is always negotiated. That is, if someone is thought to have misunderstood or misinterpreted something someone said, the first person can attempt to "correct" the hearer's misunderstanding in the ensuing conversation. Sometimes it's difficult to understand what someone meant until later. This can be due to so-called noise in the channel of communication.

Today, communication is better understood to be as much about who we are, especially in relation to each other (that is, who I think you are and who you think I am), as it is about the message, per se. Indeed, one might say that the "who we are" is a significant part of the message. These processes, termed identity work (McDermott & Church, 1976), are continually negotiated. These aspects of communication need to be taken into consideration by supervisors and other administrators in their daily activities, in their planning for meetings, and in their assessment of the "culture" or "climate" of the school in which they work.

Our understanding of interpersonal communication, in dyads and larger groups, is continually becoming more sophisticated. The work of one of the current authors (e.g., Waite, 1995a) attempted to apply these increasingly complex theoretical and empirical developments to supervision. Unlike previous research into supervision conferences, this work highlighted the unboundedness of supervision conferences (that is, that supervision conferences, no matter how formal, are never separated from the other contexts and their contextual influences). We like to think that this finding was foreshadowed by Cogan (1973) and his belief that in all contexts, all working contacts between teacher and supervisor were conferences. The finding under discussion was a little different, though, to where conferences, and we believe this to be true regardless of the definition of conference(s), are all always influenced by the multiple contexts that surround them.

Also, Waite (1995a) found that power and authority play themselves out in face-to-face interactions between supervisor and teacher, but that power and authority are negotiated continually. For example, some of this research (Waite, 1995b) countered popular misconceptions of supervisors as being always the colonizer, the aggressor, or in the one-up position in relationships with teachers. Teachers, too, have and exert power, and not all of it benevolent. This idea flies in the face of those who, shying away from a critical examination of the lived experiences of teachers and supervisors, wittingly or unwittingly perpetuate the cult of the teacher, where the lowly teacher is always the oppressed and the supervisor is the oppressor.

However, and with that said, supervision conferences, face-to-face interactions between teacher and supervisor, have the potential to be controlled by the supervisor. This potential is there whether or not the supervisor consciously wishes to exert such control. In the first place, some teachers may wish to surrender control of the conference and its agenda to the supervisor. Perhaps the teacher is obliged to engage in supervision and feels no real investment in the process. Perhaps the teacher undervalues his or her own teaching abilities, his or her abilities to reflectively analyze his or her teaching. Perhaps the teacher recognizes the supervisor as an authority—in terms of pedagogy or subject-area expertise or as a legitimate representative of the hierarchical authority. Whatever the reason, and there are many, the teacher may willingly surrender control of a supervision conference to a supervisor.

Other, interactional processes in supervision conferences could tend to disenfranchise the teacher. Teacher disenfranchisement runs counter to the spirit and purposes of supervision (if, as we believe, supervision is about teacher reflection, growth, and personal/professional development). If this is not what the supervisor wants, he or she should be aware of the tendencies present in conventional supervisory conferences and seek to unsettle them to allow the teacher more room to maneuver, more potential for growth. (It's likely that when the teacher grows professionally, the supervisor will grow too. Just as it's likely that if the teacher is repressed, oppressed, suppressed, the supervisor will be as well.)

If supervisors and administrators wish to encourage teachers to become engaged in conversation about teaching, learning (for teachers and students), and professional development, then it's to their advantage to strive to make the interactions between them as egalitarian and as open as possible. Supervisors can heighten their awareness that they need to do work, interactional work and self-work, to "level the playing field."

Imagine, to oversimplify a great deal, that a conversation between two people is like a Ping-Pong game. Think of the volleying that goes on. One hits the ball to the other, who hits it back, and so it goes, back and forth, back and forth. Conversations can go like this, too, with each person taking a turn, back and forth. Obviously it's not as simple as this, but this simplification may help you to see how it is that, as a supervisor, you might control the conference without realizing it, without wishing to do so. Who opens the conference? Who takes the first turn at talk? Who asks most of the questions, the teacher or the supervisor? The answers to these questions would reveal who is most likely to control the conference. Our observations, both empirical (Waite, 1995a) and anecdotal, indicate that usually the supervisor opens the conference and asks most of the questions. If this is the case, and we hold that it is, more often than not, then the supervisor ends up controlling the conference, whether he or she wishes to or not.

Here's how it's likely to transpire: In dyads (two-person conversations), the turns at talk alternate back and forth, as in a Ping-Pong match. If the supervisor begins, and since each person's turn at talk is expected to be conversationally relevant, the teacher in the next turn at talk is expected to respond, at least in part, to what the supervisor said. And so it goes. The teacher, unless he or she does the interactional work required (see Waite, 1995a), never gets a free, unencumbered turn at the floor to bring up his or her concerns or what interests him or her.

A similar process transpires with questions. Generally, in the supervision conferences we've observed, it's the supervisor who asks the majority of the questions. A question requires a response (or, at least, the questioner holds the questioned accountable for producing a response) (Briggs, 1986). Not only that, but the questioner is in such a position that, when the floor returns to him or her, he or she can determine the adequacy of the response and choose to re-phrase the question or otherwise follow up on the question. The questioner controls the interaction.

Are we advocating that the supervisor never use a question or that the supervisor should never be the first one to speak? No. But we are suggesting that the supervisor and teacher know what the possibilities are, given the conventional interactional processes of conferences. Elsewhere, one of us (e.g., Waite, 1995a) has advocated a dialogic approach to supervision. In this approach, every assumption, every bias is open to examination, by either the supervisor or the teacher. If we advocated that the supervisor ask no questions, he or she could not interrogate the teacher about his or her assumptions, biases, or taken-for-granted beliefs. But the supervisor must know what is likely to result if he or she unconsciously falls into a question-asking pattern.

These are some of the microcontextual factors affecting supervision and how it is enacted by its participants, but there are more.[2] The question we really need to consider here is: To what degree does postmodernity (or a radicalized modernity, if you prefer) infiltrate each of these contexts? Given this, then, the next question to ask is: If the postmodern infiltrates the contexts surrounding supervision, and to a degree which influences supervision, what are these influences?

THE POSTMODERN

Though there are those who reject the postmodern out of hand, all evidence points to the fact that the world is in the throes of a radicalized modernity or postmodernity.[3] Before discussing the conditions that characterize postmodernity and the effects these conditions have on schools, schooling and supervision, we feel a need to offer a caveat, a qualification. No epoch, no movement, no effect is so complete, so totalizing, that there are no overlaps, no leakage of one epoch, movement, or effect to another. To put it another way, though we firmly believe postmodernity is the most prevalent social trend today, its presence and its effects are nowhere complete. There are situations, places, interactions, even people that are interesting mixtures of the modern and the postmodern, perhaps mixtures of even all historically precedent time periods (traditional, modern, and postmodern, for example—perhaps you've seen those TV commercials where a monk is discussing the Internet capabilities of his laptop?). It is difficult, then, to point to something, some occurrence, some interaction and say, "That's thoroughly postmodern!" or "That's not postmodern!"

With that said, we'll proceed on the assumption that because of its ubiquity the postmodern infiltrates nearly all aspects of "modern" life, to a certain degree. What is the point then? The point of this chapter is to call to your attention what the effects of the postmodern might be in supervision you are a part of, so that you might recognize it when you see it and maybe, just maybe, act accordingly. Another possible avenue of action is for you to be able to recognize the especially debilitating aspects of postmodernity, and there are some, so that you might counteract them in an effort to make the places where you and your colleagues work more amenable to human habitation, to say nothing of conditions for the students, the children, who populate our schools. Would you want their schools to be habitable?

Having qualified our project, let us articulate the hallmarks of the postmodern and begin to identify the effects the postmodern might have on supervision.

The major characteristics of the postmodern are:

- Intensification
- Distanciation of time and space
- Infiltration of larger social concepts into the local lived experience (the Double Hermeneutic)
- Globalization

These major characteristics are interrelated, though we shall attempt to discuss them separately as a starting point.

Intensification

Intensification has to do with the sheer density of our lives, how much there is to do in the time allotted.[4] Some global trends in work and working relationships (and here we see the interrelationship of the categories mentioned earlier) contribute heavily to the phenomenon of intensification. For instance, downsizing in business and industry has left fewer workers to do the same amount of work, with fewer resources. In schools, this trend has hit central district offices the worst, eliminating many supervisory positions. In such cases, support personnel are no longer available for teachers. Long-range planning, curriculum development, and staff development, are neglected. In local schools, principals have seen their workload increase, propelled especially by more bureaucratic forms to fill out and file and more regulations to abide by. While their bureaucratic workload increases, principals' opportunities to engage in supervision of staff becomes more bureaucratic, concerned primarily with monitoring, assessment, and evaluation. Also, in some districts, positions such as the instructional lead teacher and, in some cases, assistant principal are eliminated or their numbers severely reduced, or the duties of assistant principal become primarily bureaucratic. People have to do more with less. This results in/from intensification.[5]

These work trends affect the family, and have an impact on teachers' lives and the children they teach. In the United States, more families than ever before are two-income families, with ever more women entering the workforce

(Goldscheider & Waite, 1991). However, the available evidence indicates that women still carry the burden for maintaining the home (Goldscheider & Waite, 1991). The majority of teachers are women. This means that when their children are sick or there is an emergency at home, women teachers carry more of the burden than do their husbands, and in single-mother homes they carry all the burden. Aside from the time missed at work taking care of emergencies at home, women teachers are likely to be extremely preoccupied and perhaps severely stressed by these larger workplace trends.[6] This does not bode well for the education their students receive.

We've written that everyone is a member of multiple communities, simultaneously. Principals have told one of the authors that there are two types of problematic teachers—those who are overinvolved, who hover and cannot let go, who do not trust anyone else to handle their class, and those who, in principals' eyes, are underinvolved, the "seven-thirty to three" teachers who, in principals' terms, have their bags packed ready for the ringing of the dismissal bell. Teachers who fall into this last category earn a negative reputation for committing too little to their school, especially too little of their after-school or personal time. But, given the conditions of intensification described earlier, can anyone blame them?

Teachers and other educators are being asked to give more and more, with less and less recognition, compensation, and support. You see this in school reform/restructuring efforts, where the extra work required usually comes out of teachers' hides. Teachers become exhausted in these times of accelerated change (Hargreaves, 1998). They suffer. Their families suffer. Their students suffer, and teachers feel guilty and inadequate.

Other aspects of intensification affect educators too. Basically, there's simply too much to do in too little time. Things get jammed up. We have trouble juggling all we feel we need to accomplish. We have too many choices, too many options, and what we do attempt crowds out other options, other possibilities, other ways of being in the world.

When in a hurry, you have a short fuse, lose your temper, or don't enjoy life's finer things. We're in too much of a hurry. Under conditions of modernity, relationships suffer. We suffer. Our children, our students suffer. Think of the modern high school and the difficulty teachers there have in establishing meaningful relationships with the 120 to 180 students they see each day in classes.

What effects does intensification have on supervision? Obviously, supervision suffers because it is based on establishing relationships, rapport with teachers.

Distanciation of Time and Place

Under conditions of a radicalized modernity, the significance of time and place have changed drastically. Time becomes "crunched." Computers and global telecommunications make more distant (geographically speaking)

places accessible, twenty-four hours a day. E-mail, the Internet, and such relatively simple devices as voice mail mean that any one of us can communicate
with any other almost any time we wish. What is the etiquette involved in com-
munications that are mediated by technologies? What are the rules? What are
the courtesies? For example, the game of phone tag has changed a bit with,
first, answering machines and, now, voice mail. All one needs to do is call the
other and leave a message to pass the responsibility of taking the initiative to
the other person. It's even possible to pose questions and have them answered
(essentially having a truncated "conversation") from voice mail to voice mail
without communicating with the other party in "real" time. Does this type of
communication qualify as interpersonal communication, a concept with which
we opened this chapter? Surely, electronic communication cannot substitute
for more personal, relational communication. Recent research (*Charlotte Observer*, August 30, 1998, p. 6A) points to the detrimental personal effects of
electronic communication and of electronic "communities" such as chat
groups. In accounting for how use of the Internet can increase loneliness and
depression in people, the researchers stated that "our hypothesis is there are
more cases where you're building shallow relationships, leading to an overall
decline in feeling of connection to other people." People need to connect with
other people. Supervision can and should be personal and interpersonal.

The introduction of e-mail and its widespread use has added yet another
twist to the complexity of communication. Most people who use it have committed some type of faux pas when communicating via this medium. All you
need to do to embarrass yourself is hit the reply button and reply to the whole
list of people to whom the original message was sent when you really meant to
reply only to the sender. Administrators and supervisors have become cautious
about responding openly to e-mail inquiries when with but a touch of a few
buttons that reply could be forwarded to any number of distribution lists. What
is private and what is public communication in this medium? As a society, we are
still working on these issues; the issue is unsettled, and that makes it postmodern, the unsettled, unsettling condition of rapid, accelerating change, where the
old ways are discarded but new, agreed-upon conditions are nonexistent.

What is required in these times? It seems ironic at this point to say that an
antidote to the malaise of postmodernity is communication. Communication
and more communication are what is needed to bring us closer together, but
we will have more to say about that later in the chapter.

The Infiltration of Larger Social Concepts into the Local
Lived Experience (the Double Hermeneutic)

Education, at least in its theory and theorizing, generally lags behind the
other social sciences. Postmodernity has been accepted in architecture, literature and literary studies, philosophy, anthropology, and sociology for some
time. Still, even given this lag time, philosophies and theories (explanations if

you will) from other social sciences eventually filter into the literature and the dialogue of education and educators. In a more general sense, these conceptions of social scientists percolate into the language and understanding of the general lay public, a phenomenon Anthony Giddens (1990) terms a *double hermeneutic*. In simple terms, there is a two-way (the double) understanding (the hermeneutic) continually occurring between social scientists and what/whom they study (that is, social phenomena). Social phenomena, people and their behaviors/interactions especially, are changing even as social scientists attempt to understand them. These changes are brought about, in part, because the people, the social actors, learn from the descriptions and explanations (in short, the research) done of them or similar circumstances. Take, for example, Deborah Tannen's work in *You Just Don't Understand* (Tannen, 1990) or *Talking 9 to 5* (Tannen, 1994) or John Gray's (1992) work in the *Men Are from Mars, Women Are from Venus* series. These are examples of research in social science that influences how we behave, and how we think about how we behave. At the least, familiarity with these works and others like them gives us terms and concepts with which we make sense of our lives and our work. People become aware that conversations may be dominated by men and masculine protocols and norms, and, in some cases, set out to change those norms, to make conversations more open to women and their values. Our work in supervision, hopefully, will encourage people to make some changes as well.

Science, especially social science, is inexact, built upon examination of phenomena that are ever changing. Our trust in science is tentative, since most of us have come to believe that science cannot offer us immutable, transcendent Truth, with a capital T. The dethroning of science, putting it in its place as an approximation of reality, never an accurate depiction of reality itself, is another hallmark of the postmodern. In the development (for we hesitate to use the terms evolution or progression) of civilization or the social world, certain regimes are displaced by others. The regime of religion, epitomized by the rule of the Catholic Church, was displaced by the regime of science, which, in turn, is in the process of being dethroned itself. But, recall our earlier qualification that no mode of thought, no way of thinking, and here, no regime is completely and utterly banished. Remnants of each former mode of thinking are always somewhere present in the epochs which succeed it.[7] There are aspects of religious (i.e., Catholic, Judeo-Christian) dogmatism/thought, scientism/scientific thought, and/or modern/modernistic thought present within postmodern situations, conditions, and people. It cannot be otherwise.

The skepticism with which science and other dogmas are seen contributes to other widespread social conditions, conditions of the postmodern, having to do with a crisis of authority and a crisis of representation. As these have been discussed at length elsewhere (Waite, 1995a, 1997), we shall touch upon these phenomena only briefly here. The crisis of authority or the crisis of legitimacy (Habermas, 1976) implies that authority is suspect. You've seen the bumperstickers: Question Authority! Leaders, even governments and other social institutions have to continually establish their authority. Authority and legitimacy are no longer permanent characteristics. Take, for example, the monarchy in Britain. The British monarchy has been criticized and questioned more than ever before. Tabloids in the United Kingdom and elsewhere publish intimate details of the cavorting of the prince and recently deceased princess. In the United States the papers are currently preoccupied with the intimate details of the president's life. Imagine! Lesser, more humble leaders and institutions are openly questioned just as well.

It is interesting that, here, under conditions of the postmodern, supervisors have an advantage over other administrators. Why? According to the conventional wisdom (Pajak, 1989), administrators function in line positions and exercise line authority, while supervisors are more likely to be in staff positions, exercising staff authority. Line authority, that hierarchical type, is more likely than staff authority to be under attack today because of the crisis of legitimacy just discussed. Administrators, it could be argued, are better off not depending too heavily on the power of their position (i.e, their line authority), but instead exercising more staff authority—the power that comes from personal attributes (such as charisma), persuasion, "expertise," and knowledge. If you consider the administrators you know, more and more of them are likely to be moving away from a heavy-handed wielding of authority, throwing their weight around, and are becoming "leaders." We agree with Pajak (personal communication, November 1, 1997) that supervision and educational leadership are synonymous. That is to say, supervisors were educational leaders long before the term came into vogue.

That is not to say that the conditions of postmodernity don't affect supervisors, for they do. If science and its certainty are being questioned, so-called expert knowledge is suspect as well. Supervisors, or others, who arrive on the scene and proclaim with absolute certainty that this or that way is the way to teach (or, if they carry this message to the teachers from "on high," that is, as a state or district mandate) are likely to be met with a healthy dose of skepticism. That's as it should be. Teachers are likely to respond to mandates, to one-best-way approaches, with "but it won't work with these (my/our) children"; which is to say that mandates from afar are not automatically suited to local conditions and must be adapted.

Caught up in the postmodern and connected to the crises of legitimacy and of representation is a rising tide of rejection of so-called master narratives—grand and grandiose claims, explanations, and projects. The teachers' response to the one-best-way approach is an example of this. More and more people are rejecting global solutions in favor of local remedies, tailored to fit local conditions. Wasn't it the late Speaker of the U.S. House of Representatives, Tip O'Neil, who said all politics is local?

Supervisors face another problem if they are operating from a modernist or a conventional/traditional supervision paradigm. That problem is occasioned by the interplay of the crisis of representation and the double hermeneutic.

The lay public, and this includes teachers, is coming to believe that it's darn difficult, if not impossible, to "capture reality." This results from the ever-increasingly accepted belief in the uncertainty of science and in a more widely accepted idea that there is no Truth. That is, there is no one, everlasting, eternal truth that is/will be true for everybody and for all time. On top of that, it has become accepted that our depictions of "reality" are only pale approximations of whatever it is we are trying to depict. These beliefs are summed up in such questions as: What is truth? What is reality? Whose truth is it? Whose reality is it?[8]

These phenomena combine to call data gathering during supervisory observations into question. A moment's contemplation reveals data gathering, done by a fallible human being (a supervisor) with limited abilities and operating with a set of selective perceptions, to be a tenuous platform on which to build an evaluation, an interpretation (as in a supervisor's comments on a lesson), or an intervention.[9]

To begin to counteract the effects of the crises of representation and of legitimacy, we recommend a process of Dialogic Supervision (Waite, 1995a)—a process based on mutual respect, critique, and a recognition of the positionality of each party. We will return to the discussion of Dialogic Supervision after sketching out the last of the characteristics, the hallmarks, of the postmodern—globalization.

Globalization

Work trends point to more and more globalization. Communication is more globalized, and, as pointed out earlier, this affects time and how we perceive it. Though we've written that one effect of postmodern conditions is that teachers, for example, concern themselves more and more with the local while being simultaneously influenced by distant forces, this doesn't change the fact that education is becoming more globalized. Contradictions, or what Hargreaves (1995) termed paradoxes, permeate the postmodern.

One of the paradoxes Hargreaves (1995) dealt with was that "more globalism produces more tribalism" (p. 15). Basically, this means that globalization can foster competitive rhetoric ("We'll be first in math and science by the year 2000!," for example), and gives ammunition to those who wish to scapegoat others— certain countries (such as Japan) or groups (such as "illegal" immigrants). At the same time, this fierce competitiveness, kindled by thinly veiled xenophobia and nationalism, allows certain ideological groups (the Right) to push their agenda (standards and accountability) upon the nation as a solution, or THE solution. We can't allow America to be second to anyone, now can we?!

Smyth (1992) wrote of global effects upon teachers' lives. His treatment of the "politics of reflection" actually highlighted a paradox or contradiction in current educational reform: that teachers and others are being asked to collaborate more and more on less and less. Put another way, reforms, including collaboration, site-based decision making, and shared governance, come at the same time that there is more standardization of curricula, more policies and state-mandated "reforms," "higher" standards, and "high-stakes evaluation systems" (Hargreaves, 1998). Teachers and supervisors are being asked to collaborate more and more on less and less. The situation is made worse, as pointed out by Hargreaves (1996), and the frustration of educators intensifies because, for the most part, reforms are targeted at the local school level. Our understanding of contexts, mentioned earlier, especially the mutual influence the various levels of context have, one on the other, helps to explain why this situation is so frustrating. Basically, there's only so much one can do locally. We've seen it happen time and again, where administrators at whatever level turn shared decision-making into shared blaming, where administrators wash their hands of responsibility and pass the blame on to the teachers at the local site. Again, as noted, these processes—the corruption of potentially democratic processes—can, in the wrong hands and for the wrong reasons, lend themselves to shaming and blaming, blaming the victims (teachers and supervisors) for results and outcomes over which they have little control.

Supervision and supervisors are implicated in/by the processes of globalization. How can it be otherwise when everyone else is so severely affected? Supervisors become bureaucrats, forced to implement mandates from higher organizational levels—district, state, and national. Standards and accountability (and here we include evaluation and assessment) are a part of the national agenda, stemming from a concern with global competitiveness at the national level. Local concerns get lost in the shuffle. Again, local personal and interpersonal community and local network concerns are slighted, ignored and neglected, as global issues come to take precedence over them. Supervision, its theory and procedures, fall prey to market forces. Education becomes globalized, and supervision follows suit.

DANGER AND OPPORTUNITY: DIALOGIC SUPERVISION AS AN ANTIDOTE TO THE NEGATIVE EFFECTS OF POSTMODERNITY

Perhaps you recall the reputed Chinese curse: May you live in interesting times! The times we are living in are that and more. We understand that the Chinese character for crisis is a combination of the characters for danger and opportunity. The postmodern is ripe with opportunity, even as certain dangers are present. Though we've perhaps been pessimistic in what we've written to this point, we certainly don't wish to be accused of the nihilism some consider to be an earmark of the postmodern. In change there is hope. The seeds of revolutionary transformation are to be found in times of radical change: *Carpe diem*—if we but seize the moment.

What is Dialogic Supervision? First, we must assert that we don't see Dialogic Supervision as a panacea. We don't wish, either, to perpetuate another metanarrative. Still, with these caveats, what is Dialogic Supervision and how might it serve to counter some of the negative effects of the malaise of postmodernity?[10]

Dialogic Supervision was born from an odd admixture of the postmodern, the poststructural, linguistics, philosophy, feminism, supervision theory, and empirical research. Dialogic Supervision is loosely based upon the work of the late Russian literary theorist Mikhail Bakhtin.

Dialogic Supervision is an approach to supervision that is grounded in and meant to be applied to face-to-face communication, though recently the present authors have extended Dialogic Supervision to the areas of professional development, organization development and political development at contextual levels ranging from the interpersonal to the school, and further, from the local to the global. As the name implies, Dialogic Supervision is premised on dialogue, but not just any dialogue, a dialogue that is based upon mutual respect and reflective and open critique. In Dialogic Supervision assumptions are open to question, possibilities are limitless.

With such a new approach as this, there first needs to be a certain groundwork laid. Initial (and ongoing) self-work needs to be done by all the participants in Dialogic Supervision. Supervisors need to check themselves for their assumptions and presuppositions. Supervisors need to be able to both give and receive critique (i.e., criticism) in humane and constructive ways. Supervisors, perhaps, are more adept at giving critique than they are at receiving it. Even more, supervisors must "invite" critique and, perhaps, encourage and instruct the teachers with whom they work on how to do so. A potential pitfall, which can be avoided by setting the stage and attending to the contexts of Dialogic Supervision, is that such supervisory sessions could degenerate into complaint sessions, be those sessions face-to-face clinical supervision, staff development sessions, curriculum development committee meetings, or of some other type.

Communication is always a negotiated process. The meaning of supervision is always negotiated, just as the roles of the participants are constantly being negotiated. This is the complicity to which the title of this chapter refers. Teachers are responsible for the supervision (or lack thereof) they receive, just as supervisors are. It takes two to tango.

In the beginning, a supervisor may wish to elicit the teachers' understandings of supervision. The supervisor may do so orally or in writing. This would set the stage and give each person a place to start. The supervisor, as an equal participant, may share with teachers, individually or in groups, his/her current understanding of supervision, his/her role, the process and its likely outcomes, all the while communicating that supervision is a dynamic process, negotiable and subject to change.

Our suggestion is that, especially within the postmodern, a primary role of supervisors is to help teachers deal with change, to prepare them to thrive in dynamic, shifting contexts of change. Of course, supervisors must be able to thrive in such contexts if they are to be of any assistance to others. This is another aspect of the self-work mentioned earlier. Knowledge of the teacher's understanding of supervision may give the supervisor insight into the teacher's stage of development (which would be helpful for those who believe in developmental stage theory). Essentially, then, seeking understanding of the teacher's perception of supervision could serve as an assessment tool, while opening that understanding up for negotiation.

Because of the nature of supervisory authority and the crisis of legitimacy (authority), supervisors using the dialogic approach will want to communicate their status as a learner. That is, under conditions of postmodernity, supervisory authority, what little there is, will be based upon mutual respect, vulnerability, and authenticity.[11] Within Dialogic Supervision supervisors operate from a "positionality" rather than from an organizational, hierarchical "position." Positionality speaks to the feminist standpoint view of identity and, thereby, of authority—a view very much similar to Bakhtin's concept of answerability. Both terms and their related concepts imply that when speaking to someone, the communication is targeted to a particular sociohistorical being, as the speaker perceives the other to be. In Bakhtinian terms, the communication is aimed at the hearer's conceptual horizon, with the hearer's answer already anticipated even in the framing of the speaker's utterance. For Bakhtin, words belong to neither the speaker nor the hearer, but acquire their meaning from an area somehow between the speaker and hearer, from the larger sociohistorical context(s) from which the word derives and within which the word is situated. Words come already inflected with meaning, but speakers (and hearers) can re-inflect the word. Words and their meanings are of many types, most ideologically laden. There are authoritative words, the words of the fathers, in Bakhtinian terms. There are multivoiced words and dialogues—words and dialogues that reflect the many voices in a community. These multivoiced words and dialogues are what Bakhtin termed *dialogic*. The polar opposite of a dialogic word, utterance, or dialogue is that which Bakthin terms *monologic*. The monologic is authoritarian. It is not open to inflection or interpretation and recognizes no other voices or perspectives.

Positionality and answerability, combined, call forth a person's responsibility to speak for himself or herself and from his or her sociohistorical position. People—teachers, administrators, and supervisors—must be wary of speaking for others and must beware of others' words that are spoken through them. People need to bear witness and have a responsibility to respond as only they can—from their perspective and informed by their biography, their history, their philosophy, and their beliefs. Supervisors can bear witness, as can teachers. Supervisors can witness a teaching episode or the situation or contexts in a school or district and speak authentically and forthrightly from their perspective. Teachers have this right and obligation too. Supervisors, using a dialogic approach, recognize their positionality and that of the teacher, who most likely has a different perspective, and encourage a dialogue between these perspectives, these points of view and positionalities.

In advocating a dialogic approach to supervision we mean to rehabilitate supervision to reflect more contemporary understandings of communication, while, at the same time, we attempt to open supervision up—to make it more inclusive, more democratic, more egalitarian. Supervision serves as an antidote to the negative effects of the postmodern when it recognizes and fosters authentic relationships (i.e., community). Authentic relationships do not thrive under conditions of intensification. Time and caring are needed. Respect, understanding and flexibility are needed and must be demonstrated by everyone involved—teachers, administrators, students, students' parents, supervisors, staff, and members of the local community. For what we wrote earlier as characteristic of communication is applicable to education and educational interactions: How we talk, how we teach, how we administer and supervise means as much or more as what we say and what we teach, administer, or supervise.

Perhaps it is fitting that we end this chapter by mentioning another key Bakhtinian term—*unfinalizability* (Emerson, 1993; Hall, 1995). Unfinalizability deals with the notion that no one can ever "start anything over fresh," that the past always leaks into the present and leaves traces, and with the "virtues of surprise and creativity in everyday life" (Emerson, 1993). Supervision, learning, and communication are dynamic, never-ending processes. Even though there are sociohistorical and contextual constraints at work on us, especially exacerbated in postmodern times, there are always dynamic, creative and liberating forces at play as well. *Carpe diem*. Seize the moment!

Case Study 10: A Dialogic Approach to Supervision

Rose is the new principal of a middle school in a large town in the south. This is not her first assignment as a principal, as she was a principal in another town for the past ten years. However, now that she has to start her new job, she is very anxious, because she believes she knows nothing about the new school and the environment where she has to act. As Rose is concerned about teachers' personal and professional growth, she wants to start by listening to what teachers in this new school have to say, what their needs are, and how they perceive the environment in which they act. After that, and only then, she feels, can all of them together discuss the priorities to be implemented.

While she is waiting for the teachers to come to their first meeting, and although she has strengthened her willingness and ability to listen to them, she is also thinking about some strategies to develop autonomy in children and improve their learning. Because of her past experience, Rose is very aware of the difficulties all will face in achieving this, mainly that of teachers working alone, in an isolated and private way. That is why she intends to work collegially, involving teachers in all decisions. Will teachers accept working together? Will they accept, at least some of them, working in partnership with other colleagues as their "critical friends"?

Her thoughts were interrupted by the arrival of the first teachers. While they were choosing a place to sit, other teachers arrived, and ten minutes later Rose started talking about her concerns and goals. Steve, a math teacher and an attentive listener, instead of answering her concerns, stressed the problems caused by the last changes mandated at the state level and complained that he was tired of always being ignored by policy makers. Other teachers supported his complaints and emphasized the stress caused by such changes, changes they felt were superficial or even detrimental to children's learning.

After this moment of catharsis, one teacher started talking about her own needs and about the areas of her development in which she was willing to invest. Then, a few suggestions came from some teachers, which were in the direction that Rose expected:

- Jean, a music teacher, remembered the experience she had had in helping children develop their sense of autonomy;

- William agreed to work with Mary (both are geography teachers) as her "critical friend"; and

- Pamela expressed her interest in using the Internet.

The remaining teachers kept silent. Rose had an idea of how the discussion should go, but she was afraid that some teachers would become defensive. She became aware that she had to rethink her approach to teachers' feelings. She is now sure that if she doesn't take these feelings into account, the desired changes and teachers' commitment to change won't occur. The challenge was harder than she had thought.

FOLLOW-UP QUESTIONS

1. What, in your opinion, are the main supervision roles of a principal?

2. Can Rose's approach to supervision be considered a modern or a postmodern one? Give reasons for your answer.

3. Can a collaborative culture be built without changing the isolation in which teachers usually work?

4. Are the aforementioned "critical friends" necessarily compatible with dialogic supervision? How can they become so?

5. What strategies should Rose follow to deal with the debilitating aspects of postmodernity that were brought up by the teachers? Following a dialogic approach, what are some other things Rose can do?

NOTES

1. Ideolect is the linguist's term for a person's speech—his/her own, personal dialect. Propriospect is Goodenough's equivalent term for a person's personal, unique culture. Obviously, both language and culture have some, though not all, elements that are shared by other people. Interestingly, the closer people are in physical proximity and experience, the more the various elements of language and culture are shared.

2. There are other layers or levels of context within which supervisors and teachers work; which influence them, their thoughts and beliefs, their actions, and the understandings and interpretations, each of the other and of supervision itself. In discussing anthropological and philosophical texts and textual interpretation, Scharfstein (1989) discussed five levels of context (though, he wrote, "any particular subject matter would suggest its own variation on this set" [p. 63]). These five levels are: The microcontextual, the correlative context, the macrocontext, the metacontext, and the universal context. The microcontextual level is synonymous with that which we dis-

cussed earlier, having to do with the words immediately surrounding a given passage or utterance. The correlative context is comprised of, say, an author's other work and the ideas upon which she or he draws; as such, it is the next layer or ring of an ever-widening circle, taking in more and more ideas and influences, though more removed, physically, from the immediate microcontext. For supervisors, the correlative context may include other supervisory interactions that the supervisor may have had with the present teacher and others. The macrocontext is more impersonal than the microcontext and deals with larger matters, such as disputes between schools of thought and cultural conditions. Scharfstein (p. 65) notes that "the inclusiveness of macrocontexts creates a constantly overlapping effect." The macrocontext deals with a certain phenomenon, say supervision, from above and allows for comparison among and between different overarching systems (for example, of thought or practice), of which the phenomenon of interest is but a part. The universal context is a joining together of all the other contexts, in their relations to each other, to make visible the full universe of the phenomenon, the text, or the object of interest. Surely, this taxonomy of contexts is applicable to supervision and supervisory interactions, though we simply wish to show here the complexities of the contexts affecting supervisory practice.

3. The fact that some people reject postmodernism really has to do with the confusion between poststructuralism and postmodernity and the reaction of society's conservative elements. That is to say, in the strict sense, postmodernity and the postmodern (or radicalized modernity) are terms sociologists and other social commentators employ to speak of social conditions today. These are descriptive terms, and postmodernity is a *social description*. As such, one would be hard pressed to defend a position that denied the globalization of the economy and of communication, primary contributors to the postmodern condition. Poststructuralism, on the other hand, is a more politically loaded term, a radical analysis of present conditions. Proponents and practitioners of poststructuralism are concerned with how the world is constituted through language and, especially, how power, oppression, and hegemony operate through language. The fact that poststructuralism is a radical critique of the world engenders strong reactions, and when poststructuralism is conflated with postmodernism, both are easily dismissed by reactionary elements of society.

4. Time is another interesting concept, one which we'll discuss under intensification. Suffice it to say here that time, that is, our conception of time, is a thoroughly modern concept (for example, "time is money," the notion that one can "waste" time or save time). If we are to rehabilitate the modern, we would accomplish much if we could come to other conceptions of time.

5. The impetus for downsizing is an effort to "streamline" organizations and bureaucracies, that is, to cut costs. We see here how higher, arguably more noble ideals such as education are displaced by market motives.

6. Here we are writing of large, global trends. We recognize exceptions exist (e.g., single fathers who are teachers or husbands who share equally in household responsibilities or who do a disproportionate amount of them).

7. Here it is relevant to mention the debate over the term *postmodern*. The "post" prefix implies that postmodernity comes after the modern, with a clear demarcation of boundaries between the modern and that which comes after it, the postmodern. However, and as we argue, there are no such clear demarcations. Everything is complex, dynamic, and interwoven. So, though we prefer the more accurately de-

scriptive term *radicalized modernity*, after Giddens (1990), it is sometimes more convenient to speak and write of the postmodern and postmodernity.

8. Others, critical theorists, for example, might ask the next questions: What interests does this definition of truth serve? Who benefits if we accept this definition of reality? Who is disadvantaged by acceptance of this definition of reality? Of truth?

9. See Waite (1995a) for a more thorough discussion of these issues.

10. For a more complete discussion of Dialogic Supervision, please refer to *Rethinking Instructional Supervision: Notes on Its Language and Culture* (Waite, 1995a).

11. We recognize that authenticity is troubled by poststructuralist thinkers: What about a person is "authentic," given poststructuralist assumptions that people and situations are brought into being, defined, by language? The person, poststructurally, is shifting and elusive and, therefore, has no core personality, no essential characteristics that can be "authentic."

REFERENCES

Apple, M. W. (1998). Are markets and standards democratic? (Review of the book *Devolution and choice in education: The school, the state and the market). Educational Researcher, 27,* 24–28.

Bakhtin, M. M. (1981). *The dialogic imagination* (M. Holquist, Ed.) (C. Emerson & M. Holquist, trans.). Austin: University of Texas Press.

Blumer, H. (1972). Symbolic interaction. In G. Spradley (Ed.), *Culture and cognition: Rules, maps, and plans* (pp. 65–83). San Francisco: Chandler Publishing Company.

Briggs, C. L. (1986). *Learning how to ask: A sociolinguistic appraisal of the role of the interview in social science research*. Cambridge: Cambridge University Press.

Cicourel, A. V. (1992). The interpenetration of communicative contexts: Examples from medical encounters. In A. Duranti & C. Goodwin (Eds.), *Rethinking context: Language as an interactive phenomenon* (pp. 291–310). Cambridge: Cambridge University Press.

Cogan, M. L. (1973). *Clinical supervision*. Boston: Houghton Mifflin.

Emerson, C. (1993, October). *Revolutionary dissident against the Russian idea: Mikhail Bakhtin in the perspective of American pragmatism*. Paper delivered to the University of Georgia Humanities Center, Athens.

Giddens, A. (1990). *The consequences of modernity*. Stanford, CA: Stanford University Press.

Goldscheider, F. K., & Waite, L. J. (1991). *New families, no families?: The transformation of the American home*. Berkeley: University of California Press.

Goodenough, W. H. (1981). *Culture, language, and society* (2nd ed.). Menlo Park, CA: Benjamin/Cummings Publishing Company.

Gray, J. (1992). *Men are from Mars, women are from Venus*. New York: HarperCollins.

Habermas, J. (1976). *Legitimation crisis* (T. MacCarthy, trans.). London: Hinemann.

Hall, J. K. (1995). (Re)creating our world with words: A sociohistorical perspective of face-to-face interaction. *Applied Linguistics, 16,* 206–232.

Hargreaves, A. (1991, April). *Prepare to meet thy mood?: Teacher preparation time and the intensification thesis*. Paper presented to the annual meeting of the American Educational Research Association, Chicago.

Hargreaves, A. (1995). Renewal in the age of paradox. *Educational Leadership,* 52(7), 14–19.

Hargreaves, A. (1996, April). *Cultures of teaching and educational change.* Paper presented to the annual meeting of the American Educational Research Association, New York.

Hargreaves, A. (1998). The emotional politics of teaching and teacher development: With implications for educational leadership. *International Journal of Leadership in Education, 1*(4), 315–336.

McDermott, R. P., & Church, J. (1976). Making sense and feeling good: The ethnography of communication and identity work. *Communication, 2,* 121–142.

Mead, G. H. (1934). *Mind, self, & society.* Chicago: University of Chicago Press.

Pajak, E. F. (1989). *The central office supervisor of curriculum and instruction: Setting the stage for success.* Boston: Allyn & Bacon.

Scharfstein, B. (1989). *The dilemma of context.* New York: New York University Press.

Sergiovanni, T. J., & Starratt, R. J. (1997). *Supervision: A redefinition* (6th ed.). New York: McGraw Hill.

Smyth, J. (1992). Teachers' work and the politics of reflection. *American Educational Research Journal, 29,* 267–300.

Tannen, D. (1990). *You just don't understand: Women and men in conversation.* New York: Murrow.

Tannen, D. (1994). *Talking from 9 to 5: How women's and men's conversational styles affect who gets heard, who gets credit, and what gets done at work.* New York: Murrow.

Waite, D. (1995a). *Rethinking instructional supervision: Notes on its language and culture.* London: The Falmer Press.

Waite, D. (1995b). Teacher resistance in a supervision conference. In D. Corson (Ed.), *Discourse and power in educational organizations* (pp. 71–86). Cresskill, NJ: Hampton Press.

Waite, D. (1997, November). *Supervision and the contradictions it must face.* Paper presented at the annual meeting of the Council of Professors of Instructional Supervision, Pittsburgh, PA.

11

Possibilities of Postmodern Supervision

Patricia E. Holland and Maryalice Obermiller

GUIDING QUESTIONS

1. *What concepts of postmodern theory are evident in postmodernist supervision?*
2. *What changes in the supervisor's role are reflected in the six postmodernist supervision scenarios in this chapter?*
3. *What is the teacher's role in postmodernist supervision?*
4. *How does postmodernist supervision make supervision, teaching, and learning integrated rather than hierarchically structured activities?*
5. *How does the supervisor support teachers' professional development in postmodernist supervision?*

When educators discuss postmodernism and what it means for them in their work and study, there is a marked tendency to drift toward abstraction and to focus on concepts of postmodernist theory itself, rather than to describe how these concepts are enacted in educational practice. Perhaps this drift into heady intellectual and linguistic realms occurs because the present configuration and operation of schools remains such a deeply entrenched norm and one so antithetical to postmodernism that envisioning anything different happens only in what Larry Cuban (1990) has described as "tinkering at the edges." For practitioners, administrators as well as teachers, who are working under increasingly heavy burdens of bureaucratic accountability (Seashore-Louis, 1998), it is often difficult even to imagine—much less to create—schools and classrooms that mirror anything other than modernist "metanarratives" of "linear progress, rational planning of ideal social orders, and the standardization of knowledge and production" (Harvey, 1989). Acknowledging these difficulties does not suggest, however, that educators ignore the challenges of postmodernist thought. Rather, as we will attempt to demonstrate, efforts to understand postmodernism's influence might well involve recognizing and focusing on the glimmers of postmodernism that appear in actual contexts for educational practice. Understanding postmodernism may also involve consideration of how to construct contexts for educational practice that are themselves exemplars of postmodernist concepts.

Our particular focus in this chapter is on the educational practice of supervision and on constructing and recognizing what a postmodernist version of supervision might look like. Such a postmodernist view of supervision, by its very nature, cannot be merely an abstraction. Nor can it rely on familiar descriptions of supervision as a set of principles and protocols that a supervisor selects and applies in a prescriptive manner to the particular situations these principles and protocols are designed to address and remedy. Even high points of supervision theorizing, such as models of clinical (Cogan, 1973) and developmental supervision (Glickman, Gordon, & Ross-Gordon, 1995), present supervision in what are essentially such modernist and instrumentalist terms.

Postmodernism, on the other hand, demands that the theory and practice of supervision not be viewed in isolation, but rather be seen as a part of a larger context that includes and gives equal emphasis to teaching and learning. When we asked ourselves what such a context might look like and how we could construe an educational setting where supervision, teaching, and learning become equal rather than hierarchically structured activities, we discovered one already evident in efforts to support teachers' learning and use of instructional technology. We find it interesting to adopt a pragmatic position and assume that the value of postmodern ideas for educators lies in its utility for school settings. Moreover, we believe that technology, which is itself a kind of postmodernist phenomenon in its open discontinuity, can serve as a catalyst for the development of what can be described as co-constructed postmodernist approaches to teaching, learning, and supervision. While we have observed that this catalytic potential of technology remains largely unrecognized, we contend that examining it through lenses offered by concepts of postmodernism offers a way to contextualize our thinking about supervision within settings of teaching and learning.

In the following sections of this chapter we will present six scenarios of teaching, learning, and supervision as they occur within contexts of instructional technology. These scenarios are typical examples of how technology is being used in schools across the country; in other words, they are not examples drawn from exceptional schools in the vanguard of technology equipment, knowledge, or use. Each scenario will be developed as a context featuring a particular concept associated with postmodernist theory. As we have said, our primary interest is in how such contexts foster postmodern views of supervision and in how they help us understand, recognize, and create postmodernist versions of supervision. To those ends, then, we will explore how each scenario illustrates a particular postmodernist concept and, more importantly, what that concept implies for the theory and practice of instructional supervision. We will also consider the challenges such concepts pose to current views of supervisory theory and practice.

CONTEXT SCENARIO

Two science teachers walk into a school's computer lab during their planning period. They wave to their colleague, the school's technology specialist, who is in an area of the lab where folding partitions enclose twenty or so computer stations, creating a space where an English class works on a newsletter project. The technology specialist stands beside the English teacher and listens and jots down notes while the teacher explains and then demonstrates for a student how to download graphics and position them in the newsletter. When the teacher moves on to assist another student, the technology specialist leaves the enclosed area and joins the two science teachers who have seated themselves at a table in an open area of the computer lab. The science teachers, one a veteran of fifteen years, the other a novice in her second year of teaching, explain that they have come to talk about how they might use the new science software program "Model-it." They are interested in the capabilities "Model-it" has to support learners in first building qualitative models, then providing them with assistance as they move toward developing quantitative models. "Model-it" would provide a simulation environment and a modeling environment for students to build and test their own scientific models. Together, the specialist and the teachers plan a series of lessons using the software and decide to meet to review the students' work in order to evaluate their use of the software in terms of its ability to help the students understand science concepts, not just science facts and procedures, and also for its ability to prepare students to meet certain objectives on the annual state achievement tests. The veteran teacher suggests that some consideration might also be given to what a review of the students' work suggests about the software's potential for use with younger students. Arrangements are also made for the technology specialist to present a model lesson using the software for a combined group of both teachers' students, and for the novice and specialist to co-teach the other lessons using the software.

The scenario we present is certainly not distinguished by any extreme departure from what might happen in the ordinary course of events within many school settings. Because it is so ordinary, to think of this scenario in terms of postmodernist supervision may appear at first glance somewhat odd. What does this scenario have to do with supervision? There is not even any mention of a supervisor or of supervision. The seeming absence of supervision is, in fact, one of the elements of the scenario that reflects postmodernist thinking, in that it is not disruptive to established bureaucratic power structures within which supervision is traditionally located. Supervision is instead seen as a working relationship among educators that emerges out of and is defined by

specifics of their work situations. The typical hierarchical power structure in which the supervisor holds the power to define teaching and to dictate its practice to teachers dissolves. Instead of what commonly occurs when a supervisor enters a classroom either to evaluate a teacher or to help correct deficiencies in instructional practices or in the use of curriculum materials, this scenario depicts the technology specialist's work with the English and science teachers as occurring at the teachers' behest and emerging out of what the teachers themselves identify as needs in their teaching circumstances at that particular time. This distinction is an important one for postmodernist supervision in that it shifts power and control over decisions about what and how to teach from supervisors and administrators to teachers. Familiar practices of clinical supervision (Cogan, 1973; Acheson & Gall, 1997)—planning with teachers for instruction, observing teaching, and meeting with teachers to review information about their teaching—become integral parts of *teaching* rather than a separate and external process of *supervision*.

The distinction is also important because postmodernist supervision so conceived becomes a constructivist process in which truth and knowledge are considered to be human inventions, rather than representations capturing some absolute knowledge or truth that has its own existence outside of the mind that holds it (Anderson, 1990). A corollary assumption of postmodern constructivism is that knowledge develops within communities; in other words, knowledge is socially constructed. For supervision, these assumptions mean that instead of being defined as a process that operates from the outside in, it is redefined from the inside out and comes to be seen not as an extraordinary event but as rooted in the daily life of classrooms. Supervisors and teachers, like the technology specialist and teachers in our scenario, engage with events of teaching and learning in more naturalistic ways and create "texts" (for instance, the specialist's notes on the English teacher's directions, the specialist's and teachers' judgments about the math students' projects, or the collaboratively prepared instructional materials) that recount their experiences. Teachers and supervisors establish interpretive communities and commit themselves to working relationships and open discourse in which together they seek to cull from their "texts" whatever meanings they can.

Postmodernist supervision as a constructivist process not only conceives of knowledge as socially constructed human invention, but also contends that such knowledge is specific to its setting—it is context-bound. According to this view, the postmodern supervisor is faced with what Foucault (1984) has termed "heterotopia," that is, the coexistence in "an impossible space" of a "large number of fragmentary worlds." The postmodern response to this situation is to relinquish illusions of controlling supervisory situations or of moving toward some generally accepted ideal model of teaching or learning or supervision. Instead of judging teaching performance and prescribing remedies to improve it, supervisors give up their myths of infinite progress—for either teachers' practice or their own. They come to see supervision as an opportunity to examine the ways that they and teachers construct their various realities of teaching and learning. They adopt a view that, in the words of constructivist Ernst von Glaserfeld (1984), maintains "that the operations by which we assemble our experiential world can be explored, and that an awareness of this operating . . . can help us do it differently and, perhaps, better."

HYPERTEXT SCENARIO

Using the networking capabilities of technology, student learning activities are no longer limited by textbooks, campus media, or local library resources, which in the past made it possible as well as practical to think about what students learn in standardized and uniform terms. Technology makes it possible for teachers to help students customize learning. Rather than arrive in a classroom where the curriculum has been pre-planned for an average student, age 12, seventh grade, students work as partners with their teachers to assess their needs and interests and to shape learning experiences and choose learning resources that respond to these needs and interests. Imagine, for instance, a classroom in Texas history where students are gathering information about various nationalities who settled in the state. One group of students might be researching the influences of German culture on Texas, using a map to locate communities with German names. They then use one of the four computers in the classroom to search the Web for homepages of some of these communities to see what evidence there is of continuing German influence. One of the students excitedly reports discovering a website developed by students in Germany who are gathering information about where people who emigrated from their town settled in America. Another group decides to conduct interviews of Vietnamese immigrants to Texas and seek the help of the school librarian to help them search online the archives of national and local newspapers to see how the media reported the arrival of these new citizens. They are shocked to discover reports of blatant discrimination against Vietnamese fishermen.

The teacher in this classroom helps the groups think about what resources they might use to explore their topics, keeping an open mind to letting the information gathered by the students suggest next steps for their study. The teacher also helps the students think about the meaning of the information they have gathered, not in terms of some absolute generalizations about the immigrant experience in Texas, but with an openness to what might well be conflicting and contradictory ideas. During times when the class assembles as a whole rather than in their project subgroups, these conflicting and contradictory ideas are discussed. Both the students and the teacher accept that differences of opinion may not be resolvable within the class, but that they provide ideas to think about long after the projects are complete.

We have borrowed the term "hypertext" from the language of technology to convey the sense in which classroom learning, like hypertext software, provides a nonlinear method of accessing and organizing information. Unlike traditional approaches to curriculum and teaching, which rely on a teacher's or someone else's sequential organization of information for learning, hypertext systems leave the learner free to explore and integrate information in uniquely different ways. According to Beiber (1993), such hypertext systems provide flexible access to information by incorporating notions of navigation, annotation, and tailored presentation. These notions are illustrated in the scenario, as students and their teacher explore varying information sources and construct their own interpretations of the meaning and significance of the information they gather about immigration to Texas. Diversity exists not only in different approaches and materials students use but also in differences in the outcomes of student learning.

The notion of hypertext is a postmodernist one in that it opens the way to thinking about multiple realities. In a classroom context, such multiple realities are shaped as students study different material and choose varying ways to demonstrate what they have learned. In keeping with the hypertext notion, the teacher's role in the classroom is also nonlinear and flexible, as she helps students produce and understand complex and richly referenced bodies of information. While no mention of supervision is made in the above scenario, there are postmodernist implications for the supervisor who would work with the teacher in such a classroom. In the first place, when the outcomes of learning have not been predetermined, students' and teacher's choices of resource materials for learning are based not only on the topic under study but also on their unique experience of the framing and unfolding of that learning. Put in terms of what Lyotard (1984) claims is the essential postmodernist position of "incredulity toward meta-narratives," there are no "totalizing" theories of curriculum or learning governing what occurs in the classroom, no universal teaching practices or exact specification of what all students must learn.

So how would a supervisor who holds such postmodernist views think about supervision?[1] A most fitting description is given by Judith Morgan, a teacher who writes in her journal about the notion of supervision:

> The word "supervision" is a compound word consisting of "super" and "vision." Super connotes "beyond, great" and vision connotes "an ability to see." Thus, supervision deals with the ability to see beyond the obvious, the ability to see greatly, the ability to see greatness. As with politics and governance, those who would make the best, most compassionate, astute, honest, empathetic, competent leaders, rarely desire the job. So with supervision—those who possess the ability to see have no desire to control others, to find fault, to lay blame, to condemn, to chastise, to wield power.

Underlying Ms. Morgan's thinking about supervision is an issue of power—the power of a supervisor to exercise exclusive authority and presumed superior knowledge and name what constitutes the reality of the classroom as it is and as it ought to be. Such exercise of supervisory power reflects Foucault's (1975) contention that knowledge and power are inseparable and interrelated, that they directly imply one another, and that there is no power relation without the correlative constitution of a field of knowledge or knowledge that does not presuppose and at the same time constitute power relationships. In the stance and counterstance of supervision, the encounter is stacked in favor of the one who claims expert knowledge, which comes with its own language and system of symbols and tools for conveying the power of truth (Edelman, 1977).

Postmodern supervision eschews this power position in which a supervisor provides an "objective" account of events of classroom teaching and learning, becoming instead a matter of individuals—students, teachers, supervisors—constructing and articulating their own social realities of classroom experience. The concept of "hypertext" in postmodernist supervision is about making those multiple realities public and about examining them for what they reveal about the nuances of educational practice. Postmodernist supervision extends Garman's (1982) notion of "organic reciprocity," in which a dynamic and energizing tension is maintained between a spirit of collective inquiry and respect for individuals' perspectives. Rather than being what Garman describes as a working relationship to be desired because it helps individuals and groups accomplish predetermined goals, organic reciprocity becomes the essential descriptor of the nature of the working relationships within which postmodernist supervision occurs.

MEMES SCENARIO

A committee of six teachers, the principal, the school librarian and the technology specialist meet to discuss the school's staff development program in technology. The principal reports that last year's efforts creating the infrastructure to support interconnectivity have resulted in at least one computer in every classroom with access to e-mail, the library, the school's local network, and online data. He expresses frustration, however, that despite mandatory inservices in technology, some teachers still are not using the computer for anything other than the required report-card grading. The technology specialist nods, and says that there are still teachers—probably 10 percent of the faculty—who think that it is the technology specialist's responsibility to teach students about computers and that such teaching occurs in computer labs, not in the regular classroom. Staff development for these teachers, she suggests, might involve her co-planning and co-teaching lessons that integrate technology into the curriculum. But, the technology specialist concludes, it probably makes more sense for her to spend time supporting the teachers who are already doing exciting things with technology.

One of the teachers then talks enthusiastically about how she and a number of other teachers have created mini-labs of six to eight computers in their classrooms and have restructured their teaching to make use of "centers" where different students work either individually or in groups on varying learning activities. The mini-lab is one such center, and the teacher explains how she plans activities for her fastest-learning students that use technology to enrich the curriculum for them. Staff development in technology, the teacher suggests, should focus on providing teachers with specific technology-based curriculum materials in the various academic content areas for these students.

Another teacher gently suggests that all students, not just the best ones, need to have the opportunity to use technology. She goes on to declare that if centers are utilized to their full potential and if technology is truly integrated into the curriculum, then special education students as well as gifted students can work to their own abilities within the same classroom. She describes her efforts at the beginning of the year to develop individual learning goals with students and to involve them in ongoing planning of their learning experiences. She can hardly wait, she says, for the time when every student will have his or her own personal laptop, so that students can exercise more control over the pacing and sequence of their own learning. Arriving at school without a laptop would be like arriving without pencil and paper. Staff development in technology, she concludes, should let teachers set their own professional development goals and develop their own individualized means for reaching those goals, so that teachers can become familiar with technology at their own pace.

While the notion of multiple realities that has already been described as a characteristic of postmodern thinking is obvious in the viewpoints about instructional technology and staff development represented by different individuals in this scenario, the scenario also illustrates another related concept of postmodernism. This concept affirms that the multiple realities that individuals and communities create are not just mental constructs but also signified in the ideas, materials, structures, and artifacts that make up their cultural settings. Anderson (1990) points out that this is an idea espoused by semioticists, those scholars who study signs and their meanings. According to semiotic theory, any human creation is a container of meaning. "Every object that the eye falls upon tells something about its creator, and about the society, and is used to create meaning within the mind of the beholder" (Anderson, 1990).

According to Anderson (1990) this idea that the things humans create carry meaning can be extended even further by the concept of "memes," a term coined by the British zoologist Richard Dawkins to describe the means by which the forms given to mental constructs replicate within or across cultural communities. Examples of memes include such things as "tunes, ideas, catch-phrases, clothes, fashions, ways of making pots or of building arches." We would add that examples of memes also include the ways that schools and classrooms are organized, as well as the forms of teaching and staff development that take place in schools.

These ideas, that the things people create carry meanings and that some of these things and their meanings replicate within and across communities, are powerful ones for postmodernist supervision. They draw attention below the smooth surface of objective description that has in recent decades commanded supervisors' attention. It is no longer enough to simply provide a detailed account of the contexts and events of teaching and learning that the supervisor observes. It is the meanings that those contexts and events hold, both for the observed and the observer, that become important. For a number of years now, supervision scholars working within interpretive (Eisner, 1982; Garman,

1990) and critical (Smyth, 1991; St. Maurice, 1987) traditions have urged that supervision focus on the meaning of teaching and learning; but with postmodernism it becomes clear that those meanings are actually contained *in* the context and events of teaching, rather than somewhere beyond or behind them. What this distinction means is that the professional development of educators such as those in the scenario is served by thoughtful consideration of their individual and collective practice.

The idea captured in the term "memes," that things humans create replicate within or across communities, is also a powerful idea for postmodernist supervision in that it calls upon supervisors and teachers to be mindful of the ideas, practices, structures, and materials that are ubiquitous and accepted without thought or question. Of particular importance for supervision is the way that staff development is used as a vehicle for selecting which "memes" will be supported for replication. Postmodernist supervision seeks to make the process of selection one of conscious choice rather than a mirroring of popular convention.

COMMUNITY OF DISCOURSE SCENARIO

At the end of the school day, a teacher sits down at the computer in her classroom and opens her e-mail. She reads the notices from her school principal and from the school district central office about an upcoming voluntary inservice training session on the use of "Front Page" to support classroom management and instruction. She replies to the district message to register for the training, noting that she wants to learn how to construct interactive forms for websites and how to use the web site authoring program with the students. She then sends a message to the school's technology specialist scheduling a co-taught session to help students develop their own web pages for classroom presentations. She then reads and responds to a note requesting information about some curriculum materials from a teacher colleague in another school and reads the latest postings to the listserv on feminist pedagogy to which she subscribes. After responding to the rest of her e-mail, the teacher logs on to the Internet to search for and review web sites about archeological discoveries in Peru in preparation for an upcoming study she and her students will be doing. One site is a web page developed by an archeologist and his university students. The teacher posts a request for an on-line interview between her students and the archeologist. She also posts Peruvian site URLs to her online Peru file. The file serves as the beginning of a web site she and the class will develop as part of their study of Peru. Next, she accesses the discussion group site for the mentor teacher collaborative in which she participates as part of a nearby university teacher education program. The teacher transfers from her word-processing program files to the discussion group site a think-piece she has written about beginning teachers' difficulties in conferencing with parents. While in the discussion site, she also reviews what other members of the collaborative have written and posted in response to an article that one of the university faculty members of the collaborative has recently written and posted on the site with a request for comments. Finally, she inserts the disc given to her by the novice teacher she has been assigned to mentor. On the disc is the journal that the beginning teacher keeps as part of her induction program responsibilities. The teacher reads and responds to the novice's journal, as she does on a weekly basis, and adds a reminder that the novice has made a commitment to begin journalling online by the end of the month. When she has finished, she shuts down her computer and leaves her classroom, stopping in the office on her way out to put the journal disc in the novice's mailbox.

Within postmodernism, the concept of discourse "communicates the social relatedness of the human world, and more specifically, our social relatedness as inscribed in and expressed through language" (Pinar et al., 1995).[2] While the scenario that we have presented emphasizes the use of technology to support a teacher in a series of language exchanges with other members of the related discourse communities within her professional practice, what makes these exchanges important from the perspective of postmodernist supervision is that they portray ways that discourse is shaped and controlled by the modes of knowledge production that define the teacher's particular social world. It is also important to recognize these exchanges as examples of supervision, in that they foster the teacher's professional development.

Postmodernists recognize a relationship between discourse and power. As Bove (1990) points out, the term discourse has come to include what has heretofore been an unstated kind of control which he describes as:

control by power of positive production: that is, a kind of power that generates certain kinds of questions, placed within systems that legitimate, support, and answer those questions; a kind of power, that, in the process, included within its systems all those it produces as agents capable of acting within them. (p. 54)

The implication of these ideas for postmodernist supervision is to suggest that the source of power in supervisory relations lies within the creation of discursive knowledge and that there are many ways that such knowledge can be created. Cherryholmes (1988) points out that:

Educational discourse ranges from what is *said* in elementary classrooms, teacher education classes, and research findings reported at conferences and conventions to what is *written* in high school textbooks, assessment exams, and research articles in professional journals. (p. 3)

The preceding scenario depicts a teacher engaging in various forms of educational discourse. By acknowledging and legitimating these various forms, postmodernist supervision affords teachers full participation in the creation, exchange, and interpretation of the ideas that construct the discourses that shape their professional lives. Regardless of its form, however, discourse within postmodernist supervision necessarily occurs within genuine, uncontrived, and egalitarian relationships. As Bakhtin (1981) says, "The idea begins to live, that is, to take shape, to develop, to find and renew its verbal expression, to give birth to new ideas, only when it enters into the genuine dialogic relationship with other ideas, with the ideas of *others*" (p. 188). In other words, knowledge is constructed within communities of discourse—what Stanley Fish (1980) calls "interpretive communities." It also follows from Bakhtin that if ideas live only by coming into relation with other ideas and with the ideas of others, that knowledge does not exist as some independent entity that exists outside of the community of discourse within which it is created. In the scenario, technology helps to bring the teacher's ideas into contact with the ideas of others, thus creating and maintaining various communities of discourse, and supporting the teacher's access to them.

PROCESS SCENARIO

At the request of the technology specialist, a district-level curriculum supervisor visits a middle school on what is one of several school-based staff development days throughout the year. On these days, teachers work on what they and their administrators have determined to be currently important curriculum and professional development interests at their particular school. For many of the teachers in the school the focus this year, as in the past couple of years, is on instructional use of technology as a tool and an integral part of the curriculum rather than as a stand-alone subject for teaching technology skills. As the supervisor walks by one classroom on her way to the technology lab area, she sees several teachers meeting with a colleague who has attended a regional service center workshop on brain-based learning. They are discussing ideas about how to use "Inspiration" conceptual mapping software to support brain-based learning in their teaching. In the library another group of teachers works with the librarian to become familiar with the CD-ROM materials. When the supervisor reaches the technology area, she sees a half-dozen teachers and a member of the office staff listening to the technology specialist explain and demonstrate the Excel program that is part of the Microsoft Office software being phased into the district. Another group of teachers is sitting at terminals in an open lab area and practicing with both Excel and Power Point Microsoft Office programs. Yet another group of math teachers meets in another area of the lab to plan a series of lessons requiring the use of spreadsheets. As the supervisor waits to give the technology specialist some requested curriculum materials and articles, she thinks about how different it is from the old days of staff development, when a supervisor would address the entire faculty in the auditorium about the same computer application and when faculty from other schools would be meeting at the same time in their auditoriums to hear the identical information from other supervisors.

Postmodernism acknowledges and even delights in the ampliative potential of multiple realities to unfurl in rich and intricate displays of details and interpretations. The image is of a kind of video display, an ongoing collage/montage of ephemeral, fragmented images, so framed to remind us that they are tentative and incomplete representations, producing what Derrida describes as "a signification which could be neither univocal nor stable" (cited in Harvey, 1989, p. 51). Postmodernism, it can be surmised, is concerned with "process" rather than with "product."

The effect of this concern with process on supervision is to expand it beyond the traditional practice, where teaching is observed and data are collected with the expectation that these data reveal problems that the supervisor can then help the teacher solve or at least manage. Rather than providing teachers with a pre-specified body of knowledge, supervision is instead construed more broadly in terms of the variety of ways that teachers can learn and grow as professionals. Postmodernist supervision can therefore be said to be concerned with the "ontological" rather than the "epistemological." This distinction, made by McHale (1987, cited in Harvey, 1989) in a discussion of the postmodern novel, applies equally well to teaching and supervision. Harvey (1989) describes McHale's distinction to mean:

a shift from the kind of perspectivism that allowed the modernist to get a better bearing on the meaning of a complex but nevertheless singular reality, to the foregrounding of questions as to how radically different realities may coexist, collide, and interpenetrate. (p. 41)

In the preceding scenario, technology serves not only as a context but also as a catalyst for the coexistence, collision, and interpenetration of the supervisor's, specialist's, and teachers' ideas and experiences. As they become familiar with and use technology as an instructional tool, their understanding of both the medium of technology and of how it can function within pedagogical practice develops. While such understanding may be shared—and quite readily by using forms of technology ranging from e-mail to interactive video—there is no attempt to shape a common practice—a product—that will serve as a standard against which each individual teacher's use of instructional technology will be measured. Nor is there an effort to develop uniform inservice educational programs for teachers. Instead, perhaps because the possibilities of instructional technology are still not codified within educational practice, the emphasis is on a process where supervisors and specialists experience and explore the uses of instructional technology along with teachers. As an element of postmodernist supervision, this emphasis on process defines supervision as a continual and endless experience, and one that is inextricably intertwined with the experience of teaching itself.

PLASTIC SCENARIO

Over the course of the summer, three teachers have worked to overlay five broad issues that will serve as the basis for a course on environmental biology with the national science curriculum standards. The teachers then worked with the technology specialist to develop a class web page that would serve as a vehicle for the teachers and the students to access and share assignments and information throughout the semester-long course. In addition, the teachers and technology spe-

cialist began to develop individual profiles for each student that would serve both to document students' work in terms of their own specialized interests and also, as a vehicle for the teachers, to provide students with responses to and evaluation of their work. Each student would have a password for retrieving his or her profile.

When the students arrived for the first day of class, they used their passwords to retrieve their profiles and the class web site. To prepare for a discussion at the end of the week, the students began to work on adding their ideas to the general outline that the teachers had developed of the five broad issues on which the course was based. As the students continued to work on this assignment during the following class, the teachers met with a university professor and a researcher from the district central office to begin developing a research design for comparing the knowledge these students would gain of the field of environmental biology with that of students from the previous year who had been exposed to a more traditional curriculum.

This scenario reflects two practices that are familiar within the conventional practice of supervision, that is, curriculum planning and action research (Glickman et al., 1995; Oliva & Pawlas, 1997). What moves these practices into the realm of postmodernist supervision is that they emerge out of the unfolding educational events, rather than being imposed upon those events in an effort to contain and control them.

In the case of curriculum planning, the scenario describes the teachers, students, and specialist working to create the curriculum as a kind of interactive text that will be continuously created as it is read and interpreted. The postmodernists' use of the notion of "text" to refer to the way in which knowledge is situationally constructed and interpreted has already been discussed in connection with the "hypertext scenario." The point to be added here is the idea of "intertextuality," which calls attention to the ways that texts are created and interpreted on the basis of other texts. "Intertextuality" portrays the fluid, open, protean manner in which these relationships among texts influence both their creation and interpretation. In other words, these relationships are "plastic" in that they are in a flexible or changing state and can be shaped or molded in different ways without breaking apart.

In the case of action research, while the efforts of the teachers and researchers to develop a comparative study of current and previous environmental biology students' learning may end up being a conventional piece of research, it is the way the information from the study will be used that can move it into the realm of postmodernist supervision. If it is seen as yet another text that can in some way inform the teachers' and researchers' understanding of different ways of organizing the teaching and learning of the course, then it becomes an example of the plastic nature of postmodernism.

It is important to an understanding of postmodernist supervision to recognize that inherent in both of these examples of postmodernism's plastic nature is an implicit refutation of the idea that supervision generally is about the search for educational remedies.[3] From the postmodernist position, there is no "remedy" for the predicaments we find ourselves in. We cannot speak of remedy, but rather of hope. St. Maurice (1987) suggests that hope may be embedded in the community of inquiry in which we all share our analysis and critiques, live with each other and our ambiguities, and constantly rebuild our horizons in light of our discourse. According to St. Maurice:

Collegiality and growth are made through hard, open-minded and responsible work in each classroom encounter in every school, every day. In these encounters, in these struggles for open discourse, power is made, not granted to us; truth is not mediated from any distant source, but we make it, in what we think and say, incessantly and immediately. (p. 261)

SUMMARY

In this chapter six scenarios have been presented to illustrate concepts associated with a postmodernist version of educational supervision. The first of these concepts identifies postmodernist supervision as a constructivist process located within a specific *context*. The second concept draws on the notion of *hypertext* to describe the way in which postmodernist supervision seeks to publicly recognize and examine multiple realities of classroom experience. The third concept employs the term *memes*—that is, the means by which the forms given to mental constructs are replicated within or across cultural settings— to explain the attention paid in postmodernist supervision to the ideas, structures, and materials found in schools and classrooms. Next, the concept that postmodernist supervision occurs within a *community of discourse* is discussed in terms of teachers having full participation in the creation, exchange, and interpretation of the ideas that shape their professional practice. The fifth concept illustrates that postmodernist supervision is more concerned with *process* than with product. The example helps clarify why and how postmodernist supervision is being construed in terms of a wide variety of ways that teachers can learn and grow as professionals. And finally, the concept that the form of postmodernist supervision is *plastic* recognizes the way in which understanding of educational events is ever evolving from the unfolding of those events and the discourse of educators who make inquiry into their meaning.

Case Study 11: Collaborative Visions and Challenges for the Future
of Technology in Post Middle School

The technology facilitators Phyllis and Karl worked at Post Middle School campus with the campus principals and a team of teachers during the summer in preparation for the new school year. Collaboratively they developed a plan that included a review of surveys, notes, and comments collected from the teachers about their professional development during the previous school year. In addition, the team generated a list of suggested workshop, study group, and conference opportunities to extend teachers' skills in using the additional technology resources added to the campus during the summer. The team also began conducting focus groups with teachers to discuss what would become the ongoing campus vision for the year. Consonant with the suggestions of the focus group, this year would be devoted to articulating a vision for the changes in the learning environment that the technology had the potential to create. The following quote served as a starting point: "For an innovation to be successful, it needs to be integrated into the fabric of existing practice."

The technology facilitators felt they faced several challenges, as they worked to ready the computer labs, classroom "teaching / learning" stations, and student laptops for the beginning of school. How to continue to discuss a collaborative vision for the future of technology on the campus with the total school community was an important challenge that everyone in the school would continue to deal with far into the future.

Although the teachers returning from summer break would see computer labs and the classroom "teaching / learning" stations that were installed last year, they would also see expanded computer labs, teacher workstations in every classroom and teaching space; and every eighth-grader would have a laptop computer as one of his or hers textbooks. Expansion of the computer labs would also accommodate more students, in a variety of configurations: small groups, one-class projects, one-team projects (several classes), and several-team projects. The new software would support all curriculum areas—math, science, and language arts—as well as generic tools—database, spreadsheet, presentation, and website authoring tools. Phyllis and Karl felt confident that the teachers would continue to embrace the new challenges posed by technology as a learning tool, since they had shown their willingness in previous years to risk trying the new technology for personal use and instructional support. Discussions in the focus groups suggested that teachers would view the increased capacity of technology to support curriculum development and student profiles as positive additions to classroom management and curriculum delivery.

However, Phyllis and Karl were concerned about how to shift the technology focus from the changes in the physical environment to the changes in school culture and how to use technology as a tool in accomplishing this shift. While teachers to date had responded to the changes created by the additions of new technology, they had not yet had the time to fully integrate technology into their curriculum and instruction as individuals or teams. One still-unanswered question was how teachers could be innovative and experimental in their use of instructional technology and, at the same time, be accountable on their professional evaluations for students' passing the state-mandated achievement tests and the state-mandated curriculum. Phyllis and Karl discussed how to support the teachers as they balanced these potentially conflicting demands of teaching and learning. Based on their experiences, Phyllis and Karl felt reassured that if any group of teachers could meet these challenges, those at Post Middle School could!

FOLLOW-UP QUESTIONS

1. How are the six concepts of postmodern supervision illustrated in the case study?

2. In what ways does a technology-rich school environment serve as a context for postmodern supervision?

3. How does a technology-rich environment support teachers' professional development?

4. What roles do Phyllis and Karl, as campus technology facilitators, play in "supervising" the teachers in a technology learning environment?

NOTES

1. This discussion of the issue of power in supervision is drawn from a paper presented by Patricia Holland and Noreen Garman at the 1991 annual conference of the Professors of Instructional Supervision in Houston, Texas.

2. Our discussion of the concepts of discourse and communities of discourse reflects the thinking of Piantanida and Garman (1999) on these topics.

3. This discussion of "remedy" is drawn from the paper presented by Patricia Holland and Noreen Garman at the 1991 annual conference of the Professors of Instructional Supervision, Houston, Texas.

REFERENCES

Acheson, K., & Gall, M. (1997). *Techniques in the clinical supervision of teachers: Preservice and inservice applications* (4th ed.). White Plains, NY: Longman Publishers USA.

Anderson, W. (1990). *Reality isn't what it used to be.* San Francisco: Harper & Row.

Bakhtin, M. (1981). *The dialogic imagination* (M. Holquist, trans.). C. Emerson & M. Holquist (Eds.). Austin: University of Texas Press.

Beiber, M. (1993). *Providing information systems with full hypermedia functionality.* Proceedings of the Twenty-sixth Hawaii International Conference on System Sciences.

Bove, P. (1990). Discourse. In F. Lentricchia & T. McLaughlin (Eds.), *Critical terms for literacy study* (pp. 50–65). Chicago: University of Chicago Press.

Cherryholmes, C. (1988). *Power and criticism: Poststructural investigations in education.* New York: Teachers College Press.

Cogan, M. (1973). *Clinical supervision.* Boston: Houghton-Mifflin.

Cuban, L. (1990). Reforming again, again and again. *Educational Researcher, 19,* 3–13.

Eisner, E. (1982). An artistic approach to supervision (pp. 53–66). In T. Sergiovanni (Ed.), *Supervision of teaching.* Association for Supervision and Curriculum Development Yearbook. Alexandria, VA: Association for Supervision and Curriculum Development.

Edelman, M. (1977). *The political language of the helping professions: Words that succeed and policies that fail.* New York: Academic Press.

Fish, S. (1980). *Is there a text in this class? The authority of interpretive communities.* Cambridge: Harvard University Press.

Foucault, M. (1975). *Discipline and punish.* London: Penguin Books.

Foucault, M. (1984). *The Foucault reader.* New York: Pantheon Books.

Garman, N. (1982). The clinical approach to supervision (pp. 35–52). In T. Sergiovanni (Ed.), *Supervision of teaching.* Association for Supervision and Curriculum Development Yearbook. Alexandria, VA: Association for Supervision and Curriculum Development.

Garman, N. (1990). Theories embedded in the events of clinical supervision: A hermeneutic approach. *Journal of Curriculum and Supervision, 5,* 201–213.

Glickman, C., Gordon, S., & Ross-Gordon, J. (1995). *Supervision of instruction: A developmental approach* (3rd ed.). Boston: Allyn and Bacon.

Harvey, D. (1989). *The condition of postmodernity: An enquiry into the origins of cultural change.* Cambridge, MA: Basil Blackwell.

Holland, P., & Garman, N. (1991). *Beyond the "Yes, But . . ." in supervision: A modernist and postmodernist conversation*. Presented at the Annual Conference of the Council of Professors of Instructional Supervision, Houston, Texas.

Lyotard, J. (1984). *The postmodern condition*. Minneapolis: University of Minnesota Press.

McHale, B. (1987). *Postmodernist fiction*. London: Viking Penguin.

Oliva, P., & Pawlas, G. (1997). *Supervision for today's schools* (4th ed.). White Plains, NY: Longman Publishers.

Piantanida, M., & Garman, N. (1999). *The qualitative dissertation: A guide for students and faculty*. Newbury Park, CA: Corwin Press.

Pinar, W., Reynolds, W., Slattery, P., & Taubman, P. (1995). *Understanding curriculum: An introduction to the study of historical and contemporary curriculum discourses*. New York: Peter Lang.

Seashore-Louis, K. (1998). A light feeling of chaos: Educational reform and policy in the United States. In *Education yesterday, education tomorrow. Daedalus, 1*(4), 13–40.

Smyth, J. (1991). Instructional supervision and the redefinition of who does it in schools. *Journal of Curriculum and Supervision, 7*, 90–99.

St. Maurice, H. (1987). Clinical supervision and power: Regimes of instructional management. In T. Popkewitz (Ed.), *Critical studies in teacher education: Its folklore, theory and practice* (p. 261). London: Falmer Press.

Von Glaserfeld, E. (1984). An introduction to radical constructivism. In P. Watzlawick (Ed.), *The invented reality* (p. 27). New York: W. W. Norton.

12

Communicative Action: A Postmodern Bridge for Supervision in School Organizations

Edward Pajak and Karen K. Evans

GUIDING QUESTIONS

1. *In what way(s) does postmodernism reveal weaknesses inherent in modernist philosophy?*
2. *How can a postmodern perspective provide clues to influence practice?*
3. *How would a postmodern clinical supervisor engage teachers in the improvement of instruction?*
4. *Why is Habermas' theory of communicative action integral to the authors' position?*
5. *Explain the concept of a learning organization and a learning community.*
6. *Compare and contrast this chapter with the views expressed in Chapter 10.*

WHAT IS POSTMODERNISM AND WHAT ARE ITS IMPLICATIONS FOR SUPERVISION IN EDUCATION?

The answer to this question is not as unequivocal as one would prefer. Because postmodernism emerged as a reaction against and rejection of the major tenets of modernist philosophy, a contrast between the two may be the best way to begin answering the proposed question. Modernism posited that truth and universal values could be discerned through objectified, scientific methods (Glanz, 1997). Postmodernism counters this proposition, stating that perceptions are embedded in culture and language and therefore no single truth exists; there is more than one reality (English, 1997a). That is, what may be true and right for one individual or group in a particular situation is not necessarily so for another. Knowledge and truth are not viewed as absolutes, according to postmodernism, but as constructions based on human perceptions that vary according to context. Rather than discovering truth, as modernism proposes, knowledge is viewed by postmodernist philosophy as being constructed or invented uniquely within each culture and reconstructed or reinvented over time. Postmodernism also opposes modernism's claim that scientific procedures can be objectified. Postmodernist thinkers hold that "pure objectivity" is impossible, because values and truths are always contextualized. Thus, so-called objective scientific methods and proofs inevitably contain bias and error (English, 1997a).

Propositions of postmodernism reveal weaknesses inherent in modernist philosophy and offer an expanded and more inclusive perspective from which to consider organizations, generally, and instructional supervision, specifically. However, postmodernism is characterized by inherent limitations as a guide to practice. One of the major inadequacies of postmodernism is that although it provides a broader "approach about how to *think* about theories, it does not provide an approach about how to *act*" (Tierney, 1994, p. 26). That is, it criticizes the major tenets of modernism, yet provides little of substance in their place. By holding that no metanarrative should dominate thinking about organizations (English, 1996), postmodernism leaves us with few clues to guide the processes of investigation and change.

HOW DOES POSTMODERNISM INFLUENCE OUR VIEW OF ORGANIZATIONS AND THE WORK OF CLINICAL SUPERVISORS?

The postmodern perspective changes not only the way we view organizations but also how we view organizational roles, functions, and the change process. For example, postmodernism highlights the importance of considering and understanding the unique culture and language of each organization, rather than trying to discover universal rules that apply to all (Flecha, 1996; Ryan, 1995). That is, postmodernism brings to awareness the recognition that issues, problems, and solutions found within one organization may not even be relevant for the people who inhabit another. According to this view: "The postmodern era suggests a conception of organizations as processes and relationships rather than as structures and rules. In such organizations, verbal communication and conversation are likely to be important" (Mitchell, Sackney, & Walker, 1996, p. 52). Successful change, therefore, implies broad participation and making room for dissenting voices to be heard.

Postmodernism also calls attention to the foremost limitation of modernist-based management science, its focus on the leader as an autonomous and objective agent. According to Fenwick English (1997b), one of the most prolific writers currently advocating the application of postmodernist thinking to school organizations:

Management science, as it has been defined in behavioral-structural frames in educational administration, cannot encompass the realm of leadership. The frames them-

selves eliminate that which is most important, i.e., the interaction/communication of the idiosyncratic and complex personal/character/interpersonal dimensions between leaders and followers, and these dynamic exchanges and reciprocities within a special context, culture and historical period. (p. 16)

Postmodernist understanding produces a shift in our conception of leadership, from a (modernist) single source of unilateral and universal directives, to a collaborative and consultative leadership emphasizing equity and open communication as essentials to organizational advancement.

Under modernist assumptions, the clinical supervisor in educational settings is viewed as an expert who collects data via objectified, scientific methods and subsequently recommends strategies for change. In contrast, the postmodernist perspective advocates a more collaborative approach, with the supervisor acting as a guide or facilitator in a collegial and discursive relationship with the teacher (Glanz, 1997). For example, a *modernist* clinical supervisor would enter the classroom, record some type of data related to observable behaviors, and prescribe an intervention intended to reduce the discrepancy between what he or she has independently defined as real and some abstract notion of ideal practice, typically for the purpose of establishing a more efficient learning environment for students. In contrast, a *postmodernist* clinical supervisor would consult with the teacher and together review their perceptions and interpretations of the current classroom situation. In doing so, they would consider all available information, including personal values and beliefs. Then, together, they would devise a plan to construct a new classroom reality. In addition to the collegial aspect of the interaction between supervisor and teacher, with postmodernism both the teacher and supervisor are challenged to examine the social and political context in which they work and to "take risks and construct knowledge for themselves" (Glanz, 1997, p. 12). Their purpose would be to make classroom learning more equitable as well as effective, while allowing students to participate in the construction of this reality. This collaborative postmodernist viewpoint is evident in Argyris's (1982) concept of "double-loop learning," which represents a flattening of "the organizational hierarchy in ways that support exchanges of information and collaboration in the design and implementation of innovations," a process that encourages and facilitates "development of heuristics in exploration of new meanings that support new organizational realities" (Curry, 1994, p. 148).

The two most fully developed models of clinical supervision that best represent the postmodernist viewpoint are probably those of Bowers and Flinders (1990, 1991) and Waite (1995). More recent treatments have considered the philosophical underpinnings of supervision in education (Neville & Garman, 1998) as well as the relation between supervisory practice and economic forces (Smyth, 1998) and cultural, ethnic, and gender issues (Gay, 1998).

Postmodernist assumptions also suggest a more capacious stance toward instruction in schools. Instead of favoring and confining teachers to a particular instructional approach, postmodernism implies that teachers should be urged to allow for and represent multiple narratives in their classrooms. Individual teachers and students would be permitted to analyze and select ideas and contributions from a range of learning experiences instead of having a single metanarrative of instruction imposed upon them. Such an approach to learning would help to accentuate differences and similarities as well as the positives and negatives of a range of perspectives, rather than invalidating one with another, and would provide teachers and students with a more extensive knowledge base from which to draw (English, 1996).

WHERE ARE WE NOW?

While theorists debate the appropriateness and utility of postmodernism for understanding and leading schools as organizations (see English 1998a, 1998b; and Willower, 1998, for endorsement and counterpoint), its very real impact on schools and educational leaders is difficult to dispute. The speculations of theorists represent reality for school practitioners, who daily confront problems and paradoxes arising from the postmodern condition of society (Hargreaves, 1994). Further, applications of postmodern thinking have been anticipated and even incorporated into schools for some time. For example, the need to legitimize diversity by encouraging multiple narratives is manifested in recent innovations such as decentralized district structures, an emphasis on culturally inclusive instructional practices and curricula, and teachers having greater voice in schoolwide decision-making. Mentoring and peer coaching among teachers are probably the most visible examples of how postmodern notions of empowerment, voice, and participation have directly affected instructional supervisory practice. In addition, the original formulation of clinical supervision has essentially been "deconstructed" into a multitude of competing models with diverse goals, strategies, and rationales, which essentially redefine the traditional relationship between teachers and supervisors, consistent with new and more democratic organizational structures and processes (Pajak, 2000, p. ix).

A number of authors, most prominently Foucault and Lyotard, have developed philosophical positions that are usually considered as falling under the postmodernist rubric. Each of these orientations may be viewed as expressing and highlighting different aspects of the postmodern movement. However, a detailed discussion of various adaptations of postmodernist thought is well beyond the scope of this chapter. The focus here will be on only a single theory, one associated with Jurgen Habermas—the *theory of communicative action*—and its application to district-wide supervisory practice.

THEORY OF COMMUNICATIVE ACTION

Habermas' theory of communicative action is perhaps most accurately characterized as a bridge between modernism and postmodernism, joining together major suppositions of both perspectives. Habermas (1987) detected virtue in both modernism and postmodernism and yet had reservations about both positions as well. According to Spencer J. Maxcy (1994), another prominent advocate of applying postmodern perspectives to educational leadership: "Habermas in *The Philosophical Discourse of Modernity* argues that the modern project lies incomplete and the focus upon *postmodernity* is a misappropriation of the critical posture required for any rational project to continue" (Maxcy, 1998, p. 4). Habermas' theory of communicative action recognizes the difficulty of establishing universal values, as illustrated by its rejection of the modernist notion that one subject can know the best option and legitimately choose for other people. However, proponents also assert that certain conduct can justifiably be deemed *right* and other conduct inherently *wrong* (e.g., rape). A particular option can be considered right if participants freely agree and may be deemed wrong if it imposes on others' freedoms (Flecha, 1996). Thus, communicative action accedes with the modernist position regarding the presence of universal principles; however, it advocates that the "process to establish these criteria must involve a best judgment, a consensus continuously being revised by new knowledge and points of view" (Flecha, 1996, p. 9). The theory of communicative action aligns with postmodernism in addressing many limitations of modernism (i.e., citing the difficulty of establishing universal values without considering differences of language and culture), but emphasizes striving to overcome limitations of democracy rather than turning against it, as some proponents of postmodernism suggest (Flecha, 1996).

Communicative action may also resolve the tension between two concepts—efficiency and equity—that are often viewed as mutually exclusive. Postmodernism's emphasis on equity stands in stark contrast to the single-minded emphasis on efficiency of some management theories (e.g., Total Quality Management). Efficiency and equity are frequently viewed as "either-or" propositions, with organizations focusing on one at the expense of the other. However, communicative action suggests a way to conceptualize and focus on both simultaneously. Thus, effectiveness and equity do not necessarily have to be at odds with each other (Ryan, 1998; Maxcy, 1998); rather, organizations can realistically and successfully attend to both (as is illustrated in a subsequent section).

COMMUNICATIVE ACTION AND SUPERVISORY PRACTICE

Supervision of instruction at the school district level is much more complex than the dyadic interactions of principals and teachers or between colleagues engaged in clinical supervision at the local school. District supervisors face the challenge of somehow making sense of the myriad materials, resources, ideas, programs, policies, events, and people that comprise and contribute to the instructional mission of the school. In fact, the collaborative "creation of meaning around the central value of providing high-quality instruction for students is what effective district level supervision is all about" (Pajak, 1989a, p. 2). Other research suggests that of all the organizational processes affecting instruction, clear, honest, and open *communication* is viewed by outstanding supervisory practitioners as most important to success (Pajak, 1989b).

In adapting to postmodern societal trends (including those that have resulted in families and communities no longer providing the stable environment that children need), many school districts have embraced the movement to decentralize and democratize their organizations, most notably through site-based management and shared governance at the school level. An undeniable shift from a top-down to a multi-directional flow of information has occurred in most school districts during the last five to ten years. Instructional programming, planning, and curriculum are also being decentralized, with more decisions made by teachers. Faculty and staff are motivated and organized through development of local school goals instead of policies and guidelines established at the district level. Teachers generally work more collaboratively on the improvement of instruction, coaching one another and sharing ideas informally and taking responsibility for classroom observation and conferencing. Teachers are increasingly empowered as they participate in decisions and exert more autonomy in solving problems that they face collectively. An outgrowth of such decentralization is that teachers are more often viewed as experts, whereas previously processes involving problem-solving and decision-making were viewed as operations "best handled by experts at the top of the district organization" (Pajak, 1992, p. 21). Professional development opportunities are more often tailored to the needs of individuals, with teachers playing more active roles in staff development, while research and program evaluation are conducted by school practitioners to generate new knowledge. Interaction and collaboration with parents and the community are also increasingly advocated and pursued (Pajak, 1992). Delegating responsibility for instructional improvement to schools, however, has caused a crisis for district-level supervision by usurping its purpose of creating meaning through broad-based participation.

Some advocates of postmodernism argue that establishing forms of community among teachers in schools is a key to resisting what are viewed as oppressive practices (Ryan, 1998), while others foresee the imminent demise of bureaucratic structures. Given the pernicious instability that inevitably results from radical decentralization (witness the tribulations of former communist-bloc countries), a more prudent course of action may be to encourage an "integrated decentralization" (Murphy, 1989), involving simultaneously strong local diversity and centralized coordination in order to attain an effective balance between local autonomy and district-level control (Pajak, 1992, p. 18). This assumption appears to be consistent with the theory of communicative action.

The application of communicative action for the purpose of instructional improvement on the school-district level was the brainchild of Dr. Joe A. Hairston, Superintendent of Clayton County Schools (Georgia). Dr. Hairston developed the *Teacher Think Tank* (see case study at the end of this chapter) that involved collaboration among forty-five teachers in a large metropolitan school district. These teachers were gathered to identify obstacles to teaching and learning and to develop appropriate policy recommendations for the superintendent and school board. The *Think Tank* reviewed directives and district policies, student data (i.e., achievement scores, dropout rates), and research/literature regarding instructional effectiveness. Given the traditional top-down management style that most teachers had experienced during their careers, however, a high degree of skepticism initially arose about whether the group really had any influence. Such concerns were eventually set aside and replaced by a renewed collective commitment to the well-being of students. At the first meeting of the *Teacher Think Tank*, when more seasoned teachers cynically rejected the idea that anything would come from their discussions of the problems and any recommendations they might develop, one of the newer teachers began to cry and related a description of the desperate plight faced by many of her fourth-grade students. She stated that she was willing to try anything that held even the slightest possibility of helping them. Other teachers supported her view, arguing that the group was being asked to contribute its expertise and they had a professional obligation to do so. Cynicism soon abated as the collaborative process ensued.

Postmodernism reflects "a generalized crisis of meaning" for the individual (Johnston, 1994). Thinking about educational leadership from a postmodern perspective, however, promises the possibility of restoring "human agency to the center of meaning and history." Educational leaders are freed to view all individuals as active agents "capable of altering structures and changing schools to benefit their students and the school community" (Miron & Elliott, 1994, p. 133). The construction of knowledge through discourse necessarily implies the absence of power relations and the ability to determine what "counts" as meaning (Johnston, 1994). This collaborative, communicative viewpoint was encouraged and demonstrated throughout the *Think Tank* process. At the outset of the *Think Tank*, each teacher was asked to answer the question, "What does being a teacher *mean* to you personally?" Other questions included: "What about teaching gives you satisfaction?" "How do you know when you have been successful?" The teachers' perspectives were considered essential in identifying and resolving problems; thus, power struggles were abated and solutions developed through a new and enriched channel of communication. By incorporating teachers into the policy-making process the superintendent, who initiated the *Think Tank*, was able to use his power to transform traditionally subordinated groups, such as these teachers, "into a community of intellectuals" and thus "seek to change the inherited history of the school" (Johnston, 1994, p. 137).

During the *Think Tank* the teachers identified problems that interfered with teaching and learning and developed a variety of recommendations for resolving each. "What gets in the way of doing my job as a teacher?" was the central question that guided the process. The concerns the teachers identified fell into the following eight categories: job demands, resources, curriculum, support/training services, students, home/parents, other teachers, and administrators (see Figure 12.1). The largest category by far was job demands, representing 33 percent of the responses, and the major obstacle within that category was "too much paperwork." Paperwork was followed closely by "insufficient planning time," "non-academic duties" and "interrupted instructional time." The second largest category related to resources (17%) and included "inadequate physical space," "lack of materials and other resources," and "limited access to technology." Something interesting that the teachers discovered as they discussed these findings was that limited availability of resources was not a problem in every school, suggesting that at least part of the resolution to difficulties in this area may involve more equitable distribution of what was already available in the district. The next category, support/training services, represented another 12% of responses and included: "lack of social workers, psychometrists, and school psychologists in schools," "lack of support from the community," "not enough staff development on incorporating technology into the curriculum," and "no training to implement new curriculum." The fourth category, curriculum, represented 11% of the responses and included obstacles such as: "inconsistency between curriculum and assessment," "inordinate emphasis on test scores," and "inordinate emphasis on self-esteem." The fifth and sixth categories related to students and their home situations, respectively representing 9% and 9% of the responses. Obstacles asso-

Figure 12.1
"What gets in the way of doing my job as a teacher?" (N ~ 250 teachers)

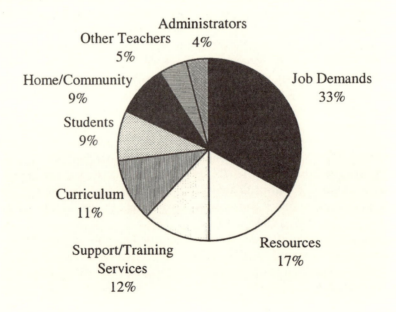

ciated with these categories were "student misbehavior," "unprepared students," and "student absenteeism," as well as "parental apathy," "instability at home," and "parental resistance to school-initiated interventions." Finally, other teachers (5%) and administrators (4%) comprised the seventh and eighth categories of obstacles. Specific concerns related to these last two groupings included "variation in teachers' levels of understanding" and "teacher negativity," as well as "poorly organized administrators" and "lack of administrative consistency in student disciplinary matters." It was gratifying to both the superintendent and the principals that administrators comprised the least frequently mentioned category of all.

Almost all of the constraints to effectiveness that teachers identified were systemic in nature. The obstacles to teaching, in other words, were generic. Furthermore, rather than being confined to a specific classroom, the concerns originated outside the classroom. The large number of issues identified by teachers as constraints to their effectiveness suggested a very real need for someone in the organization to take responsibility for improving organizational processes. A major implication for the supervisor, if this came about, would be a required shift in perspective, from viewing the teacher within the classroom as the client to viewing the teacher *within the organizational system* as the client. That is, the focus of supervision would shift to the improvement of the system that exists outside the classroom in order to improve the functioning of processes inside the classroom. This shift in perspective from the teacher in the classroom to the teacher in the organizational system would require a simultaneous parallel shift in how supervisors perceive change itself.

Some change theorists distinguish between first-order change and second-order change. A first-order change is brought about by simply increasing or decreasing the forces driving the system, which itself remains unchanged. A mechanical example might be stepping on the accelerator in order to move an automobile up a steep hill. An improvement in performance is thus achieved by expending more energy. A second order change, in contrast, is brought about by altering the relationship among the elements within the system, or actually changing the system. In the example of an automobile climbing a hill, a second-order change would be accomplished by shifting to a lower gear, thereby changing the relationship among the elements within the drive chain and achieving the purpose of getting to the top by making the mechanical system more efficient. In trying to improve instructional effectiveness, it seems that individuals most often respond by applying the principle of first-order change exclusively. People work harder as new programs or the latest innovations are introduced. A focus on removing the obstacles is rare. What is needed is a combination of second-order and first-order change, that is, shifting gears at the same time that we add more fuel.

The teachers' list of concerns provided a basis from which twenty-two specific problems were identified and recommendations for each were developed. Table 12.1 illustrates several of the proposed concerns and associated recom-

Table 12.1
Teacher Think Tank

	Problem	Recommendation
• Insufficient Time for Instructional Planning	Work days (planning time) spent in meetings or on paperwork	Reserve work days for instructional planning
		Limit number of meetings Use memos in place of informational meetings
		Use meetings for discussion and decisions
	Insufficient time for collaborative planning	Restructure schedule to allow for collaboration (i.e., exploratory classes at same time for all grade level teachers)
• Inequitable Resources	Inequitable amount of materials, resources and technology among schools due to variations in socio-economic status within the county	Curriculum coordinators should reassess the distribution of all county materials presently on-hand
		Create a cluster computer inventory to improve access to materials
	Schools within lower socio-economic areas have less opportunity to raise money for needs	Coordinators should assist schools in locating funds (e.g., grants)
		County should adopt/coordinate plan for local businesses to partner with schools in need
• Inequitable Academic Expectations	Discrepancy exists between percentages of white and minority students receiving College Preparatory diplomas	Utilize curriculum and texts that include minority struggles (i.e., civil rights, slavery)
		Institute higher teacher expectations for *all* students

mendations. For example, one identified problem was the inequitable distribution of instructional materials, resources, and technology within the county. Ironically, local site autonomy was identified as the culprit. It was noted that schools within low socioeconomic areas had less opportunity to raise supplemental money for these needs, whereas more prosperous schools had very active and involved parent and community support systems in place, able to raise thousands of dollars in discretionary funds through auctions of donated items, special dinners, and sales of miscellaneous products (e.g., gift-wrapping paper). The proposed list of recommendations called on curriculum coordinators to reassess the distribution of all materials purchased with district funds, for district coordinators to assist in locating grants for schools in need of resources, and for the district to coordinate a plan for partnering local businesses with schools in need and to create a computer inventory to improve district-wide access to materials. Another problem identified by the teachers was insufficient time for planning lessons. Recommendations generated to address this problem included reserving teacher "work days" for planning instead of in-service training, restructuring the schedule to allow for collaborative planning during the school day, reducing interruptions to instructional time, allowing reasonable lead-time for completing paperwork, limiting the number of meetings (i.e., using memos in place of informational meetings), and assigning support staff to supervise students before and after school to free teachers during this time for planning. These particular problems and the solutions developed to handle them address inequity and improve efficiency simultaneously, thus demonstrating that effectiveness and equity are not mutually exclusive, as often thought.

The *Think Tank* allowed teachers to function as experts and to actively participate and work together regarding important issues relevant to their positions. Central coordination was not abandoned for local diversity; instead, teachers were able to have control and input regarding district policies while still adhering to such policies. That is, a balance was achieved between centralized and decentralized authority. The *Think Tank* illustrates how a large school district can include teachers more to address pertinent issues, such as equity, while also making room for multiple narratives.

The case study at the end of this chapter reveals how a school district can respond to challenges occurring within its instructional systems and through a communicative action framework initiate inherent transformations that improve both equity and effectiveness. Consensus was obtained for decisions through communication and collaboration; however, the *Think Tank* necessarily became an ongoing process repeated for several years to achieve deep changes in the culture, organizational processes, and collective processes. The development of "postmodern interventions" such as this must be characterized by independent thought and critical distance, including both individual and multiple voices (Bernstein, 1992).

SCHOOLS AS LEARNING ORGANIZATIONS

The concept of a learning organization or learning community (Curry, 1994; Dumaine, 1989; Pajak, 1993) fits the emerging reality of schools and associated contextual transformations resulting from postmodern influences. A learning organization is an organization that is able to adjust quickly and meet the demands of rapidly changing circumstances (Dumaine, 1989) and seems to encapsulate the postulations of Habermas's theory of communicative action and the example presented earlier. As technological advances continue to create a state of flux and instability in the social, political, and economic environment, organizations will be required to become increasingly flexible, adaptable, and receptive to change. Decentralization and more democratic structures have helped schools to move beyond simple transmission of knowledge to structures that facilitate the generation and invention of new knowledge. But richer information must be encouraged through alternative channels, such as the *Think Tank*, to encourage collaboration among all members in the system and open communication across all levels. Thus, schools can become learning organizations engaged in the work of creating new meanings.

As the structures of the school organization transform into learning communities, the roles of all members (i.e., superintendents, teachers, parents) in the system become altered as well. The function of a school leader and, more important, who is considered a leader is probably the most notable redefinition. Leadership in the schools becomes a *process* for which *all* are responsible, instead of a trait projected onto a single individual. Work by Senge (1990a, 1990b) and Giroux (1989, 1991) suggests four elements that help define the role of a leader in the schools operating under the influences of a perpetually changing environment.

1. empowering self and others;
2. transcending superficial understanding;
3. applying knowledge to practical problems; and
4. making the future better than the present. (Pajak, 1993b, pp.173–78)

The collaborative investigation, brainstorming, and generation of solutions described in the case study to follow illustrates one organization's commitment to empowering its members. The *Think Tank* process empowered teachers and included them not only in problem analysis, but in decision-making and long-range planning as well. The school district, at the initiation of the superintendent, successfully integrated individual situations and perspectives into policy recommendations shaping both present and future goals. This "holistic and integrative" (Pajak, 1993) approach to problem and solution analysis facilitated development of designs for comprehensive and long-term systematic improvements. Accordingly, this collaborative and empowering process aided in transcending superficial understanding as new, more complex meanings were generated. Traditional interventions typically focus narrowly on present problems and applying superficial treatments, consequently failing to consider the "bigger" picture and the interconnectedness of elements within the system. The incorporation of multiple and diverse perspectives in the *Think Tank* provided a more comprehensive picture of the entire system and an increased understanding of how the parts are interrelated.

In summary, the example provides a representation of how a school district was able to enrich communication within the system by creating a space for diverse, disempowered members and a new channel of information flow from teachers directly to policy-makers (i.e., the school board). In order to deal with the new postmodernist reality, school districts must create opportunities for dialogue between and among individuals and groups within the organization beyond what traditional structures allow. Enhanced, multidirectional communication will enable collaborative construction of new meanings, ideas, and goals needed to face the challenges brought about by the transitions to a postmodernist reality.

Case Study 12: Teacher Think Tank: *Postmodern Supervision in Action*

At the direction of the school superintendent, the principals of twenty-seven elementary schools, ten middle schools, and eight high schools were each asked to nominate several teachers to participate in what was called a *Think Tank Experience*. The teacher nominees were to display personal characteristics described in a letter to principals that included being:

- intuitive, creative, and reflective thinkers
- interested in their own continued learning
- well-read
- change agents and leaders
- able to work well in groups
- willing and able to critically examine issues and offer solutions
- interested in exploring new avenues for systemic change, and
- people who consistently ask, "What if" kinds of questions.

One teacher was finally chosen to represent each school in the *Think Tank*, with the deliberate intention of assuring equitable gender, ethnic, content area, and school level representation. The *Think Tank* completed its work at ten evening meetings after school from October through March, facilitated by a professor from a nearby college of education. The teachers received staff development units and small stipends for their participation. School and district administrators were prohibited from attending these meetings, unless invited by the teachers.

Work in the *Think Tank* proceeded in two phases that focused on: (1) obstacles to teaching and (2) district-wide student achievement. A central question driving the first phase of the *Think Tank's* work was eagerly answered by the teachers, namely: "What gets in the way of your doing the kind of job as a teacher that you'd really like to do?" Responses from more than two hundred and fifty teachers were collected and categorized.

During the second phase of their work, the teachers examined data relating to student achievement, both for the county as a whole and for individual schools. The data reviewed by the teachers in the *Think Tank* included test scores for different grade levels in various academic areas, disaggregated by race and sex. Other measures included dropout rates, numbers of students suspended, percentages of over-age students by grade level, incidents of student violence, and possession of controlled substances and weapons, as well as percentages of students in advanced-placement courses, community and school collaborations, and numbers of parental contacts.

During both phases of their work, *Think Tank* participants also studied existing district documents consisting of reports, policies, and plans relating to organizational effectiveness and instructional quality. As a group, the teachers reviewed issues from the last five years of two major professional journals and conducted Internet searches for innovative ideas on how to improve teaching and learning success. In all, sixty-six recommendations for improving teaching district wide were generated, along with forty-four suggestions for improving student success in learning.

FOLLOW-UP QUESTIONS

1. Describe the process underlying the *Think Tank*.
2. What characteristics of the *Think Tank* are consistent with postmodernism?
3. How were issues of equity addressed in this case study?
4. What gets in the way of your doing the kind of job as a teacher that *you* would like to do?
5. What kinds of things get in the way of your students' success?

REFERENCES

Argyris, C. (1982). *Reasoning, learning, and action*. San Francisco: Jossey-Bass.

Bernstein, R. J. (1992). *The new constellation: The ethical-political horizons of modernity/postmodernity*. Cambridge: MIT Press.

Bowers, C. A., & Flinders, D. J. (1990). *Responsive teaching: An ecological approach to classroom patterns of language, culture, and thought*. New York: Teachers College Press.

Bowers, C. A., & Flinders, D. J. (1991). *Culturally responsive teaching and supervision: A handbook for staff development*. New York: Teachers College Press.

Curry, B. (1994). Reconceptualizing higher education organizations. In S. J. Maxcy (Ed.), *Postmodern school leadership: Meeting the crisis in educational administration* (pp. 141–152). Westport, CT: Praeger.

Dumaine, B. (1989). What leaders of tomorrow see. *Fortune, 120*(1), 48–62.

English, F. W. (1996, October). *Redefining leadership as meaning in context*. Paper presented at the meeting of the University Council for Educational Administration, Louisville, KY.

English, F. W. (1997a). The cupboard is bare: The postmodern critique of educational administration. *Journal of School Leadership, 7*, 4–26.

English, F. W. (1997b, March). *The recentering of leadership from the jaws of management science.* Paper presented at the meeting of the American Educational
Research Administration, Chicago, IL.

English, F. W. (1998a). The postmodern turn in education administration: Apostrophic or catastrophic development? *Journal of School Leadership, 8,*
426–447.

English, F. W. (1998b). Musings on Willower's "fog": A response. *Journal of School
Leadership, 8,* 464–469.

Flecha, R. (1996, May). *Traditional modernity, postmodernity and communicative
modernity: Related issues in constructing roles and learning tasks of adult education.* Paper presented at the meeting of the International Adult and Continuing Education Conference.

Gay, G. (1998). Cultural, ethnic, and gender issues. In G. R. Firth & E. F. Pajak
(Eds.), *The handbook of research on school supervision* (pp. 1184–1227). New
York: Simon & Schuster Macmillan.

Giroux, H. A. (1989). Rethinking education reform in the age of George Bush. *Phi
Delta Kappan, 70*(9), 728–730.

Giroux, H. A. (1991). *Postmodernism, feminism, and cultural politics: Redefining
educational boundaries.* Albany: State University of New York Press.

Glanz, J. (1997, March). *Supervision: Don't discount the value of the modern.* Paper
presented at the meeting of the American Educational Research Association, Chicago, IL.

Habermas, J. (1987). *The philosophical discourse of modernity.* Cambridge: Massachusetts Institute of Technology Press.

Hargreaves, A. (1994). *Changing teachers, changing times: Teachers' work and culture
in the postmodern age.* Toronto: Ontario Institute for Studies in Education
Press.

Johnston, B. J. (1994). Educational administration in the postmodern age. In S. J.
Maxcy (Ed.), *Postmodern school leadership: Meeting the crisis in educational
administration* (pp. 115–131). Westport, CT: Praeger.

Maxcy, S. J. (1994). Introduction. In S. J. Maxcy (Ed.), *Postmodern school leadership:
Meeting the crisis in educational administration* (pp. 1–13). Westport, CT:
Praeger.

Maxcy, S. J. (1998). Preparing school principals for ethno-democratic leadership. *International Journal of Leadership in Education, 1*(3), 217–236.

Miron, L. F., & Elliott, R. J. (1994). Moral leadership in a poststructural era. In S. J.
Maxcy (Ed.), *Postmodern school leadership: Meeting the crisis in educational
admnistration* (pp. 133–140). Westport, CT: Praeger.

Mitchell, C., Sackney, L., & Walker, K. (1996). The postmodern phenomenon: Implications for school organizations and educational leadership. *Journal of
Educational Administration and Foundations, 11,* 38–67.

Murphy, J. T. (June, 1989). The paradox of decentralizing schools: Lessons from
business, government, and the Catholic church. *Phi Delta Kappan, 70*(10),
808–812.

Neville, R. F., & Garman, N. B. (1998). The philosophical perspective on supervision. In G. R. Firth & E. F. Pajak (Eds.), *The handbook of research on school
supervision* (pp. 200–241). New York: Simon & Schuster Macmillan.

Pajak, E. (1989a). *The central office supervisor of curriculum and instruction: Setting the stage for success*. Boston: Allyn and Bacon.

Pajak, E. (1989b). *Identification of supervisory proficiencies project: Final report*. Arlington, VA: Association for Supervision and Curriculum Development.

Pajak, E. (1992). A view from the central office. In C. D. Glickman, (Ed.), *Supervision in transition* (pp. 126–138). Alexandria, VA: Association for Supervision and Curriculum Development.

Pajak, E. (1993). Change and continuity in supervision and leadership. In G. Cawelti (Ed.), *Challenges and achievements of American education* (pp. 158–186). Alexandria, VA: Association for Supervision and Curriculum Development.

Pajak, E. (2000). *Approaches to clinical supervision: Alternatives for improving instruction*. Needham Heights, MA: Christopher-Gordon.

Ryan, J. (1995). Order, anarchy, and inquiry in educational administration. *McGill Journal of Education, 30*, 37–59.

Ryan, J. (1998). Critical leadership for education in a postmodern world: Emancipation, resistance and communal action. *International Journal of Leadership in Education, 1*(3), 257–278.

Senge, P. M. (1990a). *The fifth discipline: The art and practice of the learning organization*. New York: Doubleday Currency.

Senge, P. M. (1990b, Fall). The leader's new work: Building learning organizations. *Sloan Management Review*, pp. 7–23.

Smyth, J. (1998). Economic forces affecting supervision. In G. R. Firth & E. F. Pajak (Eds.), *The handbook of research on school supervision* (pp. 1173–1183). New York: Simon & Schuster Macmillan.

Tierney, W. G. (1994). *Multiculturalism in higher education: An organizational framework for analysis*. (Project No. R117G10037). University Park, PA: National Center on Postsecondary Teaching, Learning, and Assessment. (ERIC Document Reproduction Service No. ED 371 675).

Waite, D. (1995). *Rethinking instructional supervision: Notes on its language and culture*. London: The Falmer Press.

Willower, D. J. (1998). Fighting the fog: A criticism of postmodernism. *Journal of School Leadership, 8*, 448–463.

PART III

PRACTITIONER RESPONSES

Introduction

In Part III, three practitioners react to the previous chapters and explore how ideas proffered by the modern and postmodern thinking affect practitioners. They describe the applicability and utility of the modern and postmodern theorists' ideas for implementation in school practice.

In the first chapter of Part III, Osborne Abby, Jr. offers a point of view based on the practical application of modern and postmodern thinking in today's classroom life. He advocates for the infusion of postmodernism in the practical application of supervision. He also suggests that the flexibility intrinsic to postmodern thinking is important in the arena of curriculum. However, he believes that systems of curriculum have become so entrenched from state and national mandates and other forms of bureaucratic machinery that although such changes are needed, they are unlikely to occur.

In Chapter 14, Frances Vandiver cautions that a preoccupation with the modern-postmodern debate may result in a lost opportunity to craft new ways of thinking about teaching, learning, supervising, and evaluating. To avert that possibility she suggests that modernists and postmodernists work together toward developing a theory that will address the needs of all students. However, she urges the inclusion of the practitioner voice in this process.

In the final chapter, Eric Nadelstern, Janet Price, and Aaron Listhaus discuss how the infusion of postmodern thinking can enable students to take ownership for their learning and support teacher collaboration and collegial relationships. Through the description of a multicultural alternative education program, they illustrate how postmodern beliefs can be used to build an infrastructure that supports interdisciplinary instruction and continuous professional development. By showcasing the seamless integration of professional development within the instructional organization and leadership of the school, they demonstrate the instrumentality of postmodernism in cultivating a consensually governed school community.

than ten years in the proverbial "pilot seat" of upper administration, where supervision was a personal bailiwick. With that level of practical experience, the challenge before me seemed far less daunting. In fact, as I prepared to write my first draft, the challenge seemed less a challenge than an opportunity to share my sage opinions.

Well, I was wrong, it was not a simple exercise. As I revisited my thoughts on the topics, reread some previous treatises, and scanned the contributions you have read while getting here, I found that my core beliefs were questioned at every turn. What was to have been that *walk in the park* became a soul-searching endeavor.

As I put pen to paper, haunting thoughts kept swirling, disrupting any attempt to put something down. Had I fallen into some Neanderthal abyss and not been aware? Had my liberal approach to wide-based educational opportunity only been a veneer hiding some deep-rooted biases? Had I lost true north on my personal compass? Was there opprobrium waiting should I continue?

The problem was that for a self-proclaimed modernist, much of what I was reading from the postmodern camp (if one can even define it as such) seemed to make sense. The more I thought about the contradictions posited by each side, the more I couldn't help but feel that my educational psalm book may have been tainted. Maybe we should throw caution to the wind and let education take an uncharted course? After all, had not similar action fostered new civilizations in the past?

I certainly was in a predicament and not sure exactly how to bring closure and move on. It was obvious that I could not straddle the two positions and contribute anything, so a decision had to be made. One was—and I hope what you read on the following pages will allow you some of the introspection I have experienced.

BEGINNINGS

Certainly, there has been a scholarly crusade to enlighten, cajole, and move the pendulum of thought from modernism to a postmodern plane. Just as certainly, the reasons for transformation are understandable, if not always practical. The cry for change has come from a wide base made up of educators, politicians, and humanitarians. Each is motivated in his or her own way to remove the hold of a centrist European structure on the educational marketplace.

Some of the flurry came from individuals and groups vested in lightening what is considered the oppression of an aged way of thinking. Other camps, more interested in creating a "new order," splintered, creating competing voices and forcing less effective efforts of change. Regardless of the genesis or impact, it is important to accept that a wave of change has been slowly and consistently growing and is becoming a tsunami with which all in education will eventually have to reckon.

Having said this, it is time to set the first of many compass points for use as guides for later discussion. *The debate on modernism and postmodernism is not*

13

Modern and Postmodern Perspectives on Curriculum and Supervision: *A View from the Top*

Osborne F. Abbey, Jr.

GUIDING QUESTIONS

1. *How does the author's professional position influence his viewpoint?*
2. *Why do you think the author states that postmodern approaches are more viable in supervision than in curriculum? Explain.*
3. *How might a modernist supervisor respond to the author's position?*
4. *Given emphases on national and state standards, can postmodern thought influence curriculum? Explain.*
5. *What would/could/should a supervisor do if a teacher did not incorporate state standards into daily lesson plans?*

OPENING THOUGHTS

When I accepted the challenge of this chapter—to provide a personal "in the trenches" view of the impact of modern and postmodern philosophies on curriculum development and supervision—I did not realize the paths that I would travel in order to frame and construct my thoughts. On the surface, the project seemed harmless enough. I did not have to provide in-depth support for my musings, for they are simply my thoughts. I did not have to judiciously critique the work of scholars, but only report on the world of curriculum and supervision from a superintendent's vantage. At first blush, the entire effort seemed a walk in the park.

After all, I have been involved in the business of developing, revising, and implementing curriculum for over twenty-three years. I have also logged more *nouveau.* Although the terms may have a millennial fragrance, the issues hold an odor of mildew and age. This debate began a long time ago and has simply continued to carry on over the past two centuries.[1] Of course, it has taken on varied formats and sub-themes, but the core issues have remained pretty much true to form.

My purpose is not to carry on the debate, but to shed some *practical* light on how modern and postmodern philosophy plays in today's trenches. The points I shall make are not research based, they cannot be tested easily through a historical review, nor can they be substantiated anywhere outside of my sphere of experience unless by coincidence or through shared beliefs. They are, however, like the warrior's tale, based on life experience. Hopefully, what I bring to the table will provide some additional insight that you will find helpful.

ISSUES

What are the issues? By now you have hopefully had time to reconcile the varied points of view presented in the first two parts of this book. Each brings strength and value to its tenets. Each makes a convincing argument for holding a status quo or furrowing the educational landscape in a different pattern. Each, although presented in late 1900s perspectives, has roots that can be traced to the emergence of formal education in America. They are valid and valued, but far too detailed and heavy to carry through our discussions.

Therefore, for purposes of this chapter, let's agree that *modernism* is synonymous with a detailed plan of action complete with defined intermediate and long-term goals, objectives, and outcomes. Let's also accept that this "plan" is one carefully guided and shaped by the dominant thinking, political and educational, of an era. *Postmodernism*, then, will represent a state of mind that finds such levels of organization constricting, limiting, and oppressive.

In the proverbial nutshell, one point of view likes order, structure, and predetermined outcomes and the other prefers free, unrestricted activity leading to wherever it ends up. One is defined by the age and controlling structures in which it occurs, and the other cares little for "the good of the order" and prefers to embrace any opportunity to its fullest regardless of the standardbearers. I realize that this is an oversimplification of very involved issues, but, as I mentioned previously, to try and maintain the level of introspection of the previous sections would only serve to tether our discussions.

CURRICULUM

How does the struggle of modernism and postmodernism play in the world of curriculum development, revision, and implementation? Before we begin this discussion, it's time for another compass point. *Curriculum is the very life-blood of an educational process.* Curriculum can be formal or informal. It can be written or passed on by word of mouth. It can be implemented in institutions of learning or on street corners. It can lead to higher levels of understanding and knowledge or simply allow for day-to-day survival. There is a curriculum for everything we know and accept, public or private.

Going back to my simplistic model, curriculum can be either defined or undefined. The defined approach guides a practitioner from a beginning to an end, using predetermined models of information, expectation, and outcome. The other allows for unstructured activity that follows any course that may strike one's fancy and may or may not reach the same end every time. One is bound by the beliefs of an era, and the other casts aside conventionalities to explore uncharted territory.

It is time for a third compass point. *Education policy is rarely determined by educators. It is most often determined by politicians, corporate and religious leaders, and local power groups.* Each of these groups has an agenda. As controlling elements, the agenda they adopt will, as a matter of course, be one that supports their particular view of the world. The goal is to pass that view on to subsequent generations in order to continue their status. The major vehicles used for passage are religious and educational institutions.

Vested in their beliefs, as each group will be, it is logical to conclude that none will readily accept too much divergence from their central theme. To do so would cloud their belief system and weaken the system's philosophical infrastructure. Therefore, it is easy to understand why postmodern thinking would not be readily acceptable to the controlling group(s) seeking to perpetuate a belief system.

If this is a valid statement, and I believe it is, then therein lies the rub that may well prevent the modern/postmodern debate from ever reaching closure in public/private education. No controlling system will readily and willingly allow the dissolution of its core beliefs to truly accommodate the levels of individuality and fluidity advocated in a postmodern environment.

To put all of this in an educational setting: In public or private schools, should what goes on within the classrooms under the guise of education be structured or unstructured? Should there be accountability to standards, or should schools allow myriad unpredictable outcomes? Should what is taught be controlled and constructed by a privileged few, or should it be open to individual interpretation? Should there be gateway measures, or should every student be allowed to travel wherever they wish? Should there be gradients of performance or should any effort be rewarded as successful? Should education be free of limiting factors such as race, culture, geographic location, and religion, or should there be criteria and defined guidelines for participation at various levels?

It is time for a fourth compass point. *Those who tell the tales define the culture.* As long as education, public or private, serves to provide new entrants into the work force, then those who have control of the marketplace will define the process for this passage. Because both the economy and an individual's success or failure in that economy depend on marketplace performance, schooling will be driven by outside influences. K-12 schooling in our society is

not truly intended to be an exercise leading to higher levels of personal understanding or scholarly knowledge, although, in fact, that may be a sidebar outcome. It is there to provide a vehicle for children to prepare for adulthood. The
expectation is that schools *in loco parentis* will develop a cadre of post-
adolescents ready to either enter the world of work at graduation or move on
to some level of post-secondary education before entering the workforce.

In this type of ecosystem, curriculum innovation or revision will be guided
by principles outside the hands of educators. "Others" and "circumstances"
will continue to define our existence and behavior as they have in the past. In
the absence of a major societal upheaval, the educational process will continue
to be oriented toward standardized and normative assessment. "Standing,"
for the foreseeable future, will remain an educational vestige. As such, it will
continue to reinforce current [modern] thinking that competition, quotas, hierarchies, and the like are a way of defining existence and, in turn, success.

Given the recent rejection of affirmative action programs, defeat for bilingual education programming, the strengthening of a conservative political
force, and the global angst of emerging world orders, I, sadly, do not see postmodernism and all its possibilities as gaining a strong foothold early in the new
millennium.

SUPERVISION

Regardless of the etiology of a curriculum, ensuring its implementation is a
challenge that falls on a supervisory team. Depending on the makeup of a
school district, this team could be simply a superintendent/principal or as
large as a series of supervisory personnel including principals and superintendents. In this arena, modernism and postmodernism take on a different hue.
The issues become ones of the levels of supervisory involvement and its intent.

I have been an observer of the supervisory process for nigh on twenty-three
years. I have been both the observed and the observer, and I have seen first
hand the problems with the traditional (modern) approach to supervision.

Modern supervisory practice holds that the supervisor follow predetermined constructs, hold to a set number of encounters defined either by contract or code/statute, and present carefully worded narratives or a checklist as
an end product. This document is filed in an individual's permanent file and is
rarely visited, with the exception of the occasional disciplinary action. Dialogue between the observed and the observer is usually minimal and the more
seasoned the dyad, the less the dialogue. Overall, humanity is the defining
driver in the observation process and, as a result, it is rare to find an observation or evaluation that is less than complimentary. People, by their nature, do
not purposely go out of their way to say negative things if positive or neutral
comments can suffice.

This approach, although it meets requirements, is not a productive one in
either the long or the short run. It simply does not provide for open professional and collegial dialogue free of an air of suspicion. It tends to create a

closed system. Observations and evaluations become things to be done or to live through and not viewed as constructive, growth opportunities.

For years I have witnessed elated teachers who proudly announce that they have had their observation(s) and can now get on with the rest of the year. Implied in this type of statement is the knowledge that the supervisor will not be visiting again, at least not without some external prodding. Likewise, I have sat among supervisors who also proudly announce that they have *completed* their observations and are "done" for the year. Either way, the educational process is the loser.

To be fair, however, I do need to say that in some cases a supervisor may have too many staff to manage to do other than a perfunctory job. In cases such as this, the culprit is usually a board of education or a superintendent who wants to keep costs down by limiting supervisory staff who are usually more highly paid. Again, the educational process is the loser. Economy of scale is not a solid rationale for undermining strong supervision.

Then what would be the alternative? Obviously, attitude, funding, and ratios are ever-present issues that impact on supervision regardless of an individual supervisor's investment in excellence. True, but I've found that if the supervisors' supervisor is doing his/her job with gusto and professionalism, then the overall process increases in its worth.

Let me share the way I approach supervision. It is a postmodern philosophy grounded in a compass point. *In order to improve, an individual must know what is expected and also receive constant feedback on performance.*

With this beacon in mind, the supervisory model must be one that is partnered. This requires a process for setting the ground rules. The best way to do this is to call all those whom you supervise together and openly discuss the importance of the process and how it will be *ongoing* and not predicated on some predetermined code or contract. If you are introducing this concept of "ongoing" for the first time, expect resistance, especially from the more seasoned staff. However, do not sway from the conviction that professional growth is predicated on feedback that is valuable and frequent.

If you are bound by guidelines to use a particular document or format, do not attempt to change the accepted approach. But, you can implement a program where you use the "standard" as often as you feel necessary and in ways that may be nontraditional.

I always have a pre-year and end-of-year feedback meeting where I solicit input as to how the observation/evaluation process can be improved and made more meaningful. It is in these sessions that you can find the greatest assistance to maintaining a solid and mutually acceptable format. Without group ownership, any process, no matter how well thought through, will falter.

You do not have to meet with every individual prior to an observation if you have provided the group with a detailed outline of your expectations and discussed the same in a group meeting. By using this approach, you have established a baseline expectation for your observation visits. However, if you have a particular issue or issues that you are attempting to change or reinforce, it is a must that you meet individually with the staff member prior to an observation and discuss specific expectations.

The observation itself is nothing more than a snapshot of what you see during the observation. It is not to be confused with *scripting* or other forms of observational techniques that are geared for instructional improvement.

Once the observation period is complete, you should assess your observation notes and draft some "talking points" that you will use during the post-observation conference. You *should not* come to a post-observation conference with a prewritten observation report. You want to be able to present your perceptions and hear what the staff member has to say. A predrafted document sets up a natural barrier to such dialogue.

When the post-observation conference is over, then write the observation report and share a copy with the observee. If you have openly and honestly developed the report in tandem, you will find all parties grow from the experience.

It is important to define the difference between formal and informal observations. Informal observations are a valuable tool for reinforcing points made in the formal one or for introducing other constructive feedback. You must be aware, however, that like the police, you are never "off duty." Should you come across an activity that goes against guideline, board policy, or statute/code, you are bound to put your observation in writing. This is a point you need to make from the very beginning with all of the staff you supervise so that there are no surprises later on.

Tantamount to the informal observation, you should constantly be introducing new ideas for instructional growth to the staff either individually or en masse. It will depend on the topic which method you use. Once introduced, you should follow up with a discussion on the relevance of the concept to the instructional process.

To be truly effective, you will need to be visible and involved. The modern supervisor is more office bound. As an advocate of a postmodern approach, you need to be out in the classrooms. Not only will your presence help you to monitor what is happening, but also it will reduce the anxiety of your visits. It will allow you to "nip" things in the bud before they arrive at a stage that requires a heavier, more uncomfortable approach.

"All roads lead to Rome," as they say, and so do all observations lead to the annual performance report. This is one of the more critical moments in the supervisory process. It is when you will summarize a year's performance and make recommendations on employment that can be negative, neutral, or positive. It is not a process to be taken lightly. However, if you have worked through a positive observation program, this final phase will not be uncomfortable for you or the staff member.

The annual evaluation is a document that is comprised of information that has been shared with the individual over the course of the year. It is not a time to introduce surprises or criticisms not previously shared. Nor is it a time to bring forth information in a formal manner that you shared in an informal way over the course of the year. That informal data is just that, and unless you placed it in a memorandum or in some other format accepted by the bargaining unit, you may not use it now. Like the observation report, you most likely will be using a pre-adopted document. This should not be a problem, and I have never found it to be one. You can say what you need to regardless of the format required.

Finally, there ought to be a professional improvement plan. This is a plan that is mutually developed and aside from the observation/evaluation process. It is designed to improve an individual's level of instruction and may be related to areas of growth or concern or may be totally independent of the observation/evaluation statements. The key component is that it is related in some way to the individual's job performance and not some farfetched tangent not directly linked to employment.

Although much more involved and certainly more consuming, a postmodern approach to supervision, from my perspective, is the most productive. To follow the traditional modern approach simply does not provide the support or commitment required to manage a school or department in the most effective way.

CLOSING THOUGHTS

Writing this chapter has been an interesting experience for me, and I hope that it has been of benefit to you as well. As a member of upper management for the past ten years, I have experienced firsthand many postmodern influences as they've moved through the various levels of education. I have watched as principals and classroom teachers have tried to implement pied piper activities, to no avail. I have also witnessed the destructive force of modernistic entrenchment and inflexibility toward divergent populations and new ways of thinking.

For many reasons, I would have liked to have come down more on the side of postmodernism in the curricular arena. Unfortunately, I am just too integrally involved in the day-to-day machinery of school systems to see it taking a strong hold in the long run. It is unfortunate, as many tenets of postmodern thought are important to remodeling our society. However, national and state pressure to use standardized gateway intermediate and graduation examinations precludes the flexibility needed to sustain postmodern possibilities.

Supervision, on the other hand, is ripe for change. For far too long, the passive, modern supervisory approach has been the norm. It is time to bring in a "new wave" and to vitalize supervision in the name of excellence. Postmodernism can be successful and sustained in this arena through commitment, courage, and integrity.

NOTE

1. For some insight into the level of debate on curriculum and supervision, you may find Tanner & Tanner's *Curriculum Development: Theory into Practice* (3rd ed.), Merrill–Prentice Hall, helpful.

14

Paradigms of Curriculum and Supervision: A Practitioner's Viewpoint

Frances M. Vandiver

GUIDING QUESTIONS

1. *What is the author's position on modern/postmodern debates in curriculum and supervision?*
2. *How does the ever-increasing diversity of the student body in our nation's schools impact curriculum and supervision?*
3. *How does the author's position as a principal influence her view of modern/postmodern curriculum and supervision?*
4. *How effective was this principal in achieving her purposes?*
5. *React to her conclusions. What does she consider to be our most urgent agenda?*

As I read the chapters regarding the modern and postmodern paradigm curriculum debate, I was heartened to realize that the theorists are also struggling with the complexities of the situations being faced by schools and school practitioners. Those of us whose primary work is in schools know full well that we are in the "eye of the storm" around student achievement, accountability, unfunded mandates, and a national conversation around education. As practitioners, we know that the student body in America becomes more diverse yearly in cultural backgrounds and academic readiness at all levels. We know that the teachers in America no longer reflect many of the students they teach and that there is a looming teacher shortage of grave proportions. We know that more and more students are leaving elementary school without the proper foundations in reading and math. We know that the traditional home environment that supports student learning is no longer the norm and that many of our students' families do not speak English. We know that the traditional structure of our schooling does not meet the needs of many of our students. The complications of our students' lives and the diversity of their backgrounds render the old model of a time-centered, teacher-delivered curriculum not only out of date but also ineffective for many students.

The postmodern theorists have enumerated many of the current conditions that make questioning the modern curriculum pedagogy a reasonable exercise. In this information age, schools are no longer the depositories of "all that we need to know." Our ethnic, racial, economic, and cultural diversity make it more difficult to accept the traditional modern paradigm for curriculum. Regardless of intent, the taught curriculum in most instances did not account for these individual differences. The current turmoil over curricular paradigms is played out in our schools as uncertainty on the part of practitioners, frustration on the part of many students, and a lack of success for many schools.

The current national focus on school reform was triggered by the report *A Nation at Risk*. There are many competing views regarding how we can improve our nation's schools. The plans being offered are not unlike a buffet menu from the modern and postmodern descriptors of curriculum. While the debate continues, schools are besieged by all sides of the reform agenda. Some educators believe that no changes are needed in the ways that teachers and principals perform their work; they claim that demanding unquestioned discipline, drill, and rote learning are the key to survival in the twenty-first century. The voice of the business community is heard through the SCANS competencies and the demand for students who are ready for the job market. Our increasingly complex and diverse populations demand sensitivity to their children's abilities, cultures, and areas of interest. Higher education continues to demand students whose SAT and ACT scores continue to be higher each year. Government at local, state, and national levels has entered the conversation with a continual accountability dialogue that is often focused on punishment for lack of student achievement. When all of the layers of conversation are peeled away, the reform agenda is really about curriculum. We just aren't sure anymore about what should be taught, how it should be taught, and who should teach it. As I continued to read the previous chapters in the volume, classroom images danced through my mind and the theoretical considerations gave way to practical applications.

CLASSROOMS AND PARADIGMS

Students in the second-floor classroom were eagerly following the cues from the teacher who was standing in the front of the room. I marveled at their intensity and her enthusiasm. She was leading the class in a simple word-recognition exercise. She gave lavish praise when the students were correct and gentle corrective feedback when they were not. She spoke to them in their native language as well as in English. She lived in their community; she knew their families. The students took great pride in their successes and were eager learners. Nevertheless, I wondered how could they possibly be ready to pass the state high school competency test in the next three years? The curricular demands seemed out of synch with the needs of these students.

As I walked into the large double room with fifty students, two teachers, and a classroom set up both for individual computer work and classical whole-group instruction, I was struck by the orderliness and the time-on-task behavior that was purposeful and engaging. The two teachers functioned as a team, and all the students were aware of their performance levels in reading comprehension and math application. Both teachers and students were working rigorously so that the students could reach the mastery levels needed in order to receive high school credit. Mastery was established as the constant, and time as the variable for these students. The average age of these freshmen was almost sixteen, each with minimal school success in the past. When I asked the lead teacher how she spent her day, she replied that she spent most of her time convincing the students that they could be successful. Most of them, she said, had lost hope and did not see themselves as successful in the future. They did not see reason to put forth much effort; her job was to convince them otherwise. Curriculum in this setting was aligned with hope for survival.

The special education resource teacher worked with the biology teachers to develop needed accommodations for the students mainstreamed into the class. She worked with the students on their reports, making sure they had needed time in the media center and helping them access Internet resources. She talked about the success her students were having and their boost in self-esteem as they were successful in the regular classrooms. In this context, curriculum first meant access.

The earth science students were presenting their depictions of the water cycle, complete with characters and a story line. Once the key concepts were presented by the teacher, the students had worked in groups to develop their own interpretations of the information. As I talked with them, I asked how they liked this kind of assignment. They said that they liked being able to take the information and then "make sense of it on their own." The teacher talked with me later about how students of varying abilities were able to function well with this type of assignment. In this context curriculum had moved from presentation of material to include active student engagement in a constructivist modality.

The language arts and social studies teachers had developed an integrated course for tenth-grade students. The course was titled "American Studies" and used essential questions as the entry points for each unit. The students were responsible for creating much of their own learning. Today, they were dressed in the garb of the period they had chosen for concentrated study and had a visual display along with original writing as part of their exhibition. I talked with several groups of students about this experience. They said that deciding what to study, how to study, and how to present their learning was frustrating at first. Once they got started, they generally reported that they learned a lot and enjoyed the freedom to venture into areas that interested them. These teachers believed that the students should be active participants in choosing learning activities, content, and display.

These scenarios occurred at the high school where I was the principal, where we focused on developing organizational structures and curricular models to meet with needs of our diverse student population. They are not presented here as examples of best practices as much as they are presented to demonstrate the variety of curricular contexts that exist within one school setting. Each of these classes represents only a small picture of the diversity of students and teachers who were this high school. Together, these classes represent a mosaic of modern and postmodern curriculum paradigms.

TEACHERS AND CHANGING PARADIGMS

Over a five-year period, this school had experienced a dramatic demographic change without any corresponding change in teaching to accommodate the students. When I arrived, the faculty lamented this change in their school as a personal loss, as many of the teachers' children had gone to school there—when it was a "good" school. None of these teachers wanted their beloved school to fail; they just were not equipped with the tools and strategies necessary to make these new students successful. Secondary teachers were never trained to teach basic reading comprehension and math skills. They were taught to deliver *the* curriculum—usually that was defined as going through the textbook sequentially—beginning at the beginning and finishing at the end by the end of the year. Secondary teachers were not prepared to teach culturally and economically diverse students who could not comprehend the information in the textbook.

This predominately white, middle-class faculty, who had been trained to deliver curriculum regardless of who the students were, did not understand why the students were unsuccessful and in many cases appeared unmotivated. Their curricular content and delivery model had worked in the past; these new students just didn't care about their education. There was no debate at this high school regarding the "one best way" to deliver curriculum to this variety of students. There was not even a conversation about "one best" curriculum for these students. The concern was centered on declining student achievement, the low reading ability of the students, and the cultural diversity within the school. Change in its student body and its community was forcing this school to reexamine what should be taught, how it should be taught, and who should teach it. This faculty had to deal with the fact that the student diversity—culturally, racially, and academically—would not be able to respond to the singular curricular paradigm of their own training.

This is not unlike what is happening in many schools across the country. Whether reading professional journals or the local paper or talking with colleagues at regional and national meetings, the focus of concern is searching for ways to insure academic success for all students. Educators talk about strategies to assist the myriad of diverse students while the general public, and lawmakers in particular, talk about making schools more accountable. Could it be that the current clash is a manifestation of trying to use the nineteenth-century technology of schooling with the students of the twenty-first century?

The postmodernists' notion of a need for a new curriculum that is "emancipatory, empowering, and liberating" can be helpful as a way to think creatively. However, my experience has taught me that creative endeavors flow from a firm foundation, they do not just happen. This underscores the importance of creating theoretical frameworks for curriculum content and delivery to enable our current and future teachers to be better equipped to help all students achieve at high levels. Many of the suggestions offered by Behar-Horenstein, for example (see Chapter 1), to assist teachers in developing a working knowledge of curriculum precepts with a practical application are encouraging. Teachers need to enter the profession with a practical understanding of curriculum, preparation to teach a rich diversity of students, and practical experiences that they can use as a foundation for their teaching.

TEACHERS AND CURRICULAR REFORM

Over the past decade, I have been a principal at a middle school in a high socioeconomic area and at an urban high school in an inner-city area. I have learned that the greatest resource for improving teaching and learning through curriculum inquiry is the faculty. However, there are many structural and cultural constraints of schooling that have to be overcome in order to allow teachers to be active participants in curricular reform. Individuals become teachers because they are learners themselves and because they want to help others enjoy the thrill of learning. The system of schooling dims this inner passion in many of our teachers as they are reduced to roles that do not include decision-making or meaningful leadership opportunities. Adult learning during the working day is not a focus in most systems of schooling. Additionally, there is little structured time for interaction, conversation, and planning between teachers about teaching or students during the working day. Teachers' learning had to be addressed before student achievement would improve. Opportunities for teachers to learn together, share student work, observe each other, and learn outside the school have to become part of the school culture. We have to energize the teaching context before we can energize the learning context.

The need for a common language of instruction for students that would enable them to see connections between classes and grade levels became a focus of our conversations. Time was provided for teachers within grade levels to explore commonalties and develop integrated approaches within their curricular areas. Time was provided for teachers within a discipline to discover the expectations—generally unspoken—that the grade levels had for each other. This enabled the teachers to know what mastery levels were expected for the next level of the subject. These conversations about horizontal and vertical curriculum articulation helped us go beyond the intended curriculum of the county scope and sequence and the state course frameworks, to the taught curriculum within the school. These conversations allowed the teachers to construct their own sense of the curriculum that was appropriate for the students they taught.

At the same time, opportunities for our teachers to learn during the school day had to be provided. A weekly schedule was developed whereby for one day a week, each period of the day, teachers had an opportunity to learn together. We committed an instructional position to a teacher who served as our Staff Development Facilitator (SDF). The SDF organized the learning sessions and led them until other teachers felt comfortable enough to share strategies and student work. A professional library was established and the SDF office had an area for small groups of teachers to meet together and work. The learning sessions began to develop a school culture with an expectation of adult learning and conversations about teaching and learning. The commitment of funds to release teachers for conversation and planning along with funding the staff development facilitator provided concrete evidence of the importance of adult learning in the school. Teachers got excited when they were given the freedom to learn, question, make decisions, and develop as professionals. These activities were the catalyst that moved these faculties from passive recipients of curriculum from outside sources to active participants in creating a variety of models that were useful in the context of each school and for its students.

TEACHER-TO-TEACHER SUPERVISION

The conversations around new ideas, new strategies, and new successes needed a new forum for more in-depth and focused work. Our affiliation with the Coalition of Essential Schools led us to develop a study group format for teachers to work in small groups. These groups became known as Critical Friends Groups (CFG) and functioned as peer observation and feedback components for our continued focus on improving curricular models and increasing student achievement. Each CFG had a teacher who served as the group's coach/facilitator and received training through the Annenberg Institute for School Reform program. After watching this structure for teacher observation and feedback of each other's work in two very different school contexts, I am convinced that a new model of supervision must be teacher-focused and teacher-directed.

The traditional role of the administrator as supervisor is often played out in an infrequent visit to the teacher's classroom with an "evaluation instrument in hand." In reality, the administrator often knows little about the context of the classroom, has had little if any contact with the teacher around instructional issues, and may not have a strong instructional background. This scenario does not instill much pride in the "evaluation" and holds little hope for instructional improvement. The reliance on an administrator, whose own responsibilities preclude active involvement in teaching or the daily conversations about students and achievement, to be a pivotal player focusing on supervision for individual teacher growth is open to question in my mind. While principals need to provide leadership, expectations, vision, and re-

sources enabling a school to develop a climate for continuous improvement of both teaching and learning, their role in effective supervision for instructional improvement may need to be restructured.

I have seen tremendous growth in teacher effectiveness using a formative approach with a teacher-to-teacher model. The ease of interaction with trusted colleagues, the exchange of ideas, approaches, and the sharing of successes and failures develop a continuous improvement mindset that is often missing in the supervisor-to-teacher model. In any effective supervision model, expectations need to be articulated, protocols need to be developed, instruments need to be chosen, and timelines need to be determined. Once these structures are in place, I believe that developing teacher leaders, who are effective teachers themselves, as facilitators for instructional supervision may be a model that is worth consideration. This model does not remove supervision from the administrators' responsibilities; it suggests a shift in what the role might be. Utilizing expertise from the community in collaborative endeavors, as suggested by Ovando (see Chapter 6), would become more specific to the needs of each small teacher group and would be driven by their identified needs. Supervision in a collaborative and formalized teacher-to-teacher model is an extension of the Critical Friends Group process described earlier.

TEACHERS, THEORIES, AND URGENCIES

The modern curriculum view has served us well for generations. Certainly there has been poor interpretation and implementation but by and large our schools have done what they were supposed to do—provide an education for our students in order for them to be productive citizens and continue our democratic way of life. I believe that the modern and postmodern views of curriculum will meld into a new view of curriculum that will provide grounding in the modern view while adopting the flexibility needed to account for the diversity of needs identified by the postmodernists. The questions that Behar-Horenstein (see Chapter 1) developed to guide curriculum development serve as a practical approach for making this transition. The questions can provide specific curricular parameters while providing flexibility for different teaching contexts.

The urgency of the situation cannot be overstated. Schools, for the most part, are struggling individually to make sense of the reform whirlwind around them. Inservice opportunities are often focused only on ways to improve test scores. Many reform initiatives are little more than packaged curriculum to be "delivered" to all students. The depersonalization of both students and teachers in the rush to accountability is frightening. Many teachers and principals are concerned about the trend toward summative evaluations as the only indicator of student and school success. They do not want to be subjected to a "teach to the test" mentality that predetermines the curriculum.

The curriculum theorists need to combine their best thinking and create models that can better meet the needs of our diverse students. Practitioners need to be collaborators in this endeavor as they can provide the grounding in practice that is needed to develop appropriate models. The debate over what should be taught, how it should be taught, and who should teach it will continue. However, we need to ensure that the strongest voices in the debate are educators rather than policy-makers, religious leaders, and business corporations. If we become preoccupied with a modern-postmodern debate rather than forging new models, we may lose the opportunity to direct the conversation.

15

Student Empowerment through the Professional Development of Teachers

Eric Nadelstern, Janet R. Price, and Aaron Listhaus

GUIDING QUESTIONS

1. *What characterizes this high school's innovative approach overall and particularly as related to professional development?*
2. *According to the authors, what makes their approach to professional development successful?*
3. *Describe some postmodern influences that have likely shaped the International High School's approach to professional development.*
4. *What would it take for your school to model many of the approaches taken by the International High School?*
5. *What role, if any, would/could modernist approaches to curriculum and/or supervision play at the school?*

The International High School (IHS), a multicultural alternative educational environment for recent arrivals, serves students with varying degrees of limited English proficiency. A collaborative project between the New York City Board of Education and LaGuardia Community College of the City University of New York, this school offers a high school/college curriculum combining substantive study of all subject matter with intensive study and reinforcement of English. Our mission is to enable each of our students to develop the linguistic, cognitive and cultural skills necessary for success in high school, college and beyond.

IHS is a learning organization in which professional development is not a separate initiative but, rather, is built into everything we do. Our current overall organization, including our professional development program, is based on our ongoing evaluation of student performance and faculty effectiveness and reflects an evolution over time.

THE BASIC UNIT FOR PROFESSIONAL DEVELOPMENT: THE INTERDISCIPLINARY TEAM

The faculty and the student body are organized into six interdisciplinary teams. On each team, four teachers (math, science, English and social studies teachers) and a support services coordinator are jointly responsible for a heterogeneous group of about seventy-five ninth-through twelfth-grade students. The faculty works with the same group of students for a full year providing a complete academic program organized around themes such as "Motion," "Conflict and Resolution," or "The American Dream." Teams also provide affective and academic counseling.

The interdisciplinary teams provide an ideal infrastructure for professional development. Significant decision-making power over curriculum, budget and scheduling is delegated to the teams and three hours of meeting time are built into each faculty team's weekly schedule. Team members use this time to develop and revise curriculum, to plan schedules and allocate available resources, to discuss students with special needs and jointly devise ways of better meeting those needs, and to share successful practices and trouble shoot problems.

Team members also team teach, particularly when new teachers are hired. The faculty evaluation process includes both self-evaluation and evaluation by peers on the team.

CROSS-TEAM PROFESSIONAL DEVELOPMENT

The policy-setting body for the school is the Coordinating Council which includes administrators, student government representatives, parents' association representatives, the union chapter leader, and a representative from each interdisciplinary team. Issues for the council may first surface in individual team discussions, such as reporting on a successful innovation by one team for possible adoption schoolwide. Conversely, the council regularly identifies schoolwide issues that need discussion and action at the team level, such as how best to provide guidance services or how to align the curriculum offered by each team with state and city graduation standards. The council meets at least monthly. A steering committee, comprised of the school's principal and two assistant principals and two elected teacher representatives, takes care of day-to-day school management and sets agendas for Coordinating Council meetings.

A schoolwide Curriculum and Assessment Committee includes representatives from each instructional team. Its current charge is to oversee schoolwide efforts to refine performance-based assessment practices culminating in graduation by portfolio and to align curriculum and assessment standards across instructional teams.

A schoolwide Personnel Committee also includes representatives from each instructional team and determines faculty hiring and evaluation procedures. It oversees the "Peer Evaluation" process through which untenured faculty present a portfolio of their work every year to a faculty committee. Tenured faculty present their portfolio every three years. This process not only holds teachers responsible for demonstrating continued growth and improvement, it also provides a valuable forum for sharing best practices. In addition, faculty are regularly observed and coached by members of their instructional team and by the steering committee.

Monthly faculty meetings are devoted to professional development across teams and focus on those topics deemed most central by the Coordinating Council, Steering Committee, and Curriculum and Assessment Committee. Recently, the emphasis has been on aligning curricula with external standards and internal assessment practices, and meeting agendas are carefully planned to move this effort forward (IHS, 1991).

CROSS-SCHOOL PROFESSIONAL DEVELOPMENT

Several professional development days are built into the school year. Generally, these are held jointly with two newer schools, established with assistance from the IHS staff. Brooklyn International (established in 1994) and Manhattan International (established in 1993) also serve new immigrants through similar teaching methodologies, organizational structures, and assessment strategies. These joint staff development days supplemented by regular meetings of representatives from the three schools provide opportunities to share and generalize successful practices across schools. Faculty also serve on the graduation portfolio panels at these sister schools, an effective way to jointly develop performance standards and share curriculum.

IHS shares students, resources, faculty, and facilities with its host, LaGuardia Community College. Several teachers from IHS teach courses in the college, and several faculty from the college teach within the interdisciplinary team structure. This serves to narrow the gap between high school graduation requirements and college entry requirements. College faculty assist the high school faculty in preparing students for college level work and in counseling students to register for the appropriate level courses as high school juniors and seniors. On occasion, professors from the college as well as visiting artists and scientists team teach instructional units with IHS faculty, building the school's capacity to integrate the arts and scientific method across the curriculum. Instructional teams also work with community-based organizations and businesses to provide internships for our students.

ESSENTIAL ELEMENTS OF EFFECTIVE PROFESSIONAL DEVELOPMENT

What makes this approach to professional development successful? The answer lies in a variety of factors, including:

- It is built, seamlessly, into the governance and instructional organization of the school;

- It gives teachers the necessary time and decision-making authority to support each other's professional development on and across teams;

- It supports individual professional growth and the sharing of best practice through peer coaching and evaluation by other team members, regularly scheduled teacher portfolio presentations and team-teaching opportunities for new faculty members;

- It provides regular opportunities for collegial collaboration and the sharing of successful practice both within the school and with other schools serving similar students;

- It allows for regular, systematic interaction with the college and with businesses and community organizations, helping faculty constantly reassess how we are preparing students for higher education and the world of work;

- It shares best practices with the larger educational community through hosting a constant flow of American and international visitors, collaboration with outside researchers, membership in citywide and national networks, and faculty participation as instructors in various university teacher education programs and presenters at a wide range of conferences;

- Its content is determined collaboratively by representative bodies based on the school community's ongoing assessment of the instructional program;

- It promotes a climate of inquiry and continuous improvement, as evidenced by a series of performance-driven organizational reforms implemented over the past fourteen years; and

- It is driven by a coherent long-term strategy working backward from graduation requirements to ensure that all students have the necessary supports to meet rigorous graduation criteria.

GOALS AND OUTCOMES

Our overriding goal for professional development is to ensure that every faculty member is fully equipped to support students in meeting increasingly rigorous graduation requirements. This means that teachers must be providing learning opportunities designed to move our students towards specific proficiencies from the moment they enter our school.

Our goal for student achievement is to improve student attendance, retention, course pass rates, and graduation rates while simultaneously raising standards, consistent with the State Education Department's decision to require Regent-level work from all high school graduation candidates and our own mission to prepare students for success in college and beyond.

To meet these goals, our teachers must be actively and collaboratively engaged in ongoing efforts to understand and internalize standards and to align curriculum and classroom assessment to graduation standards. To adequately support all students, our faculty must continue to hone its proficiency in the following teaching strategies:

- Managing a student-centered classroom, facilitating cooperative learning within small groups of students engaged in projects where they construct their own learning in small groups with careful coaching by the teacher;

- Accommodating heterogeneity by designing and modifying curriculum so that it is accessible but challenging for all students, from the immigrant who is attending an American school for the first time and may not be fully literate in his or her native language to a student who has achieved near native fluency and received excellent academic preparation in the home country;

- Integrating both first- and second-language development with content areas in classrooms where students speak many different languages and have widely varied levels of proficiency in English; and

- Constructing an interdisciplinary course of study that permits students to make connections, solve meaningful problems and apply learning to new areas without sacrificing the rigor of the individual disciplines.

These are the basic strategies that IHS teachers have always been encouraged and supported to develop and that have led to our outstanding student outcomes, ones in which any school could take pride but that are particularly noteworthy when compared to outcomes of other Limited English Proficient students. Our current challenge is to adapt these strategies to a more demanding curriculum to prepare our students for more rigorous graduation standards.

PROFESSIONAL DEVELOPMENT DESIGN AND IMPLEMENTATION

Every aspect of the school, including professional development, is grounded in a set of research-based principles. The work of James Cummins (1995) informs our perspective that limited English proficient students require near-native fluency in English to realize their full potential within an English-speaking society; but, at the same time, in an increasingly interdependent world, fluency in a language other than English must be viewed as a precious resource for the student, the school, and the larger society. As per Chamot and O'Malley (1994), we believe that language skills are most effectively learned in context and emerge most naturally in purposeful, language-rich, interdisciplinary study. John Slavin's (1987) work confirms that students (and teachers as well) learn best from each other in heterogeneous, collaborative groupings. Linda Darling-Hammond (1994) has actually used data from our school to develop her conclusion that the most successful educational programs are those which emphasize high expectations coupled with effective support systems. Finally, Theodore Sizer (1984) and Deborah Meier (1995) have demonstrated that the most effective instruction takes place when teachers are actively involved in the decision-making processes.

Over the past fourteen years, our research-based professional development design has resulted in a series of instructional reforms affecting all students and faculty. They were arrived at through careful experimentation and evaluation and agreed to by faculty consensus after discussion and consultation with parent and student representatives. For instance, in 1988 faculty decided to lengthen the class period from thirty-five- to seventy-minute periods after participating in a "student for a day" exercise, where teachers shadowed a specific student for a whole day. The faculty overwhelmingly concluded that giving students more time in fewer classes would result in a more coherent, less disjointed learning experience.

The shift from "singleton" classes to the current organization in interdisciplinary teams began in 1990, when an IHS math teacher attended a math/science conference and came back excited about the possibilities for interdisciplinary learning. She enlisted a physics teacher to collaboratively develop a set of activities that engaged students in applying math to solve real world science problems. In 1991, these two teachers then joined up with humanities teachers and, with the full support of the administration, created a trimester-long interdisciplinary block program for a group of students, organized around the theme of "Motion." Evaluating student performance, they found attendance and course pass rates improved, cutting decreased, and the overall level of sophistication of student work improved when the students' school day was coherent, interrelated, and interdisciplinary. A second interdisciplinary team formed in the fall of 1992 and enjoyed similar success. Consequently, the school community decided to reorganize the entire school into interdisciplinary teams in the spring of 1993.

Originally, the school year was divided into three cycles and students remained with one interdisciplinary team for only one-third of the year. One team, believing that if they had longer to get to know their students they could accomplish more with them, proposed to enroll a sixth of the student population, with student and parent agreement, for a full year's program. Again, the success of this experiment convinced the representative Coordinating Council to adopt an annualized approach to instruction for the entire school, beginning in the 1996–1997 school year. Similar processes resulted in the decision to provide guidance services within the interdisciplinary team structure, where a team of teachers is responsible for the same group of students all day for a full year. The Assistant Principal for Guidance and the two experienced guidance counselors on staff provide coaching, technical assistance, and regular training sessions to designated members of the six instructional teams who, beginning in this current school year, have each taken over college advisement, personal and academic counseling, and crisis intervention for the 75 students served by their team.

There is a great deal of cross-fertilization between the organization of student instruction and assessment and how we develop and evaluate our faculty. For instance, one impetus for reorganizing into teaching teams was that faculty concluded they should model the cooperative learning they expected of students working in small groups in their classrooms. Conversely, after we developed our portfolio reviews of teachers, one team began experimenting with adapting that system to student assessment. The practice soon spread informally to other teams and the Curriculum and Assessment Committee developed a guide to assessment standards entitled "Performance Based Assessment Standards." This guide (IHS, 1998) outlined what we expected of our students over and above passing the state's basic competency tests at exemplary rates.

This process culminated with IHS requesting and receiving a variance from the State Education Department, permitting us to replace the usual Regents Competency Test program with graduation by portfolio for a five-year trial period beginning in the spring of 1996. Since then, the State Education Department has decided to phase out basic competency testing and will eventually require the more rigorous Regent exams for high school graduates beginning with the class of 2001, our current freshmen. Consequently, our long-term goal must be to enable students to graduate with a portfolio of best work that meets or exceeds the work produced in Regents-level classes and that demonstrates mastery to an extent comparable to passing scores on the Regents exams.

At every level, our professional development program is now organized around this long-term goal. The Curriculum and Assessment Committee, which includes student representatives and teachers from every instructional team, has taken the lead in developing assessment standards and rubrics to assess student performance tasks, organizing teacher meetings to test the rubrics on actual student work, supporting team efforts to revise curriculum to ensure that every student has adequate learning opportunities to put together a satisfactory senior portfolio, and preparing guides and protocols for faculty mentoring seniors and chairing graduation portfolio panels. The PTA and student government are regularly consulted on graduation portfolio issues and brief their constituencies through articles in their respective newsletters.

The monthly faculty staff development meetings are now devoted to working back from exit criteria to evaluate and improve instruction. Faculty are systematically comparing school curricula and student work to state content standards and to the performance standards contained in the New Standards Project (1997). For instance, beginning last spring, instructional teams were paired to compare their curricula to state standards for content learning. This helped teams identify and address gaps in their curricular offerings as well as share best practices in a collaborative setting. At our last faculty meeting, teams compared strategies for mentoring seniors in preparation for graduation portfolio presentations. At the next meeting, faculty will meet in small discipline-based groups to identify which projects and assignments are adequately rigorous for purposes of including in graduation portfolios. It is anticipated that as a result of these discussions, instructional teams will continue to revise some student assignments as required to meet our increasingly rigorous graduation standards.

The interdisciplinary instructional teams carry the greatest responsibility and receive the bulk of the resources for implementing the necessary professional development to support more rigorous exit criteria. At their regularly scheduled weekly meetings, team members both revise student assignments to better prepare all students for senior portfolio and employ a case management approach to adapt those assignments to the needs of specific students. A typical instructional team meeting might include a discussion about how to help a student with reading problems or limited English complete a demanding research project, how to help students frame their own questions to explore in science experiments, how to use a grant to integrate technology into the curriculum, or how to upgrade a literature assignment to meet graduation requirements.

OBJECTIVE EVIDENCE OF SUCCESS

The International High School at LaGuardia was created to address the achievement gap between limited English proficient students and native speakers of English. Our initial success is documented by the following statistics. Using a cohort analysis of the class of 1993, the Office of Research, Evaluation, and Assessment (OREA), New York City Board of Education, found that 34% of all LEP students graduated in four years; 44% of all students in NYC graduated in four years. However, 54% of International High School students graduated in four years.

In another analysis (OREA) of the percentage of students graduating as a factor of total enrollment last year, the International High School compares to some of the finest, competitive, specialized high schools in the city as follows: 23.2% at Stuyvesant High School, 20.9% at Brooklyn Tech High School, 20.4% at Bronx High School of Science, 20.0% at the International High School, 18.8% at F. H. LaGuardia High School of Music and Art.

These results are especially encouraging considering the other schools are specialized schools requiring rigorous entrance exams for admission. International High School admits students based not on achievement but rather on need, admitting only students identified by the Language Assessment Battery as limited English proficient. It is our mission to narrow the existing gap of achievement for immigrant students such that they may successfully compete on a level playing field with native speakers of English.

Interdisciplinary instruction has long been known to increase language acquisition as well as deepen the understanding of academic concepts. New learners of English are better able to make gains in language proficiency and master high school subject content when classes are thematically connected. Our students continue to make greater gains in English language acquisition than their peers in other schools throughout New York City. In the 1994–1995 school year, 69.2% of our students achieved mandated gains in English language proficiency compared to 61.4% of students in New York City. In the 1995–1996 school year, 70.5% of IHS students achieved mandated gains compared to 65.4% of students in New York City (1995–1996 Annual School Report, New York City Board of Education).

Our team approach to case management has enabled us to close the achievement gap within our extremely heterogeneous student population. At weekly team meetings, teachers share classroom practices that enable less well prepared students to meet more rigorous standards and devise and assess intervention strategies for specific students having difficulty. As a result of this student-centered approach, course pass rates have increased. In the school year 1994–1995, 91% of students passed all of their classes. In the last two years, 1995–1997, the course pass rate has been 93%. Citywide, two-thirds of all students fail one of their classes, and almost half of all students fail more than one of their classes. Not surprisingly, student daily attendance at IHS has also increased. During the 1994–1995 school year, our daily attendance rate was 93.2%. During 1995–1996 it rose to 93.9%. Last year student daily attendance was 94.8% (Office of Data Analysis of the Office of the Chief Executive for School Programs and Support Services, 1996–1997).

In addition to high course pass rates, we also have a high retention rate. During the last three years, our dropout rate has continued to be well below the dropout rate for New York City. For students entering International's ninth grade in 1992 and tenth grade in 1993, our dropout rate was 1.7%, as compared to New York City's 16.4%.

Our students also graduate at higher rates than their counterparts in New York City. Typically, 42% of LEP students graduate after four years; 49% of all students graduate after four years. At IHS, 72% of students who entered in 1992 graduated four years later. The four-year cohort graduating in 1995 was 60.6%, the four-year cohort graduating in 1994 was 54.8% (Office of Data Analysis of the Office of the Chief Executive for School Programs and Support Services, 1996–1997).

Annually, 92–95% of our limited English proficient graduates apply and are accepted to college. Two-thirds attend four-year colleges; one-third attend two-year colleges. Of our graduates, 80% attend City University of New York (CUNY); 20% attend state or private colleges. Among the college acceptances for the class of 1997 are Columbia, Cornell, Fordham, MIT, New York University, Rutgers, University of Chicago, and University of Pennsylvania, as well as most of the State University of New York campuses.

Our professional development has not only led to student achievement, it has also led to better ways of assessing student achievement while supporting teacher development.

The faculty's peer support, review, and evaluation system became a powerful force in shaping a common set of strongly held values and principles for guiding both the design and the practice of student assessment. Over time, student assessment practices have evolved from traditional, periodic tests and quizzes to a continuous process of self-reflection, peer assessment, and teacher assessment organized around collaborative performance tasks and individual portfolio development. Both the substance and the process of the assessments are authentic rather than contrived or removed from the act of learning. . . . A richly interwoven array of formal and informal occasions for evaluation creates the expectation that learning is a process of continual reflection and improvement in which every member of the school community is constantly involved. (Ancess & Darling-Hammond, 1995)

Our teacher collaboration also fosters good learning habits in our students. As the school's peer review policy states:

Shared leadership in a high school can foster the professional growth and development of teachers, leading to the empowerment of students as successful learners. . . . If we view ourselves as true educators, we must also view ourselves as learners. . . . If we model self-improvement in an atmosphere of sharing, that is what our students will learn. (Ancess & Darling Hammond, 1995)

The collaborative atmosphere is conducive to high morale and low absenteeism. Our teachers are absent because of self-treated illness on average 2.7 days per year as compared to the New York City average of 6.2 days per year. In the thirteen years of existence, no staff member has ever left for a comparable position in another New York City public school. As one staff member wrote in her self-evaluation:

An American education is one that fosters competition. Competition leads to hostility, isolation, secretiveness, and shame. Collaboration, on the other hand, provides many benefits, as it has done for me. First and foremost, it promotes a feeling of self confidence. It provides a supportive environment to help me feel secure not only in presenting what I know is good, but also in allowing me to feel secure in examining my weaknesses on my own and with others. . . . Collaboration furnishes recognition for everybody, because each party naturally acknowledges the contributions of the others. It helps me to think because I receive input from others and am exposed to a greater variety of ideas and information. So it also broadens the scope of what I can produce. It provides a feeling of community, which I haven't experienced in other work environments. Experiencing that environment myself makes it possible for me to provide it to my students. (Self-Evaluation, Nancy Dunetz, 1990)

THE ROLE OF THE PRINCIPAL IN A FACULTY-GOVERNED SCHOOL

Eric Nadelstern, the current and founding principal of IHS and coauthor of this chapter, is fond of saying that the most important role he plays in the fourteenth year of the school is that he keeps someone else from sitting in his office. In more reflective moments, he points out that the principal's role in a consensually governed school community is to provide teachers with the support necessary to be as good as they are and to continuously remind them just how good that is. This entails:

- establishing a schoolwide focus on teaching and learning,
- building a powerful community of leaders and learners,
- modeling in interactions with teachers the kind of relationships they should develop with students,
- developing a collegial vision and purpose,

- serving as a resource for solving problems and implementing new programs,
- focusing faculty on their own growth and development as well as that of their students,
- evaluating new initiatives in relation to student learning outcomes,
- communicating the mission and philosophy of the school to internal and external audiences, and
- enlisting a broad base of political and financial support for ongoing experimentation and innovation.

Democratic schools in postmodern times require stronger leadership than traditional, top down, autocratic institutions. The nature of that leadership, however, is markedly different, replacing the need to control with the desire to support. Ironically, such leaders exercise much more influence where it counts, creating dynamic relationships between teachers and students in the classroom and resulting in high standards of academic achievement.

REFERENCES

Ancess, J., & Darling-Hammond, L. (1995). *Authentic teaching, learning, and assessment with new English learners at International High School.* New York: National Center for Restructuring Education, Schools, and Teaching.

Chamot, A. U., & O'Malley, J. M. (1994). *The CALLA handbook: Implementing the cognitive academic language learning approach.* Reading, MA: Addison Wesley.

Cummins, J. (1995). *Negotiating identities: Education for empowerment in a diverse society.* Ontario: California Association for Bilingual Education.

Darling-Hammond, L. (1994). Performance-based assessment and educational equity. *Harvard Educational Review, 64*(1), 5–30.

Meier, D. (1995). *The power of their ideas: Lessons for America from a small school in Harlem.* Boston: Beacon Press.

International High School (IHS). (1991). *Personnel procedures for peer selection, support and evaluation.* New York: In-house publication.

International High School (IHS). (1998). *Performance based assessment standards.* New York: In-house publication.

New standards: Performance standards, Vol. 3. (1997). Washington, DC, and Pittsburgh, PA: National Center on Education and the Economy and the University of Pittsburgh.

Sizer, T. (1984). *Horace's compromise: The dilemma of the American high school.* Boston: Houghton Mifflin.

Slavin, R. (1981). Cooperative learning and desegregation. In W. Hawley (Ed.), *Effective school desegregation*, pp. 225–244. Beverly Hills: Sage Publications.

Afterword: Closing Reflections

Modern and postmodern perspectives clearly influence the way in which we conceive of and practice curriculum and supervision. Contributors to this volume have expressed their views on a fundamental question: To what extent is curriculum/supervision inquiry directed toward the problems of curriculum/supervision practice? Practitioner contributors have affirmed that modernist/postmodernist thinking has indeed influenced curriculum and supervisory practices in schools. Practitioner and professor contributors have articulated varied ways classroom practice has been influenced by these paradigms and have proffered different directions needed to enhance the quality of schooling via curriculum and supervision. Regardless of orientation, each contributor, more specifically, has offered strategies and ideas aimed at improving curriculum inquiry, teaching in the classroom, school leadership, and a plethora of challenges facing education in the new millennium.

Each author presents a thoughtful, well-reasoned exposition that attempts to recover meaning and value in supervision and curriculum through an understanding of how modernist and postmodernist perspectives affect practice and theory. Each contributor addresses key issues related to the efficacy of curriculum and supervision paradigms and their influence on practice. In many cases, contributors state their views forthrightly:

1. "Modernism and postmodernism have advantages and disadvantages and each can contribute to sound curriculum practice. Ultimately, however, practitioners are left to decide which paradigm offers the best advice for practice." (Behar-Horenstein)

2. "It's a different world for both curriculum practitioners and curriculum researchers." (Short)

3. "The time has come to find a common unity in the field of curriculum," yet postmodernism, as "ideological criticism" although important, has little to offer to those interested in practice. (Hlebowitsh)

4. "I assert, however, that the postmodern proclivity to completely eschew supervision, evaluation, and judicious and intelligent use of directive supervision is misguided, potentially limiting, and yes, even dangerous." (Glanz)

5. "In sharp contrast, fusion leadership, a modernist paradigm, builds partnerships, joins parts of an organization into a cohesive unit by eliminating boundaries." (Zepeda)

6. "These two supervision perspectives [modern and postmodern] appear to be contradictory at first; however, a closer look at their underlying assumptions and propositions reveals that they are not mutually exclusive but complementary of each other." (Ovando)

7. "I hope that this chapter will convince you that postmodernism has much to offer the educational community and the global society. In the upheaval and conflict of the modern world, maybe postmodernism offers a fresh way to look at our sociopolitical, economic, ethical, religious, psychological, ecological and educational dilemmas." (Slattery)

8. "I write from the perspective of affirmative postmodernism. . . . I feel fortunate to be born in a culture that has been deeply influenced by" modernism, yet "I am not completely satisfied with" this approach. Having been coerced to work in a school as a teacher where the principal urged compliance "with the school district's instructional goals, I found their rationales deeply authoritarian, irrational, unethical, and unwise." (Henderson)

9. "Multicultural education has a similar mission, and therefore can be seen as an ideological analogue of, and methodological tool for putting postmodern ideals into pedagogical practice." (Gay & Hart)

10. "Our suggestion is that, especially within the postmodern, a primary role of supervisors is to help teachers deal with change, to prepare them to thrive in dynamic, shifting contexts of change." (Waite & Ramires Fernandes)

11. "From the postmodernist position, there is no 'remedy' for the predicaments we find ourselves in. We cannot speak of remedy, but rather of hope." (Holland & Obermiller)

12. "Propositions of postmodernism reveal weaknesses inherent in modernist philosophy and offer an expanded and more inclusive perspective from which to consider organizations, generally, and instructional supervision, specifically." (Pajak & Evans)

13. "It is unfortunate, as many tenets of postmodern thought are important to remodeling our society. However, national and state pressure to use standardized gateway intermediate and graduation examinations precludes the flexibility needed to sustain postmodern possibilities. Supervision, on the other hand, is ripe for change. For far too long, the passive, modern supervisory approach has been the norm." (Abbey)

14. "I believe that the modern and postmodern views of curriculum will meld into a new view of curriculum that will provide grounding in the modern view while adopting the flexibility needed to account for the diversity of needs identified by the postmodernists." (Vandiver)

15. "Democratic schools in postmodern times require stronger leadership than traditional, top-down, autocratic institutions." (Nadelstern, Price, & Listhaus)

What are the implications of such divergent views? Perhaps a modernist view, with its penchant for dualisms and proclivity for unity, might offer a resolution so that a synthesis of principles will advance practice and scholarship. Perhaps through some form of consensus building or amalgamation of insights (clearly, according to a postmodern thinker, these are modernistic ploys), common purposes will be identified. Yet, this approach may be considered too simplistic by some postmodernists since their perspectives are grounded in a complex and rigorous body of knowledge. Rejecting modernism with its pronouncements of certainty, knowledge, and truth, postmodernism questions the given and thrives on its critique of the modern. As Slattery has so eloquently reminded us: "We will have to live with certain tensions, ambiguities, chaos and contradictions that are not fully resolvable. Working comfortably within ambiguity and complexity rather than lusting after certainty and reason is a postmodern response to questions of progress and justice."

We realize the limitations of modernism, with its historic connection to Cartesian positivist traditions. We realize that modernist propositions and practices have not solved all the major sociopolitical and instructional problems of schooling. Yet, we realize that modernism is not so oppressive as its critics would have us believe. Modernist scholarship has moved beyond mere adherence to positivist inquiry to curriculum and supervision work founded on democracy and participative leadership. At the same time, we realize the potentiality and very substance of a postmodern critique. Varied and multidimensional in terms of its ideology, epistemology, and ontology, postmodernism, as Gay and Hart have pointed out, "resists all types of educational fragmentation, and related linear and hierarchical rankings of knowledge." Notwithstanding this logic, postmodernists, by in large, have not adequately addressed practical issues of curriculum and supervision. Postmodernism has in fact been criticized for exhibiting a regular set of features consonant with a metanarrative. We understand those who criticize postmodernism for its lack of guidance in day-to-day classroom work. Indeed, practitioners and modernist and postmodernist scholars alike, who work together, have to grapple with everyday curriculum and supervision realities.

We believe most fundamentally that paradigm debates over modernist versus postmodernist conceptions of curriculum and supervision help further invigorate our respective fields of study and practice. We caution that common unity and purpose must be identified if we plan to forward scholarship and improve practice in curriculum and supervision. Each contributor in this volume passionately articulates her/his vision for better supervisory and/or curriculum practices. To the extent to which such disagreements deepen our commitments and further our understanding of the intricacies of supervision and curriculum theory and practice, then the debates are warranted, worthwhile, and should be encouraged (see, e.g., English, 1998; Willower, 1998).

What educators in curriculum, instruction, supervision, and teaching do is ultimately entwined with the context and opportunities we provide for growth. Curriculum and supervision are tools by which we assist people to acquire not simply requisite skills but also ways of developing a sense of self, a sense of meaning, human intelligence, and purpose. In doing so, we fulfill our mission to encourage our students and ourselves to reflect, renew, and evolve as practitioners, scholars, and individuals. We realize that teaching is much more than merely transmitting knowledge and utilizing scientifically derived teaching skills. Fundamentally, effective teachers (as well as those of us who struggle with curriculum and supervision) are trying to help the young grow and develop as human beings. In the end, what loftier pursuit and more meaningful goal is there than engaging our students in exploration of self, identity, and purpose?

Conceiving curriculum and supervision in critical ways enables the individual to explore and become conscious of one's sensibilities and cognitive capabilities. The responsibility is surely awesome. But what are the alternatives? We believe that our energies would be better spent in considering the following questions among others: How can we, as committed beings, encourage students and ourselves to get in touch with our existential reality? How can we best urge our students and ourselves to become spontaneous, creative, and conscious?

REFERENCES

English, F. W. (1998). The postmodern turn in educational administration: Apostrophic or catastrophic development? *Journal of School Leadership*, *8*, 426–447.
Willower, D. J. (1998). Fighting the fog: A criticism of postmodernism. *Journal of School Leadership*, *8*, 448–463.

Index

Acheson, K. A., 78
Adult learning, 97–98, 261–62
Affirmative postmodernism, 152–60, 278
African Americans, 175, 182
Alexander, W. M., 10
American College Test (ACT), 258
"American Studies," 259
Anderson, W., 219
Annenberg Institute for School Reform, 262
Apple, Michael W., 15, 18, 24, 65
Appley, D. E., 112
Argyris, C., 231
Aronowitz, S., 19
Aronson, J., 183
Art, 134, 158
Association for the Accreditation of Colleges of Teacher Education, 176
Autobiography, 177–78

Baker, E. L., 10
Bakhtin, Mikhail, 144, 191, 205, 206, 207, 221–22
Balliet, T. M., 72
Banks, J. A., 177, 180
Bataille, G., 143–44

Beauchamp, G., 10, 13
Behar-Horenstein, Linda S., 27–28, 261, 263
Behaviorism, 182
Beiber, M., 217
Bellon, E. C., 99
Bellon, J. J., 99
Bennett, Lerone, 180
Berman, Morris, 159
Bestor, A., 10
"Beyond High School Graduation Requirements: What Do Students Need to Learn at the International High School?" 271
Birth of a Nation, 176
Block scheduling, 143
Bobbitt, John Franklin, 13, 18, 65, 66, 73
Bode, Boyd, 65
Bolin, F., 72
Bondi, J., 12, 13, 19
Borgmann, A., 159–60
Bove, P., 221
Bowers, C. A., 231
British monarchy, 202
Britzman, D. P., 137

Bronx High School of Science, 272
Brookfield, S. D., 97, 99
Brooklyn International, 267
Brooklyn Tech High School, 272
Brooks, J. G., 95–96
Brooks, M. G., 95–96
Brophy, J. E., 117
Bruekner, L. J., 110
Burton, W. H., 110

Capitalism, 135
Carl D. Perkins Vocational Education
    Act, 24
Carlson, D., 142–43
Cartesian philosophy, 71, 135
Catholic Church, 201
Chamot, A. U., 269
Charlotte Observer, 200
Charters, W. W., 13, 18
Cherryholmes, C., 221
Child study movement, 59
Christianity, 155
City University of New York, 265. *See
    also* Professional development
Civil rights, 139, 176
Clandinin, D. J., 40
Coalition of Essential Schools, 262
Cogan, M. L., 195
Collaborative supervision: benefits of,
    117–20; characteristics of, 113–17;
    collegiality and, 11–13; cooperation
    and, 111–13; defined, 111, 112;
    equality and, 114; evolution of su-
    pervision and, 108–11; feedback
    and, 117–18; formative evaluations
    and, 114–15; observation/data
    gathering and, 115–16; peer super-
    vision and, 114; process for, 117; re-
    search implications and, 120–21
Committee of Ten, 58
Common unity of curriculum field,
    55–56, 67; behavioral objectives
    and, 63–65; curriculum objectives
    and, 62–65; design inevitability and,
    60–62; origins of field and, 56–59;
    postmodern view and, 55–56; public
    school mandate and, 59–60; recon-
    ceptualization of field and, 65–67;

school experience and, 62–65; Tyler
    rationale and, 62–63
Communalism, 172
Communication: Dialogic Supervision
    and, 206, 207; globalization and,
    203; supervision and, 191, 192,
    194–95, 199–200
Communication revolution, 139
Communicative action, 232–39, 240
Community, 172–74, 193–94
Connelly, F. M., 40
The Constructivist Leader, 94–95
Constructive postmodernism, 136, 138
Constructivist approach to supervision:
    adult learning principles and, 97–98;
    job-embedded learning and,
    100–102; knowledge acquirement
    and, 215–16; leadership develop-
    ment and, 94–95; learning commu-
    nities and, 98–100; power structure
    and, 215; practice overview and,
    96–97; theory overview and, 95–96
Cooperation, 111–13
Coordinating Council, 266, 267, 270
Copernicus, 140
Counts, G. S., 13
Critical Friends Groups (CFG), 262,
    263
Critical pedagogy, 170
Crow, G. M., 100
Cuban, Larry, 212
Cultural pluralism, 18, 24, 28
Cummins, James, 269
Currere, 56–57
Curriculum: changing student bodies
    and, 260–61; classroom scenarios
    and, 258–60; controllers of, 264;
    debate outcomes and, 251–53, 256;
    definition of, 56; development guide
    for, 27–28; education reform agenda
    and, 258; fundamental factors of,
    three, 59, 65–66; as life-blood of
    education, 251–52; premodern,
    161, 163; student diversity and,
    260–61, 263–64; teacher learning
    and, 261–62; *Teacher Think Tank*
    study and, 236. *See also* Modern
    curriculum; Postmodern curriculum

Curriculum and Assessment Committee, 266, 267, 271

Curriculum contemplation, 155, 156

Curriculum deliberation, 154, 155, 156

Curriculum interpretation, 154–55, 156

Curriculum research-practice relationship, 34–35; application-of-research paradigm and, 41–43; common domains and, 37; concept changes in, 43–46; decision-making and, 36–37; deliberation process and, 44–45; differences and, 35; empirical studies on, 35–37; encyclopedias/research handbooks and, 40–41; knowledge types and, 46–48; needs for new paradigm and, 48–49; paradigm changes in research and, 46–48; research topic guidelines and, 38–40; situation analysis and, 48; synthesis of domains and, 41

Daft, R. L., 104

Daigle, K., 61–62

Darder, A., 176

Darling-Hammond, Linda, 96, 99, 269

Davis, J. H., 141

Dawkins, Richard, 219

Deconstruction, 133–34, 136, 137, 177

Department of Superintendence, 109

Derrida, Jacques, 136, 137, 222

Descartes, René, 144, 153

Desrochers, C. G., 81

Developmental Teacher Evaluation Kit, 116

Dewey, Evelyn, 58

Dewey, John: constructivist theory and, 95; curriculum contemplation and, 155; curriculum deliberation and, 154; democratic principles of education and, 12, 21; developmental curriculum and, 12; essence of philosophy and, 160; fundamental factors of curriculum and, 65–66; history of curriculum development and, 57–58, 59; positivism and, 138;

reconceptualization of curriculum and, 66; supervision and, 74

Dialogic Supervision, 77–78, 192, 203, 204–7

Discipline and Group Management in Classrooms, 116

Doll, W. E., 12–13, 19, 22–23, 137

"Doublespeak and Euphemisms in Education," 80

Education and Experience, 95

Education policy controllers, 252

Edwards, R., 144–45

Eight Year Study, 57

Eisner, E. W., 15, 71, 140–41, 145, 155, 158–59

Elliot, Charles, 11, 58

Ellis, C., 117, 120, 140

Ellsworth, E., 137

The Encyclopedia of Educational Research, 36

English, Fenwick, 230–31

Enlightenment, 153, 157, 159, 163

Epistemology, 8

Essentialism, 9, 137

Ethnic Notions, 176

Eurocentrism, 157

Family structure, 193

"Fantasia," 134

Feedback, 102, 117, 254–55

Feeling, Tom, 180

Feminists, 17

F. H. LaGuardia High School of Music and Art, 272

Fission, 104

Fitzpatrick, J. L., 8

Flanders, N., 116

Flax, J., 156, 157, 158

Flinders, D. J., 231

Flossie & the Fox, 180

Forest, L., 99

Forms of Curriculum Inquiry, 35

Fosnot, C., 95

Foucault, M., 137, 215, 217, 232

Franklin, John Hope, 180

Franseth, J., 110

Freire, Paulo, 19, 170

Fundamentals of Curriculum, 161
Fusion, 104
*Fusion Leadership: Unlocking the Subtle
    Forces That Change People and Or-
    ganizations*, 104

Galileo, 140
Gall, M. D., 78
Gardner, H., 176–77
Garman, N. B., 71, 113, 218
Gay, Geneva, 279
Gender discrimination, 198–99
Giddens, Anthony, 193, 201
Giroux, H. A., 18, 19, 24–25, 177,
    240
Glanz, J., 111, 117, 121
Glaserfeld, Ernst von, 216
Glatthorn, A. A., 114, 119
Glickman, C. D., 71, 99, 78, 82, 115,
    121
Globalization, 203–4
Goodlad, J. I., 38, 39, 40
Gordon, Stephen P., 71, 78, 115, 121
Gray, John, 201
Greene, Maxine, 14, 15, 138, 160
Greenwood, James M., 72
Griffin, D. R., 137, 138
Grove, R. W., 39

Habermas, Jurgen, 232–33, 240
Hairston, Joe A., 234–39
Hall, G. S., 12
Hameyer, U., 40
Hammill, P. A., 18
Handbook of Research on Curriculum,
    36, 41
Harding, S., 157, 158
Hargreaves, A., 156, 203, 204
Harris, Ben M., 83–84, 115
Harris, William Torrey, 58
Hart, Pamula, 279
Harvard Educational Review, 21–22
Harvey, D., 223
Hawthorne, R. D., 45
Heidegger, Martin, 137
Heller, D. D., 114, 117, 120
Henderson, J. G., 45, 165
Heterotopia, 215

Hill, Sallie, 73
Historians, 17
Hlebowitsh, P. S., 20
Honebein, P., 96–97
Hosic, James, 74
Huckleberry Finn, 175
Huebner, D., 176
Hunkins, F. P., 18, 37
Hunter, Madeleine, 63
Hutchins, R. M., 10
Hypermodernism, 159–60

"Identity Politics," 139
Ideological imperialism, 61
Impressionism, 134
Individualism, 172, 191–92
Institutional change, 169–70
Intensification, 198–99
Interaction Analysis Category System-
    FIAC, 116
*International Encyclopedia of Educa-
    tion*, 36
International High School (HIS), 265.
    See also Professional development
International Olympic Committee, 134
Internet, 200
Intertextuality, 224
Irish immigrants, 176
"Is a Collegial Relationship Possible be-
    tween Supervisors and Teachers?"
    83–84
Isolation, 102
Italian Americans, 176

James, S., 114, 117, 120
Japanese Americans, 176
Jencks, C., 18, 137
Jenkins, D., 40
Jigsaw learning activities, 172–73
Jipson, J., 142, 145
Job analysis, 65
Job-embedded learning, 100–102
Johnson, Charles, 180
Johnson, Lyndon, 153
Johnson, M., 11

Kendler, H. H., 14
Kesson, K. R., 159, 165

Killian, J., 101
Kilpatrick, William, 57
Kimpston, R. D., 38, 39
Kincheloe, J. L., 61, 141
"Knowledge Production and Utilization in Curriculum," 34–35
Kosmoski, G. J., 109, 111
Krajewski, R. J., 115, 116

LaGuardia Community College, 265. *See also* Professional development
Lambert, L., 94–95, 98
Language, 139, 140
Lasley, T. J., 80
Lather, P., 137, 141
Lawrence-Lightfoot, S., 141
Lawson, H., 157–58
Learning communities, 98–100
Lengel, R. H., 104
Lewis, A., 10
Liberatory ethics, 136
Lincoln, Y. S., 20, 142, 146
Little Red Riding Hood, 180
Lortie, D. C., 102
Lyotard, Jean-François, 133, 137, 145, 157, 217, 232

McCall, J., 97–98
McCutcheon, G., 154
Macdonald, J. B., 160, 176
McHale, B., 223
Machiavelli, Niccolò, 104
McLaren, P. L., 170
McLeod, J., 141
McNeil, J. D., 13
Manhattan International, 267
Martin, J., 14
Marx, Karl, 157
Marxists, 17
Maxcy, Spencer J., 232–33
May, W. T., 78
Mead, George Herbert, 191
Media revolution, 139
Meier, Deborah, 269
Men Are from Mars, Women Are from Venus, 201
Messick, S., 15
Messinger, L., 85

"Middle Passage," 180
Modern curriculum: contemporary conceptions and, 9, 11–13; contributions of, 16–17; as defined approach, 252; experience and, 11–12; historic basis of field and, 55; influences on, 6; instruments of control and, 55; limitations of, 13–15; measuring curriculum effectiveness and, 14–15; postmodern synthesis with, 26–27, 28–29, 263–64; postmodernist criticism of, 6–7, 17–19, 20, 25–26; power relationships and, 15; student diversity and, 258; success of, 263; teacher accountability and, 6; teacher role in development and, 15, 16; technocratic approach and, 10; traditionalist view and, 8–9, 10–11. *See also* Common unity of curriculum field
Modern Educational Theories, 65
Modernism: advances of, 279; communicative action and, 232–33; debate benefits and, 279–80; influence of, 277; limitations of, 279; objectivity and, 230; postmodernism's relation to, 135–36, 163; summary of contributors' positions on, 277–79; synthesis with postmodernism and, 279; truth and, 229
Modern supervision: advantages of, 84; aim of supervision and, 74, 75; applied science approach and, 78–79; collaboration and, 231; cooperation and, 75; definitions of supervision and, 75, 76; democratic principles and, 73–77, 108, 109, 110; effectiveness of, 253–54, 256; evolution of schools and, 94; fusion leadership and, 104; influences on, 74; interpretive-practical approach and, 79; limitations of, 84; pedagogical correctness and, 80; postmodernist criticism of, 70; scientific knowledge and, 109, 110; task-oriented approach and, 77. *See also* Collaborative supervision
Morgan, Judith, 217

Moss, Alfred, 180

Multicultural education: autobiography and, 177–78; border crossing and, 181–82; community building and, 172–74; emancipation and, 182–83; empowerment and, 182–83; goal of, 170; holistic approach and, 175–76; implementation implications and, 186–87; literature evaluation and, 176; multiple knowledge sources and, 176–81; resistance/struggle and, 184–86; school culture and, 179; shifting centers and, 181–82; success perception and, 184; as transformative, 170. *See also* Professional development

Multiculturalism, 139, 140

Nadelstern, Eric, 274

A Nation at Risk, 258

National Commission on Teaching and America's Future, 96

Newlon, Jesse, 57, 74, 109

New Standards Project, 271

New York City Board of Education, 265. *See also* Professional development

New York State Education Department, 272

Nietzche, Friedrich W., 137

North Carolina, 192

O'Malley, J. M., 269

O'Neil, J., 100

O'Neil, Tip, 202

Objectivism, 153

Office of Research, Evaluation, and Assessment (OREA), 272

Oliva, P. F., 10, 12, 13

Ontology, 8

Organic reciprocity, 218

"Organizing What We Know about Curriculum," 36

Ornstein, A. C., 37

Ovando, M. N., 115, 119, 263

Paino, J., 85

Pajak, E. F., 82, 100, 202

Paley, N., 142, 145

Palmer, P. J., 153, 158

Panaritis, P., 72

Paradigm defined, 8

Payne, W. H., 72

Pedagogical correctness, 80–81, 82

Peer supervision, 114

Perennialism, 8–9;

Personnel Committee, 267

Phenix, P., 10

Phenomenologists, 17

Pinar, William F.: autobiographies/journals and, 22; curriculum development and, 55, 59, 61, 65; curriculum theory projects by, 164–65; curriculum understanding and, 155; gender and, 137; intellectual freedom and, 23; modern curriculum limitations and, 154; race/class issues and, 61; social psychoanalysis and, 23; teacher autonomy and curriculum and, 18

A Place Called School, 38

Pohly, K., 80

Polyfocal conspectus, 45

Ponticell, J. A., 95, 103, 120, 121

Popham, W. J., 10

Positionality, 206

Positivism, 138

Posner, G. J., 38–39, 40

The Postmodern Condition, 157

Postmodern curriculum, 145–46; centrality of literature and, 61; classifications of, 17; contributions of, 24–25; creative thinking and, 261; critically informed practice and, 164–65; criticism of modern view and, 6–7, 17–19, 20, 25–26; cultural study of, 155–60; curriculum contemplation and, 155, 156; curriculum deliberation and, 154, 155, 156; curriculum implications and, 143–45; curriculum interpretation and, 154–55; curriculum understanding and, 154–55; deconstruction and, 133–34; democratic principles and, 160; design inevitability and, 60–62; developmental implications and, 7; effective evaluation and, 22–23; Eurocentrism and, 157; fundamentals of curriculum and, 163–64; historic basis of field and, 21, 55–56; hypermodernism and, 159–60; imperialistic position of, 21–22; individuality of student and, 19–20; integrated theory and, 23–24; knowledge hierarchy and, 158–59; language and, 144; limitations of, 19–24, 25; methodological integrity and, 20–21; modernist criticism of, 25; paradigm shifts and, 161, 163; postmodern skepticism and, 157–58; power and, 156; practical application of, 22–23; psychoanalysis and, 144–45; public school mandate and, 59–60; research and, 140–43, 145; scheduling and, 143; self-actualization and, 12; synthesis with modern view and, 26–27, 28–29, 263; systemic educational reform and, 161; teacher role and, 24; teacher training and, 23; teaching practice and, 160; theory application and, 132–33; totality of representation and, 138; transformative curriculum leader and, 163–64; as undefined approach, 252

Postmodern education, 171–72; holistic approach and, 174–76; information gathering and, 216–17; multiple narratives and, 231–32; principles of, 171. *See also* Multicultural education

Postmodernism: affirmative, 152–60, 278; collaborative approach and, 241; communication/media revolution and, 139; communicative action and, 232–39; debate benefits and, 279–80; deconstruction and, 133–34, 136; defining, 135–36; democratic principles and, 136–37; discourse on, 138–40; efficiency and, 233; equity and, 233; influence of, 232, 277; language and, 139; learning organization/community and, 240; limitations of, 230; modernism's relation to, 135–36, 163; multiculturalism and, 139, 140; multiple realities and, 229–30; multiple understandings of, 137–38; objectivity and, 230; paradigms of, 136–37; pedagogical correctness and, 80; postmodernity and, 156; psychology and, 139; reason and, 139; shortcomings of, 279; summary of contributors' positions on, 277–79; synthesis with modernism and, 279; types of, 132; view of organizations and, 230–31

Postmodernity, 197–98; authority and, 201–2; globalization and, 203–4; intensification and, 198–99; local remedies *v.* global solutions and, 202; postmodernism and, 156; social science influences and, 200–201; time/place significance and, 199–200

Postmodern skepticism, 157–58

Postmodern supervision, 225; collaborative approach and, 108, 115, 231; community of discourse and, 220–22; crisis of representation and, 202–3; criticism of modern view and, 70; Dialogic Supervision and, 77–78, 204–7; directive *v.* nondirective approach and, 80–82; effectiveness of, 80–82, 84–85, 256; formal/informal observations and, 255; globalization and, 204; instructional leadership, and, 71, 80; interaction and, 192–93; memes scenario and, 218–20; modern complement to, 121; multiple realities and, 217–18, 219; "plastic" scenario and, 223–25; postmodernist theory and, 212–14; power relations and, 70–71, 202, 214–15, 217–18; process scenario and, 222–23; reconceptualization of field and, 82–83; scientific knowledge and, 108

Poststructuralism, 137

Power relationships, 15, 156, 217, 221–22

The Prince, 104

Professional development, 265–66; cross-team, 266–67; design/implementation of, 269–72; essential elements of, 267–68; goals of, 268–69, 271; interdisciplinary team and, 266; objective success evidence and, 272–74; outcomes and, 269; principal role and, 274–75
Progressivists, 9, 11, 59, 142–43
Project Method, 57
Psychoanalysis, 144–45
Psychology, 139, 144
Pulley, Jerry, 80

"Queer Theory," 139

Racism, 175, 183
Rationality, 153, 159
Realism, 137
Reason, 139
Reconstructionists, 9, 13
Red Scare, 176
The Reenchantment of Science, 138
Reflection, 101
Regents Competency Test, 271
Reid, W., 154
Relativism, 203
Releasing the Imagination, 138
Religion, 201
"Reorganizing City School Supervision," 74
Resnick, D., 15
Resnick, L., 15
Review of Educational Research, 36, 40–41
Review of Research in Education, 36, 40–41
Reynolds, W. M., 154
Richardson, L., 141–42
"The Rite of Spring," 134
Rogers, K. B., 38, 39
Rorty, R., 137
Rosales-Dordelly, C. L., 37
Roseneau, P. M., 152
Ross-Gordon, J. M., 78, 115, 121
Rugg, Harold, 13, 57–58

St. Maurice, H., 225

Sanders, J. R., 8
Sarason, S., 161
Sarup, M., 144
Saylor, J. G., 10
Scheduling, 143
Scholastic Aptitude Tests (SAT), 258
Schubert, W. H., 12, 13, 40
Schwab, J. J., 43, 48, 154
Science, 135, 201, 203, 230
Scott, Z. E., 109–10
Sears, J. T., 137, 163
Seigfried, C. H., 164
Semiotic theory, 219
Senge, P. M., 240
Sergiovanni, T. J., 80, 100, 116, 120–21, 155
Shores, J. H., 11
Short, E. G., 20, 37, 39–40
Shumaker, A., 58
Simpson, I. J., 109–10
Situation analysis, 48
Sizer, Theodore, 269
Skin Deep, 176
Slattery, P., 18, 21–22, 61–62, 154, 156, 158, 183
Slavin, John, 269
Sleeter, C. E., 170
Smith, B. O., 11
Smith, D. G., 154–55
Smyth, J., 71, 203
Social change, 170
Social efficiency movement, 65
Something Strong Within, 176
Spears, H., 110
Staff Development Facilitator, 262
Stanley, W. O., 11
Starratt, R. J., 100, 116, 120–21
Steele, C. M., 183
Steering Committee, 267
Stravinsky, Igor, 134
Stuyvesant High School, 272
Subjectivity, 153
Sugarman, J., 14
Supervision: annual performance report and, 255–56; applied science approach and, 78–79; collegial relations and, 83–84; communication and, 191, 192, 194–95, 200; com-

municative action and, 233–39; community and, 193–94; critical-emancipatory approach and, 79–80; democratic principles and, 72, 84, 99; directive *v.* nondirective approach and, 80–82; early clinical processes of, 93; economy of scale and, 254; evolution of schools and, 93–94; feedback and, 102, 254–55; fusion/fission principles and, 104; growth-oriented practices and, 102–3; individualism and, 191–92; inspection and, 72, 73; interaction and, 190, 191–97; interpretive-practical approach and, 79; isolation and, 102; modern-postmodern synthesis and, 78; pedagogical correctness and, 80–81, 82; power/authority and, 195–96; premodern view of, 71–73, 84, 104; professional improvement plan and, 256; reform strategies and, 94; shortcomings of current, 104; supervisor-teacher collaboration and, 97, 103 (*see also* Collaborative supervision); teacher disenfranchisement and, 196; teachers' rights and, 96; teacher-to-teacher, 262–63; terminology and, 71–72, 80; tofu metaphor and, 85–86; traditional, 104. *See also* Constructivist approach to supervision; Modern supervision; Postmodern supervision

Taba, H., 10
Talking 9 to 5, 201
Tannen, Deborah, 201
Tanner, D., 12, 20
Tanner, L., 12, 20
Taubman, P. M., 154
Taylor, Frederick, 73
Teachers College, 58
Teacher Think Tank, 234–39, 240–41
Technicism, 14–15

Technology, 213, 216, 218–19, 223
The Three Little Pigs, 180
Tierney, W. G., 142, 146
Tofu, 85–86
The Tofu Book, 85
Tribalism, 203
The True Story of the Three Little Pigs, 180
26th Yearbook of the National Society for the Study of Education, 57–58
Tyler, Ralph W. (Tyler Rationale): behavioral objectives and, 63–65; criticism of, 62–63; evaluation and, 63; experience and, 62; guidelines and, preferences for, 45; history of curriculum development and, 57; modern reasoning and, 154; postmodern curriculum and, 7, 62; postmodernists' criticism of, 18, 20–21; purpose of schools and, 19–20; reconceptualization of curriculum and, 66; school purpose and, 62; traditionalist view of curriculum and, 10

Usher, R., 144–45

Vocationalism, 182
Vygotsky, L. S., 95

Walker, D. F., 71–78, 95, 154, 195, 231
Wang, H., 144
Wiles, J., 12, 13, 19
Winder, A. E., 112
Wittgenstein, Ludwig, 138
Wood, F. H., 101
Worthen, B. R., 8
Wraga, W. G., 58

You Just Don't Understand, 201

Zemke, R., 97
Zemke, S., 97
Zepeda, S. J., 95, 120, 121

About the Contributors

Jeffrey Glanz is Associate Professor in the department of Instruction, Curriculum, and Administration at Kean University, located in Union, New Jersey. He is currently Executive Assistant to the President of Kean University. He has authored *Bureaucracy and Professionalism: The Evolution of Public School Supervision*, authored *Action Research: An Educational Leader's Guide to School Improvement*, coauthored *Supervision that Improves Teaching: Strategies and Techniques*, and co-edited *Educational Supervision: Perspectives, Issues, and Controversies*.

Linda S. Behar-Horenstein is Associate Professor in the department of Educational Leadership Policy, and Foundations at the University of Florida in Gainesville, FL. Some of her published work has appeared in *Curriculum & Teaching*, *Elementary Guidance & Counseling*, *Journal of Educational Administration*, *Peabody Journal of Education*, and the *High School Journal*. She has authored *The Knowledge Base of Curriculum: An Empirical Analysis*, coauthored *The Art and Practice of Dance/Movement Therapy*, and co-edited *Contemporary Issues in Curriculum*, now in its second edition.

Osborne F. Abbey, Jr., is currently the Assistant Superintendent, Township of Union Public Schools, New Jersey. He has served as a superintendent, as a New Jersey Department of Education official, and as a special education instructor. He is also an adjunct professor at Kean University. He has written articles on a wide range of educational issues, including supervision, budgeting, public relations, and management.

Karen K. Evans has been a full-time doctoral student and recently completed her Ph.D. in Educational Psychology at the University of Georgia. She assists Edward Pajak in directing the Northeast Georgia PreK-16 Education Reform Initiative. Her interests include school reform and research regarding classroom-based interventions, particularly solution-focused approaches.

Margarida Ramires Fernandes is Professor of Curriculum Studies in the School of Education at the University of the Algarve, Portugal. Her research interests include curriculum development and evaluation, supervision in teacher education, and school-based research and development. She has authored numerous academic papers, articles, chapters, monographs and books in these areas, in English and Portuguese. She is Vice President of the Portuguese Association of Sciences in Education.

Geneva Gay is Professor at the University of Washington-Seattle. She is nationally and internationally recognized for scholarship in multicultural education. Her writings include more than 100 articles and book chapters, the co-editorship of *Expressively Black: The Cultural Basis of Ethnic Identity*, and the authoring of *At the Essence of Learning: Multicultural Education*.

Pamula Hart is an elementary school teacher in the Upper Dublin (Pennsylvania) School District and a Ph.D. student in the Multicultural Education Program at the University of Washington, Seattle. Her special interests are multicultural classroom practice, biraciality, professional staff development, and building level administration.

James G. Henderson is Professor of Curriculum and Instruction in the College of Education at Kent State University. He is the author of two texts on reflective teaching, and he is coauthor of *Transformative Curriculum Leadership* that presents a postmodern interpretation of curriculum leadership. He recently co-edited a text that is designed to support democratic curriculum practitioners' continuing critical studies. His articles have appeared in the *Journal of Teacher Education, Teaching Education, Journal of Curriculum and Supervision*, and *Journal of Curriculum Theorizing*.

Peter S. Hlebowitsh is Associate Professor in the College of Education at the University of Iowa. He is currently co-managing several large-scale democratic school reform projects in the Newly Independent States of the former Soviet Union. With the support of funds provided by the United States Information Agency, he has helped to produce national curriculum materials for the Czech Republic and the republics of Armenia and Bulgaria. He is also the author of *Radical Curriculum Theory Reconsidered*, coauthor of *American Education: Purpose and Promise*, co-editor of the *Annual Review of Research for School Leaders*, and editor of the John Dewey journal, *Education and Culture*.

Patricia E. Holland is Associate Professor in the department of Educational Leadership and Cultural Studies at the University of Houston. She has authored and coauthored articles appearing in the *Journal of Curriculum and Supervision, American Educational Research Journal, Peabody Journal of Education, Journal of Staff Development*, and *Journal of Curriculum Theorizing*. She is coauthor of *Collaborative Leadership and Shared Decision Making*.

Aaron Listhaus is a faculty-elected school administrator at the International High School at LaGuardia Community College, and chair of the school leadership team. He has taught English, math, science, and history to immigrant students for the past thirteen years. He conducts national staff development workshops on topics such as ongoing professional development, authentic assessment, interdisciplinary curriculum, and democratic school governance.

Eric Nadelstern is Principal of the International High School at LaGuardia Community College, an innovative public secondary school for limited English proficient youngsters that he founded in 1985. He has served as a teacher, staff developer, central office administrator, and supervisor. He is an outspoken advocate for transforming schools into democratic learning communities.

Maryalice Obermiller is Assistant Professor in the department of Educational Leadership and Cultural Studies at the University of Houston. She has twenty-five years of educational experience that includes teaching and administration at K-12 levels. She has developed programs and courses for developing administrators, including integration and conceptualization of the impact of technology on teachers and administrators for the future.

Martha N. Ovando is Associate Professor in the department of Educational Administration at the University of Texas at Austin. Some of her published work has appeared in the *Journal of School Leadership, Urban Education, Journal of Personnel Evaluation in Education*, and *Wingspan*.

Edward Pajak is Professor of Educational Leadership in the College of Education at the University of Georgia. His articles have appeared in the *Journal of Curriculum and Supervision, American Educational Research Journal, Sociology of Education*, and the *Journal of Psychoanalytic Anthropology*. He is co-editor of the *Handbook of Research on School Supervision* and is author of *The Central Office Supervisor of Curriculum and Instruction* and *Approaches to Clinical Supervision: Alternatives for Improving Instruction*.

Janet R. Price teaches career development, American history, and literature at the International High School at LaGuardia Community College, where she also serves as union chapter leader and arts coordinator. She is the author of numerous reports and articles on school reform issues and the co-editor of *The Rights of Students*, an ACLU handbook. Some of her published work has appeared in *Yale Law and Policy Review* and *Encounter*.

Edmund C. Short is Professor of Curriculum Studies at Georgia Southern University and Professor Emeritus of Curriculum and Supervision at the Pennsylvania State University. He served as founding editor and editor of

ASCD's scholarly journal, the *Journal of Curriculum and Supervision,* for eight years, until 1993. He has edited *Forms of Curriculum Inquiry.*

Patrick Slattery is Associate Professor at Texas A&M University. He has authored *Curriculum Development in the Postmodern Era* and coauthored *Understanding Curriculum* and *Contextualizing Teaching.* His articles have appeared in *Harvard Educational Review, JCT, Curriculum Inquiry,* and *Childhood Education.* He is editor of *JCT: Journal of Curriculum Theorizing.*

Robert J. Starratt is Chair of the Department of Educational Administration and Higher Education at the Graduate School of Education at Boston College. He served previously on the faculty of Fordham University (1976–1997), where he helped redesign their doctoral and master's programs in educational administration. He has lectured internationally (Canada, Ireland, Australia, Hong Kong, India, Malaysia, New Zealand, etc.) on educational leadership, school renewal, ethics in educational administration, and human resource development. The author and coauthor of many books, he is currently working on a book that uses metaphors from drama to develop a philosophy of education for schooling to themes of critical theory, postmodern frameworks, the new science, and philosophical anthropology.

Frances M. Vandiver has twenty-six years of experience, which includes teaching at the junior high, middle school, and high school levels as well as six years in higher education. She has spent ten years as a principal at both the middle and high school levels. She was a contributor to a recent Jossey-Bass publication, *On Being a Principal.* She recently joined the University of Florida as Director of the P. K. Younge Developmental Research School and Lecturer in the College of Education.

Duncan Waite is Professor of Educational Leadership at Southwest Texas State University. He is founding editor of the *International Journal of Leadership in Education.* His articles have appeared in the *Journal of Curriculum and Supervision, American Educational Research Journal, Teaching & Teacher Education, Urban Education,* and *Theory into Practice.* He authored *Rethinking Instructional Supervision: Notes on Its Language and Culture.*

Sally J. Zepeda is Assistant Professor of Educational Leadership in the College of Education at the University of Georgia. She has authored and coauthored articles in the *Journal of Curriculum and Supervision, Journal of Staff Development, International Journal of Educational Management, Journal of School Leadership,* and *Kappa Delta Pi Record,* among others. She authored *Staff Development: Practices That Promote Leadership in Learning Communities* and coauthored four books: *Special Programs in Regular Schools; Historical Foundations, National Standards, and Contemporary Issues; The Reflective Supervisor: A Practical Guide for Educators;* and *Hands-On Leadership Tools for Principals.*